Questions and Answers on Life Insurance

Questions and Answers on Life Insurance

The Life Insurance Toolbox

Anthony Steuer

iUniverse, Inc.

New York Lincoln Shanghai

To My Wife Cheryl
And to my son—Avery

Families are what life insurance is about and
my family is what life is about.

Once in a while
you get shown the light
in the strangest of places
if you look at it right

Scarlet Begonias—Robert Hunter

Questions and Answers on Life Insurance
The Life Insurance Toolbox

iUniverse books may be ordered through booksellers or by contacting:

iUniverse
2021 Pine Lake Road, Suite 100
Lincoln, NE 68512
www.iuniverse.com
1-800-Authors (1-800-288-4677)

ISBN-13: 978-0-595-32147-6 (pbk)
ISBN-13: 978-0-595-76954-4 (ebk)
ISBN-10: 0-595-32147-X (pbk)
ISBN-10: 0-595-76954-3 (ebk)

Printed in the United States of America

CONTENTS

CHAPTER 4: HOW TO CHOOSE A LIFE INSURANCE COMPANY

PREFACE

Whether or not you know anything about life insurance, there is something in this book for you. This book is designed with the question and answer format so that you can access the specific information you would like to review. You only have to look at what you want to look at. It's designed to be painless.

It's widely known that life insurance is one of the least exciting topics to think about. However, a significant percentage of people have a life insurance policy. With any product that you are paying hundreds to thousand of dollars for, you should know what you are getting. In working with clients and advisors, I have discovered a lack of knowledge.

As a consumer you can learn about life insurance from the ground up or just a specific topic. Life insurance is a topic that is often designed in a confusing manner.

As an advisor, this book will assist you in finding answers about areas that will allow you to better work with your clients.

For both consumers and advisors, this will also allow you to double check any information you are told and find any additional resources you may need.

Why did I write this book? In my close to 20 years in the life insurance industry I have found a lack of resources and knowledge for consumers and advisors. Life insurance can be confusing and this book will help you to better understand this valuable financial tool.

In California, the Department of Insurance offers a license that is held by less than forty people (including myself), known as the Life and Disability Insurance Analyst License. I hold the Chartered Life Underwriter (CLU) designation, discussed in Chapter five.

Leadership roles include serving on the board of the San Francisco Life Underwriters Association. As well as serving as President of the Leading Life Insurance Producers of Northern California and as President of the San Francisco Chapter of the American Society of CLU & ChFC.

My other activities include numerous speaking engagements for professional associations, providing articles for professional publications and serving as a technical editor for the insurance sections for *The Retirement Bible* and *The Investing Bible* both by Lynn O'Shaughnessy.

My goal is for you to find this book useful as a reference. I feel that the more informed you are, the better choices you can make.

CHAPTER 1: INTRODUCTION TO LIFE INSURANCE

QUESTION 1: What is Life Insurance, Where did it come from and why should I Care?

Life insurance is a type of insurance that pays money when someone passes away. That's simple. However, to understand what life insurance is today you should look at how life insurance originated. Life insurance is one of the very oldest types of insurance/financial products in existence. It stems from the old principle that if a villager's house burned down, and then the other villagers would help to rebuild the house.

The first life insurance came from this concept. Then a concept known as the tontine annuity system was founded in Paris by the 17th-century Italian-born banker Lorenzo Tonti. Although essentially a form of gambling, this system has been regarded as an early attempt to use the law of averages and the principle of life expectancies in establishing annuities. Under the tontine system, associations of individuals were formed without any reference to age, and a fund was created by equal contributions from each member. The sum was invested, and, at the end of each year, the interest was divided among the survivors. The last remaining survivor received both the year's interest and the entire amount of the principal.

However, as the amount of money that people wished to be insured for increased, the greater the risk as well as the potential for violent fluctuations for those involved. To minimize this effect, it was necessary that the law of large numbers be applied to this situation. This is where we see the first roots of the actuarial practice. An actuary is defined as a mathematician employed by an insurance company to calculate premiums, reserves, dividends and insurance, pension and annuity rates, using risk factors obtained from experience tables. These tables are based on the company's history of insurance claims as well as other industry and general statistical data.

This is an example of the principle known as the law of large numbers. This principle states that the greater number of similar exposures (in this case-lives insured) to a peril (e.g. death), the less the observed loss experience will deviate from the expected loss experience. Basically, the more people that the risk is spread out over, the more money (premiums) will be coming in; that when a person does die, it will not be as big of a burden to the rest of the insured's. Of course, in certain circumstances, there will not be much that can be done.

The function of insurance is to safeguard against misfortunes by having the losses of the unfortunate few paid by the contributions of the many that are exposed to the same peril. This is the essence of insurance—the sharing of losses and, in the process, the substitution of a certain small "loss" (the premium payment) for an uncertain large loss. (Reference—Black, H. & Skipper, K.; *Life Insurance*, Twelfth Edition, Prentice Hall (Englewood Cliffs, NJ), p. 18)

Life insurance, like any other financial product is a tool to assist you in accomplishing a specific goal (or goals). As such, it will assist the beneficiary when there is an economic loss, due to the death of the insured that extends well beyond just funeral or final medical expenses. The loss of future income, due to the death of a breadwinner can have a severe impact on the lifestyle of the surviving family members. Debt owed by the deceased may become due and payable as well as possible estate or inheritance taxes. Life insurance can create an immediate source of funds to enable the payment of these expenses and to provide a source of future income.

Benjamin Franklin helped found the insurance industry in the United States, in 1752, with the Philadelphia Contributionship for the Insurance of Houses from Loss by Fire. The current state insurance regulatory framework has its roots in the 19th century with New Hampshire appointing the first insurance commissioner in 1851. Insurance regulators' responsibilities grew in scope and complexity as the industry evolved. Congress adopted the McCarran-Ferguson Act in 1945 to declare that states should regulate the business of insurance, and to affirm that the continued regulation of the insurance industry by the states was in the public's best interest.

The purchasing of life insurance is an uncomfortable task for many people and the image of most life insurance advisors leave something to be desired with examples such as Bill Murray in "Groundhog Day" and Mel Brooks in "High Anxiety". Typically, there is recognition of an obligation to protect one's dependents from the financial hardship an untimely death may cause, however no one likes to think about the fact that they will die someday. This is another reason aside from the potential discomfort of dealing with a life insurance advisor that can make it easy to delay and put off the decision to purchase life insurance.

Keep in mind that as you go through this process that life insurance is not for you, it is for your survivors. Therefore, you typically will only have a need for life insurance when you are leaving behind someone or some entity that is dependent on your income.

"Any road will get you there as long as you don't know where you're going"—Socrates.

QUESTION 2: Why Do I Need Life Insurance?

Times have changed and the reasons why people buy life insurance have grown from the original purpose. The following is a list of some of the more common reasons:

- **Income Replacement**—Protect the premature death of a spouse or parent so that the loss of income is not devastating to the family.

- **Payment of Outstanding Debts**—Such as mortgages, car payments, credit cards

- **Final Expenses**—Funeral and other administrative expenses, etc.

- **Education Funding**—The death of a parent may mean that the quality of education, intended for a child, may be out of reach.

- **Emergency Fund**—Any adjustment expenses, such as time off work, medical and counseling expenses.

- **Special Needs Child**—The use of life insurance provide a guarantee that the funds will be there to care for those special needs.

- **Business Continuation**—To provide funding to assist in orderly transfer of business ownership, in the case of an owner's death—life insurance guarantees that the business is transferred as intended.

- **Business Insurance**—Key Person, Executive Bonus, Split Dollar, and Deferred Compensation funded with life insurance.

- **Estate Taxes**—Under current tax law life insurance can provide liquidity at death to pre-fund the estate tax liability. This may not be necessary if the Estate Tax is permanently repealed.

- **Charitable Giving**—A charitable-minded client may leave a gift to a favorite organization, without significantly reducing the size of the estate by using the death benefit to replace the value of the property gifted to heirs.

- **Equalizing Inheritance**—provides additional liquidity to assist in providing each child with equal shares of their parents' assets.

- **Income In Respect of a Decedent**—People die owning assets that have not yet been taxed; these taxes then become the obligation of the beneficiary. Life insurance provides liquidity to assist in the payment of these taxes.

- **Second Marriages**—There can be conflict when a parent with children remarries. Life insurance on the parent provides the new spouse financial security from the insurance coverage. And at the same time allowing the children to receive the parent's estate immediately. This can avoid unwanted animosity between the children and the new spouse and allow them to live in harmony.

Please note that that life insurance is commonly used for business reasons. Further information is in Question #129.

Is proper planning for everyone?

As the famous saying goes—only two things in life are certain death and taxes. This table looks at the fact that no matter how rich and famous you are, that you should always expect the unexpected.

Florence Griffith Joyner	Olympic Track Champion	Age 38	Died from suffocation from an epileptic seizure on Sept. 21, 1998
Phil Hartman	Comedian and Actor	Age 49	Gunshot on May 28, 1998
Linda McCartney	Photographer and spouse of Paul McCartney	Age 56	Breast Cancer on April 17, 1998
Ray Nitschke	Football Legend	Age 60	Heart attack on March 8, 1998
Sonny Bono	Celebrity and Congressman	Age 62	Skiing accident on January 5, 1998
Brandon Tartikoff	NBC Television Executive	Age 48	Hodgkin's Disease on August 27, 1997
Princess Diana	Princess of England	Age 36	Car Accident on August 31, 1997
Chris Farley	Actor and Comedian	Age 33	Drug overdose on December 18, 1997
Michael Landon	Actor	Age 54	Cancer on July 1, 1991
Lee Remick	Actress	Age 55	Cancer on July 2, 1991
Jim Henson	Creator of the Muppets	Age 53	Pneumonia on May 16, 1990

QUESTION 3: How Much Life Insurance Do I Need?

This is an excellent question to which there are as many answers as there people whom you ask. Every advisor, financial columnist and relative has a formula that they consider is the best. This section is designed to present the various different methods that are used, as well as the pros and cons of each method ranging from the simple to the extremely complex calculation. As these issues, deal with how to value a life, it is indeed a very complex proposition.

The method that makes the most sense to you is probably the one that may work the best for you. No method is perfect, as you are trying to hit a moving target. Life brings many changes and your needs will change with them. The more assumptions then the more complex you'll make your planning, and the more chances there are that something will not work as planned. This does not mean that you should only use the simplest methods—it is to give you a concept of why it is important to actively participate in all of your planning, fully understand it and constantly monitor it. After all, it is your money. Remarkably, the simplest formulas can often be the best.

All of the issues discussed in this question will have an impact on the amount of life insurance and, other assets needed. Often the desired goals may not be financially feasible. These issues are not only financially based; they can also be extremely emotional.

Another thought to keep in mind is that as your other assets grow, such as retirement plans, investments, etc, your need for life insurance will decrease.

These are some of the more commonly used approaches.

Basic Approaches

Multiple of Income:

This method (also known as the "human capitalization value") uses the approach of a multiple of your annual income typically ranging from five to eight times your annual income. This is one of the oldest and best known methods to determine how much life insurance you need, as well as one of the easiest to use. It's also the most frequently mentioned by financial columnists in consumer publications.

While simple, this earnings-multiple method misses a range of important factors. For example, it ignores household demographics, past savings, Social Security offsets, housing expenses, taxes, etc. It also ignores expected life changes and individual preferences about sustaining the living standards of survivors. It is simply a "best guess".

Cover Your Debts

This entails buying only enough life insurance to cover debts such as your mortgage, student loan bills or outstanding car notes. The issues are similar to the issues for the multiple of income approach discussed above in that it misses a whole range of factors, such as not considering any future debts or needs such as child care or college education costs. This method is also too simplistic to provide any real value.

Human Life Value Concept

The human life value concept deals with human capital. Human capital is a person's income potential. We all have a human life value. In wrongful death litigation, human life value is measured daily in court (however, the litigation value tends to be significantly different). Insuring human life value is the primary purpose of life insurance. The human life value concept goes beyond numbers and considers the entire impact caused by the loss of a human life and the value to a person's loved ones. Here are some questions to give you a start:

- If you had been killed in a car accident last week, and someone else had been responsible for your death, how much money would your family sue the responsible party for?

- If you had been killed in a car accident last week, and you had been responsible, how much money would you want your family to receive?

- If you died of cancer last week, how much money would you have wanted your family to receive?

- How much are your tomorrow's worth? What is your Potential Earning Power (PEP)?

Here are the steps to use the human value approach. The future expected earnings of the insured needs to be capitalized and the present value of income flow to the family (for the time frame needed) determined. This generally involves a multi-step process:

1) Estimate the insured's earnings for the period of time replacement would be needed. When estimating earnings, future increases in salary may be considered and an "average" annual salary used. Whether or not to include "growth" of earnings has a significant impact on the amount of coverage that will be needed.

2) Subtract from earnings, a reasonable estimate of annual taxes and living expenses spent on the insured, in order to arrive at the actual salary needed to provide for family needs. Commonly, this is a percentage of salary. Rather than calculating a composite of each separate need, it is often suggested that the survivors will need about 70% of the pre-death income to carry on after the insured's death. A higher or lower percentage may be needed depending on a particular family's circumstances. The percentage of salary needed can be more accurately determined through a detailed examination of the family budget.

3) Determine the length of time the net earnings need to be replaced. This could be until the insured's dependents are assumed to be grown and to no longer need the financial support of the insured, or until the assumed retirement age of the insured.

4) Select a rate of return with which to discount the future earnings. A conservative estimate on rate of return would be the return on US Treasury bills or notes, or the rate of return paid for death proceeds left on deposit with the insurance company. A life insurance company will leave a death benefit in an interest bearing account. The rate paid on this type of account is the rate that should be used. A safe assumption would be the rate on a money market or certificate of deposit (CD) account.

5) Multiply the net salary needed by the length of time needed, to determine the future earnings. Then calculate the present value of the future earnings using the assumed rate of return. This calculation can be performed using a spreadsheet, specialized software, a financial function calculator, or by using discount interest tables.

For example: let's assume you are age 40 and make $65,000 per year. By examining your family budget, it is determined that $48,500 per year is needed for family support. It is also determined that this income would need to be replaced until retirement at age 65 (25 years). If we assume a 5% discount rate, the present value of your future net salary would be $683,556. Stated another way, it would take this amount to pay $48,500 per year for 25 years based on a 5% rate of return. This assumes that the insurance proceeds will be liquidated over the needed period of income (the capital liquidation method). A more conservative approach would be to keep the principal intact and live off the income generated (the capital preservation method). See discussion under life needs analysis below.

The human value method is useful in situations where replacing the income lost due to the death of a breadwinner is the primary concern. However, this method only factors in the replacement of income and does not take into account any lump sum needs at death. In addition, a client's financial situation may be more complex and additional analysis may be required. For example, the issues of funding a college education, integration with Social Security benefits, paying estate tax, and determining what other sources of income are available are not included in the human value approach. In situations where a more detailed calculation is needed, the life needs analysis method can be used.

This method will provide only a rough sense of your human life value, which can be a factor in determining the amount of insurance you should have in your financial portfolio. It is most useful in situations where replacing the income lost due to the death of a breadwinner is the primary concern. Typically, the amount of life insurance indicated under this method is less than the actual need, as it does not take into account any lump sum needs at death as well as college education funding, estate taxes, integration with social security, existing life insurance and forth. See the next section where we will discuss a needs analysis approach.

Capital Preservation and Capital Liquidation

This method can be used in conjunction with a needs analysis approach or separately as a quick calculation, if you have just want do an income replacement approach on its own. Whether you are using this method strictly on its own or in conjunction with a needs analysis, once the amount of income that needs to be replaced is determined, a decision must be made as to whether the pool of capital to provide this income will be preserved or liquidated.

Capital Preservation:

The capital used for income replacement is left intact and the beneficiaries live off the income it produces.

Pros:

- Optimally provide an income stream indefinitely as the principal (death benefit) remains intact.
- Simple to calculate.
- The longer the payout period, the better this method becomes.

Cons:

- If the rate of return is lower than the assumed rate, the beneficiaries could run out of money prematurely the interest rate chosen is up to you, however a conservative and realistic interest rate will have a greater chance of meeting your goal. A good guide might be the historical rate of return on U.S. Treasury Bills.
- The amount of money needed to fund income replacement is typically greater than that of other methods, as the beneficiaries live off income only (optimally) rather than principal and income.

How to calculate: Arrive at the annual income (either before tax or after tax) needed using any suitable method, including your own estimate, if you wish. Divide this figure by the assumed after tax rate of return (conservative) that can be earned on the income replacement fund.

Example: For an annual income need of $100,000 (after taxes) and an assumed after-tax rate of return on the principal (death benefit) that is presumed to be 5%, the replacement need would be $2,000,000 ($100,000 divided by 5% (.05)).

Capital Liquidation:

The length of time of income needs to be replaced becomes a major factor in determining the capital needed for income replacement.

Pros:

- Typically requires less money than the capital preservation method as both principal and income are used.

Cons:

- The length of time that the proposed insured's salary needs to be replaced is highly subjective.
- Requires all the factors mentioned on the worksheet and human value needs to be examined.
- The survivor can outlive the income stream.
- More complex to calculate.

How to calculate:

1) Determine the number of years of income replacement needed.
2) Multiply the net income shortage by number of years of income replacement.
3) Add immediate cash needs and any new capital needed to determine total capital needs.
4) Subtract existing capital from total capital needs to arrive at additional capital required.

Because the family (in the prior example)lives off income only rather than both principal and income, $2,500,000 would be needed to generate $100,000 per year using capital preservation, while only $1,562,208 would be needed using capital liquidation (assuming 4% after-tax return for both).

However, as the period of income replacement lengthens, the difference between income preservation and liquidation narrows. For instance, if we assume a 35 year income replacement need for the above example, the capital preservation value does not change while the capital liquidation value becomes $1,866,461.50.

Capital Liquidation:

As this example demonstrates, the capital liquidation approach requires a lower income replacement need. However, this example assumed the income replacement fund would be consumed over 20 years. If earnings are less than expected, the fund could be depleted sooner. Also, if the 20 year figure is based upon the spouse's life expectancy, the spouse could live beyond that expectancy and there would not be any money available after 20 years. This points out the inherent risk of the capital liquidation approach, while also assuming a 4% after tax rate of return.

Assumptions about rate of return and life expectancy must be very conservative in order to avoid premature depletion of the fund. The capital liquidation method may be appropriate in situations when the income replacement period is certain or is short term. An example would be when income replacement would continue only until the children reach a specified age.

Life Cycle Model of Consumption and savings

As shown in the prior methods, planning can vary in complexity. These prior approaches on a static predictable future and are based on rough calculations.

The life-cycle model of consumption and savings is a new approach that is based on the life-cycle model which was developed in the 1950s and 1960s by Professor Franco Modigliani and his colleagues at Massachusetts Institute of Technology. Modigliani won the Nobel Prize in 1985 for developing the model, which built on early work by Yale economist Irving Fisher in the 1920s.

This model assumes that an insured's goals are to secure the living standards of the household and ensure comparable living standards for his or her survivors. In the economic approach, spending targets are derived by calculating how much the household can afford to consume in the present and still be able to preserve the same living standard in the future. Although spending targets under the Capital Needs Analysis approach can be adjusted to approximate those derived under the economic approach, there are practical limits to doing so. This is particularly true in the case for households experiencing changing demographics or facing borrowing constraints.

This approach is based on the fundamental goal of saving money and having insurance—the desire to avoid major disruptions in a household's standard of living. This approach uses advanced mathematical techniques to calculate the savings and life insurance needed to balance consumption in the present with consuming in the future and to preserve a household's living standard for survivors. This method describes how life insurance holdings are adjusted as life insurance needs change. All economic resources, tax liabilities and benefits—Social Security retirement benefits and survivor benefits, etc.—are taken into account in the calculation, along with family demographics, tax-deferred savings, housing plans, special expenditures, estate plans, capacity to borrow and lifestyle preferences.

This type of modeling includes contingent planning, which recognizes that survivors may have special needs and different incomes. Key variables—age of retirement, Social Security benefits and tax-deferred asset withdrawals, for example—can be changed to determine how these factors alter the maximum sustainable living standard. The insurance recommendations are substantially different from those of the conventional methods. This type of approach (in theory) would allow the agent/representative to use a more comprehensive base to determine life insurance needs rather than the historical guessing/estimating theory. Without an economic modeling process, there is no mathematical ability for determining an appropriate amount of insurance.

A benefit of this approach is that it incorporates the fact that as other assets grows; the need for life insurance to replace income will diminish.

The downside of this approach is that it depends on a large number of assumptions and the more assumptions that are relied upon, the greater the chance that the calculations will be further off. The other issue is the complexity of this type of model.

To the best of my knowledge, the only software currently available for this type of calculation is ESPlanner available on the web at www.esplanner.com.

The (Capital) Needs Analysis method

The (Capital) Needs Analysis method is used by most insurance agents/planners and at most financial-planning Web sites. Chartered Life Underwriters (CLUs) know the method as the Human Life Value Concept or the Human Capitalization Method. These methods give you the income you will earn from your present age until your retirement age, assuming a rate of interest that represents salary increases through that period. These concepts are sometimes treated as one and the same and sometimes as differing methods.

Like the earnings-multiple method, the Capital Needs Analysis method projects the income the insured will earn between now and retirement (or later) and sometimes discounts these flows. But this procedure goes further; it calculates the net contribution of the insured to the family's living standard by subtracting the insured's present values of future tax payments and living expenses from his or her present earnings. The net contribution of the insured is then compared with today's spending needs of potential survivors. Such a needs analysis incorporates factors such as mortgage payments, other household expenses and special expenditures.

Here are some of the factors that are considered (if not all):

The method of calculating this value is as follows:

1) Estimate the individual's average annual earned income from the person's present age to the age of retirement.
2) Deduct the amount that is not allocated to others. Money spent for income taxes, life and health insurance premiums, and all other self-maintenance expenses should be deducted in this step.
    Typically this is a percentage of salary. A good starting point is this Consumer Expenditures Survey by the Bureau of Labor Statistics, where the percentage of income required after taxes and expenses would be:

| | Percentage of Gross Income |
Annual Gross Income:	Required:
Under $48,000:	70%
$48,000 to $53,000:	66%
$53,000 to $59,000:	63%
$59,000 to $65,000:	60%
Over $65,000:	57%
All Two Income Families:	70%

Please keep in mind that these are only averages. This table also assumes that educational expenses are taken care of separately and the mortgage is paid for.

3) Using a reasonable rate of interest, determine the present value of the amounts allocated to others for the working period used in step 1. Most financial calculators can perform this equation for you.

However, the Capital Needs Analysis method raises several concerns:

- If the household sets a spending target too high for survivors, the method will generate a larger amount of life insurance than is appropriate. This will cost the household too much in life insurance premiums. If the spending target is set too low, the recommendation would leave the household underinsured.
- It does not take into account what your beneficiary's needs will be.
- Please keep in mind that these are only averages. Also it assumes that educational expenses are taken care of separately and the mortgage is paid for.
- It does not integrate with Social Security.
- Other sources of income.

This method only factors in the replacement of income and does not take into account any lump sum needs at death.

Sample Worksheet (see after worksheet for more information on the various factors):

INCOME NEEDS:

1. Annual income your family would need if you die today (typically between 60%-80% of total income)
Consider any lifestyle changes, and include any current expenses such as mortgage/rent, groceries, clothing, utility bills, entertainment, travel, transportation, child care, etc: $_____

2. Annual income available to your family from other sources—include all salaries, dividends, interest, current (or estimated) social security benefits along with all other sources of income: $_____

3. Annual income to be replaced (Subtract line 2 from line 1.):
$_____

4. Funds (Capital) needed to provide income for your required number of years? $_____

Multiply line 3 by the appropriate factor* below:
  * 10 YEARS X 8.1; 15 YEARS X 11.1; 20 YEARS X 13.6; 25 YEARS X 15.6; 30 YEARS X 17.3; 35 YEARS X 18.7 and 40 YEARS X 20.0

EXPENSES:

5. Funeral expenses—average cost of an adult funeral is about $10,000:
$_____

6. Administrative Expenses (also referred to as an Emergency Fund and/or Final Expenses (approximately six months—50% of the higher wage earner's salary);—can vary for cleaning up the affairs of the deceased, e.g., advisor fees, filing taxes: $_____

7. Mortgage and other outstanding debts (credit card debt, car loans, home equity loans, etc). It may make sense to pay off these debts, considered if the survivor will have a substantial income:
$_____

8. College costs**: 2002-2003 cost of a *four-year* education: public college-$51,346; private college $109,412 multiply by number of children, costs are increasing more rapidly than inflation

$_____

9. Capital needed for college—Multiply line 8 by the appropriate Years before college Factor:
* 5 years X .82; 10 years X .68; 15 years X .56 and 20 years: X .46

$_____

10. Total capital required Add lines 4, 5, 6 and 9

$_____

ASSETS: Keep in mind that current asset value may be considerately different at time of liquidation as well as the value may be significantly discounted due to forced sale such as real estate, family business or other investments:

11. Bank accounts, money market accounts, CDs, stocks, bonds, mutual funds, real estate: $_____

12. Retirement savings IRAs, 401(k)s, Keoghs, pension and profit sharing plans: $_____

13. Present amount of life insurance (including group life insurance assumes that it will continue): $_____

14. Total income producing assets—Add lines 11, 12 and 13

$_____

15. Life insurance needed—Subtract line 14 from line 10

$_____

*   Factors: Inflation is assumed to be 3%. College costs indexed at 6%. The rate of return on investments is assumed to be 6% after tax.
** Source: The College Board, Trends in College Pricing 2002
Information and factors are based on information from the Life and Health Insurance Foundation for Education; a nonprofit organization

An application of the capital liquidation/preservation model will assist in a more detailed analysis. A custom worksheet will allow you to include what is important to you and to control the degree of complexity. Please note that a separate worksheet should be required for each spouse.

This can be done by using all or some of the following steps as they apply; the factors are discussed previously and are listed for you to keep in mind:

Outflows:

ONE-TIME (LUMP SUM EXPENSES):

1) Funeral Expenses (See following pages)
2) Estate Administration, Final and other Miscellaneous Expenses— (See following pages)
3) Estate Taxes (See following pages)
4) Emergency Fund/Readjustment Period (See following pages)
5) College Fund(s) (See following pages)
6) Debt Resolution (See following pages)
7) Uninsured Medical Costs
8) Workforce Retraining
9) Offset for any assets included below
10) Home Mortgage Pay-Off
11) Property Taxes

TOTAL ONE-TIME (LUMP SUM EXPENSES):

INCOME NEED (ONGOING EXPENSES)

1) Annual Income Replacement Needed by Survivor(s); (including special needs dependents)—this includes all day to day expenses such as groceries, etc.)
2) Multiply by % Reduction, typically 60-70% (lower since one less person)
3) Multiply Line 2 by ___ (use factor/discounted rate of return) years required

TOTAL ANNUAL INCOME NEEDS (ONGOING EXPENSES): TOTAL OUTFLOWS:

TOTAL INFLOWS:

1) Social Security Benefits (See following pages)
2) Savings and Investments (See following pages)
3) Retirement Assets (See following pages)
4) Present Amount of Life Insurance (See following pages)
5) Non-Cash Assets that could/would be liquidated
6) Total any Lump Sum Assets
7) Multiply Line 6 by same factor __ as line 3 above

TOTAL INFLOWS

TOTAL LIFE INSURANCE NEEDED (SUBTRACT TOTAL INFLOWS FROM TOTAL OUTFLOWS:

Keep in mind that your insurance needs will change from year to year and when you have any major changes in your life such as a marriage, divorce, birth of a child, a child moving out, retirement, purchase and/or sale of a home, changes in occupation, business relationship, worth, disability and death. These are just some changes to keep in mind. Basically, any change that affects any of the factors above or any factor you add in will call for a reevaluation of your life insurance needs. In any event, it would be optimal to review your needs annually and at a minimum of every three years. If you know when certain life events will be occurring then you may have an idea of how long you will need certain amounts of life insurance. This can help you make the decision of whether you need permanent life insurance and/or term life insurance (and the number of level premium years). Keep in mind also that as your asset base grows, your need for life insurance will most likely decline; however, protecting against estate taxes may become a concern.

Funeral Costs:

These can vary depending on location, type and many other reasons. More than 2,000,000 funerals are arranged by Americans every year; they can cost $5,000 to $10,000 or more. The average cost of an adult funeral is about $10,000. This is often a difficult subject to talk and think about. Nevertheless, it is a critical area to include in your life insurance planning as well as in your overall financial strategy. The Federal Trade Commission (FTC) has developed an extensive consumer guide. This guide and the following resources will allow you to estimate the potential cost. The guide can accessed from the FTC web site at: http://www.ftc. gov/bcp/conline/pubs/services/funeral.htm

Highlights of the guide include:

- Pre-need-planning and prepaying
- Different types of funerals
- Choosing a funeral provider
- What funeral costs include and calculating the actual cost
- Services and products
- Other resources
- Solving problems
- Worksheet of prices to check
- Glossary of terms

Administrative, Final and other Miscellaneous Expenses—can vary for cleaning up the affairs of the deceased, advisor fees, filing taxes and a number of other reasons can typically reach 50% of the higher wage earner's salary

Estate Taxes:

"Two weeks of solid work on his estate may be worth more to an executive than his financial gains of the past ten or fifteen years"— Price Waterhouse

Please note that this is a quote and applies to all, whether or not they are an executive, male or female—the Tax Code is non-discriminatory.

"The legal right of a taxpayer to decrease the amount of what otherwise would be his taxes, or altogether avoid them, by means which the law permits cannot be doubted"
Gregory vs. Helvering, 293 U.S. 465; 55 Supreme Court Reporter 266

"Over and over again, courts have said that there is nothing sinister in so arranging one's affairs to keep taxes as low as possible. Everybody does, rich and poor, and all do right because nobody owes any public duty to pay more than the law demands. Taxes are enforced exactions, not voluntary contributions." Judge Learned Hand

Estate Tax Table:

The Economic Growth and Tax Relief Reconciliation Act of 2001 has changed the federal estate tax numbers. Below are the non-guaranteed changes:

Year	Exemption	Maximum Tax Bracket	Unified Credit
2005	$ 1.5 Million	47 percent	$ 555,800
2006	$ 2 Million	46 percent	$ 780,800
2007	$ 2 Million	45 percent	$ 780,800
2008	$ 2 Million	45 percent	$ 780,800
2009	$ 3.5 Million	45 percent	$1,455,800
2010	N/A	N/A	N/A
2011	$ 1 Million**	55 percent**	$ 345,800**

**The Taxpayer Relief Act of 1997 numbers will be reinstated provided that The Economic Growth and Tax Relief Reconciliation Act of 2001 is not extended. Under current law, the federal estate tax is cancelled for only the year 2010.

How to do a rough calculation of your potential estate tax:

1. Total your gross estate. Typical items include anything of value in which you have an ownership interest. Examples: Home and other real estate, Retirement Plan Balances, Stocks, Mutual Funds, other investments, businesses, life insurance proceeds (not held outside your estate), etc.

2. Subtract from your gross estate, all allowable deductions such as funeral and administrative expenses (See Above), mortgages, other loans, credit card debt, other debts/claims against the estate, charitable deductions, Adjustable Taxable gifts (post 1976 lifetime taxable transfers not included in gross estate), gift taxes paid on post 1976 taxable gifts, any applicable tax credits such as unified tax credit, state death tax credit, foreign tax credit, tax on prior transfers credit, and, if applicable (you must be married), the marital deduction and any other applicable expenses.

3. If you have a positive net estate then this would be your net taxable estate.

4. Use the table above to calculate your tentative estate tax.

Notes:

Your unified credit is subtracted from your tentative tax, if unused during your lifetime. The unified tax credit means that no federal estate tax is payable on a taxable estate equal to your exemption equivalent. Estate taxes are due when your tentative tax is greater than your unified credit.

Your estate may be valued at death or six months later, whichever is more beneficial. If you own a farm or closely held business, your method of paying tax will be different. This will depend on the estate at death and what the executor decides; based typically on advice from attorneys and other professional advisors.

Please note that this is to generate a rough idea of a potential estate tax. Please be sure to check on whether this is the current tax table by visiting the IRS web site at www.irs.gov. You should consult with a properly certified estate planning advisor.

Emergency Fund/Readjustment Period—

Consider at least two to six months, to cover time off from work and other expenses that may need to be covered (replaced).

College Costs

Knowing how much college costs is to some degree an uncertainty, as it will depend on many factors, including tuition, room and board, books and expenses.

There are two types of college costs for which you will need to plan:

- **Direct costs**—fixed charges established by the college; such as tuition, room and board (on-campus student housing and meals).
- **Indirect costs**—expenses controlled by the student; such as personal expenses, books and transportation. The college may be able to give you some guidelines on typical indirect expenses at their campus.

Estimate your expenses for one year, or you can request expense lists from colleges that interest you and adjust them for anticipated transportation and personal expenses.

If college is a few years away, you'll need to build future cost increases into your planning. If you have a particular college in mind, you may want to use current costs at that college to forecast your future expenses. College tuition costs increased 5% annually on average between 1997 and 2000, according to the College Board.

This is only an estimate of your educational expenses. The actual cost may vary depending on many factors. This section provides a limited overview of different resources for you to ascertain possible higher education costs, as well as how to plan for them.

Quick Facts:

- College costs roughly $120,000 for four years at a private school and $55,000 for four years at a public school (1)
- In 2020, four years at a private university will cost $270,000. (2)
- College costs are increasing almost twice as fast as the inflation rate. (3)
- The odds of winning a full athletic scholarship are less than 1%. (4)

(1) Source: *The College Board for the 2001-2002 school year*
(2) Source: *Smartmoney.com*
(3) Source: *The College Board, Trends in College Pricing 2000*
(4) Source: *National Collegiate Athletic Association, Division I Facts and Figures 2000; NCAA, Division II Facts and Figures, 2001; National Center for Education Statistics, Digest of Education Statistics 2000*

There are a tremendous number of resources available on the Web. These are just a few of them. For more, simply go to any search engine and type in College Costs. You may want to visit:

http://www.smartmoney.com/college/investing/index.cfm?story=save —This site has a number of resources and a full planning center. The main site is www.smartmoney.com

Another helpful site is www.collegeboard.com. This is one of the most comprehensive sites for figuring savings for future education.

Confusion occurs because there is much discussion of using life insurance as a funding vehicle for college. This is not applicable towards the purpose discussed here, where we are looking strictly at the death benefit rather than the cash value of a life insurance policy. Of course, if there is significantly more assets than you would need, then you will need either less or no life insurance at all, for the purpose of college costs. That said a word of caution here is that, as most web sites are built for sales purposes, their information may be biased towards their company and services. However, they can assist you in determining a range of appropriate costs and savings plans.

Debt Resolution:

Short term obligations ranging to long term obligations. Paying these off is not always a necessity and may not be the best option. Include mortgage balance, credit card debt, car loans, home equity loans, etc.

The Home Mortgage:

This is an issue that should be addressed during the planning process. There are two options:

1) Pay off the mortgage—the advantage is that this reduces the overall debt load. The disadvantage is that this can use a sizeable chunk of the death benefit. This would be listed under one time expenses and would reduce the income replacement/survivor living expense need.
2) Continue with the mortgage—Allows you to have more funds available for other purposes and to continue having the income tax deductions.

Determining the Income Replacement/Survivor Living Expenses:

Consider any lifestyle changes (impact at the insured's death), what portion of your income the survivor is dependent upon, etc., include any current expenses such as mortgage/rent, groceries, clothing, utility bills, entertainment, travel, transportation, child care, etc. There are two different methods, as discussed previously in this question. You can multiply the proposed insured's income by a certain percentage (70% can be a typical number). Or, if you would like, you can perform a more detailed analysis with these steps:

1. Determine the gross income of the insured. This can be difficult due to potential promotions and cost of living increases in the

future. It may be appropriate to assume that the insured's income conservatively increases, each year to keep pace with inflation and then take an average income based on the period that needs to be replaced. Factoring in future increases provides a measure of inflation protection for the family.

2. Consider how many years the survivor will require financial support—if they are a non-working spouse, will they go back to work, is there an adjustment for remarriage and when will the children no longer need any financial support, also consider if there is a special needs child.

3. Subtract from the insured's gross income, any costs associated with the self maintenance of the insured. Examples would include employment taxes, medical costs, insurance premiums, food, clothing, contributions to retirement plans and discretionary funds set aside as savings. These costs can be arrived at through a detailed examination of the family budget. This should leave the net income that is needed to provide support for the family.

4. Ascertain any other sources of income that will be available to the family. These would include survivor benefits from deferred compensation plans, income from pension plans and IRAs, income from investments, plus any Social Security survivor benefits.

5. Decide whether the capital needed for income replacement will be preserved or liquidated. As discussed earlier, under the capital preservation approach, income can be provided to the family indefinitely. However, if capital liquidation is used, the length of time income needs to be replaced becomes a major factor in determining the capital necessary for income replacement.

Adjust the number of years of funds needed by investment growth:

Discount the sum by the net (after tax and inflation) rate of return to arrive at new capital needed.

Inflows:

With any inflow, consider that there may be penalties, or other charges or other reductions for early withdrawal:

- Social Security Benefits—Survivor's Income
- Retirement Assets—IRA's, 401(k) plans, Keoghs, pension and profit sharing plans, etc.
- Savings and Investments—bank accounts, CD's, stocks, bonds, mutual funds, real estate/rental property, etc.
- Present amount of life insurance—Include group insurance and personal insurance purchased on your own
- Other Assets (keep in mind that assets should grow, hopefully reducing the future amount of needed life insurance (however the may increase the need for survivor life insurance) and only include liquid assets (not assets that would change your lifestyle, such as a car or home).
- Other sources

Social Security Benefits:

Please note that as indicated above, that this is based on information at the time of the writing of this book. Please contact the Social Security Administration to confirm this information. Their Web Site is www.ssa.gov and their toll-free number that operates from 7AM to 7PM, Monday to Friday: **1-800-772-1213**.

Social Security will provide a survivor's benefit upon the death of a worker eligible for Social Security. Of course, you will have to make a decision as to how you feel about the future of Social Security and consider the political risk (Congress) as well. Any Social Security benefits payable will reduce the amount of income that will need to be replaced.

Social Security Benefits are also available to the surviving spouse if there are children under the age of 16. Social Security is also paid to a child (or children) until they turn age 18 or 19 if still in high school. Also, note that Social Security is available to widows or widowers at age 60 if the spouse had been covered. The period when no social security benefits are available is called the "blackout period".

Calculating the amount payable is complex and is best done by contacting the Social Security Administration directly.

Retirement Plans:

Retirement plans, which are usually defined as pension plans, 401(k) and other profit sharing plans, along with tax sheltered annuities (TSA's), SEP, Simple Plans and IRA's can all be used as a source of income replacement. Distributions from retirement plans require careful planning and thought in order to receive the maximum benefit from the plan. Besides the issues of Capital Preservation as opposed to Capital Liquidation; there is the issue of whether these funds should be left to grow on a tax deferred basis as well as the issues of avoiding any income tax on the gain from the funds.

Current Life Insurance:

This includes any personal, individual insurance as well as any group life insurance (through an employer, etc). With group life insurance, you may also choose to not include it as usually it is only effective while you are with your current employer.

Life Expectancy and Mortality Issues

When faced with designing a life insurance portfolio (as well as for any financial planning), an important factor is estimating your life expectancy. This is a guessing game as much as a science.

There are a number of resources, tables and web sites (with simple to complex calculators), available for this purpose. Please keep in mind that, the more variables you introduce the greater the likelihood that your estimate will be wrong.

A good starting point is the table issued by the U.S. Government, for use by life insurance companies in determining a basis for life insurance premiums. This table is updated every few years and is called the Commissioners Standard Ordinary Mortality Table (see the 2001 version on the next page).

Commissioners 2001 Standard Ordinary Mortality Table
(Society of Actuaries)

AGE	MALE Average Future Lifetime	FEMALE Average Future Lifetime		AGE	MALE Average Future Lifetime	FEMALE Average Future Lifetime		AGE	MALE Average Future Lifetime	FEMALE Average Future Lifetime
0	76.62	80.84		41	37.39	41.05		81	7.01	9.35
1	75.69	79.88		42	36.46	40.11		82	6.57	8.81
2	74.74	78.91		43	35.53	39.17		83	6.14	8.29
3	73.76	77.93		44	34.61	38.23		84	5.74	7.79
4	72.78	76.95		45	33.69	37.29		85	5.36	7.32
5	71.80	75.96		46	32.78	36.36		86	5.00	6.87
6	70.81	74.97		47	31.87	35.43		87	4.66	6.43
7	69.83	73.99		48	30.97	34.51		88	4.35	6.02
8	68.84	73.00		49	30.07	33.60		89	4.07	5.64
9	67.86	72.02		50	29.18	32.69		90	3.81	5.29
10	66.88	71.03		51	28.28	31.79		91	3.57	4.96
11	65.89	70.05		52	27.40	30.90		92	3.35	4.61
12	64.91	69.07		53	26.52	30.01		93	3.15	4.28
13	63.93	68.08		54	25.65	29.14		94	2.96	3.93
14	62.95	67.10		55	24.79	28.27		95	2.78	3.63
15	61.98	66.13		56	23.94	27.41		96	2.62	3.38
16	61.02	65.15		57	23.10	26.57		97	2.47	3.18
17	60.07	64.17		58	22.27	25.73		98	2.32	3.02
18	59.12	63.20		59	21.45	24.90		99	2.19	2.82
19	58.17	62.23		60	20.64	24.08		100	2.07	2.61
20	57.23	61.26		61	19.85	23.27		101	1.96	2.42
21	56.29	60.28		62	19.06	22.47		102	1.86	2.23
22	55.34	59.31		63	18.29	21.68		103	1.76	2.06
23	54.40	58.34		64	17.54	20.90		104	1.66	1.89
24	53.45	57.37		65	16.80	20.12		105	1.57	1.74
25	52.51	56.40		66	16.08	19.36		106	1.48	1.60
26	51.57	55.43		67	15.37	18.60		107	1.39	1.47
27	50.62	54.46		68	14.68	17.86		108	1.30	1.36
28	49.68	53.49		69	13.99	17.12		109	1.22	1.25
29	48.74	52.53		70	13.32	16.40		110	1.14	1.16
30	47.79	51.56		71	12.66	15.69		111	1.07	1.08
31	46.85	50.60		72	12.01	14.99		112	0.99	1.00
32	45.90	49.63		73	11.39	14.31		113	0.92	0.93
33	44.95	48.67		74	10.78	13.64		114	0.85	0.86
34	44.00	47.71		75	10.18	12.98		115	0.79	0.79
35	43.05	46.75		76	9.61	12.34		116	0.72	0.73
36	42.11	45.80		77	9.05	11.71		117	0.66	0.67
37	41.16	44.84		78	8.50	11.10		118	0.61	0.61
38	40.21	43.89		79	7.98	10.50		119	0.55	0.56

The following are some of the many factors that can impact your life expectancy:

- **Gender**—males generally have shorter life expectancies than females as shown in the mortality table.
- **Tobacco Use**—if you use tobacco, your life expectancy will be shorter than for those who don't use tobacco. Smoking will especially shorten your life expectancy.
- **Build**—being overweight can reduce your life expectancy. Your target weight is determined by your height and weight, exceeding that weight reduces your life expectancy. Please see Question 77 for further information.
- **Alcohol use**—excessive alcohol drinking can reduce your life expectancy.
- **Driving**—unsafe driving indicates a greater risk of accidents and death and will therefore reduce your life expectancy.
- **Blood pressure**—especially uncontrolled high blood pressure will reduce life expectancy.
- **Family medical history**—if a parent or sibling has/had a history of heart disease, cancer, diabetes or high blood pressure prior to age 60 then life expectancy may be lower and is a factor though it is hard to measure.

A good resource is the life tables available from the U.S. Department of Health and Human Services—Center for Disease Control and Prevention (CDC). Annually, they publish a life expectancy table on their web site. This table can be a valuable resource and is found at—http://www.cdc.gov/nchs/fastats/lifexpec.htm

Here Are Some of the Life Expectancy Final Data 2000 Highlights:
(All figures are for the U.S.)

- All Americans, at Birth: **76.9 (2000)**
- All Americans, at Age 65: **17.9 (2000)**
- All Males, at Birth: **74.1 (2000)**
- All Males, at Age 65: **16.3 (2000)**
- All Females, at Birth: **79.5 (2000)**
- All Females, at Age 65: **19.2 (2000)**

*Source: **National Vital Statistics Reports, Vol. 51, No. 3***

Other sites of interest include:

http://www.retireweb.com/death.html: This site features a life expectancy calculator which is a simple calculation and is based on a specific mortality table used by actuaries for retirement planning purposes. The mortality table is called GAM 83 and is based on insured group annuity experience from the 1970s. The table only varies by sex and by age. Actuaries use this table to help determine how much a pension plan should hold for retired individuals. The calculation uses the probabilities of living from the mortality table for a given age and sex and then determines how long that individual is expected to live. The table will not be accurate for any given individual but is correct when considering large groups of people. Any given individual will have a 50% chance of living longer than the given life expectancy and a 50% chance of dying earlier than the given life expectancy. On average, the table will produce the correct value. Of course, (as many users have pointed out) individual health and other circumstances vary. This calculator is not supposed to calculate your *exact* time of death but merely give you a rough estimation of how long you can expect to live, in order to help you in the retirement planning process.

www.livingto100.com—The Living to 100 Life Expectancy Calculator© was designed to translate what has been learned from studies of centenarians and other longevity research into a practical and empowering tool for individuals to estimate their longevity potential. The average person is born with a set of genes that would allow them to live to 85 years of age and maybe longer. People who take appropriate preventive steps may add as many as 10 quality years to that. People who fail to heed the messages of preventive medicine may subtract substantial years from their lives.

www.longtolive.com—As described on their site—Haven't you ever wondered what your Life Expectancy is? Now you can find out using our Life Expectancy Calculator. This tool will also show you easy ways to extend your life with minor changes, like taking a multi-vitamin every day. After you calculate your Life Expectancy, you will also get your very own Life Clock (Death Clock). You can now watch time slip away…Long to Live is just for fun, although it is based on statistical life expectancy data. These numbers are REAL, but they are just statistics. Some people live longer than others, and some are hit by busses, etc...Everybody has their own death clock. What is yours?

A search on any internet search engine will find a multitude of sites and calculators on the web. Almost everyone will give you a different estimate. Therefore, in doing your planning, the best option will typically be the one you best understand and makes the most sense to you.

CHAPTER 2: TYPES OF LIFE INSURANCE

QUESTION 4: What Are The Basic Types Of Life Insurance Products Out There?

There is a confusing array of life insurance products, almost rivaling the mutual fund industry and its bewildering variety of choices. With over 1,500 life insurance companies active in the business and with each company usually offering several different types of policies/contracts,—you can see that there are many thousands of different contracts available.

No guide, advisor or reference can feasibly cover every type of policy and every nuance. Yet there are major similarities between certain types of life insurance contracts. For example, a universal life policy issued by company A will be similar to a universal life policy issued by company B. State Insurance Regulations make this so. This chapter is designed to help you with the differences between the different types of policies.

All life insurance policies promise to pay an agreed sum of money if the insured person should die while the policy is in-force, but all life insurance policies are not the same. A wide variety of plans are available. Some policies provide permanent coverage while other coverage is only temporary (i.e., term life insurance). Some policies build cash values (i.e., "permanent" life insurance) while others do not. Some policies combine different kinds of insurance (e.g., a permanent base policy with a term "rider"), and yet others let you change from one type of insurance coverage to another. Your choice should be based on your needs and what you can afford. Some permanent life insurance policies allow you to add additional, term life insurance during the period of your greatest life insurance need. Usually the term insurance is on your life, but it can also be bought for your spouse and children if needed.

QUESTION 5: How do I tell the Basic Differences between Term and Permanent Life Insurance?

Let's look at the differences between term and permanent life insurance. For our present purpose, permanent life insurance includes any policy that is not term life insurance (i.e., one that gradually accumulates a cash value). Typical examples include whole life, universal life and variable life policies). Unfortunately, it can get confusing. When a term policy accumulates a cash value, then it is typically a form of universal life policy and not term insurance at all. But there are exceptions. For example, a "term to age 65" policy will typically accumulate a cash value in the intermediate in-force years. This cash value will then gradually reduce to zero by age 65, when the coverage automatically ends.

Here is a summary of each of these kinds of insurance:

TERM INSURANCE:

- As the name implies, it is purchased for a specified term of years.

- The cost (premium) is lower, especially for younger applicants.

- Premiums systematically increase year by year as you get older.

- Term insurance has no residual value. That is, it expires without value at the end of the term.

- Less than 1% of term policies ever pay a death benefit, according to a 1993 study of over 20,000 policies by Penn State University. Don't be misled by this statistic. Most term policies cannot be renewed beyond age 75, but annual renewal term policies ("ART") may usually be renewed to age 100. However, ART policies become prohibitively expensive at the older ages, so renewing them much beyond age 70 or 75 is impractical for most people.

PERMANENT INSURANCE:

- Premium payments usually (but not always) remain the same each year.
- Premium payments generally are considerably higher than for term life insurance policies in the early years of the contract.
- Premium payments may be discontinued under certain circumstances. Some policies provide significant degrees of flexibility.
- Interest or other earnings on the cash value is tax deferred.
- Permanent policies typically make no sense without a long term commitment from the buyer, since little or no cash surrender value accumulates in the first few years in (most cases).
- Coverage may stay in-force to age 95 or greater and the policy will have a residual value (cash value—sometimes called cash surrender value).
- Access to the cash value is available through loans and withdrawals.

QUESTION 6: The $64,000 question—Should I Buy Term Life Insurance or Permanent Life Insurance and Invest the Difference?

This the perhaps the most controversial question of all when it comes to selecting a life insurance policy. Life insurance people generally line up in one of two "camps": The whole life "camp" consists of True Believers, to whom buying permanent life insurance is the answer to every problem except cancer (and maybe that,too). These people have some valid points in their favor, but neither "camp" owns the moral high ground on this issue. The term insurance "camp" is often referred to in derisory terms by the permanent folks as "termites"—those whose recommendation is "buy term and invest the difference." This means investing the difference between the (cheap) term life insurance premium and the (expensive) permanent policy in stocks or mutual funds. The theory is that, over time, the investment component of the two will accumulate more money than the permanent policy would accumulate. There is little or no love lost between the two sides on this issue.

As you might expect, the truth often lies somewhere in between the two opposing points of view. The two sides have polarized the issue into a dichotomy—an either/or situation, when in reality very often a combination of term and permanent life insurance is the most appropriate recommendation. So which is better for you depends on your specific needs and circumstances. There is no one size-fits-all solution to the life insurance planning problem.

Term insurance is generally agreed to be an excellent short term solution to a temporary need for life insurance coverage, while permanent life insurance is intended to remain in-force until your death or until your needs change. The one that is better suited for your needs depends on your particular situation. If you would like assistance in making this determination, please contact me.

Most people need some life insurance. As Dr. Joe Belth, Indiana University Professor Emeritus and one of the most respected critics of the life insurance industry, pointed out some years ago, there is no substitute for life insurance. No other financial product will do what life insurance accomplishes. It becomes a question of determining a specific life insurance solution for you. While you are young, with a growing family and limited budget, you will probably need a higher death benefit than you could afford if you purchased only permanent insurance. Term insurance makes sense for you at this stage in life. Rates are low and benefits are high. At some point, however, you will probably need to own some permanent coverage in order to accomplish the intended purpose that life insurance is designed to fill. Permanent insurance provides coverage for the rest of your life prospectively. It is a vehicle for cash accumulation, it can provide liquidity to pay estate taxes, and it is a method for leveling out premiums. The last point can be very important.

While term insurance is very cheap if purchased at younger ages, it becomes prohibitively expensive much beyond age 70 or 75. Buying permanent life insurance early helps to ensure its affordability. The invested cash value element accumulates over time, helping to cover the increasing cost of the pure life insurance protection element in the later years. The tradeoff is paying a higher, more or less level premium for many years, to avoid the problem of un-affordability in the later years. Term insurance, then, is temporary coverage intended to meet a short term need over a specific time horizon. Permanent insurance is a long term solution for lifetime needs. Again, which one is right for you depends on your individual situation.

QUESTION 7: What are the different types of Term Life Insurance?

With that brief overview of term and permanent coverage in mind, now let's take a more in-depth look at each type of insurance. Term insurance provides coverage for a specified period (term) of one or more years. It pays a death benefit only if you die during the specified term and if you have paid the required premiums to keep it in-force for the term. Term insurance usually provides the largest amount of death protection for your premium dollars. Most term policies are guaranteed renewable for one or more additional terms, even if your health has changed. Each time you renew the policy for a new term, the premium payment will be higher and it will usually remain level for the balance of the term. If you are considering term insurance, be sure to check the premium schedule at the specified renewal ages, and find out for how long the policy can be renewed, if you decide to keep it.

Many term insurance policies can be exchanged for a permanent policy during the term period. This conversion privilege could prove to be very important, especially if your health deteriorates and you are unable to qualify for a new permanent policy. Be sure to check the conversion eligibility period as you review the coverage, before applying for a policy. Common types of term insurance include:

- Annual Renewable Term (also known as yearly renewable term, "ART" or "YRT")—features an annually increasing premium and a level death benefit.

- Level Premium Term—features a level premium for a specified number of years (the premium may or may not be guaranteed to remain level). At the end of this level premium period, some policies allow you to renew coverage for another term at very favorable rates, provided that you meet the company's underwriting criteria (i.e., your health remains good). This type of coverage is known in the industry as re-entry term. If you don't meet the company's current underwriting standards and thereby do not qualify for the re-entry term rate, you can still keep the coverage in-force for a specified period of years by paying a higher rate set forth in the policy.

- Decreasing Term Insurance (sometimes known as Mortgage Insurance because this type of coverage is often used for mortgage cancellation in the event of the premature death of the family's primary wage-earner)—features a level premium and a decreasing death benefit. Since coverage decreases gradually over the years, the premium will be considerably lower than level premium term.

- Return of Premium Term—allows the policy owner to receive the sum of premiums paid (sometimes with interest) after a certain term of years, usually the end of the level premium period.

QUESTION 8: How do I recognize the Advantages and Disadvantages of Term Life Insurance?

Advantages of Term Life Insurance:

- Premiums are lower than permanent insurance, allowing younger people to buy more coverage when the need for protection is usually greatest.

- Term is also useful for insuring specific needs that will disappear in time such as mortgages or loans. Mortgage cancellation insurance, for example, is decreasing term coverage whose face amount (i.e., insurance amount) at any given time roughly approximates the amount of the outstanding mortgage. If the insured person dies, the insurance proceeds are used to pay off the mortgage.

Disadvantages of Term Life Insurance:

- Premiums increase over time as the insured person grows older. This is also true of level term coverage; at renewal time, the premium goes up and remains level for the next term.

- Coverage ceases when the term ends. Even when the policy may be renewed for another term, the ever increasing premium may make coverage too expensive to continue.

- Generally, term policies don't offer cash value or a reduced paid up insurance option.

- According to a 1993 Penn State University study covering more than 20,000 policies, only 1% of the policies resulted in a death claim.

QUESTION 9: What Are Some of the Characteristics of Permanent (Cash Value) Life Insurance?

Permanent life insurance refers to any cash value type of insurance that provides continuous coverage to age 95 or 100. This type of policy generally has a level premium that must be paid to keep the coverage in-force. Under some circumstances, premium payments may be reduced or stopped, but this cannot be counted upon. Permanent policies typically will accumulate a cash value, which is tax deferred. Most permanent policies allow you to borrow against the policy value or withdraw all or a portion of the cash value.

Premiums are higher than you would pay for the same face amount of term insurance, but they are less than the cumulative premiums you would eventually pay if you were to keep renewing a term policy into advanced age. This is because interest earned on the cash value helps to offset the higher cost of pure life insurance protection as the insured person grows older.

Some policies (e.g., universal life) allow you to vary your premium payments every year and even skip a payment if you wish. The premiums you pay (less expense charges deducted from the premium payments) go into an accumulation account that earns interest. Mortality (insurance) charges are deducted from the account. Insurance coverage continues as long as there is enough money in the account to pay the insurance charges.

The cash value of many life insurance policies may be affected by an insurance company's actual experience over time. For example, mortality expense charges are based on actuarial assumptions that may require periodic adjustment as national mortality experience gradually changes. Likewise, expense charges are affected by such factors as how efficiently the company operates, economies of scale, overall company expenses and so forth...Policy loans will also affect the long term performance of a policy.

QUESTION 10: What are the Types of Permanent (Cash Value) Life Insurance?

There are many types of permanent life insurance including:

- Endowment
- Whole, Ordinary or "Straight" Life (terms are synonymous)
- Limited Pay
- Adjustable Life
- Adaptable Life
- Universal Life
- Joint or Survivorship Life
- Variable Life
- Variable Universal Life

The barrel below is a basic portrayal of how a cash value life insurance policy works:

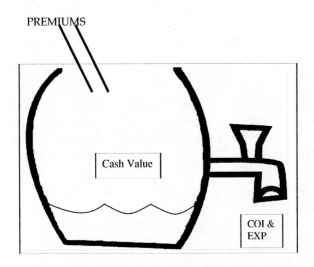

Every so often (annually, semi-annually, quarterly or monthly); premiums are paid into the policy. This increases the level of water of barrel.

Monthly, the insurance company turns the spigot and takes out their expenses (EXP) and the mortality charges (cost of insurance/COI). If there is not enough water in the barrel, the policy will lapse/terminate.

The remaining water in the barrel is the accumulated value. Subtract the surrender fees and this is your surrender value

QUESTION 11: What are Endowment Life Insurance Policies?

Endowment policies are infrequently sold today, yet many of these policies remain in-force. An endowment policy is similar to a whole life policy (described below), in that the face amount of coverage is paid to the beneficiary upon the death of the named insured. The difference is that at the specified time the face amount is paid as a living benefit to the person designated to receive it, as long as the insured person is living at that time. Endowment policies have a number of variations. Some run for 30 years or so and then "endow" for the face amount, while others set the maturity or endowment date at attainment of a specified age (e.g., 65). Usually, premiums must be paid for the entire in-force period, but a few limited pay endowment policies exist.

QUESTION 12: How Can I Tell The Difference Between The Many Types of Whole Life Insurance?

Whole life—often called ordinary life and sometimes straight life—is the original permanent life insurance coverage and is still the most commonly found in-force life insurance policy today. The concept is simplicity itself: (1) Premium payments are made for life at a rate fixed by the company and agreed to by the applicant; (2) When the named insured dies, the company pays the face amount to the named beneficiary. It's that simple. The company can never raise the premium rate nor can it cancel the policy as long as the premium is paid on a timely basis (absent fraud, in which case the policy can be rescinded, but fraud claims are very rare). The insurance company is therefore promising to pay the face amount upon death, whether that occurs the day after coverage becomes effective or at age 99. To keep this promise, the company employs actuaries who determine the premium payment levels that will be adequate to fund the guarantees in the policy. Life insurance company actuarial science is, as the term implies, very scientific and fairly precise. It involves the pooling of risks over a large population of insured persons. The company has no idea which specific insured persons will die in any given year, but it knows with considerable accuracy how many will die each year, and their likely age distributions. This knowledge allows actuaries to calculate premiums and set adequate reserve levels necessary to keep the promises made by the company. Although this is not usually specified in the policy, if the insured person lives to the end of the specified mortality table, the company usually considers the policy "endowed" and pays the full face amount to the policy owner.

Whole life has become much less popular over the past 20 years, with the introduction of universal life, variable life and variable universal life. Whole life policies are more rigid than adjustable life, universal life and variable universal life in the sense that premiums must be paid on time or else the policy "lapses" (i.e., ceases or goes into a so-called non-forfeiture option mode, such as extended term coverage or reduced paid up life insurance). Whole life policies usually included the "automatic premium loan" feature that would allow the company to pay any overdue premium payments by making a loan from the cash value. The distinguishing feature of the whole life policy is its simplicity. Pay the premiums on time and the policy will pay off upon the insured's death, period. The main disadvantage of whole life is the premium payment, which is higher than for 14universal life, variable universal life and their variants. If the policy owner is unable to pay the premiums due to job loss, illness or other circumstances then the policy will lapse.

Policy loans are usually available, but borrowing from a policy can lead to its eventual lapse if the loan is not repaid. For more information on policy loans, please refer to Chapter 10; Question #'s 106-109 which discuss policy loans in detail as policy loans can be a very complex and destructive factor to your coverage.

The cash value in a whole life policy is invested by the insurance company through its general investment portfolio. In contrast, variable universal life policies have the cash value component invested in separate accounts (more on this later).

Whole life policies are either participating or non-participating (par v. non-par). A participating policy charges a higher premium and in return, pays regular dividends to the policy owner. Non-par policies pay no dividends and premiums are usually lower than par policies. Dividends can be utilized in several different ways. Dividends are not guaranteed and depend on the company's actual experience with the book of in-force business. Dividend options include (a) cash; (b) purchase of fully paid-up life insurance in small increments with each dividend; (c) reduction of the next premium payment; (d) retained by the company at interest; (e) purchase of one-year term insurance in an amount equal to the then cash value (the so-called fifth dividend option; that was popular with policy owners who wanted to maximize the face amount of coverage during the early in-force years). It is important to understand that dividends are bought and paid for when you apply for a participating policy. The trade-off for dividends is higher premiums.

Here is a brief overview of the many types of whole life insurance:

Ordinary Life provides permanent lifetime coverage with premiums payable for the whole of life. This is the original whole life policy also known as straight life and continuous premium whole life. Ordinary life policies provide permanent protection for a level annual premium outlay (the mortality costs are spread over the life of the policy). Cash values normally increase at a fairly constant rate, equaling the face amount at age 100. Cash values in early years are typically low, due to the high costs of policy sale and issuance. These costs include underwriting and administrative expenses, with the largest portion represented by the agent's commission, ranging from 40% to 80% or more of the first year premium.

Limited-Payment Whole Life pays the face amount at death, but the premium payments are compressed into a shorter payment period. At the end of the premium payment period, the policy becomes paid up for its full face amount. This limited payment period is expressed as "paid up at age X" or by the number of years premiums must be paid—(e.g., 20 pay life or paid-up-at-65). Since the premium paying period is shortened, the annual premium is higher and is the actuarial equivalent of lifetime premium payments. This category also includes single premium whole life, which is no longer popular due to changes in the tax laws several years ago that established the so called Modified Endowment Contract Rules ("MEC"). In general, however, MEC rules involve a calculation to determine whether a life insurance policy will be treated for tax purposes as an insurance contract or an investment contract. If the former, withdrawals are treated as a tax free recovery of the contract's original cost basis until the entire basis has been withdrawn. Subsequent withdrawals are fully taxable at ordinary income tax rates. If the latter, withdrawals are treated for tax purposes on a last in, first out basis. This means that all withdrawals are treated as taxable interest until they cumulatively equal all interest earnings in the contract. Further withdrawals are then treated as non-taxable recovery of basis.

Indeterminate Premium Whole Life sets the premium payment at a rate lower than the maximum rate that the company reserves the right to charge. Usually, the actual premium rate represents a significant discount from the maximum premium the company may charge, and this discounted premium rate may be guaranteed for several policy years. Thereafter, the company annually declares (sets) the premium rate, which is usually lower than the maximum rate but may be more than the initial rate. The policy is designed and priced so that when the company has favorable mortality, investment and expense experience, the policy owner shares in that favorable experience in the form of lower premium payments.

Current Assumption Whole Life is a whole life variant that makes use of a current interest rate in setting the cash value, along with an indeterminate premium structure (see the explanation above). This coverage type is also commonly referred to as "Interest Sensitive Whole Life." Most of these products take into account current mortality and expense charges rather than those guaranteed by the contract.

The policies described above work as follows: The premium is paid to the insurance company, which deducts expense charges (the contract specifies the maximum that can be charged; however, most companies usually charge less). Many of these types of policies have no stated expense charges; instead there are higher mortality charges and a margin built into the interest earnings credited to the cash value. The net amount remaining is added to the preceding year's accumulated fund balance to come up with a beginning year balance. Interest is added to the balance based on the insurer's current rate. Then mortality charges are deducted (these charges are calculated based on the maximum permissible rates as set forth in the contract or, more often on lower current rates). This rate is applied to the policy's net amount at risk (face amount less cash value). Typically the contracts stipulate that surrender charges will be levied against the fund balance to arrive at the net surrender value. This value is never less than that required by non-forfeiture law.

These come in many variations, such as limited pay and lifetime pay premiums. The shorter the premium payment period, the higher the premium. The company sets the premium rate, and deducts certain expense charges from premiums received. The contract states the maximum premium that can be charged; although companies often charge less.

The net amount remaining is added to the preceding year's accumulated fund balance to constitute a beginning year balance. Then the insurer credits interest to this balance and then mortality charges are assessed. These charges are calculated based on the maximum permissible rates allowed in the contract or, as is typical, on lower current rates. Most of these contracts stipulate that surrender charges will be levied against the fund balance to arrive at the net surrender value. This value is never less than that required by the standard non-forfeiture law. The surrender charges decline in percentage annually and usually last for ten to sixteen years.

Variable (Whole) Life Insurance—See Question 14

Single Premium Whole Life ("SPWL") policies never really caught on with the public, probably due to the high initial outlay (often approaching 50% of the initial face amount for an insured at age 35). An exception is the early 1980s, when this type of policy was heavily promoted for its then favorable tax treatment (which Congress changed in the mid-1980s). At that time, the policy owner could pay a single premium and then borrow the interest earnings each year, while deducting the loan interest. The modified endowment contract ("MEC") rules adopted in 1987 ended this practice (The MEC rules are addressed later in this report). With SPWL, the purchaser pays a single premium to the insurance company, which credits current rates of interest to the fund value. Instead of mortality and expense charges being deducted annually from the cash value, they are netted against the interest credited to the fund. Unfortunately, this tends to create the appearance that there is no deduction for these charges.

Other, less common types of Whole Life policies include Modified Life, the so-called 'Economatic' policy, Indexed Whole Life, Graded Premium Whole Life and, as briefly discussed above, Single Premium Whole Life.

QUESTION 13: What is Universal Life Insurance?

Universal Life arrived on the insurance scene in the early 1980s. It was billed as the ultimate in life insurance flexibility, because it gives the policy owner considerable flexibility as to the amount and timing of premium payments and the face amount of coverage can be changed (down at any time; up with evidence of continued insurability).

Universal Life—popularly known as "UL", is unique in the sense that a UL policy "unbundles" the pricing elements that make up a traditional cash value policy (interest earnings, mortality costs and company expenses) and prices them separately.

Think of a UL policy as a bucket into which you pour liquid money. The bucket has a spigot at the bottom, and the company turns the spigot to drip money out of the bucket to pay for the expenses associated with the policy. Meanwhile, money left in the bucket earns interest at a rate declared by the company. It is the policy owner's responsibility to keep enough money in the bucket (by making adequate, timely premium payments) to pay the policy expenses as they come due. While the policy owner must put enough money into the bucket to keep the policy in force (otherwise, it will lapse), otherwise there is complete discretion as to when premium payments will be made and in what amounts.

Alas, while UL policies are appropriate in the right circumstances, they have failed to live up to their initial billing as the complete solution to most permanent life insurance needs. To better understand why, think of a traditional whole life policy. The policy owner has but one responsibility—to pay the premiums when due. If premiums are paid when they come due, the policy will never lapse and eventually it will mature as a death claim, period. UL is different. If the policy owner fails to fund it adequately, UL may turn out to be temporary rather than permanent life insurance. On a traditional whole life policy, the pricing elements are bundled together and guaranteed for the life of the policy. On a UL policy the company may change pricing elements subject to certain limits set forth in the policy. Thus, the company may raise the expense charges and mortality costs and lower the amount of interest credited to the accumulating funds "bucket". Many

UL policy owners have been disappointed to learn that what they thought was permanent life insurance turned out to be unaffordable as they grew older. Moreover, the life insurance industry generally did an inadequate job of educating their customers about UL. As a result, thousands and perhaps tens of thousands of policy owners today own UL policies that are ticking away like time bombs destined to explode (lapse) because of inadequate cash value.

UL policies were designed to be transparent to the consumer in the sense that the policy owner sees exactly how much money is put into the bucket, how much interest is credited on the bucket funds, and how much is withdrawn periodically by the company to pay the expense elements in the policy. In theory, this is a major step forward, but the problem is one of communication. In reality, many policy owners do not understand how their UL policies work and therefore are unaware that their policies are likely to lapse before life expectancy has been attained. Companies report to their policy owners by means of periodic statements showing the amount of money in the bucket, interest earned and amounts withdrawn. Inevitably, these statements are complex and not easily understood. While these periodic reports are useful, their main benefit is the comparison between actual results achieved with forecast results.

UL policy owners are well advised to ask the company for a so-called in-force illustration at least every two or three years. An in-force illustration is a printout that consists of several columns of numbers based on current values and assumptions compared with guaranteed minimum values. Some such illustrations provide three separate projections, including a minimum guaranteed projection, a favorable projection and a slightly pessimistic one. An in-force illustration is essential because it is the only effective way to monitor the progress of a UL policy. Keep in mind that most UL policies sold prior to the mid-1990s were based on the assumption that the higher interest rates of that era would continue indefinitely. Falling interest rates mean that many of those policies are destined to lapse long before the policy pays off as a death claim due to inadequate premium funding. Furthermore, some UL companies have subsequently increased their mortality and expense charges to levels higher than those illustrated when the policies were originally issued.

QUESTION 14: What are Variable Life and Variable Universal Life and why are they different?

Variable Life and Variable UL provide death benefits and cash values that vary with the performance of an underlying portfolio of investments. These are some of the most difficult policies to understand. UL policies earn interest on the cash value bucket, as described above. The company invests the premium dollars as part of the company's so-called General Account. In other words, the insurance company bears the risks inherent to investing and credits in-force UL policies with interest based on the company's investment results. There is, however, no direct link between the company's investment portfolio and the declared interest rate on UL policies. There is a relationship between what the company earns on its investments and the interest it credits to UL policies, but this relationship is indirect. In contrast, Variable Life and Variable UL policies invest the cash value bucket in a variety of investments from which the policy owner chooses. These are usually referred to as investment sub-accounts. There is a direct link between the performance of the investment sub-accounts and the amount earned on the cash value bucket. For example, if the policy owner chooses one or more sub-accounts that are invested in the stock market, and the market drops, the policy may be inadequately funded and the policy owner will have to put in additional funds to keep it in-force. On the other hand, if the stock market does well, the earnings on the cash value bucket may well exceed considerably the amount that would be earned on a UL cash value bucket.

Variable Life comes in both UL and whole life versions. Usually, the policy owner has a choice of investment sub-accounts that range from the conservative (bond or money market funds) to aggressive (growth stock funds). Variable Life and Variable UL must by law be sold with a prospectus, and you will definitely want to read the prospectus before buying one of these policies. The prospectus is a lengthy document and it is tedious to pore through it. Nonetheless it will disclose vitally important information that will affect the policy's future performance. If you cannot or do not want to bother with the prospectus, it is essential that you seek competent advice from someone qualified to help you choose the right policy for your circumstances. Because of the direct link between performance of the investment sub-accounts and the cash value bucket, the cash value of a Variable Life/Variable UL policy is not guaranteed and the policy owner bears that risk. However, by choosing among the available fund options, the policy owner can create an optimum allocation of funds to the available investment sub-accounts in order to best meet the stated objectives and risk tolerance. Good investment performance leads to higher cash values and, ultimately, higher death benefits. On the other hand, poor investment performance leads to reduced cash values and death benefits. Some policies guarantee that death benefits cannot fall below a minimum level.

When you are discussing the possibility of purchasing a Variable Life or Variable UL policy, you will be provided with a proposal and the prospectus. Because the policy owner decides how the cash value bucket will be invested, there are more choices to make than on a UL policy—and more things that can go wrong. On the other hand, the policy owner has more control over the cash value bucket. Whole Life, UL, as well as Variable Life and Variable UL all permit policy loans. Keep in mind that taking out a loan puts the policy at much higher risk of lapsing prematurely. A loan can also result in adverse tax consequences under certain circumstances. A Variable Life or Variable UL policy may be surrendered for its cash value at any time and the policy owner also has the option of exchanging the policy for an annuity contract. It is always a good idea to be mindful of the fact that buying any form of permanent life insurance and keeping it only a few years will prove to be an expensive way of buying temporary life insurance. Term life insurance is extremely cheap and, if the need for insurance is temporary, term is the preferred solution.

Issues to consider with Variable Universal Life that can offset the tax advantages of life insurance are the following charges:

- Federal and state premium taxes that vary among states but average around 3 percent of premiums;
- M&E (mortality and expense) charges assessed against cash values that range, among policies studied, from 60 to 90 basis points (with 100 basis points equaling 1 percentage point);
- Investment management assets charges that vary, among policies studied, from 20 to 162 basis points; and
- Surrender charges that typically exceed the first year's premium and last from 10 to 15 years.

(These issues are from a report on Variable Universal by James Hunt; Consumer Federation of America.)

Before allocating future premium payments to the investment sub-accounts, check them out carefully. Make sure they fit the policy owner's risk tolerance. Are they well balanced? Is there a range of investment choices that suits all risk tolerances? There are many factors that affect the performance and well being of a Variable Life or Variable UL policy. Please note that this is not investment advice and is strictly advice from the life insurance perspective. For advice on the investment accounts, please consult a properly licensed financial/investment advisor.

QUESTION 15: What Are No-Load/Low-Load Life Insurance Products?

There is one other type of life insurance coverage and those are No-Load life insurance products which are designed for advisors who are compensated on a fee basis. At least in California, this is limited to those who meet the criteria discussed in Question 60. However this regulation is frequently broken. You may wish to check with your State's Insurance Department (See Appendix A for a directory with contact information). Some states do not have any type of regulation for fee-based life insurance advising and consulting.

These products were designed to help reduce policy costs, allow more of each premium to be credited to the policy and enable cash values to grow quickly. Some of the products have no percent of premium charges, no policy charges, and no surrender charges. The companies do take a cost of insurance charge and credit interest (to the client).

Traditional "Load" policies pay a first year commission ranging from 25% to 90% or more (of the premium). Renewal commissions (on future premiums) range from 2% to 5%. On most term policies, there is no renewal commission paid.

On the traditional "load" policies there are very high (up to 100%) surrender charges for at least the first five years. After the first year, the surrender charges decrease at a faster rate until they become non-existent anywhere from the tenth up through the 20th year (usually). A surrender charge is the percentage that a company deducts from your cash/accumulation value.

As no-load policies have no first year commissions, there are much higher early cash values. Usually, there are minimal if any surrender charges. Depending on the situation, the first year cash value may exceed the premium.

Very few life insurance companies (less than 1%) have no-load life insurance policies. This is due to the fact that there has not been a high demand for these products. It is basically a Catch-22 situation; the companies do not introduce these products as they say that the advisors are not interested; which is true because most advisors are not properly licensed (which does not stop many of them) and also because, the agents are not willing to forgo the high first year commission. If the companies introduced a wider selection of products and worked with the agents as discussed in Question 60.; then the advisors might get properly licensed and be able to sell these products.

The other issue at this time is that, for the most part, while the cash value of a no-load/low-load policy for the first few years is significantly higher than with a traditional product, over the long term the cash values become similar. The concept of these products is excellent; however their day has not come yet.

QUESTION 16: What are some Advantages and Disadvantages of Permanent (Cash Value) Life Insurance:

Advantages of Permanent (Cash Value) Life Insurance:

- As long as the necessary premiums are paid, protection is guaranteed for life.
- Premium payments can be fixed or flexible to meet personal financial needs.
- The policy accumulates a cash value that may be borrowed against. (Loans must be paid back with interest or else the benefi-

ciary will receive a reduced death benefit.) You may borrow against the policy's cash value to pay future premiums or use the cash value to provide paid-up insurance (with certain policies).

- The policy's cash value may be surrendered partially or wholly—for the cash value or it may be converted to an annuity. (An annuity is an insurance product that provides an income for a person's lifetime or for a specific period of time.)
- A "rider" (additional feature) can be added to a policy, giving you the option to purchase additional insurance without taking a medical exam or having to furnish evidence of insurability.
- It pre-funds rising high insurance costs.
- The cash value accumulates on a tax-deferred basis in most cases (based on current tax law, which could change).

Disadvantages of Permanent/Cash Value Life Insurance:

- Higher premium payments, compared to term life insurance, may make it hard to buy enough protection.
- It may be more costly than term insurance if you don't keep it long enough. Premiums are higher than term in the early years of the contract.

Questions 9 through 15 are an overview of the various types of policies available. Since there are many unique products available in the marketplace, be sure that you are making a valid, "apples to apples" comparison between policies.

QUESTION 17: What is a Policy Rider?

A policy rider is an optional benefit that can be added to a policy for an extra premium. Legally, it is defined as a document that amends the policy or certificate. It may increase or decrease benefits, waive the condition of coverage or, in any other way, amend the original contract. Examples are:
- Accelerated Death Benefit Rider—Rider that allows payment of a portion of the face amount prior to the death of the insured, if the insured is diagnosed with a terminal illness or injury.

- Accidental Death Benefit—A benefit in addition to the face amount of a life insurance policy, payable if the insured dies as the result of an accident. Sometimes referred to as "double indemnity."
- Annual Renewable Term Rider—Term life insurance that is "blended" into the policy, which reduces the premium and will reduce the cash value.
- Child Rider—Rider which provides insurance to the insured's child(ren).
- Cost-of-Living Rider: Benefit that can be added to a life insurance policy under which the policy owner can purchase one-year term insurance equal to the percentage change in the consumer price index with no evidence of insurability.
- Disability Income Rider (generally on older policies)—This rider typically pays a monthly benefit of 1% of the death benefit of the coverage, in the event of permanent and total disability.
- Guaranteed Insurability Option—Allows the purchase (optional) of additional coverage at certain intervals without providing evidence of insurability (no underwriting).
- Living Benefits Rider: A rider that allows insureds who are terminally ill or who suffer from certain catastrophic diseases, to collect part of their life insurance benefits before they die, primarily to pay for the care they require.
- Other Insured Rider: Rider which provides coverage to an eligible business or family member other than the insured
- Spousal Rider: Rider which provides coverage to the insured's spouse.
- Terminal Illness Rider—See Living Benefits Rider above
- Waiver of Cost of Insurance Rider (Universal Life policies generally): Waives the cost of insurance in the event the insured becomes totally and permanently disabled during the life of the policy.
- Waiver of Premium Rider (term and whole life policies generally): Provides that in the event the insured becomes totally and permanently disabled before a specified age premiums on the contract will be waived during the continuance of the contract.

Keep in mind that many of these riders are more profitable for the insurance carrier. Each carrier only offers certain riders per policy.

QUESTION 18: Are there any other types of Life Insurance?

- **Credit life insurance**—This insurance is designed to pay off the balance of a loan if you die before you have repaid it. Credit life insurance is available for many kinds of loans, including student loans, auto loans, farm equipment loans, furniture and other personal loans, including credit cards. Credit life insurance can be purchased by an individual. Usually it is sold by financial institutions making loans, like banks, to borrowers at the time they take out the loan. If a borrower dies, the proceeds of the policy repay the loan directly to the lender or creditor. For more information about credit life, call the Consumer Credit Insurance Association at 312-939-2242 (http://www.cciaonline.com). This type of insurance is not considered a good buy as evidenced in the following press release dated April 3, 2003 from the California Department of Insurance:

  > SACRAMENTO, CA—Responding to a lawsuit filed against the California Department of Insurance (CDI) by the Consumer Credit Insurance Association in California Superior Court, Commissioner John Garamendi issued the following statement: "Credit insurance has been a monumental rip-off of consumers. In 1999, the Legislature recognized this fact and moved to protect consumers by regulating the premium rates charged by companies selling credit insurance. CDI studied these rates under the Low administration and confirmed the Legislature's findings. I am not surprised these rip-off artists have filed suit in an attempt to continue to scam California consumers."

- **Family income life insurance**—This is a decreasing term policy that provides a stated income for a fixed period of time, if the insured person dies during the term of coverage. These payments continue until the end of a time period, specified when the policy is purchased.

- **Family insurance**—A whole life policy that insures all the members of an immediate family—husband, wife and children. Usually the coverage is sold in units per person, with the primary wage-earner insured for the greatest amount.

- **Juvenile insurance**—This is life insurance on a child. Coverage is paid for by an adult, usually the parents or guardians. Such policies are not considered traditional life insurance because the child is not producing an income that needs to be protected. However, by buying the policy when the child is young, the parents are able to lock in an extremely low premium rate and allow many more years of tax-deferred cash value buildup.

- **Mortgage insurance**—This decreasing term coverage is designed to pay off the unpaid balance of a mortgage if you die before the mortgage is paid off. Premiums are generally level throughout the term of the policy. The policy is usually independent of the mortgage, meaning that the financial institution granting the mortgage is separate from the insurance company issuing the policy. The proceeds of the policy are paid to the beneficiaries of the policy, not the mortgage company. The beneficiary is not required to use the proceeds to pay off the mortgage

- **Senior life insurance**—Also known as graded death benefit plans, they provide for a graded amount to be paid to the beneficiary. For example, in each of the first three to five years after the insured dies, the death benefit slowly increases. After that period, the entire death benefit is paid to the beneficiary. This might be appropriate if the beneficiary is not able to handle a large amount of money soon after the death, but would be in a better position to handle it a few years later.

According to consumer organizations, some of these can the worst types of products in the financial world; so if you are considering one of these products, be sure to compare it with a traditional life insurance product.

QUESTION 19: How do I Make a Cost Comparison between Life Insurance Policies?

Making a cost comparison between permanent life insurance policies is difficult even for trained professionals. The good news is that comparing the cost of term life policies is relatively easy. First we will address term life insurance coverage and then we'll look at permanent life insurance coverage. After that you will find different methods of comparing permanent life insurance policies.

CHAPTER 3: CHOOSING AND EVALU-ATING A LIFE INSURANCE POLICY

QUESTION 20: How do I choose a Term Life Insurance Policy?

Being human, we crave simplicity because it is, well, simpler that way. Term life, is frequently put forward as the easy answer for any person who is not interested in learning the intricacies of various life insurance policies. With term, it is easy for it to be the right answer since term insurance is perfectly adequate in the majority of situations.

So with that being said, how do you evaluate the various term policies available in the marketplace as well as monitor your existing term policy?

Much has been written about how to compare the costs of different life insurance policies. With term life insurance, this is very simple as long as you ensure that you are comparing similar policies. Make sure that you are comparing different policies offering identical coverage. For example, compare the cost of a 10-year level premium term policy only to another 10-year level premium term, not to a 5-year term or decreasing term policy. The policy with the lowest cost is the one with the lowest premium. The term period is the number of years that premiums remain level until the policy expires or is up for renewal for another term: currently either 1, 5, 10, 15, 20, 25 or 30 years. Again, with term life insurance, the policy with the lowest cost is the one with the lowest premium.

The challenge comes when you are comparing dissimilar term policies, such as comparing an Annual Renewable Term Policy with a Guaranteed Level Premium Term. Then you have the variations among level premium term policies with different guaranteed periods (e.g., 5 years, 10 years, 15 years, etc.), and you have to use your best judgment in determining whether you wish to compare guaranteed or projected rates.

An informed comparison should consider any differences in company ratings from the insurance rating agencies (e.g., A.M. Best, S&P, and Moody's). As well as such intangibles as how well each company has treated policy owners in the past. It is also helpful to keep in mind that competition for term business has been aggressive in intensity for a number of years, and company actuaries have been aggressively pricing their policies to attract new business, anticipating favorable long term mortality experience. This premium rate cutting may work out or it may turn out, in retrospect, to have been overly aggressive. In other words, there is no way to know what will happen in the future.

Factors to consider:

- How many years the premium is guaranteed
- Strength of company, as measured by the insurance rating agencies
- Convertibility (option to exchange without evidence of insurability, at the same rate class, to a permanent/cash value policy)
  - o Length of Time Convertibility Option may be exercised
  - o Products Available for conversion: (some companies give you a number of choices, while some limit you to one policy that is typically not a good value compared to other available policies)
  - o Disability Options, if any
- Conversion Credit (i.e.: reduction in first year premium as an incentive to convert to permanent insurance)
- Extra cost riders available such as: Disability Waiver, Return of Premium, Family Rider, Accidental Death Benefit, Guaranteed Insurability Option, Child Rider and Terminal Illness Rider.

QUESTION 21: What Are Life Insurance Illustrations and How Can They Help?

Before life insurance illustrations were introduced, life insurance agents (that's what they called themselves in those days—nowadays an agent is more likely to use a title like financial consultant or financial planner) used something called a rate book. The rate book contained virtually everything the agent and the prospective customer needed to know about the proposed life insurance policy. Because there was no such thing as indeterminate premiums and adjustable life in those days, the cash value increased at a rate that could easily be shown as a value per $1,000 of face amount in the rate book. Term insurance was not typically used except for group term life insurance for employee benefit purposes.

QUESTION 22: How do I read a Typical Term Life Insurance Illustrations?

The term illustration below provides information about all facets of this product. The first page shows the factors that the illustration is based on. It continues with renewable period and the conversion period. The next pages illustrate the premium. The third page is a continuation of the second page and is not shown for that reason.

Life Insurance Company
olicy Illustration and Explanation
- Term Life Insurance Policy

f_____
___ a renewable and convertible term life insurance policy providing a level death benefit with guaranteed level premiums for the first ten years. After the 10th policy year premiums will increase annually.

Underwriting Class
Premiums and policy charges illustrated for this coverage are based upon Male, Age 45 Preferred Plus. Actual premiums for the insurance coverage may vary from the illustration depending on the outcome of the underwriting process.

Initial Death Benefit
The death benefit illustrated is $500,000. This benefit may be continued to age 95 if appropriate premiums are paid.

Initial Premium
This illustration is based on the premium of $375.00. The payment frequency you selected is Annual. Premiums can be paid annually, semi-annually, quarterly, or monthly by pre-authorized checking. If you elect to pay the premium more frequently than annually, the total yearly outlay will be greater than the annual premium.

Guaranteed Renewable
This policy may be renewed annually without evidence of insurability to the insured's age 95 provided appropriate premiums for each renewal period are paid.

Guaranteed Conversion
Upon request you have the right to convert all or part of the death benefit to a permanent life insurance plan for the duration of the guaranteed level premium period, or the insured's age 70, whichever comes first. Policies issued at the insured's age 66 or older are convertible during the first five policy years. Evidence of insurability is not required. The conversion must meet company rules at the time of the conversion.

This policy does not provide any nonforfeiture benefits (such as cash surrender values) during the level term period. This means that if you fail to pay a premium within a specified time of its due date, this policy will lapse without any value. You should compare this policy to other level premium life insurance policies. Other policies may provide identical coverage with nonforfeiture benefits, however, such policies may have higher premiums than the premiums for this policy. When considering the purchase of this policy, you should compare the value of having nonforfeiture benefits (such as cash values)

Life Insurance Company

icy Illustration Detail

- Term Life Insurance Policy

This illustration assumes that premiums are paid at the beginning of each payment period. The payment period for each policy year is Annual.

Policy Year	Insured Age	Annualized Premium	Death Benefit
1	45	375.00	500,000
2	46	375.00	500,000
3	47	375.00	500,000
4	48	375.00	500,000
5	49	375.00	500,000
6	50	375.00	500,000
7	51	375.00	500,000
8	52	375.00	500,000
9	53	375.00	500,000
10	54	375.00	500,000
11	55	5,915.00	500,000
12	56	6,525.00	500,000
13	57	7,170.00	500,000
14	58	7,865.00	500,000
15	59	8,655.00	500,000
16	60	9,530.00	500,000
17	61	10,855.00	500,000
18	62	12,385.00	500,000
19	63	14,165.00	500,000
20	64	16,215.00	500,000
21	65	18,540.00	500,000
22	66	21,110.00	500,000
23	67	23,970.00	500,000
24	68	27,125.00	500,000
25	69	31,430.00	500,000
26	70	35,545.00	500,000
27	71	40,905.00	500,000
28	72	45,800.00	500,000
29	73	52,235.00	500,000
30	74	59,585.00	500,000
31	75	67,670.00	500,000
32	76	76,495.00	500,000
33	77	86,020.00	500,000
34	78	96,175.00	500,000
35	79	107,200.00	500,000
36	80	119,480.00	500,000
37	81	133,324.99	500,000
38	82	149,140.00	500,000
39	83	167,165.01	500,000
40	84	187,199.99	500,000

QUESTION 23: What should I look for in a Term Life Insurance Illustration?

Reading a Term Life Insurance Illustration or Spreadsheet is not always as straightforward as it may seem. The following factors are important to consider when evaluating and comparing term life insurance illustrations. Usually only a few of these will apply to a particular policy, also some are rarely, if ever used:

- **Carrier Ratings and Financial Profile**—See Chapter 4, Questions 43-54.
- **Cash Value**—This policy generates a guaranteed cash value after a certain year.
- **Conversion/Exchange Option**—Term Life Insurance Policies are usually convertible for a specified number of years or to a specified age. The number of years varies from company to company. Convertible means the policy owner has the right to exchange the policy for a permanent insurance policy regardless of changes in health or finances and with no suicide and contestable periods (a period where the policy is negated if the insured commits suicide or there is fraud). If the policy is converted, the new policy will be issued with the same rate classification as the term policy. Some carriers will you a number of choices to convert to, while some limit you to one policy (this can sometimes the company's less competitive policy). Oftentimes there is conversion credit (i.e., reduction in first year premium).
- **Current with Re-Entry Premiums**—assumes the purchase of a brand new policy, with premiums based on then current rates at the insured's attained age, with the insured providing evidence of insurability. Rates shown assume the insured re-qualifies for the same rate classification. Re-entry is assumed to occur at the end of the policy's level period or year 10 for ART/YRT products. Note that there may or may not be a new suicide and contestability period. It is important to understand that, if the policyholder's health declines by the time of re-entry, he/she may have to pay higher premiums than the "With Re-Entry" premiums shown in order to purchase a new policy. In addition, if the insured's health declines substantially, the insured may not be

able to obtain a new insurance policy at any price. Carriers that do not have a re-entry provision will not show any re-entry rates after the initial level period. The right to apply for re-entry may or may not be guaranteed. *It is the policy owner's responsibility to initiate the application for re-entry.*

- **Current Without Re-Entry Premiums**—These premiums do not require re-qualification (providing evidence of insurability) after the policy is issued. Future premium rates shown, beyond the guaranteed level period, are not guaranteed and may be changed by the carrier, without notice subject to the maximum guaranteed premiums. Guaranteed and non-guaranteed rates are shown on the carrier's compliance illustration, along with additional important information.

- **Dividends**—Dividends illustrated are based upon the current dividend scale and can be changed by the company.

- **Guaranteed Premiums**—Guaranteed premiums are the carrier's published, guaranteed premiums and are those shown under the heading "Guaranteed" (or "Maximum") premium rates. At the end of the level period, the "Guaranteed" rates shown are the highest premiums that the carrier will charge the policyholder. Actual premiums will be the then current premiums, which may be less than but never more than the guaranteed rates shown.

- **Insurance Age**—Depending on whether a carrier uses Insurance Age (your actual age plus six months and one day), Age Nearest Birthday (the typical methods used by almost all carriers), actual age, or age last birthday will have an effect on the desired effective date of your policy. The company's pricing reflects its age rating method. This can be offset by backdating a policy to "save insurance age"; i.e., having a policy backdated to just prior to an insurance age change, which would mean a lower premium for the life of the policy. I have never found a reasonable answer as to why insurance carriers all don't simplify this by going with actual age and date of birth.

- **Modal Factor (How often you pay the premium)**—this is a factor applied to the annual premium to derive the premium due for Semi-Annual, Quarterly and Monthly Bank Draft Payments. The Modal factor for semi-annual premiums ranges from 51% to 53%, which means that you can end up paying an extra 2% to 6% if you don't pay the premium annually. The modal factor for quarterly premiums ranges from 26% to 30%, which means that you will pay anywhere from an extra 4% to 20%, by paying quarterly. The modal factor on Monthly Bank Draft premiums ranges from 8.66% to 9% which means that you will pay anywhere from an extra 3.92% to 8%. The carriers impose these factors because they do not have the use of the money for the entire year, and because they find that, depending on the mode, there is a higher chance that the policy will lapse. This is discussed in greater detail in Question 66.

- **Policy Fees**—The annual policy fee typically ranges from $45 to $90. The policy fees are added on top of the rate per thousand. The major impact is to the seller of the policy as policy fees are usually non-commissionable. That is, the carrier keeps the policy fee and the agent's commission is not paid on the fee.

- **Premium Level Number of Years**—the premium can be for 1, 5, 10, 15, 20, 25 or 30 years; of these options, how many years are guaranteed?

- **Rating Bands**—Bands are classes of amount of coverage where the higher the amount of coverage, the lower the cost per thousand dollars of coverage.

- **Renewability**—The policy is guaranteed to be renewable for a certain number of years (or to a specified age), upon timely payment of the premiums, regardless of any changes in health or finances.

- **Riders**—what optional benefits are available; for example: Disability Waiver, Return of Premium Rider, Family Accidental Death Benefit, Guaranteed Insurability Option, Child Rider and Terminal Illness Rider? Have these been shown on the illustration? These should be considered separately. Keep in mind that many of these riders are more profitable for the insurance carrier, than for the policy-owner.

- **Risk Class**: Companies differentiate not only between smoker and non-smokers. Each of these classes is further divided into four or five classes. Recently, available classes were: Best Available, Preferred Better Non-Smoker, Preferred Non-Smoker, Standard Better Non-Smoker, Standard Non-Smoker, Tobacco(Non-Cigarette), Preferred Smoker, Standard Better Smoker and Standard Smoker. What does the designated rate class mean? Are there better rate categories? What qualifications must be met to be qualifying for the class illustrated?

- **Suicide and Contestability clause**—Claims are denied for suicide occurring within 1 to 2 years upon issue of the policy (this is the typical range). Claims may also be contested during this period (usually the same number of years). New suicide and contestability clauses may be imposed only if the company requires new evidence of insurability (such as for reinstatement or a request for a lower rate classification, including a request for reentry rates).

QUESTION 24: What Should I Consider In Choosing And Evaluating A Permanent (Cash Value) Life Insurance Illustration And Prospective Policy?

Since there are many unique products available in the marketplace, be sure that you are making a valid, "apples to apples" comparison between policies. Evaluating any type of whole life insurance or other permanent coverage (which encompasses all types of cash value policies) can quickly become a complex and daunting task. Today's permanent life policies are so complex, with so many moving parts, that elaborate computerized sales illustrations are essential.

Life insurance pricing (i.e., the process of rate setting) is done both prospectively (i.e., making educated guesses about future variables) and retrospectively (i.e., looking back on actual experience and making appropriate adjustments in the premium rate and other factors). Pricing the product requires evaluation of several key factors, which can be summed up under these four basic non-guaranteed risk categories: mortality experience, investment performance, policy lapse rates and expenses. In the long term, the actual cost of a product will be determined by the company's actual performance in each of these areas. Information on these four factors is typically available from insurance industry resources such as A.M. Best and Standard & Poor's. These also can be found at public libraries and from the insurance companies themselves. After this next question, we will take a closer look at these categories.

Life insurance companies generally do not like to divulge details about their products in terms of their components.

QUESTION 25: What are the four basic components that compose and dictate the performance of a life insurance policy?

The four basic components that determine how the policy will perform are:

1. Earnings—Interest Rates, Dividends, etc.
2. Mortality—this is the cost of pure life insurance protection—basically, how much the company charges for providing the insurance (i.e. how much they feel there is at risk, how much they can lose).
3. Administrative and overhead expenses.
4. Persistency (sometime referred to as lapse component)—how many policies stay in-force?

Interest rates tend to change the most and can have a greater impact on the performance of a policy than the other components listed above. However, a small change in mortality rates will have a greater impact on the policy performance; though this does not occur very often.

Over the next few questions we will look at each of these components in depth and will be technical in some cases.

QUESTION 26: What Is Really Important In an Illustration/Product Analysis?

Permanent Cash Value Life Insurance sales are usually based on illustrations prepared by the company or by the agent using software supplied by the company. The illustration typically highlights projected interest rates and estimates policy values in future years. The illustration is a sales tool, so it naturally accents the positive aspects of the proposed policy. The consumer is naturally led to believe that there is greater assurance that the illustrated values will be achieved, than is likely in the real world. There are so many variables that can adversely affect the long term performance of the policy. Mortality costs, expense, and other charges, future investment experience—all of these are, to some extent, not directly controllable by the insurance company. Results can vary—and they certainly will. So think of the illustration more as a convenient way of showing how the policy works, than as a reasonable estimate of future values.

Understanding how all the components interact is integral to understanding how and why the policy performs as it does. When a policy is issued, the company is at risk for the entire death benefit. That's because the early premium payments go to cover mortality and other expense charges, leaving little or nothing to apply to the cash value. When a cash value starts to accumulate, this gradually reduces the company's net amount at risk.

For example, we'll use a policy issued for $100,000. When it is issued, the entire $100,000 figure is at risk to the insurance company. The cash value of the policy acts as a reserve account, reducing the amount at risk to the insurance company. Therefore, if the cash value in the 30th year of the policy is $60,000 at a certain point, then the net amount at risk to the insurance company is $40,000 ($100,000 of death benefit less the $60,000 of cash value).

The mortality cost is applied to the net amount at risk based on the insured's attained age. With increasing age, the mortality cost per thousand of net amount at risk increases. The theory is that the total mortality cost will decrease as the cash value increases. As long as increases in the cash value (derived from premiums paid in and from investment earnings) are greater than the mortality costs and other expense charges, the policy should continue to grow and remain in-force. When the increases in the policy do not offset the charges, the cash value will commence a rapid descent leading to policy termination with no value.

It is also necessary to understand how the various factors are applied to the policy every month: First, the premium paid is added to the cash value from the end of the prior period. Then mortality costs and other expense charges are subtracted. Interest is credited to this value (after costs). Therefore, the interest credited applied to the policy is not the actual internal rate of return. The internal rate of return, an important financial yardstick, is always less than the current interest crediting rate.

QUESTION 27: What Type of Earnings are there on a Life Insurance Policy?

There are three basic types of earnings—dividends and credited interest rates on traditional life insurance products. On Variable life insurance products, there are two types of accounts on a variable life policy. The first is the fixed account and this account ears interest at the current rate. The other type is a variable account which has variable accounts whose earnings/loss is the net gain or loss from amounts invested in the Variable Accounts.

QUESTION 28: What Are Dividends?

A "dividend" on a life insurance policy is unlike the dividend you receive on a share of stock or a stock mutual fund. For tax purposes, dividends are considered a return of a portion of the premiums paid for the policy. Basically, the insurance company receives the premium payments and invests them. If mortality and expense experience is favorable (i.e., the company keeps expenses down and the investments do well), the company declares a dividend, which returns a portion of the surplus to policy owners.

Only participating policies pay dividends. Basically, these policies are priced to pay dividends. In effect, the company charges a higher premium, and then returns a portion of it to policy owners. Dividends have always been a controversial topic within the life insurance industry. There is no need to get into the details here, but you should understand what a dividend is and what it is not. In Great Britain, life insurance policies are sold "with profits" (i.e., with dividends), and "without profits" (i.e., no dividends). As you might expect, policies that pay no dividends are less expensive. However, both in the U.K. and in the U.S., over long periods of time the participating policy issued by a reputable company stands a very good chance of outperforming a nonparticipating policy. The key words are "over long periods of time." Although both term and permanent policies can be participating, as a practical matter dividends are suitable only for permanent policies, with their long in-force horizons.

Typically, when the policy is purchased the policy owner is allowed to elect their form of dividend option and most insurers allow the dividend option to be changed once the policy is in-force. The policy owner can also elect a combination of options. The most common dividend options are:

1. **Payment in cash**—the insured may choose to receive policy dividend as cash payments like dividends on ordinary corporate stock. If this option is selected, the insurer will pay dividends to the policy owner in cash usually beginning at the end of the first or second policy year. Although life insurance dividends are treated as a tax free return of premiums (IRC Sec. 72(e) (1), 7702(f)); most policy owners do not choose to take dividends this way because the other options are much convenient or favorable.

2. **Reducing subsequent premiums**—the policy owner can choose to have the insurer automatically (and at no charge) apply any dividends to reduce future premiums. As dividends increase, the policy owner's required premium payments decrease. If the insurer's investments perform very well, at some point the premiums can equal and even exceed the amount of the premiums. Therefore, if the dividends were high enough to offset future premiums totally and, with any remaining excess dividends, another option would be selected.

3. **Leaving the dividends with the insurer at interest**—a policy owner can choose to leave the dividend to be retained by the insurer, accumulating and earning interest. The interest rate payable on the policy owner's accumulated account is guaranteed to equal or exceed a specified minimum. Cash can be withdrawn from the dividend accumulation account at any time. When the insured dies or the policy is surrendered, the policy pays the face value or the net cash surrender value plus the value of this account. Interest earned on accumulated and retainer dividends is fully taxable to the policy owner as soon as the policy owner has the right to withdraw it, even if the policy owner elects not to withdraw it. If the policy owner can only withdraw the interest on a specific date (usually the policy anniversary date), the interest is taxable in the policy owner's taxable year with which the date falls.

4. **Buying paid up additional insurance**—this option allows the policy owner to use dividends to purchase small amounts of completely paid-up (i.e. single premium) additional insurance coverage of the same type as the basic policy. The insurer will add the additional amount of coverage that the dividend can purchase at the insured's attained age. This is purchased at net rates with no commission paid. There is no extra premium. This requires no further evidence of insurability. These paid up additions can generate dividends of their own.

5. **Buying additional one year term insurance**—this option allows using the dividends to purchase as much additional one year term life insurance coverage as possible as allowed based on the insured's age. This option also does not have any commission paid and no evidence of insurability is required. Many insurers limit the amount of coverage that can be purchased to the cash value that year.

6. **Repaying policy loans**—Some insurers will allow policy owners to elect to use dividends to be applied directly against any interest and/or principal of a policy loan before being used in one or more other dividend options.

Terminal Dividends—most participating policies will pay a "terminal dividend" at the termination of the contract. The longer the policy has been kept in premium paying status, the larger the terminal dividend. Although most ordinary level-premium whole life policies have no explicit surrender charges, the terminal dividend is, in a sense, a form of surrender charge, since the insurer is withholding the policy owner's money instead of paying it currently. Those policy owner's who terminate their policy in the first few years will receive a relatively small terminal dividend, while those who continue to pay premiums on their policies for a longer period of time receive a larger terminal dividend. The terminal dividend therefore rewards long-term policy holding and discourages early policy lapses. (*Tax Planning with Life Insurance Second Edition 2003/2004 Financial Professionals' Edition—Published by Warren, Gorham and Lamont, RIA by Howard Zaritsky and Stephan R. Leimberg*)

QUESTION 29: What Are Interest Rates And How Are Interest Earnings Credited?

Declared Interest Rate (for traditional non-variable policies)—is the amount that the investment committee of the life insurance company determines can be credited to its in-force life insurance policies. This means, in effect, that policy owners must accept the rate declared by the company. Interest is usually credited on the accumulated value after policy expenses (mortality/risk charges and overhead expenses) have been deducted, so the actual return is less than the credited rate.

Life insurance companies generally adopt one of two general interest crediting methods that are in widespread use throughout the industry. These are the portfolio method and the banded method. Under the former system, the company credits interest to in-force policies based on a percentage of the earnings on the company's entire investment portfolio. Under the banded system, interest credited is based on the actual performance of specific pools or buckets of money that are received by the company at different times and invested at current market conditions. Since interest rates rise and fall over time, different buckets earn different interest rates. Neither the portfolio nor the banded interest rate system can claim overall superiority.

In fact, over long periods of time, the two systems tend to even out, yielding somewhat similar results. Since a permanent life insurance policy should not be bought for a temporary need, the long term nature of such contracts tends to make it somewhat less important whether the company uses the portfolio or banded system.

Market Rate—**(for Variable policies)**—The reader will recall that on variable life and variable UL policies the policy owner directly bears the investment risk. That's because the policy owner is in a position to choose specific investment sub-accounts. Usually, funds may be moved between the investment sub-accounts, sometimes with some restrictions.

QUESTION 30: What is the Difference between Gross and Net Interest Rates?

A company should disclose whether the interest rates credited are:

- gross (before any expenses being subtracted), or
- net of investment expenses, or
- net of investment expense, other company expenses and profit loads.

Participating products' dividend interest rates are most often net of investment expenses, but prior to other company expenses and profit loads being deducted. Universal life products' declared interest rates, on the other hand, are net of investment expenses, other company expenses and profit loads. Thus, two companies, both basing their interest rates on equal 9 percent total investment income returns, both having .5 percent investment expenses and 1.25 percent for other expenses and profit loads, might declare interest rates as follows:

- The mutual company would declare an 8.5 percent dividend interest rate.
- The universal life product would declare a 7.25 percent net interest rate.

Neither company might say any more regarding how their rates were declared. More importantly, both products will perform identically assuming that both have equal mortality and other charges. Yet the consumer and producer will look more favorably, although incorrectly, on the mutual company with its 8.5 percent dividend rate. Adequate disclosure by the companies will help remedy this misperception.

QUESTION 31: On what are the Interest Rate Assumptions in an Illustration Typically Based?

1. Interest earned by the company on:
   a) all investments now held
   b) new investments,

     c) new investments over a certain number of past years,

     d) other combinations of actual investments

2. An independent index such as:

     a) Treasury Bills,

     b) Moody's long-term bond index,

     c) Other indices.

3. Another basis not tied to company results or an index

4. Interest rates may be the gross interest rate resulting from investments, indices, or other measures, or the gross interest rate reduced by:

     a) Investment expenses

     b) Investment expenses and other expenses

     c) Expenses and profit

     d) A fixed amount or percentage.

QUESTION 32: What other questions should I consider regarding interest rates and dividends?

Basically, what you are looking for is whether or not the company is using numbers and facts that are realistic, while also considering the company's history.

Basis for dividends, interest rates and non-guaranteed factors:

- Are any of the underlying experience factors significantly different from current experience? If so, examine which ones and how they differ.
- If the policy is participating, is there a substantial probability that the current illustrative dividend scale cannot be continued, if current experience holds?
- If the policy is nonparticipating, is there a substantial probability that current illustrations cannot be supported by currently anticipated experience?
- Is the policy of the traditional participating variety, or does it contain non-guaranteed pricing elements using a means other than dividends?

- If the policy is not participating, what are the non-guaranteed elements involved? These are usually non-guaranteed interest crediting rates, mortality charges, loadings, etc.?
- If the policy is participating, does the company state that the contribution principle (i.e., aggregate divisible surplus should be distributed in the same proportion as the policies are considered to have contributed to the company's divisible surplus) is being followed in the illustrative dividend scale? If it is not, how does it differ?
- If the policy is nonparticipating, what is the company's practice with respect to determination and re-determination of non-guaranteed pricing elements, with particular reference to (a) the degree of discretion reserved by the company and (b) whether any of the elements are guaranteed to follow an outside index

QUESTION 33: How is a mortality charge determined?

As discussed earlier, the mortality charge is the cost of pure life insurance protection, based on experience tables developed by actuaries and on actual mortality experience. It is the amount the company charges the policy owner periodically for the insurance element in the policy. Other expense charges include a fee for policy administration, company overhead and taxes.

Each company determines its own mortality charges based on these tables and other factors. Larger companies determine their own mortality charges based on these tables, their experience and other factors, while smaller companies rely on industry wide statistics. There are considerable rate variations between companies. At first glance, that might seem curious since the industry uses pretty much the same data to develop their mortality rates. In practice, however, the differences in rates are quite logical. Some companies specialize in writing coverage on those whose health is substandard, while other companies take on specialized risks such as smokers and those in hazardous occupations. Even so, there are still some curious anomalies. For example, Company A might be more competitive at issue age 40, while Company B is more competitive at issue age 50. A company's mortality experience is measured (by A.M. Best) by the rate at which death benefits are paid, compared to the company's own actuarial expectations used to price the premium.

The difference in mortality results among life insurance companies can have a greater impact on a policy's performance than any interest rate return/dividend.

What should I ask about a company's mortality experience?

- Is the company projecting actual current experience or better than current experience?
- Do the mortality rates vary by product, and, if so, why?
- Does the company project an unrealistic increase in mortality expenses, and if so is it guaranteed?

The key is to determine which method is being utilized in a particular illustration; however this is not an easy task. The only method that I currently use is to ask, and then get it in writing if you can.

QUESTION 34: What are overhead and administrative expense charges?

Overhead Expenses include all the operating costs that the life insurance carrier incurs in the course of doing business. These costs fall into four basic categories:

(1) Cost of facilities;
(2) Data processing;
(3) Employees (labor);
(4) Sales expenses (Includes commissions, marketing costs, sales offices, etc.).

As with all of the components, these expense factors will vary widely with every life insurance company.

Commissions are a significant part of the overhead expense factor primarily in the first year, and can have a significantly negative impact on the long term performance of a permanent life insurance product, especially in the first few years. An agent's first year commission including any bonuses or allowances can exceed 100% of the first year premium (although this is not always the case). This is why most traditional cash value life insurance policies have no to almost any cash surrender value for the first few years. Policies typically pay a renewal commission from 2% to 10% for 10+ years.

Most carriers also offer their permanent life insurance policies with the option of adding in term life insurance which reduces the commission. Some have also lowered the "target" premium, which is the level to which the carrier will pay the maximum commission. In my mind, there is skepticism that this provides additional profits for the company rather than a benefit for the consumer. This will depend on the carrier and it is always a good idea to get proposals from at least two companies and use the tools in this book. You may want to cap the number of companies that you look at, as the more companies looked, the greater the chance it may become overwhelming.

A consumer also now has the option of a no-load or low-load policy refer to policies that pay a reduced commission or no commission. Some "no-load" policies do, however, pay a commission, which is usually referred to as a marketing allowance. Low load and no load policies are tend to be more competitive from the standpoint of a consumer. This is especially true during the first few years, because of the lower surrender charge (than on a traditional, load policy) or lack of any surrender charge. Most such products (there are exceptions) have other built in charges that tend to make long term performance and cost more closely approximate traditional "load" policies. Perhaps, one day in the near future, there will be more no-load and low-load life insurance policies from which to choose. Unfortunately, at present there are only a few of these.

Here some other issues to consider in reference to expense charges:

- Are expense charges consistent for new and existing policies of the same type? If they are not, this is an indication that old policyholders are subsidizing the company's attempt to capture new business.

- Do expenses vary by product or underwriting class? This is reasonable only if justified by a company's actual or reasonably anticipated experience. Otherwise it is an indication of overly aggressive marketing and subsidization of the product with the lower expenses.
- Are expenses, in an illustration that discloses them, adequate and realistic? If not, it is likely they will be subsidized by higher charges for mortality or a lower interest-crediting rate. Conversely, an unrealistic and overly aggressive projection of mortality charges could be offset by higher expense charges, or, again, a lower interest rate.

QUESTION 35: What are Persistency and Lapses?

Persistency is a measure of how long a life insurance company's policies are staying in-force (active). This is an important consideration for life insurance companies and has an impact on them. Many policy owners fail to keep their policies in-force long enough to realize the intended benefits. Another word used for a policy that terminates is "lapse". Poor persistency is a perpetual problem for the life insurance industry. When policy owners terminate their coverage prematurely, this can result in a loss to the company, especially on permanent policies that have only been in-force for a short while. Regulators and rating agencies closely monitor company persistency. If a company has a high level of early lapses (the same as a low persistency rate), then there is a problem somewhere. Watch out if this is the case with a company you plan on applying to.

QUESTION 36: What is Lapse Support?

Traditionally, a life insurance product will generate a series of annual gains in policy years after the first year. These gains are used to make up for the loss that the insurance company usually faces in the first year, when expenses are highest (mostly due to commissions, underwriting and policy issue). It can take 10-20 years for a policy to break even. Policyholders who lapse in the early years leave the company with unrecovered expenses. This is borne by the existing policyholders.

The technique to watch out for is the lapse support. A lapse supported product involves shifting expenses between policy-owners; however, in this case, the burden is shifted to those who lapse. This generates very large gains for the insurance company in the first ten to fifteen years (the policy's cash value remains artificially low) and very large losses thereafter (by increasing the policy's cash value by more than its interest earnings). Under this pattern, policyholders who lapse early will generate huge profits for the company. These profits are used to offset the losses that will occur when persisting policyholders reach the years when the policy "super performs". The net result is that lapsing policyholders subsidize persisting policyholders, making long term performance look better for those who never lapse.

Some carriers use a pricing technique wherein the products are designed to recover the initial loss very quickly. This way the products are generally lapse insensitive. It does not matter when policy owner's lapse the policy, in this situation.

These products can be identified by an illustration with very low early cash values (the cash surrender value in year 10 is less than the sum of premiums paid), and tremendous annual cash value growth in later years (the annual growth in cash value is consistently greater than what the life insurance company could reasonably earn on its investments, given the assumed policy credit rate).

QUESTION 37: Why I should watch out for lapse supported products?

- Additional Risk—The lapse support technique is based on a certain number of lapsing policyholders making contributions to a "pot". The funds in the pot will be distributed to a certain number of persisting policyholders in the later years. If the actual lapse rate is less than the assumption behind the illustration, there will be too few policyholders making contributions into the pot in the early years. There will also be many policyholders looking for distributions, from the pot, in the later years. The company would not be able to afford the illustrated super-performance in the later years.

- Short Term Product Performance—A lapse supported product shows improved long term performance only if short term performance is impaired. If you happen to be one of the unfortunate policyholders who find they must lapse early, your surrender value will be very small, if any at all. And, even with a 3% annual lapse assumption, 46% of all policyholders will have lapsed by the end of the 20th year (ignoring mortality, i.e. dying and using the life insurance)

- Policyholder Service—A policyholder who buys a lapse supported product will find himself in a strange position—the company will actually prefer that he lapse. This is not a comfortable thought when future dividends, policy enhancements and other types of policy service are considered. A lapse supported product creates a Catch-22 situation. If the insurance company is correct and lapses do materialize at the assumed level, then clients who may have thought they would never lapse, will lapse—at a great cost. If, on the other hand, the clients are right and lapses rarely occur, the company will not be able to afford to live up to the illustration. Unfortunately, the only sure thing with a lapse supported product is that short term surrender values will be very low

In a way, this is similar to gambling.

This is a brief overview of the factors that can affect the performance of a permanent life insurance policy. More detailed information will be featured in upcoming specific reports focusing on maintaining and monitoring specific types of policies. This overview is intended to give you a general idea of what might affect your policy. All of the factors previously discussed help determine the premium you pay for life insurance.

QUESTION 38: How Do These Factors Affect The Performance of a Permanent Life Insurance Policy?

This overview is intended to give you a general idea of how all of the factors previously discussed may affect your policy and how they are relevant to the actual premium you pay for life insurance. If you purchase permanent life insurance, the premiums you pay may fluctuate from year to year if any of these four factors change:

- Mortality experience improves or worsens
- Expenses grow or are reduced
- Interest credits rise or fall
- Persistency increases or decreases

Your premium outlay may potentially be reduced if:

- Interest Rates rise, or
- Mortality Experience improves, or
- Persistency is stable, or
- Expenses drop

Conversely, your premium outlay may potentially increase if:

- Interest Rates decrease, or
- Mortality Experience worsens, or
- Persistency is negative, or
- Expenses increase

QUESTION 39: What are some other Considerations and Situations?

- The Surrender Charge is the difference between the accumulated value and the surrender value. Depending on the policy, this can be 100% for the first two to five years the policy is in-force, meaning that there would no be no cash value should the policy be surrendered during this period. The surrender charge gradually reduces according to a table included in the policy. Typically, the surrender charge reduces to zero sometime between the 10th and 15th anniversary of the policy.

- Some contracts provide for future benefit increases. It is important to know in advance whether or not such increases are subject to evidence of insurability. If the insured person's health deteriorates in the meantime, and evidence of insurability is required before a scheduled benefit increase occurs, this could present a problem.

- Some disability premium waiver provisions waive premiums for the pure term cost of insurance and some waive premiums for the level (permanent) cost. You should know what cost is waived on your policy.

- The mode of premium payment deserves careful consideration. Please see "QUESTION 66: Is There A Difference In How Often I Pay My Premiums" for a full discussion and important information on this topic.

- Premium rating bands are ranges of coverage amount (e.g., $100,000 to $249,999, $250,000 to $500,000, etc.) in which the higher the amount of coverage, the lower the cost per thousand dollars of coverage.

- The annual policy fee ranges from $45 to $90 on the policies I surveyed for this report. The policy fees are added on top of the rate per thousand of coverage face amount. As a matter of interest, agents generally do not like policy fees because they are usually excluded for the purpose of determining the agent's commission. The company usually retains 100% of the policy fee to offset expenses, and the agent's commission is not paid on the fee, only on the premium payment itself.

QUESTION 40: What Is A Universal Life Insurance Policy Illustration?

Over the last few questions we have discussed the various types of permanent (cash value) life insurance policies along with the various components. An illustration is a projection of how a policy will perform based on those components. With any type of policy, it would be impossible to cover every type of policy and every nuance of each type. An exhaustive review would require volumes of dense text. Keep in mind, that there are similarities between coverage types among companies. For example, a universal life policy issued by company A will be similar—but not necessarily identical—to a universal life policy issued by company B, a five year term will compare to another company's five year term, and so on. All life insurance policies agree to pay an amount of money when you die. All policies are not the same. A wide variety of plans are available. Some provide permanent coverage and others temporary coverage. Some build up cash values and others do not. Some policies combine different kinds of insurance and others let you change from on kind of insurance to another.

The illustration below is for a universal life policy with the same parameters as the term illustration in Question 22. Please note that these illustrations are from companies. The first difference from the term insurance to be noted is that the premium is almost 10 times higher than the term premium. The reasons being are that the premium is projected to remain level to age 99 rather than for ten years and that there is a cash value. On the illustration, the difference between term and universal life is seen with the death benefit type described as Type A (Fixed); this means that the death benefit is projected to remain level. There are two other types—Increasing, where the death benefit increases by the amount that the cash value increase by and Variable, where the death benefit will vary per a chosen schedule. These can be changed during the policy's life depending on the carrier and certain guidelines and if increased subject to underwriting. The minimum premium is the minimum premium that can be paid. The initial premium outlay is what is projected to be paid. As shown in the second paragraph, an annual premium of $11,931 will guarantee the initial basic face amount (guaranteed premiums and coverage are discussed in the next question). You can elect to pay a lower premium, however the guarantee period on the policy will be shorter. The ability to pay a higher premium and have the death benefit guaranteed is fairly new and is a welcome addition for universal life policies.

The illustration discusses information about the proposed universal life policy, and is mostly self-explanatory. On Page 6, you will note that there are guaranteed results and non-guaranteed results. With the guaranteed results, it is not just the interest rates; it's also the mortality charges and the overhead expenses. A change in the mortality costs will have a greater effect on policy performance than a change in the interest. A case study in QUESTION 90 shows this on an actual policy.

Universal Life Insurance Illustration
Narrative Summary

Proposed Insured: John Doe	Initial Annual Premium: $3,050.00
Male 45 Nonsmoker	Initial Death Benefit: $500,000
Riders: None	

Basic Life Insurance Illustration

Generic Name:	1	Jc Life	Policy Form Number:	. . .
Initial Face Amount:	$500,000		Initial Death Benefit Option:	A. Level

General Information

This illustration has been provided to help you understand the life insurance policy and to allow you to compare the policy with other policies. This illustration is based on information that you provided and on certain assumptions that are not guaranteed.

This illustration assumes that the currently illustrated non-guaranteed elements will continue unchanged for all years shown. This is not likely to occur, and actual results may be more or less favorable than those shown. Non-guaranteed elements, such as interest and cost of insurance rates, are subject to change by the Company.

In general, a universal life insurance policy is flexible, allowing you to increase or decrease your premium outlay and your available death benefit.

Required California Disclosure (Form U-613)

This policy is guaranteed to stay in force for a specified number of years as long as you meet the requirements of the Policy, including the Minimum Monthly Premium provision found in the policy contract. This provision is also known as a no-lapse guarantee, and a general description of the provision is included in the Narrative Summary section of the Basic Illustration.

While this policy provides a no-lapse guarantee, it may provide nonforfeiture benefits, such as cash surrender values, which are less than those that would be provided if the guarantee were issued as a separate policy, such as a term policy. If a separate term policy has higher nonforfeiture benefits, the premiums for the separate policy might be higher than the premiums for the no-lapse guarantee provided in this policy. Therefore, when considering the purchase of this policy, you should compare the value to you of higher nonforfeiture benefits, such as cash surrender values, versus the premiums required to keep your insurance coverage in force.

Premium Outlay

Premium outlay is the amount of money assumed to be paid out-of-pocket. The amount, timing and frequency of each premium outlay may be varied and will affect the policy value and length of coverage. Each premium outlay is subject to any minimum requirements of the policy and maximum limits set by the Internal Revenue Service. This illustration assumes that any lump sum payments are received by the Company prior to the issue date of the policy and that periodic premium outlays are received by the Company at the beginning of each policy year.

The Guideline Level Premium, which is the maximum level annual premium permitted under federal tax law, is $9,625.95. In all years assuming payment of the Guideline Level Premium, guaranteed interest rates, guaranteed cost of insurance rates, no policy loans, no partial surrenders, and no policy changes, the policy will not terminate before age 120.

Minimum Monthly Premium Provision

The minimum monthly premium is $161.67. The policy will not terminate during the first fifteen policy years if, on each monthly anniversary day: (a) the total premiums paid, less any partial surrenders and policy debt, equals or exceeds (b) the minimum monthly premium times the number of months the policy has been in force, including the current month. The minimum monthly premium may change if there is a change in benefits.

Death Benefit

The death benefit is the amount of money payable to the beneficiary if the proposed insured dies while the policy is in force. The death benefit includes the base policy benefit amount plus any primary covered insured rider benefit amount. The death benefit will be reduced by any policy debt and overdue monthly deductions. This illustration shows the death benefit at the end of each policy year.

Under the level death benefit option, the base policy benefit amount will equal the face amount on the date of

Current, Specified, and Midpoint assumptions are not guaranteed. They assume that scales for interest and cost of insurance rates will continue unchanged by the Company for all years shown. This is not likely to occur because interest and cost of insurance rates are subject to change by the Company based on various factors such as claims and investment experience, persistency, expenses, taxes, and the overall economic environment. Actual results may be more or less favorable than those shown.

Universal Life Insurance Illustration
Narrative Summary

Proposed Insured: John Doe	Initial Annual Premium:	$3,050.00
Male 45 Nonsmoker	Initial Death Benefit:	$500,000
Riders: None		

death.

Terminal Illness Accelerated Death Benefit
This policy has an Accelerated Death Benefit feature for a qualifying terminal illness. Subject to a maximum benefit amount, the accelerated death benefit will be based on a portion of the in-force face amount. A lien equal to the accelerated death benefit will be established against the policy and will accumulate interest. The primary impact of the lien and any accumulated interest will be reduction of the death benefit. The Accelerated Death Benefit feature may be subject to state variations and may not available in all states.

Consult your representative and review the policy and any endorsements for complete limitations, terms and conditions. Due to possible tax consequences of the Accelerated Death Benefit feature, please consult your tax advisor.

Surrender and Policy Values
The surrender value is the amount of money you will receive if you cancel the policy. It is equal to the policy value less a surrender charge and less any policy debt. There is a surrender charge for the first 14 policy years.

The policy value will vary based on (1) the amount, timing and frequency of each premium outlay, (2) monthly deductions, (3) credited interest, (4) policy debt, and (5) partial surrenders. Each month, premiums received (less a premium expense charge) and interest are added to the policy value while monthly deductions and partial surrenders are subtracted from the policy value. This illustration shows the policy and surrender values at the end of each policy year.

Termination
Unless all requirements of the Minimum Monthly Premium Provision have been satisfied, the policy will terminate without value if there is not enough surrender value to cover the monthly deductions.

Interest
The interest rate credited to your policy value can be changed at the sole discretion of the Company but not below the guaranteed interest rate of 4.00%. The current interest rate is 5.10%. The interest rates shown in this illustration are annual effective rates.

Whenever the current interest rate is greater than the guaranteed rate, the following percentages will be added to the current interest rate as indicated:
(a) 0.5% when the policy value exceeds $10,000

Additional Key Terms
"Age" means the issue age plus the number of years the policy is assumed to have been in force. This is the age at the end of the policy year.

"Cost of Insurance" is the amount charged by the Company for providing life insurance coverage under the base policy. The cost of insurance rates may be changed by the Company, but not above the rates shown in the Table of Guaranteed Maximum Insurance Rates in the policy schedule.

"Current Assumptions" illustrate values based on current interest rates and current cost of insurance rates. Current rates are subject to change and are not guaranteed.

"Guaranteed Assumptions" illustrate values based on guaranteed interest rates and guaranteed cost of insurance rates.

"Issue Age" means the age nearest birthday of the proposed insured at the assumed effective date of the illustrated policy.

"Midpoint Assumptions" illustrate values based on interest rates and cost of insurance rates that are the average of the current and guaranteed rates. These assumed rates are not guaranteed.

Current, Specified, and Midpoint assumptions are not guaranteed. They assume that scales for interest and cost of insurance rates will continue unchanged by the Company for all years shown. This is not likely to occur because interest and cost of insurance rates are subject to change by the Company based on various factors such as claims and investment experience, persistency, expenses, taxes, and the overall economic environment. Actual results may be more or less favorable than those shown.

Life

niversal Life Insurance Illustration

Narrative Summary

Proposed Insured: John Doe	Initial Annual Premium:	$3,050.00
Male 45 Nonsmoker	Initial Death Benefit:	$500,000
Riders: None		

"**Monthly Deductions**" are policy charges including the cost of insurance, the cost of any additional benefits and riders, any monthly expense charge applicable to the initial face amount, any monthly expense charge applicable to an increase in face amount, and the monthly administrative charge.

"**Non-Guaranteed Assumptions**" illustrate the current, specified and midpoint assumptions. These assumptions are not guaranteed.

"**Non-Guaranteed Elements**" are the premiums, benefits, values, credits or charges that are not guaranteed or cannot be determined at issue.

"**Rate Class**" means the risk class of the proposed insured. After the application is underwritten, a revised illustration will be delivered with the policy if the actual rate class differs from the one illustrated.

Current, Specified, and Midpoint assumptions are not guaranteed. They assume that scales for interest and cost of insurance rates will continue unchanged by the Company for all years shown. This is not likely to occur because interest and cost of insurance rates are subject to change by the Company based on various factors such as claims and investment experience, persistency, expenses, taxes, and the overall economic environment. Actual results may be more or less favorable than those shown.

fe
Universal Life Insurance Illustration
Numeric Summary

Proposed Insured: John Doe
Male 45 Nonsmoker
Riders: None

Initial Annual Premium: $3,050.00
Initial Death Benefit: $500,000

| | | Guaranteed Assumptions | | Non-Guaranteed Assumptions | | | |
| | | | | Midpoint | | Current | |
Year	Premium Outlay	Surrender Value	Death Benefit	Surrender Value	Death Benefit	Surrender Value	Death Benefit
5	3,050	0	500,000	0	500,000	1,469	500,000
10	3,050	0	500,000	5,550	500,000	12,835	500,000
20	3,050	0	0	0	0	31,427	500,000
Age 70	3,050	0	0	0	0	31,584	500,000

Based on guaranteed assumptions, the illustration terminates in year 16.
Based on midpoint assumptions, the illustration terminates in year 20.
Based on current assumptions, the illustration terminates in year 47.

The benefits and values shown under the "Non-Guaranteed Assumptions" heading are not guaranteed. The non-guaranteed elements are subject to change by the Company. Additional premium payments may be required to keep the policy in force or to achieve desired results.

The **Guaranteed** columns assume an initial interest rate of 4.00%. The **Midpoint** columns assume an initial interest rate of 4.55%. The **Current** columns assume an initial interest rate of 5.10%.

I have received a copy of this illustration. I understand that this illustration assumes non-guaranteed elements continue unchanged for all years shown and that this is not likely to occur. The agent has told me that these elements are not guaranteed and are subject to change. I understand that actual results may be higher or lower than those shown.

Applicant or policyowner   Date

I certify that this illustration has been presented to the applicant or policyowner. I have explained that this illustration assumes non-guaranteed elements continue unchanged for all years shown, that these elements are subject to change, and that actual results may be higher or lower than those shown. I have made no statements that are inconsistent with the illustration.

Agent or other authorized representative   Date

Anthony Steuer
8363 Greenback Lane. PMB 207
Orangevale, CA 95662
916-989-3938

Current, Specified, and Midpoint assumptions are not guaranteed. They assume that scales for interest and cost of insurance rates will continue unchanged by the Company for all years shown. This is not likely to occur because interest and cost of insurance rates are subject to change by the Company based on various factors such as claims and investment experience, persistency, expenses, taxes, and the overall economic environment. Actual results may be more or less favorable than those shown.

⸺ J Life
Universal Life Insurance Illustration
Tabular Detail

Proposed Insured: John Doe	Initial Annual Premium:	$3,050.00
Male 45 Nonsmoker	Initial Death Benefit:	$500,000
Riders: None		

				Guaranteed Assumptions			Non-Guaranteed Assumptions Current		
Age	Year	Premium Outlay*	Cumulative Premium	Policy Value	Surrender Value	Death Benefit	Policy Value	Surrender Value	Death Benefit
46	1	3,050	3,050	1,267	0	500,000	1,767	0	500,000
47	2	3,050	6,100	2,456	0	500,000	3,628	0	500,000
48	3	3,050	9,150	3,551	0	500,000	5,389	0	500,000
49	4	3,050	12,200	4,537	0	500,000	7,655	0	500,000
50	5	3,050	15,250	5,391	0	500,000	9,869	1,469	500,000
51	6	3,050	18,300	6,097	0	500,000	12,224	3,824	500,000
52	7	3,050	21,350	6,611	0	500,000	14,520	6,220	500,000
53	8	3,050	24,400	6,890	0	500,000	16,719	8,499	500,000
54	9	3,050	27,450	6,899	0	500,000	18,914	10,714	500,000
55	10	3,050	30,500	6,577	0	500,000	20,985	12,835	500,000
56	11	3,050	33,550	5,872	0	500,000	22,939	16,139	500,000
57	12	3,050	36,600	4,722	0	500,000	24,731	19,631	500,000
58	13	3,050	39,650	3,084	0	500,000	26,305	22,905	500,000
59	14	3,050	42,700	890	0	500,000	27,605	25,905	500,000
60	15	3,050	45,750	0	0	500,000	28,553	28,553	500,000
61	16	3,050	48,800	0	0	0	29,511	29,511	500,000
62	17	3,050	51,850	0	0	0	30,277	30,277	500,000
63	18	3,050	54,900	0	0	0	30,861	30,861	500,000
64	19	3,050	57,950	0	0	0	31,252	31,252	500,000
65	20	3,050	61,000	0	0	0	31,427	31,427	500,000
66	21	3,050	64,050	0	0	0	31,942	31,942	500,000
67	22	3,050	67,100	0	0	0	32,242	32,242	500,000
68	23	3,050	70,150	0	0	0	32,315	32,315	500,000
69	24	3,050	73,200	0	0	0	32,115	32,115	500,000
70	25	3,050	76,250	0	0	0	31,584	31,584	500,000
71	26	3,050	79,300	0	0	0	30,630	30,630	500,000
72	27	3,050	82,350	0	0	0	29,129	29,129	500,000
73	28	3,050	85,400	0	0	0	27,010	27,010	500,000
74	29	3,050	88,450	0	0	0	24,155	24,155	500,000
75	30	3,050	91,500	0	0	0	20,173	20,173	500,000
76	31	3,050	94,550	0	0	0	14,720	14,720	500,000
77	32	3,050	97,600	0	0	0	7,640	7,640	500,000
78	33	5,408	103,008	0	0	0	1,031	1,031	500,000
79	34	14,041	117,049	0	0	0	1,371	1,371	500,000
80	35	15,002	132,051	0	0	0	1,333	1,333	500,000
81	36	16,628	148,680	0	0	0	1,568	1,568	500,000
82	37	18,085	166,764	0	0	0	1,667	1,667	500,000
83	38	19,829	186,593	0	0	0	1,859	1,859	500,000
84	39	21,603	208,196	0	0	0	2,068	2,068	500,000

Current, Specified, and Midpoint assumptions are not guaranteed. They assume that scales for interest and cost of insurance rates will continue unchanged by the Company for all years shown. This is not likely to occur because interest and cost of insurance rates are subject to change by the Company based on various factors such as claims and investment experience, persistency, expenses, taxes, and the overall economic environment. Actual results may be more or less favorable than those shown.

Life
Universal Life Insurance Illustration
Tabular Detail

Proposed Insured: John Doe
Male 45 Nonsmoker
Riders: None

Initial Annual Premium: $3,050.00
Initial Death Benefit: $500,000

| | | | | Guaranteed Assumptions | | | Non-Guaranteed Assumptions Current | | |
Age	Year	Premium Outlay*	Cumulative Premium	Policy Value	Surrender Value	Death Benefit	Policy Value	Surrender Value	Death Benefit
85	40	23,551	231,747	0	0	0	2,300	2,300	500,000
86	41	25,744	257,491	0	0	0	2,575	2,575	500,000
87	42	28,611	286,102	0	0	0	2,946	2,946	500,000
88	43	31,356	317,458	0	0	0	3,321	3,321	500,000
89	44	34,094	351,552	0	0	0	3,706	3,706	500,000
90	45	36,818	388,370	0	0	0	4,110	4,110	500,000
91	46	42,654	431,025	0	0	0	5,030	5,030	500,000
92	47	21,395	452,419	0	0	0	0	0	0

Current, Specified, and Midpoint assumptions are not guaranteed. They assume that rates for interest and cost of insurance rates will continue unchanged by the Company for all years shown. This is not likely to occur because interest and cost of insurance rates are subject to change by the Company based on various factors such as claims and investment experience, persistency, expenses, taxes, and the overall economic environment. Actual results may be more or less favorable than those shown.

Life
Universal Life Insurance Illustration
Additional Information

Proposed Insured: John Doe	Initial Annual Premium: $3,050.00
Male 45 Nonsmoker	Initial Death Benefit: $500,000
Riders: None	

The first year premium outlay includes a(n) Annual premium of $3,050.00

The **Guaranteed** columns assume an initial guaranteed interest rate of 4.00% and guaranteed cost of insurance rates.
The **Current** columns assume an initial current interest rate of 5.10% and current cost of insurance rates.

*   Even if the premium outlay is zero, monthly deductions will continue. Depending on actual results, additional premiums may be needed to avoid termination of the policy. Monthly deductions will cease at attained age 100.

Life Insurance Cost Information

	Net Payment Cost Index		Surrender Cost Index	
	Guaranteed	Current	Guaranteed	Current
Year 10	6.100	6.100	6.100	4.156
Year 20	N/A	6.100	N/A	4.290

Indices assume the time value of money to be 5.0% The Net Payment Cost Index and the Surrender Cost Index are measures of the relative cost of similar plans of insurance. A low index number represents a lower cost than a high index number. A more detailed explanation of the intended use of these indices is provided in the Life Insurance Buyer's Guide.

While the illustrated premium outlays have been tested for compliance with current Federal Tax Law, neither Empire General Life Assurance Corporation nor its representatives offer legal or tax advice. Any compliance tests applied and any tax-related statements made in this illustration represent only one interpretation of current federal tax law as it relates to life insurance. In addition, the tax treatment of life insurance is subject to change. We recommend that you consult your legal or tax advisor before making any financial decisions.

Guideline Level Premium:	$9,625.95	7-PAY Premium: $26,131.90
Guideline Single Premium:	$107,135.88	

Current, Specified, and Midpoint assumptions are not guaranteed. They assume that scales for interest and cost of insurance rates will continue unchanged by the Company for all years shown. This is not likely to occur because interest and cost of insurance rates are subject to change by the Company based on various factors such as claims and investment experience, persistency, expenses, taxes, and the overall economic environment. Actual results may be more or less favorable than those shown.

Agent: Anthony Steuer
January 13, 2004 8:07am   Page: 8 of 8   State: CA

QUESTION 41: Is There Any Way To Guarantee the Death Benefit On My Cash Value Life Insurance Policy?

An issue that has always caused concern with Universal Life (UL) is that the death benefit is not guaranteed for the life of the policy. Insurance companies are now starting to offer policies that continue past age 95/100 up to age 120. Most insurance policies will terminate (mature) at age 95 or 100 and cash out at that time leaving the insured to self-insure. This leaves the client with the cash value which often is lower than the death benefit after years of paying premiums. This payment is also reported to the Internal Revenue Service, on a 1099 form for the amount of cash value less the basis (typically the sum of premiums paid). This potentially widens the gap further between the cash value at that time and the death benefit of the policy.

A number of carriers are offering and/or deferring the maturity of a life insurance policy beyond age 100. There are two methods that are used-the Death Benefit Guarantee and the No-Lapse Guarantee. With either method, carriers may charge nothing, expense costs only, or expense charges plus cost of insurance. At this time, there are no actuarially calculated Cost of Insurance charges for ages greater than 100.

With secondary guarantee-supported universal life, the few carriers that offer the death benefit extension, as opposed to the cash value extension, provide an enormous consumer benefit. In the case of our 50-year old male again, his $12,607 premium purchased $1 million of death benefit with cash values in the guaranteed column that zero out at age 71. Cash value at age 100 is obviously still zero. A number of carriers provide a death benefit extension, though, which supports the death benefit until death actually occurs.

No-Lapse Guarantee clause—under a typical clause; the policy would be guaranteed to stay in-force for a number of years, as long as you have paid at least as much as the required premiums. This is called a no-lapse guarantee. Even though it contains the no-lapse guarantee, this policy may provide non-forfeiture benefits (such as cash surrender values) which are less than those that would be provided if the no-lapse guarantee were issued as a separate policy (for example, as a term policy). However, the premiums for the term policy might be higher than those for the no-lapse guarantee in this policy. When considering the purchase of this policy, you should consider the value to you of higher non-forfeiture benefits versus the level of the premiums required to keep your insurance coverage in-force.

Death Benefit Guarantee—This is a guarantee that the policy will remain in effect, provided you pay sufficient premiums and you do not take loans. This guarantee will depend on such factors as the amount and timing of premiums paid and withdrawals taken, and changes made to the policy. The premiums shown on an illustration with the death benefit guarantee, which is based on the initial basic insurance amount, will guarantee the contract will remain in effect for the periods shown, if these premiums are paid exactly on the first day of each policy year and no loans or withdrawals are taken. These premium amounts can be affected by policy changes. The premiums for this option are usually not much higher than a policy without a death benefit guarantee.

Question 42: Is There Any Oversight Of Policy Illustrations?

Policy Illustrations have been evolving over the last few years, with new regulations from the National Association of Insurance Commissioners. The following discusses what is being done by regulators in order to assist consumers by providing guidelines for life insurance companies and life insurance advisors. Prior to this regulation, there was a combination of lack of information provided by insurance companies to agents and agents to consumers. Agents were also allowed by the carriers, and by themselves, to provide their own "custom" illustrations that were misleading to consumers. When the National Association of Insurance Commissioners (NAIC) adopts a model regulation, it is up to each State Department of Insurance whether or not to adopt it. Therefore, you would have to check with the NAIC or your State Insurance Department (Contact Information can be found in Appendix A).

In December 1995; the National Association of Insurance Commissioners (NAIC) adopted the Life Insurance Illustrations Model Regulation. Up until this time, there was no oversight for ensuring that the presentation of illustrations was fair and appropriate. Various states have adopted this regulation with certain state by state modifications.

The Model Regulation's stated purpose is to provide rules for life insurance policy illustrations that will protect consumers and foster consumer education". Its goals are "to ensure that illustrations do not mislead purchasers of life insurance and to make illustrations more understandable".

The regulation creates standardized procedures that must be followed during the sale of all "life insurance policies except; variable life insurance, individual and group annuity contracts, credit life insurance and life insurance policies with no illustrated death benefits on any individual exceeding $10,000."

The Model Regulation sets standards for initial compliance and for annual reporting. It also sets forth, in conjunction with the Actuarial Standards Practice Number 24, rules for acceptable assumptions that underlie an illustration. Illustration defined: According to the Model Regulation—an illustration is any presentation or depiction that includes non-guaranteed elements of a policy of life insurance over a period of years. In other words, if it assumes an interest rate higher than the guaranteed rate and projects accumulated values based on the higher rate, it contains "non-guaranteed elements" and is therefore an illustration subject to the Model Regulation. An illustration is further defined as either a basic or supplemental illustration, as defined by the appropriate state's version of the NAIC Life Insurance Illustration Model Regulation.

- Basic Illustration—a ledger or proposal used in the sale of a life insurance policy that shows both guaranteed and non-guaranteed elements. A Basic Illustration must always accompany or precede any Supplemental Illustration. The Basic Illustration consists of the following components:
  o Narrative Summary—describes any policy features, riders or options (guaranteed or non-guaranteed) shown in the Basic

Illustration and the impact that they have on the benefits and values of the policy; in addition, defines the column headings and key terms used in the illustration.

o Numeric Summary—summarizes death benefits, values and premiums for three or four particular policy years using guaranteed, midpoint, and current assumptions; includes statements of understanding that must be signed by both the applicant and the agent.

o Tabular Detail—shows death benefits, values, and premiums for all policy years until age 100, policy maturity, or final expiration.

- Revised Basic Illustration—an updated version of the Basic Illustration, which illustrates the policy as issued.
- Supplemental Illustration—an illustration furnished in addition to a Basic Illustration that may be presented in a format differing from the Basic Illustration, which can only depict the same underlying premiums and a scale of non-guaranteed elements that is not more favorable than these same components in the Basic Illustration. The regulation mandates specific footnotes that must be included in the Supplemental Illustration. The Supplemental Illustration gives the company more flexibility, in explaining to the applicant or prospective applicant as to how its product works.

CAVEATS—WHAT AN AGENT CANNOT DO

The NAIC regulation clearly states that, during the sales process, an agent may not do any of the following. Doing so constitutes a violation of these regulations. If an agent violates any of these rules, you should immediately find another agent and, if necessary, contact your State's Insurance Department. The agent may not:

- Illustrate the non-guaranteed elements of a life insurance policy in a format that is not compliant with the regulation (as discussed above)
- Represent the policy as anything other than life insurance.
- Use or describe non-guaranteed elements in the policy that are misleading or could mislead.

- Imply that the amount or payment of non-guaranteed elements is guaranteed.
- Represent that premium payments are not required.
- Use the terms "vanish", "vanishing premium", or similar terms, which imply that policy becomes paid up (that no further premiums will be required after a certain number of years).

Copyright NAIC. Permission for this reprint granted by NAIC.

CHAPTER 4: HOW TO CHOOSE A LIFE INSURANCE COMPANY

QUESTION 43: Where Do I Start In Choosing A Life Insurance Company?

Choosing a life insurance company is an essential and challenging part of the process. More than 1,600 life insurance companies offer thousands of life insurance products to residents of the United States. Choosing the right company and right product from this bewildering array is a challenging task. Fortunately, there are some common sense guidelines that will help you narrow the field to a more manageable selection of companies and products. Let's cover briefly how to evaluate a life insurance company from a financial perspective.

If you think you might need your insurance coverage for more than 10 or 15 years, it is imperative that you choose your insurance carriers carefully and continue to monitor those companies on a regular basis. While no one can accurately predict a company's viability twenty, thirty, or forty years down the line, you should do everything you can to avoid the time and expense of watching your carrier struggle through receivership and sale. Just ask the policyholders at Mid-Continent Life, an Oklahoma-based life insurance company which was taken over by the state Insurance Department in 1997. Almost four years later, the fate of the 130,000 policy owners is murky at best.

While those who are making a substantial commitment to invest in a large portfolio may want to consider the services of an insurance analyst or independent consultant, a growing number of consumers are turning to the Internet for their information.

Many "net-savvy" consumers are pros when it comes to looking up and analyzing financial data on stocks, bonds, and mutual funds.

Performing insurance company due diligence, however, presents a new challenge. Fortunately, many of the leading sources of information have recently made their ratings and "analysis" available to the online public and almost all of it is free. Most likely this will change as the rating services will view this as an income stream.

Don't get caught in the trap of simply comparing two companies and choosing the better one. Instead, hold each company up to a predetermined set of benchmarks. If an insurance agent wants to sell a particular company or product, it is not uncommon for the agent to offer two or three alternatives that look worse than the one the agent wants to sell.

Finally, don't assume that it costs more to purchase insurance from a top-rated company. Remember, product illustrations are poor indicators of how a policy will perform. Since insurance companies generally have comparable expenses, reserve requirements, and overall investment strategies, buying from the best does not necessarily result in higher premiums.

QUESTION 44: What Is a Rating?

When selecting or evaluating a life insurance company, a logical place to begin is by reviewing the ratings given by the five major insurance company rating services. In a rating, the rating company or agency expresses its opinion of the life insurance company's financial soundness and creditworthiness. In some cases, the life insurance company will ask one or more rating companies for an evaluation and rating, and the company will then pay a fee ($25,000 to $30,000 is common) to the rating agency. Generally speaking, this fee does not compromise the rating because rating companies are extremely protective of their reputation for objectivity. Without public credibility, a rating is useless, so rating companies strive to maintain their credibility.

QUESTION 45: Who Are The Rating Agencies?

Five firms currently rate insurance companies. They are A.M. Best Company, Standard and Poor's Corporation, Moody's Investors

Service, Fitch, and Weiss Research. Each firm employs its own rating system, and some rating agencies are considered to be more stringent than others.

Not all insurance companies are rated by each agency. Each agency employs its own techniques for determining a given insurance company's rating. Areas of consideration may vary and these include financial leverage, management stability, recent performance, and the rated company's overall financial situation. External factors such as competition, diversification, and market presence may also be considered.

Each rating agency provides a description of its analysis and defines the meaning of each rating from the highest to the lowest. Since there are differences between rating agencies, this can make a fair comparison between different ratings somewhat confusing. Information on how to contact each rating service will be found below (including some useful links). The chart at the end of this report compares the ratings given by each agency. To obtain the latest ratings, please check with the appropriate rating service.

The following summary describes each rating service and the rating criteria used, along with a brief explanation of how insurance companies initiate the rating process. It is important to keep in mind that these criteria may change.

Third Party Ratings and Financial Data

There are five major rating firms that analyze life insurance companies on a regular basis, and they offer their ratings and analysis online:

- **AM Best Company**—Simply enter the name of your company under the "Search Ratings" category and in addition to providing you with an up-to-date rating, under the various folder tabs you will find the following: 1) the age of the company (a minimum of 50 years' experience is recommended); 2) the corporate address; 3) the company ownership structure (stock or mutual); 4) the Financial Size Category (recommended minimum is IX); 5) the business overview, and 6) the history of the company including any mergers and acquisitions. In addition to this free data, AM Best also offers a complete company report for $19.95 which provides financial statistics for the past five years. But unless you're proficient at interpreting insurance company financials, this report may prove rather overwhelming. (Web site is: www.ambest.com).

- **Standard & Poor's**—To access the Insurer Financial Strength Ratings, click on the "Ratings Lists" link, and then choose the "Insurance" category. When you have located your company, the resulting report is quite detailed. In particular, pay attention to the following data: 1) total assets for five years (goal is moderate growth over this period with a recommended minimum of $2 billion in assets); 2) total liabilities (should experience roughly the same growth rate as total assets); 3) net income (should remain relatively stable); 4) business review and history; and 5) a pie chart indicating the company's product sales. This last category is particularly important in times of change. If a company sells too much of any one product type (individual annuities, or permanent life insurance, for example) a sudden shock to the marketplace, such as a change in the economy or tax system, could result in a sharp decline in the company's business. Lack of product diversification was a leading factor behind the failure of Mid-Continent Life. The company primarily marketed one policy type and, when that product proved to be under priced, the entire company was at risk. (Web site is: www.standardand-poors.com)

- **Fitch**—The Financial Strength Ratings Reports can be found under the "Insurance" category. In addition to a letter rating, the Fitch website will provide you with a detailed business review and overall outlook for the company. In particular, you should pay attention to the following: 1) the product mix (life, annuities, group insurance); 2) the company's marketing focus (upscale and advanced marketing is usually a sign that much of the company's business is tax-oriented; 3) the primary states where the company sells insurance (diversification between several states is advised); 4) the company's reinsurance practices, and 5) the quality of the assets in which the company invests. High-risk investments (junk bonds and defaulted mortgages, for example) have caused the downfall of several large insurance companies such as Executive Life, First Capital Life, and Monarch Life, and a company's exposure to such investments should be very limited. (Web Site is at www.fitchratings.com)

- **Moody's**—Insurance Financial Strength Ratings can be found under the "Insurance" category. (Web Site is at (www.moodys.com)
- **Weiss**—Weiss is the only major rating service that charges for its current ratings. The cost is currently $7.95 per company and the only information you will receive for that price is the letter rating. To purchase a rating, click on the "Ratings Online" button. (www.weissratings.com).
- The web site addresses given here are the main home page for each rating service. It can sometimes be a challenge to find the page on each site; however keep looking as the information is there. At the time of the writing of this book, you do need to establish a free account for some of these services.

QUESTION 46: How Do I Find Out More About Each Rating Service?

As a good rule of thumb, only companies who have received one of the top two ratings from at least three independent rating companies should be considered.

- **A.M. Best Company**—has the most experience rating insurance companies, having been in the business since 1906. Each year Best publishes Best's Insurance Reports, a multi-volume set in two editions—life and health insurance companies and property/casualty companies. Many large public libraries subscribe to Bests Insurance Reports. Best rates each company on either an alphabetical (A++ to F) or a numerical scale. The latter is the Best Financial Performance Rating ("FPR"), with 9 being the highest rating and 1 being the lowest.

  An alphabetical Best Rating is an opinion based on a comprehensive quantitative and qualitative evaluation of a company's balance sheet strength and operating performance. An FPR is an opinion based primarily on a quantitative evaluation of the company's financial strength and operating performance for companies that do not meet the minimum size and/or operating experience requirements for an alphabetical Best Rating.

In 1999, Best's introduced the Best's Security Icon, which is awarded to companies in the Best "Secure" rating category (A++, A+, A, A-, B++ or B+). This emblem displays the company's rating and the evaluation category into which the company falls (Superior, Excellent, or Very Good).

You can view the latest Best Ratings and Best Company Reports (which include Best's Ratings) by visiting the A.M. Best web site at www.ambest.com. You can also obtain Best Reports by calling their Customer Service Department at 908/439-2200, ext. 5742. There is no charge for this service, because A.M. Best bills the rated insurance companies.

- **Standard and Poor's Corporation**—rates what it refers to as the claims paying ability of insurance companies that request and pay for a rating. Standard and Poor's also publishes "Security Circle" and "Financial Enhancement Ratings". An S&P Financial Strength Rating is the agency's current opinion of the financial security aspects of an insurance company, with a specific focus on the company's ability to pay claims on its insurance policies.

This opinion is not specific to any particular policy or contract, nor does it address the suitability of a particular policy or contract for a specific purpose or purchaser. Furthermore, the opinion does not take into account deductibles, surrender or cancellation penalties, timeliness of payment, or the likelihood of the use of a defense such as fraud to deny claims. For organizations with cross-border or multinational operations, including those conducted by subsidiaries or branch offices, the ratings do not take into account the potential that foreign exchange restrictions may prevent the company from meeting its financial obligations.

Insurer Financial Strength Ratings are based on information furnished by rated organizations or obtained by Standard & Poor's from other sources it considers reliable. Standard & Poor's does not perform an audit in connection with any rating and may on occasion rely on un-audited financial information. S&P ratings may be changed, suspended, or withdrawn as a result of changes in or unavailability of such information or based on other circumstances.

S&P recently introduced its Security Circle designation, awarded to insurers that voluntarily undergo S&P's most comprehensive review and have achieved one of S&P's four top rating categories (AAA, AA, A, BBB). The Security Circle emblem displays the assigned rating and category (Extremely Strong, Very Strong, Strong or Good). Any company awarded the "Security Circle" designation must agree to cooperate with S&P's ongoing monitoring of its financial condition.

In 2000, S&P introduced Financial Enhancement Ratings to review insurer capacity and readiness to meet financial commitments. This rating assesses the company's willingness to make timely payment of claims. S&P describes the criteria for this rating on the company's web site. These criteria provide an inside look at the methodologies employed in order to compare the financial and liquidity risks undertaken by the company, along with underwriting expertise.

For the latest Standard and Poor's Ratings, visit the agency's web site at www.standardandpoor's.com. You can also get information about a company's S&P rating by calling 212-438-2400.

- **Moody's Investor's Services**—assigns what it refers to as financial strength ratings that measure the insurance company's ability to meet its senior policyholder obligations and claims. The rating analysis is similar to Moody's well-known and respected bond ratings. Most companies that are rated by Moody's request the rating and go through an interview process similar to Standard & Poor's. A Moody's Insurance Financial Strength Rating is an opinion of the insurer's ability to repay senior policyholder claims and obligations punctually.

Moody's employs rating symbols for its Insurance Financial Strength Ratings that are identical to the company's bond credit quality ratings. The rating gradations provide investors with a simple system to measure an insurance company's ability to meet its senior policyholder claims and obligations.

The rating gradations are broken down into nine distinct symbols, with each symbol representing a group of ratings in which the quality characteristics are broadly the same. The symbols, comprising two distinct rating groups of strong and weak companies, range from those used to designate the greatest financial strength (i.e., highest investment quality) to those denoting the least financial strength (i.e., lowest investment quality).

Numeric modifiers are used to refer to the ranking within the group—with 1 being the highest and 3 being the lowest. The financial strength of companies sharing a generic rating symbol (Aa, for example) is roughly the same with only minor differences.

For the latest Moody's Rating, visit the company's web site at www.moodys.com. You may also find out a Moody's rating by calling 212-553-0377.

- **Fitch's Insurer Financial Strength Ratings**—In the summer of 2000, Fitch merged with Duff & Phelps Credit rating company and announced a new rating system. A Fitch insurer financial strength rating (IFS rating) provides an assessment of the financial strength of an insurance organization, and its capacity to meet senior obligations to policyholders on a timely basis. The IFS rating is assigned to the insurance organization itself, and no liabilities or obligations of the insurer are specifically rated unless otherwise stated (for example, Fitch may separately rate the debt obligations of an insurer). An IFS rating can be assigned to insurance and reinsurance companies in all insurance sectors, including the life & health, property & casualty, mortgage, financial guaranty and title insurance sectors, as well as managed care companies, such as health maintenance organizations.

The IFS rating does not address the willingness of an insurance organization's management to honor its company's obligations, nor does the IFS rating address the quality of an insurer's claims handling services. In the context of the IFS rating, the timeliness of payments is considered relative to both contract and/or policy terms and also recognizes the possibility of acceptable delays caused by circumstances unique to the insurance industry, including claims reviews, fraud investigations and coverage disputes.

The IFS rating is based on a comprehensive analysis of relevant factors that in large part determine an insurance organization's financial strength, including its regulatory solvency characteristics, liquidity, operating performance, financial flexibility, balance sheet strength, management quality, competitive positioning and long-term business viability.

The IFS rating is an international-scale rating, and incorporates relevant economic and political risks that could impair an insurance organization's capacity to meet its obligations. As a result, in most cases, it would be rare for an insurance organization to achieve an IFS rating that would be higher than the long-term, international-scale local currency ratings assigned to the obligations of its sovereign state of domicile. One exception could be cases in which foreign parental support commitments are in place. Other exceptions could include cases in which, due to the international nature of an insurer's business, a major portion of its business and financial resources is not exposed to the economic and political risks of its sovereign state.

Since the IFS rating is not assigned to any specific obligations of the insurer, the rating does not take into account the potential for government restrictions that could prevent specific obligations from being met on a timely basis. An example might be exchange controls placed on obligations owed in a foreign currency.

The IFS rating uses the same ratings scale and symbols as those used by Fitch for its international ratings of long-term debt obligations and issuers. However, the definitions associated with the ratings reflect the unique aspects of the IFS rating within an insurance industry context. Ratings in the 'AA' through 'CCC' categories may be amended with a plus or minus sign to show relative standing within the major rating category. Ratings of 'BBB-' and higher are considered to be 'Secure", and those of 'BB+' and lower are considered to be "Vulnerable".

Fitch ratings provide an overall assessment of the financial strength and security of insurance companies and are used extensively in the insurance marketplace to support insurance carrier selection and placement decisions. In addition to its traditional rating services, Fitch introduced the Fitch Security Seal in October 2000 to augment its Insurer Financial Strength Ratings. The Seal was designed to provide a simple indication for users of ratings. The seal is awarded to insurers meeting several criteria that Fitch believes indicate that the insurer offers a high level of security. Most companies that are rated by Fitch request the rating and go through an interview process. According to the Fitch website, as of January 23, 2001, about 220 large, medium, and small sized life and health insurers, making up close to 85% of the total industry based on assets, have Fitch ratings.

For the latest Fitch Ratings visit the Fitch web site at www.fitchratings.com. You can also find out a company's Fitch rating by calling 800/753-4824.

- **Weiss Research**—provides what it describes as safety ratings of insurance companies. Weiss accepts no compensation from the companies rated and does not allow companies the opportunity to preview the ratings or suppress their publication if they are unfavorable, as some of the other rating agencies do.

  Weiss reviews the financial safety of approximately 1,500 U.S. life, health and annuity insurance companies quarterly and then issues Weiss Safety Ratings, based on their analysts' review of publicly available information collected by the NAIC and supplemented by data they collect directly from the companies themselves.

The rating agency may publish a periodic watch list identifying companies whose ratings, the agency plans to review for one reason or another. For example, if one insurance company acquires another, this usually results in both companies being placed on the rating agencies' watch lists.

The watch lists usually indicate the expected direction of movement in the underlying rating. For example, watch list positive (+) means a rating upgrade can be expected, while watch list negative connotations (-) usually means a downgrade can be expected. In some cases, companies are placed on the watch list with unknown connotations. That means the rating agency does not know what the implications of the change will be until it completes its review. For example, Best uses an "under review" (U) modifier to identify companies whose rating opinions are under review and may be subject to near-term change.

As you can see, the rating agencies use different criteria and they offer an assortment of ratings. A high rating is not a guarantee that a company will meet its projected earnings or that it will survive. Similarly a low rating does not mean that a company will not meet its projected earnings or that it will fail. A rating is simply an expression of opinion about selected aspects of the current financial condition of an insurance company. Each rating service also has extensive information on their philosophy and the criteria on their website.

With permanent life insurance, it is especially crucial to go beyond the ratings and also analyze the insurance company's investment portfolio. Some of the rating agencies do this—A.M. Best for example. A life insurance policy can be in-force for many years so long term company solvency is very important. The insurer must be able to perform on its promises for decades into the future.

For the latest Weiss Rating visit their web site at www.weissratings. com. You may find out a company's Weiss Rating by calling 800/289-9222. However, you will be expected to pay for the information. Weiss is currently the only rating agency that charges the public for its ratings. At the time of the writing of this book the fee is $7.95 for the rating on each company you are interested in, and Weiss will fax or mail you a report.

QUESTION 47: How Do I Compare The Ratings From Each of The Five Major Rating Services on a Relative Basis?

Here is a table that does so:

RANK	A.M. Best	Standard & Poor's	Moody's	Fitch	Weiss
1	A++ Superior	AAA Extremely Strong	Aaa Exceptional	AAA Exceptionally Strong	A+ Excellent
2	A+ Superior	AA+ Very Strong	Aa1 Excellent	AA+ Very Strong	A Excellent
3	A Excellent	AA Very Strong	Aa2 Excellent	AA Very Strong	A- Excellent
4	A- Excellent	AA- Very Strong	Aa3 Excellent	AA- Very Strong	B+ Good
5	B++ Very Good	A+ Strong	A1 Good	A+ Strong	B Good
6	B+ Good	A Strong	A2 Good	A Strong	B- Good
7	B Fair	A- Strong	A3 Good	A- Strong	C+ Fair
8	B- Fair	BBB+ Good	Baa1 Adequate	BBB+ Good	C Fair
9	C++ Marginal	BBB Good	Baa2 Adequate	BBB Good	C- Fair
10	C+ Marginal	BBB- Good	Baa3 Adequate	BBB- Good	D+ Weak
11	C Weak	BB+ Marginal	Ba1 Questionable	BB+ Moderately Weak	D Weak
12	C- Weak	BB Marginal	Ba2 Questionable	BB Moderately Weak	D- Weak
13	D Poor	BB- Marginal	Ba3 Questionable	BB- Moderately Weak	E+ Very Weak
14	E Under State Supervision	B+ Weak	B1 Poor	B+ Weak	E Very Weak
15	F In Liquidation	B Weak	B2 Poor	B Weak	E- Very Weak
16		B- Weak	B3 Poor	B- Weak	F Failed
17		CCC+ Very Weak	Caa1 Very Poor	CCC+ Very Weak	
18		CCC Very Weak	Caa2 Very Poor	CCC Very Weak	
19		CCC- Very Weak	Caa3 Very Poor	CCC- Very Weak	

Ratings are useful, but—a rating is not a guaranty of an insurer's financial strength or security. These tools are not always foolproof with regard to a specific company. Selecting an insurance company is an exercise in common sense. It is a task requiring research and an understanding of the rating systems and various financial measures. Once you have selected an insurance company, you should continue to monitor the company because financial data and ratings change.

QUESTION 48: What Are The Definitions For Each Rating?

These were current as of the time of the writing of this book.

A.M. Best Company

Secure Best's Ratings

A++ and A+ (Superior)—Assigned to companies that have, in our opinion, a superior ability to meet their ongoing obligations to policyholders.

A and A- (Excellent)—Assigned to companies that have, in our opinion, an excellent ability to meet their ongoing obligations to policyholders.

B++ and B+ (Very Good)—Assigned to companies that have, in our opinion, a good ability to meet their ongoing obligations to policyholders.

Vulnerable Best's Ratings

B and B- (Fair)—Assigned to companies that have, in our opinion, a fair ability to meet their current obligations to policyholders, but are financially vulnerable to adverse changes in underwriting and economic conditions.

C++ and C+ (Marginal)—Assigned to companies that have, in our opinion, a marginal ability to meet their current obligations to policyholders, but are financially vulnerable to adverse changes in underwriting and economic conditions.

C and C- (Weak)—Assigned to companies that have, in our opinion, a weak ability to meet their current obligations to policyholders, but are financially very vulnerable to adverse changes in underwriting and economic conditions.

D (Poor)—Assigned to companies that, in our opinion, may not have an ability to meet their current obligations to policyholders and are financially extremely vulnerable to adverse changes in underwriting and economic conditions.

E (Under Regulatory Supervision)—Assigned to companies (and possibly their subsidiaries/affiliates) that have been placed by an insurance regulatory authority under a significant form of supervision, control or restraint, whereby they are no longer allowed to conduct normal ongoing insurance operations. This would include conservatorship or rehabilitation, but does not include liquidation. It may also be assigned to companies issued cease and desist orders by regulators outside their home state or country.

F (In Liquidation)—Assigned to companies that have been placed under an order of liquidation by a court of law or whose owners have voluntarily agreed to liquidate the company. Note: Companies that voluntarily liquidate or dissolve their charters are generally not insolvent.

S (Rating Suspended)—Assigned to rated companies that have experienced sudden and significant events affecting their balance sheet strength or operating performance whose rating implications cannot be evaluated due to a lack of timely or adequate information.

Not Rated Categories (NR)

NR-1 (Insufficient Data)—Assigned predominately to small companies for which A.M. Best does not have sufficient financial information required to assign rating opinions. The information contained in these limited reports is obtained from the several sources, which include the individual companies, the National Association of Insurance Commissioners (NAIC) and other data providers. Data received from the NAIC, in some cases, is prior to the completion of the cross-checking and validation process.

NR-2 (Insufficient Size and/or Operating Experience)—Assigned to companies that do not meet A.M. Best's minimum size and/or operating experience requirements. To be eligible for a letter rating, a company must generally have a minimum of $2 million in policyholder's surplus to assure reasonable financial stability and have sufficient operating experience to adequately evaluate its financial performance, usually two to five years. General exceptions to these requirements include: companies that have financial or strategic affiliations with Best's rated companies; companies that have demonstrated long histories of financial performance; companies that have achieved significant market positions; and newly formed companies with experienced management that have acquired seasoned books of business and/or developed credible business plans.

NR-3 (Rating Procedure Inapplicable)—Assigned to companies that are not rated by A.M. Best, because our normal rating procedures do not apply due to a company's unique or unusual business features. This category includes companies that are in run-off with no active business writings, are effectively dormant, underwrite financial or mortgage guaranty insurance, or retain only a small portion of their gross premiums written. Exceptions to the assignment of the NR-3 category to run-off companies relate to those that commenced runoff plans in the current year or are inactive companies that have been structurally separated from active affiliates within group structures that pose potential credit, legal or market risks to the group's active companies.

NR-4 (Company Request)—Assigned to companies that were assigned a Best's Rating but request that their ratings not be published because the companies disagree with Best's rating conclusion. The NR-4 will be assigned at the request of the company following the dissemination by A.M. Best of the latest letter rating assignment.

NR-5 (Not Formally Followed)—Assigned to insurers that request not to be formally evaluated for the purposes of assigning a rating opinion. It is also assigned retroactively to the rating history of traditional U.S. insurers when they provide prior year(s) financial information to A.M. Best and receive a Best's Rating or another NR designation in more recent years. Finally, it is assigned currently to those companies that historically had been rated, but no longer provide financial information to A.M. Best because they have been liquidated, dissolved, or merged out of existence.

Rating Modifiers and Affiliation Codes

Under Review (u) Rating Modifiers are assigned to Best's Ratings to identify companies whose rating opinions are Under Review and may be subject to near-term change. Best's Public Data (pd) Rating Modifiers may be assigned to Health Maintenance Organizations (HMOs), Canadian, UK and other European insurers that do not subscribe to our interactive rating process. Best's Public Data Ratings reflect both qualitative and quantitative analysis using publicly available data and other public information. Syndicate (s) Rating Modifiers are assigned to syndicates operating at Lloyd's. Affiliation Codes are based on a Group (g), Pooling (p) or Reinsurance (r) affiliation with other insurers.

FITCH RATING COMPANY

Insurer Financial Strength Ratings:

AAA—Exceptionally strong. Insurers assigned this highest rating are viewed as possessing exceptionally strong capacity to meet policyholder and contract obligations. For such companies, risk factors are minimal and the impact of any adverse business and economic factors is expected to be extremely small.

AA—Very strong. Insurers are viewed as possessing very strong capacity to meet policyholder and contract obligations. Risk factors are modest, and the impact of any adverse business and economic factors is expected to be very small.

A—Strong. Insurers are viewed as possessing strong capacity to meet policyholder and contract obligations. Risk factors are moderate, and the impact of any adverse business and economic factors is expected to be small.

BBB—Good. Insurers are viewed as possessing good capacity to meet policyholder and contract obligations. Risk factors are somewhat high, and the impact of any adverse business and economic factors is expected to be material, yet manageable.

BB—Moderately weak. Insurers are viewed as moderately weak with an uncertain capacity to meet policyholder and contract obligations. Though positive factors are present, overall risk factors are high, and the impact of any adverse business and economic factors is expected to be significant.

B—Weak. Insurers are viewed as weak with a poor capacity to meet policyholder and contract obligations. Risk factors are very high, and the impact of any adverse business and economic factors is expected to be very significant.

CCC, CC, C—Very weak. Insurers rated in any of these three categories are viewed as very weak with a very poor capacity to meet policyholder and contract obligations. Risk factors are extremely high, and the impact of any adverse business and economic factors is expected to be insurmountable. A 'CC' rating indicates that some form of insolvency or liquidity impairment appears probable. A 'C' rating signals that insolvency or a liquidity impairment appears imminent.

DDD, DD, D—Distressed. These ratings are assigned to insurers that have either failed to make payments on their obligations in a timely manner, are deemed to be insolvent, or have been subjected to some form of regulatory intervention. Within the 'DDD'-'D' range, those companies rated 'DDD' have the highest prospects for resumption of business operations or, if liquidated or wound down, of having a vast majority of their obligations to policyholders and contract holders ultimately paid off, though on a delayed basis (with recoveries expected in the range of 90%-100%). Those rated 'DD' show a much lower likelihood of ultimately paying off material amounts of their obligations in a liquidation or wind down scenario (in a range of 50%-90%). Those rated 'D' are ultimately expected to have very limited liquid assets available to fund obligations, and therefore any ultimate payoffs would be quite modest (at under 50%).

Notes:

"+" or "-" may be appended to a rating to indicate the relative position of a credit within the rating category. Such suffixes are not added to ratings in the 'AAA' category or to ratings below the 'CCC' category.

Ratings of 'BBB-' and higher are considered to be "secure", and those of 'BB+' and lower are considered to be "vulnerable".

A Rating Outlook indicates the direction a rating is likely to move over a one to two-year period. Outlooks may be positive, stable or negative. A positive or negative Rating Outlook does not imply a rating change is inevitable. Similarly, ratings for which outlooks are "stable" could be upgraded or downgraded before an outlook moves to positive or negative if circumstances warrant such an action. Occasionally, Fitch Ratings may be unable to identify the fundamental trend, and in these cases, the Rating Outlook may be described as "evolving".

Rating Watch: Ratings are placed on Rating Watch to notify investors that there is a reasonable probability of a rating change and the likely direction of such change. These are designated as "Positive", indicating a potential upgrade, "Negative", for a potential downgrade, or "Evolving", if ratings may be raised, lowered or maintained. Rating Watch is typically resolved over a relatively short period.

MOODYS

Insurance Financial Strength Ratings:

Aaa—Insurance companies rated Aaa offer exceptional financial security. While the credit profile of these companies is likely to change, such changes as can be visualized are most unlikely to impair their fundamentally strong position.

Aa—Insurance companies rated Aa offer excellent financial security. Together with the Aaa group, they constitute what are generally known as high-grade companies. They are rated lower than Aaa companies because long-term risks appear somewhat larger.

A—Insurance companies rated A offer good financial security. However, elements may be present which suggest a susceptibility to impairment sometime in the future.

Baa—Insurance companies rated Baa offer adequate financial security. However, certain protective elements may be lacking or may be characteristically unreliable over any great length of time.

Ba—Insurance companies rated Ba offer questionable financial security. Often the ability of these companies to meet policyholder obligations may be very moderate and thereby not well safeguarded in the future.
B—Insurance companies rated B offer poor financial security. Assurance of punctual payment of policyholder obligations over any long period of time is small.

Caa—Insurance companies rated Caa offer very poor financial security. They may be in default on their policyholder obligations or there may be present elements of danger with respect to punctual payment of policyholder obligations and claims.

Ca—Insurance companies rated Ca offer extremely poor financial security. Such companies are often in default on their policyholder obligations or have other marked shortcomings.

C—Insurance companies rated C are the lowest-rated class of insurance company and can be regarded as having extremely poor prospects of ever offering financial security.

Note: Moody's appends numerical modifiers 1, 2, and 3 to each generic rating classification from Aa through Caa. Numeric modifiers are used to refer to the ranking within a group—with 1 being the highest and 3 being the lowest. However, the financial strength of companies within a generic rating symbol (Aa, for example) is broadly the same.

Standard & Poor's:

Insurer Financial Strength Ratings:

AAA—An insurer rated 'AAA' has EXTREMELY STRONG financial security characteristics. 'AAA' is the highest Insurer Financial Strength Rating assigned by Standard & Poor's.

AA—An insurer rated 'AA' has VERY STRONG financial security characteristics, differing only slightly from those rated higher.

A—An insurer rated 'A' has STRONG financial security characteristics, but is somewhat more likely to be affected by adverse business conditions than are insurers with higher ratings.

BBB—An insurer rated 'BBB' has GOOD financial security characteristics, but is more likely to be affected by adverse business conditions than are higher rated insurers.

An insurer rated 'BB' or lower is regarded as having vulnerable characteristics that may outweigh its strengths. 'BB' indicates the least degree of vulnerability within the range; 'CC' the highest.

BB—An insurer rated 'BB' has MARGINAL financial security characteristics. Positive attributes exist, but adverse business conditions could lead to insufficient ability to meet financial commitments.

B—An insurer rated 'B' has WEAK financial security characteristics. Adverse business conditions will likely impair its ability to meet financial commitments.

CCC—An insurer rated 'CCC' has VERY WEAK financial security characteristics, and is dependent on favorable business conditions to meet financial commitments.

CC—An insurer rated 'CC' has EXTREMELY WEAK financial security characteristics and is likely not to meet some of its financial commitments.

R—An insurer rated 'R' has experienced a REGULATORY ACTION regarding solvency. The rating does not apply to insurers subject only to non-financial actions such as market conduct violations.

NR—An insurer designated 'NR' is NOT RATED, which implies no opinion about the insurer's financial security.

Plus (+) or minus (-) signs following ratings from 'AA' to 'CCC' show relative standing within the major rating categories.

Weiss Rating

A+, A, A- : Excellent. The company offers excellent financial security. It has maintained a conservative stance in its investment strategies, business operations and underwriting commitments. While the financial position of any company is subject to change, we believe that this company has the resources necessary to deal with severe economic conditions.

B+, B, B- : Good. The company offers good financial security and has the resources to deal with a variety of adverse economic conditions. It comfortably exceeds the minimum levels for all of our rating criteria, and is likely to remain healthy for the near future. However, in the event of a *severe* recession or major financial crisis, we feel that this assessment should be reviewed to make sure that the firm is still maintaining adequate financial strength

C+, C, C- : Fair. The company offers fair financial security and is currently stable. But during an economic downturn or other financial pressures, we feel it may encounter difficulties in maintaining its financial stability.

D+, D, D- : Weak. The company currently demonstrates what we consider to be significant weaknesses which could negatively impact policyholders. In an unfavorable economic environment, these weaknesses could be magnified.

E+, E, E- : Very Weak. The company currently demonstrates what we consider to be significant weaknesses and has also failed some of the basic tests that we use to identify fiscal stability. Therefore, even in a favorable economic environment, it is our opinion that policyholders could incur significant risks.

F: Failed. The company has failed and is either (1) under supervision of state insurance commissioners. (2) is in the process of liquidation, or (3) has voluntarily dissolved after disciplinary or other regulatory action by state insurance commissioners.

QUESTION 49: What Would Be of Assistance In A Financial Analysis?

Financial considerations play varying roles in the comparative tools used by the various rating agencies as we've discussed over the last few questions. These financial considerations can usually be, but not always analyzed on a relative basis between carriers and the industry as a whole. Please keep in mind that individual circumstances vary among companies such as size, etc. These are some of the factors you might want to review, but you should keep in mind that there are many more. These factors are provided for those who are comfortable with financial analyses. If you are not comfortable or do not understand these factors, then you should not use them as they will cause more harm than good.

Asset Analysis

- **Total Admitted Assets:** Total assets reported including separate accounts.
- **Total Liabilities:** Funds required for payment of future claims and expenses, including Asset Valuation Reserve (AVR).
- **Separate Accounts:** Assets dedicated and matched to specific liabilities, such as variable life insurance policies.
- **Total Surplus & AVR:** Total capital, surplus and Asset Valuation Reserve (AVR). AVR is the reserve for potential losses in invested assets.
- **Surplus & AVR as % of General Account Assets:** Total Surplus & AVR as a percent of general account assets. Higher numbers represent greater protection for the policyholder.

- **Invested Assets:** Total assets under investment.
- **Distribution of Invested Assets:** The percentage of each category of investments to the total invested assets.
- **Net Yield on Mean Invested Assets:** Net Investment Income divided by the average of the current and prior year's invested assets.
- **Asset Growth:** 1-year and 3-year compound growth for Total Admitted Assets and Total Surplus & AVR.

Asset Quality Analysis

- **Non-Investment Grade Bonds (Class 3-6):** The NAIC divides bonds into six categories. Classes 1 and 2 are considered investment grade, classes 3 through 6 are below investment grade.
- **Non-Investment Grade Bonds/Total Bonds:** The sum of bonds in classes 3 through 6 divided by Total Bonds.
- **Non-Investment Grade Bonds/Surplus & AVR:** The sum of bonds in classes 3 through 6 divided by Surplus & AVR.
- **Non-Performing Bonds/Total Bonds:** Class 6 bonds are "In or Near Default". This is the percentage of the bond portfolio that is considered non-performing.
- **Non-Performing Bonds/Surplus & AVR:** Class 6 bonds divided by Surplus & AVR.
- **Non-Performing Mortgages & Real Estate/Total Mortgages & Real Estate:** This is the percentage of the mortgage and real estate portfolio that is considered non-performing. This includes mortgages that are 90 days overdue or in foreclosure and real estate acquired through foreclosure.
- **Non-Performing Mortgages & Real Estate/Surplus & AVR:** Mortgages 90 days overdue or in foreclosure and foreclosed real estate divided by Surplus & AVR.
- **Non-Performing Assets/Surplus & AVR:** Bonds in or near default (Class 6), Mortgages 90 days overdue or in foreclosure, and real estate acquired by foreclosure are each presented as a percent of Surplus & AVR.
- **Total Non-Performing Assets/Surplus & AVR:** Total non-performing bonds, mortgages and real estate as a percent of Surplus & AVR, and then as a percentage of invested assets.

Bond Portfolio Analysis

- **Total Bonds Book and Market Value:** The total book value and market value of bonds, and the ratio of market value to book value.
- **Bond Quality Distribution:** The percentage of bonds in each of the six NAIC classes.
- **Weighted Bond Class:** Indicates the average NAIC class for each dollar invested in bonds.
- **Bond Maturity Distribution:** The distribution of bonds by number of years to maturity.
- **Weighted Bond Maturity:** Indicates the average number of years to maturity for each dollar invested in bonds.

Operating Income Analysis

- **Total Income:** Total income from all sources.
- **Total General Expenses:** Total general expenses incurred. This includes investment expenses.
- **Total General Expenses/Total Income:** Total general expenses as a percent of total income.
- **Earnings Before Policy Dividends and Taxes:** Net gain from operations before policy dividends and federal income taxes.
- **Policy Dividends:** Amount paid out as policy dividends, and as a percent of earnings.
- **Pretax Earnings from Operations:** Net gain from operations after policy dividends and before federal income taxes.
- **Federal Income Taxes:** Amount paid in federal income tax, and as a percent of pretax earnings.
- **Net Earnings from Operations:** Earnings before policy dividends and taxes minus policy dividends and federal income taxes.
- **Net Realized Capital Gains:** The total capital gain (or loss) on assets sold during the year.
- **Net Income:** Net Earnings plus Net Realized Capital Gains.
- **Net Income as % of Admitted Assets:** Net Income divided by total admitted assets.

- **Unrealized Capital Gains:** The total capital gain (or loss) on assets that remain in the investment portfolio.

Premium Growth

- **Premium Growth:** 1-year and 3-year compound growth for Total Premium Income (premiums and annuity considerations only) and Ordinary Life Premium.

Profitability

- **Return on Assets:** Net Earnings from Operations divided by the prior year's Invested Assets.
- **Return on Equity:** Net Earnings from Operations divided by the prior year's Capital & Surplus.
- **Lapse Ratio:** The percentage of ordinary life policies that lapsed during the year and the average for three years.
- **Interest Margin:** Net Investment Income and Required Interest are as reported. The Interest Margin is the Net Investment
- **Income less Required Interest as a percent of Required Interest.**
- **Ordinary Life Expenses/Premiums:** Ordinary Life insurance expenses as a percent of Ordinary Life Premiums.
- **Total General Expenses/Total Income:** Total general expenses as a percent of total income.
- **Commissions & General Expenses/Total Income:** Commissions and total general expenses as a percent of Total Income.

Analysis of Face Amount of Insurance

- **Total Insurance In-force:** Total face amount of insurance in-force.
- **In-force Distribution:** Each category (ordinary, group and other) is presented as a percent of the total amount in-force.
- **Total Reinsurance Ceded:** Total face amount of insurance ceded to re-insurers.
- **% of In-force Ceded:** Each category (ordinary, group and other) is presented as a percent of the total face amount of insurance in-force in that category.

- **Average Policy Size:** The number of ordinary life policies and the average policy size for total in-force and new policies issued.

Analysis by Line of Business

- **Net Premiums Written:** Total premium and annuity considerations plus deposit-type funds.
- **Distribution:** Each category is presented as a percent of the net premium income.
- **Net Earnings from Operations:** Net earnings after dividends and taxes.
- **Distribution:** Each category is presented as a percent of the net gain from operations

(The financial definitions and ratios for this question are based from those used by LifeLink Vitalsigns Software)

QUESTION 50: Who is IRIS (Insurance Regulatory Information Reports)?

Another useful resource are the Insurance Regulatory Information (IRIS) reports issued by the National Association of Insurance Commissioners (NAIC). IRIS reports are comprehensive analyses of the financial status of life insurance companies. The NAIC routes its IRIS reports to the various state insurance commissioners. The IRIS testing process has been used since 1972 to help insurance regulators evaluate the financial condition of insurance companies that they regulate. More than 5,000 companies file their financial statements with the NAIC each year. The IRIS financial ratios serve as an early warning system to spot troubled companies. Ratios measuring such things as profitability, solvency, and liquidity are analyzed in detail. Poorly performing companies are recommended for immediate regulatory action, while others are recommended for less urgent ("targeted") regulatory action. A booklet with more information about IRIS is available on the NAIC web site at www.naic.org.

There are currently twelve IRIS ratios calculated for life and health companies. The basis for each ratio is reviewed annually to ensure its currency and continued relevance for solvency monitoring. The ratios are revised as necessary. There is a "usual range of results" that is used as a starting point. The ratios and trends are valuable in identifying companies likely to experience financial difficulties. They are not in themselves indicative of adverse financial condition. The ratios and range comparisons are computer generated.

The IRIS report is available to the public, and can be ordered from the NAIC on their Web Site for $125. This report lists ratio results for each filing company and includes industry mean and median ("average" and "typical") ratios for comparison. A narrative explanation of each of the ratio formulas, benchmarks and worksheets is also included.

A useful explanation of the IRIS system is found in the NAIC report. The ratios are grouped into four categories. These include Overall Ratios (ratios numbered 1, 2, and 3), Investment Ratios (4, 5, 6, and 7), Surplus Relief Ratio (8) and Changes in Operation Ratios (9, 10, 11, and 12). The individual ratios are:

1. Gross and Net Changes in Capital and Surplus
2. Net Income to Total Income (Including Realized Capital Gains and Losses)
3. Commissions and Expenses to Premiums and Deposits (Discontinued)
4. Adequacy of Investment Income
5. Non-Admitted to Admitted Assets
6. Total Real Estate and Total Mortgage Loans to Cash and Invested Assets
7. Total Affiliated Investments to Capital and Surplus
8. Surplus Relief
9. Change in Premium
10. Change in Product Mix
11. Change in Asset Mix
12. Change in Reserving Ratio

Copyright NAIC. Permission for this reprint granted by NAIC.

QUESTION 51: What Is The Risk Based Capital System?

This is a system used currently only by the State Insurance Regulators, it is hoped that it will be available to the public soon. It is in the book for the purpose of showing the tool used by insurance commissioners in determining whether or not to act with an insurance company that may be or is at risk.

In 1992, the NAIC developed yet another standard—Risk Based Capital or RBC for short. RBC was designed as a means of gauging the appropriate minimum amount of capital for a given life insurance company. It was designed to identify inadequately capitalized life and health companies. RBC was intended to provide a uniformly applied guideline for regulatory intervention and to enable regulators to take specific action before a company becomes insolvent.

Risk Based Capital is the amount of capital (assets minus liabilities) deemed to provide a minimum financial cushion in light of a company's size and risk profile. It is calculated by applying factors to various asset, premium and reserve items found in the company's Annual Statement. The Annual Statement is a voluminous document that each company must file with every state insurance department in which the company has a certificate of authority to do business. RBC factors are higher for items with greater underlying risk and lower for less risky items. For example, some lines of coverage are considered riskier than others, and RBC takes the relative risk into consideration.

The company's calculated RBC is compared to actual capital. RBC is not meant to be a measure of the appropriate amount of capital, but rather the minimum amount with which state insurance regulators feel comfortable.

The RBC standard measures four primary risks—asset default risk, adverse experience risk, interest rate risk caused by changes in interest rate levels, and general business risk. Actuaries refer to these as the C-1, C-2, C-3 and C-4 risks. RBC is designed to penalize companies with major investments in real estate and common stock, or those that are engaged in riskier lines of business. Conversely, RBC rewards companies with more conservative investments or in less volatile lines of business.

The RBC system is a spectrum or continuum of increasingly stringent regulatory responses for companies that trigger one of the following RBC action levels:

1. Company Action Level: At this RBC level the insurer must submit to the insurance commissioner a comprehensive financial plan. The plan must identify the conditions contributing to the company's financial condition, contain proposals to correct the company's financial problems and provide projections of the company's financial condition both with and without the proposed corrections.

2. Regulatory Action Level: In addition to requiring the insurer to submit a comprehensive financial plan, the insurance commissioner performs any examinations or analysis of the insurer's business and operations that are deemed necessary and issues any appropriate corrective orders to address the company's financial problems.

3. Authorized Control Level: In addition, the commissioner may place the insurer under regulatory control.

4. Mandatory Control Level: The insurance commissioner is required to place the insurer under regulatory control.

There are differences in the makeup of Risk Based Capital by asset size. This rein-forces the difficulty of making meaningful comparisons between an individual insurer's RBC results and those of the industry. The NAIC stresses that the RBC system is unsuitable for making qualitative comparisons between insurers. Its purpose is to identify under-capitalized companies only and RBC does not address quality of capital or other related issues. Because of the risk that RBC ratios will be misinterpreted by the general public, they are not released to the general public. In fact, release of RBC data to the public is specifically prohibited. RBC ratings are designed for use by State Insurance Commissioners and affected companies only. Limited information about RBC can be found on the NAIC website—www.naic.org.

QUESTION 52: Are The Carriers Held to any Ethical Standard?

Every carrier does adhere to their own ethical practices as well as to basic guidelines, dictated by the Department of Insurance in their state. A list of each state's insurance departments contact information can be (found in Appendix A). A relatively newer entity is IMSA which stands for the Insurance Marketplace Standards Association. IMSA promotes high ethical standards in the sale and service of individually-sold life insurance, annuity and long-term care products. IMSA member companies are insurers who have agreed to adopt and abide by IMSA's Principles and Code of Ethical Market Conduct in order to earn your trust and gain your confidence.

IMSA's Principles and Code of Ethical Market Conduct:

Each IMSA member life insurance company subscribing to these principles commits itself in all matters affecting the sale of individually-sold life, annuity, and long-term care products:

1. To conduct business according to high standards of honesty and fairness and to render that service to its customers which, in the same circumstances, it would apply to or demand for itself.
2. To provide competent and customer-focused sales and service.
3. To engage in active and fair competition.
4. To provide advertising and sales materials that are clear as to purpose and honest and fair as to content.
5. To provide for fair and expeditious handling of customer complaints and disputes.
6. To maintain a system of supervision and review that is reasonably designed to achieve compliance with these Principles of Ethical Market Conduct.

IMSA's standards help assure that a company continues to commit itself to honesty, fairness and integrity in all customer contacts involving the sale and servicing of individual life insurance, long term care insurance and annuities. As part of that commitment, the company carefully monitors the sales process, its employees and agents on a regular basis.

The company develops policies and procedures to assure that customers receive information they need to make decisions about purchasing and/or replacing policies. The company also maintains a system to respond expeditiously to customer concerns and complaints.

IMSA's standards complement those required by state regulation, but in some instances are more rigorous than current regulatory requirements. IMSA member companies agree to set up and follow procedures specifically designed to promote ethical market conduct and agree to monitor those procedures to verify continued compliance with IMSA standards.

An insurer becomes a member by adopting IMSA's Principles and Code and by implementing policies and procedures to meet IMSA's rigorous standards. To demonstrate its commitment, the insurer undergoes an assessment by an outside, independent examiner such as an accountant, attorney, actuarial or management consultant who is certified to assess that the company has met these standards. If the independent assessor determines that the insurer's systems and programs to promote and maintain ethical behavior meet IMSA's standards, the insurer earns an IMSA membership for three years. The assessment and review process must be repeated every three years in order for a company to remain a member of IMSA.

Choosing a life insurance company is an important decision, and you should consider many factors. A number of legitimate business decisions may have guided a company's decision not to qualify for IMSA membership at this time. IMSA membership is not the only indicator of a company's commitment to ethical market conduct. However, IMSA membership could be an important consideration for you. It is further evidence that a company is committed to high standards and has established market conduct policies and programs to recognize customers' needs.

A complaint against an IMSA Member Company should be directed to your insurance company and follow their complaint handling procedure. In many cases, people find that insurers are eager to resolve customers' problems and complaints.

Should you not receive a satisfactory response to your complaint, you may then forward a copy of your original letter to IMSA. It is our policy to forward all complaints to our member companies and request that they respond directly to the customer and copy IMSA on that response.

IMSA can be found online at www.imsaethics.org or at:
Two Wisconsin Circle, Suite 320
Chevy Chase, MD 20815
240-497-2900 (Phone) or 240-497-2901 (Fax)

(The above information is from the IMSA website.)

QUESTION 53: How Do I Find Out About Any Complaints Filed Against My Insurance Company Or File My Own Complaint?

Each State Department of Insurance maintains data on the number of complaints filed against an insurance company, as well as pending Class Action Lawsuits. To find your State Department of Insurance, go to the National Association of Insurance Commissioner's (NAIC) web site—www.naic.org or Appendix A. Your State Department of Insurance is also where you can file a complaint, if you feel you have gone through your other resources, such as trying to work with your life insurance company or there is some reason why you cannot approach them. Or contacting IMSA (Insurance Marketing Standards Association)—contact and other information about them can be found in the prior question #52. Other options are many depending on your state, your research and any other factors. An attorney is always an option if the situation warrants it and the amount at stake exceeds the fees.

QUESTION 54: So, What is the Best Way to Select An Insurance Company?

Ratings are useful, but—a rating is not a guaranty of an insurer's financial strength or security. These tools are not always foolproof with regard to a specific company. Selecting an insurance company is an exercise in common sense. It is a task requiring research and an under-standing of the rating systems as well as various financial measures. Once you have selected an insurance company, you should continue to monitor the company because financial data and ratings change.

CHAPTER 5: FINDING A LIFE INSUR-ANCE AGENT

QUESTION 55: How Do I Evaluate a Life Insurance Advisor?

Life insurance has traditionally been sold and serviced by a traditional life insurance agent. Over the last few years, this has changed. There are very few traditional life insurance agents who only sell life insurance and other related insurance products. Almost all are now called by such descriptions as financial advisors, financial consultants and financial planners. The advisors who traditionally had those titles have now expanded more significantly into life insurance. CPA's, also, are now in the life insurance sales business. It has become very difficult to evaluate a life insurance advisor. As with any area, receiving good advice is crucial. The following are some issues to keep in mind.

The agent system has also changed; historically almost all agents were what are called "captive". This means that they only sold products for the company with which they were affiliated. Today, there are still quite a few "captive agents"; however, the majority are brokers who represent multiple carriers. Some "captive" agents can sell other companies' products; however some can only sell their own products. This is important to find out and be aware of. If an advisor can only sell one company's product then they are trying to make one size fit all. This is one more reason for you to shop around.

QUESTION 56: What are the Regulatory Resources for Researching a Life Insurance Advisor?

Any person selling life insurance (and/or annuities) must be licensed with their State Department of Insurance. Contact information for State Departments of Insurance is located in Appendix A

With insurance departments, the resources and compliance can sometimes be more lax in some states than others. On most insurance departments' web sites, you can research whether or not an insurance representative is licensed. The representative has to be licensed in the state where the insured either works or lives. You can also see on some web sites, their history of continuing education. As with any field, a practitioner, who is up to date on the latest techniques, is most likely more proficient.

With Variable Products, they are also overseen by the NASD (National Association of Securities Dealers—www.nasdr.com) whom is generally tougher with the representatives that they oversee. On the NASD web site, you can research whether or not an insurance representative is licensed. With variable insurance products representatives have to be licensed with both the NASD and the State Insurance Department.

The NASD also maintains the qualification, employment, and disclosure histories of the more than half a million registered securities employees of member firms. For an overview of all the current services that the NASD provides to investors, you may go directly to http://www.nasdr.com/investors.asp. The list of services is lengthy.

QUESTION 57: What Else Do I Need To Know About My Insurance Advisor?

In addition to their record with their State Insurance Department and the NAIC if it applies; take a look at their qualifications:

- How long have they been a life insurance advisor?
- What percentage of their practice is life insurance?

- Do they have the Chartered Life Underwriter (CLU) designation which is the only educational rather than sales driven life insurance designation?

The following questions discuss compensation issues which can play an important role in life insurance purchasing.

QUESTION 58: How is the Agent compensated and how Will That Affect the Advice you're Given?

For an agent, compensation disclosure is an important issue, which is not currently the case. The current compensation system invites replacement and poor persistency (the percentage of policies that stay in-force—see question 35. It fails to align the interests of producers and life insurance companies. Consider the producer's perspective: Selling life insurance is a tough job. Few consumers seek out life insurance or annuities; the product must persuade a prospect to buy. Prospecting for business is hard, unpleasant work. Successful producers understandably feel deserving of their financial rewards.

From the opposite side, life insurance companies must write enough business and keep it in-force long enough to make a profit. Since a career agency force is almost prohibitively expensive, most companies are forced to compete for independent producers. This intense competition creates enormous pressure to pay the highest possible commissions. Unrestricted competition does not always serve the public interest. The present agent compensation system is based upon the fact that life products are hard to sell. The more difficult the sale, the higher the commission—and the more inefficient the product is from a consumer standpoint.

QUESTION 59: How Is The Current Compensation System Harmful to Agents and Consumers?

Regulatory help is needed to facilitate a new compensation model that serves the agents of the insureds as well as the industry. High, or "heaped," first-year commissions are common throughout the industry. Producers then receive smaller commissions, if any, each year, as long as a policy is in-force. This model encourages sales but discourages persistency (keeping policies in-force). While the need for change has been apparent for several years, insurers cannot afford to act unilaterally, and antitrust implications prevent them from acting in concert.

Surely, here is an opportunity for state insurance regulators. Life insurance companies should support a coordinated state regulatory initiative limiting up-front producer compensation. There is no need, however, to limit the ultimate commission payout. Let competition take care of that.

Specifically, producer compensation should be split into a selling fee and a service fee. The selling fee would be whatever amount an insurer deems appropriate, but it would have a ceiling on how much is payable within the first year the policy is in-force. For example, a selling fee may be payable over five years, contingent on the policy staying in-force and with up-to-date premium payments. A service fee, on the other hand, would be paid to the agent who services the policy—who may not necessarily be the selling agent.

Regulators could also exercise control over the commission structure by limiting product approvals. Companies must design products attractive to the consumer while satisfying producer commission demands. This virtually impossible task produces a competitive landscape in which products are studiously differentiated.

Good product design and pricing lead to persistency—and ultimately, profitability. It is unrealistic, however, to link producer compensation with profitability. The producer does not control these factors. Producers should not be penalized for home office management failures.

Companies, nonetheless, can tap producers to help encourage persistency. For example, producers could be required to meet with each policy owner at least once each year or forfeit their right to ongoing compensation. Producers who have an assured interest in their in-force business will strive to maximize their compensation by encouraging persistency.

Life insurers should enter into good-faith, profit-sharing agreements with their producers. If producers are expected to forgo heaped first-year commissions, they must be confident of a long-term financial reward commensurate with their contribution and commitment. Permanent life insurance is profitable for companies achieving sufficient sales volume. The same is true for annuities. Producers can make or break persistency; therefore, companies have an incentive to compensate agents based on persistency.

So where do insurance companies begin in aligning their interests with those of their producers? An excellent starting point is mandatory commission disclosure at the point of sale. Making producer compensation and overall marketing allowances transparent to the buyer would help bring about lower first-year commissions and more emphasis on long-term relationships.

It is not that difficult to design a viable commission disclosure standard. Commission disclosure can and should be made as simple as possible. For example, the producer's first-year compensation should be disclosed as a dollar amount and as a percentage of the first-year premium. Renewal commissions should be disclosed in like manner. All other marketing costs, such as general agent allowances and other selling expenses, should be disclosed to the consumer at the point of sale. If it is administratively difficult to provide these disclosures at the point of sale, they should be mailed to the applicant by the home office. The applicant should then be given the opportunity to ask questions or cancel the application.

Developing a much-needed new producer compensation model will require a cooperative effort between the industry and its regulators. Producers and companies would adapt accordingly, consumers would be better served and this would enhance the industry's public image.

The point is that the current compensation system has built in conflicts of interest that a fiduciary should bear in mind in analyzing and/or monitoring a life insurance policy…

Something to keep in mind is that commissions are often quite different than thought of. Often with non-variable life insurance, there are other types of compensation, such as sales conventions and other sales prizes.

QUESTION 60: Can an Advisor Accept Both A Fee and A Commission?

Due to the potential conflict of interest involved with commissions, there is little movement towards fee based planning with no-load/low-load products. In the review of in-force products where a fee is charged, only a properly licensed fee based planner can be retained. Only some states have a separate license that allows Life Insurance Advisor or other Financial Advisor (anyone who sells life insurance) to charge a fee for their services. Please visit your state's Department of Insurance website to see if your state offers such a license. In States that do not, it is a gray area.

For example, my home state, the State of California issues a little known license called the "Life and Disability Insurance Analyst" which is discussed in California Insurance Code Sections 1831-1849 found on their website. This license was first conceived and introduced into the insurance code in 1984 and, when I attained this license in 1998, I was only the 39th person in the state to attain it.

This is the only section of the State Insurance Code that allows any-one to charge a fee for the analysis of life and disability insurance prod-ucts. There are a few exceptions (see below). The code is very clear that when you receive any fee from a client, you are prohibited from receiv-ing any commission for that same client. At one time, I called a compli-ance attorney at the Department of Insurance and they verified that that is exactly what the code intends. The reality of the matter is that there is currently widespread abuse (most of it unintentional) of this little known section of the code, and that these are planners who collect a fee from their client, as well as commissions on the sale/implementa-tion of an insurance product. I will not address the ethical issues here, strictly the compliance issues What is interesting is that most advisors who are exempt under the code, with whom I've met, are so concerned with their liability that they no longer will review a life insurance product. The following are, as examples, the exemptions to the Code in the State of California. This is to give you the idea that if somebody wishes to charge you a fee, make sure that they are properly licensed to do this by checking with your State Department of Insurance and, if there is no such license, then ascertain their qualifications as best you can. This could be a challenge in states where no such license exists.

Exemptions to California Insurance Code Sections 1831-1849—Life Analyst—Charging a fee:

- Active members of the State Bar of California
- Any person who has passed all of the qualifying exams necessary to become an associate of the Society of Actuaries
- An officer or employee of any bank or trust company who receives no compensation from sources other than the bank or trust company for activities connected with his employment, which would otherwise subject him to this chapter.
- An investment advisor, as defined in Section 25009 of the Corporations Code, when acting in that capacity
- Complex exception—see the code.

Fee-Only Life Insurance planners will also be the advisors who will offer you Low-Load Life Insurance Products. As discussed in Question 16, these products pay no commission, therefore advisors charge a fee and can be more objective. Some products do pay a minimal marketing fee.

QUESTION 61: Is There A Code of Ethics for Life Insurance Agents?

There are many gags both in the movies and by comedians about life insurance agents. Two of the more well-known are the life insurance agents in Woody Allen's "High Anxiety" and the character in Bill Murray's "Groundhog Day". The most likely reason is that agents, at one point, rated as low as used car salesmen in consumer confidence ratings (of course, no offense intended to any used car salespeople). Agents today (for the most part) are professionals and have high standards to which they hold themselves.

To give the reader some idea, a number of professional financial advisor groups have a Code of Ethics. The following is from the American College which is provides professional designations and the Master of Financial Service degree:

Professional Pledge and Canons of Ethics:
All students who matriculate with The American College and earn any of its designations are required to comply with the College's Code of Ethics and Procedures. Included in the Code are the Professional Pledge and the Canons.

The Professional Pledge:
"In all my professional relationships, I pledge myself to the following rule of ethical conduct: I shall, in light of all conditions surrounding those I serve, which I shall make every conscientious effort to ascertain and understand, render that service which, in the same circumstances, I would apply to myself."

I.   Conduct yourself at all times with honor and dignity.

II.   Avoid practices that would bring dishonor upon your profession or The American College.

III.   Publicize your achievements in ways that enhance the integrity of your profession.

IV.   Continue your studies throughout your working life so as to maintain a high level of professional competence.

V.   Do your utmost to attain a distinguished record of professional service.

VI.   Support the established institutions and organizations concerned with the integrity of your profession.

VII.   Participate in building your profession by encouraging and providing appropriate assistance to qualified persons pursuing professional studies.

VIII. Comply with all laws and regulations, particularly as they relate to professional and business activities.

An association that I am proud to be a member of is the Society of Financial Service Professionals. The Society of Financial Service Professionals consists of advisors such as Chartered Life Underwriters (CLU's), CHFC's, CFP's, CPA's and others involved with some aspect of financial services. Typically most of these advisors will have some knowledge and hands-on experience with life insurance. The inclusion of this code of professional responsibility is to give the reader a sense of what they should expect in their life insurance advisor as this is the expected manner of performance.

CODE OF PROFESSIONAL RESPONSIBILITY OF THE SOCIETY OF FINANCIAL SERVICE PROFESSIONALS:

The Code of Professional Responsibility of the Society of Financial Service Professionals is divided into five components, as follows:

- Preamble—a brief introduction to the Code of Professional Responsibility, including its history and purpose.
- Canons—aspirational model standards of exemplary professional conduct.
- Rules—specific standards of a mandatory and enforceable nature.
- Applications—practical examples of how the canons and rules apply in given situations.
- Disciplinary Procedures—the mechanisms for enforcement of the Code of Professional Responsibility.

PREAMBLE

The Society of Financial Service Professionals is dedicated to setting and promoting standards of excellence for professionals in financial services. In fulfillment of this mission, the Society's Board of Directors has adopted this Code of Professional Responsibility. All Society members are automatically bound by its provisions.

The ultimate goal of enacting the Code is to serve the public interest. The path to fulfilling the goal is the fostering of professionalism in financial services. A profession has been defined in the writings of Solomon S. Huebner as possessing four essential traits:

- knowledge or expertise
- service to others
- working with other professionals to enhance the practice and reputation of one who is a member
- self-regulation

Through its Code of Professional Responsibility, the Society strives to improve the level of ethical behavior among its members by articulating standards that are aspirational in nature, that is, by identifying the lofty, altruistic ideals that define a true profession, and by delineating and enforcing minimum standards of ethical conduct.

This Code of Professional Responsibility has its origin in the code of ethics of the American Society of CLU & ChFC, the predecessor organization of the Society of Financial Service Professionals. The members of the Society created and adopted a code of ethics in 1961. With a name change in the fall of 1998, and a broadened membership constituency, it became appropriate to create this new Code of Professional Responsibility.

The Society acknowledges the diversity of its membership...from those that serve the public directly, as advisors, to those that serve indirectly through companies, educational organizations, and the like. Whatever role he or she plays within the financial services industry, it is the responsibility of each Society member to understand and adhere to the Code of Professional Responsibility.

From time to time, a Society member may be unclear about the ethical implications of a given course of action. In such cases, a Society member may request an advisory opinion from the Society; or may seek confidential advice through the Society's Ethics Information Line. Advisory opinions will be unpublished and specific to the inquiring member. However, there may be instances in which the subject matter of the advisory opinion has broad, general application and in such cases, at its discretion, the Society may chose to publish a given opinion for the benefit of all members, preserving the anonymity of those involved.

An alleged violation of the Society's Code of Professional Responsibility will result in an enforcement action, carried out in accordance with the Disciplinary Procedures. The procedures ensure that any member charged with ethical misconduct is afforded appropriate due process. The procedures also provide for appropriate sanctions, such as reprimand, censure, and revocation of membership, should a member be found to have acted in violation of the Code.

True enforcement of ethical behavior must come from the personal conscience of each individual, rather than external forces. Nevertheless, as an organization that promotes its members' education and expertise to the consumer, the Society believes it is essential that it act in an enforcement capacity.

CANONS

CANON 1 *Fairness*

A member shall perform services in a manner that respects the interests of all those he/she serves, including clients, principals, partners, employees, and employers. A member shall disclose conflicts of interests in providing such services.

Fairness requires that a professional treat others as he/she would wish to be treated if in the other's position. A professional also strives to avoid unfairness by inflicting no unnecessary harm on others and, when possible, shielding others from harm.

RULES

R1.1 A member shall not engage in behavior involving concealment or misrepresentation of material facts.

Applications for Rule 1.1:

A1.1a. In the sale of financial products, the use of product projections that are more aggressive than the company's current assumptions—without offering alternate illustrations/projections using more conservative assumptions—is a form of misrepresentation. It is best to show a range of assumptions for each product to illustrate the impact of changes on the rate of return and other expenses.

A1.1b. To avoid misrepresentation, the financial services professional is advised to use unbiased historical illustrations, show past performance, and to educate the consumer on the difference between past results and projections, and actual future results.

A1.1c. Improper replacement is a form of misrepresentation. When considering the replacement of one insurance, annuity, or other financial product for another, a thorough comparison of both products, including surrender charges, incontestable clauses, expenses, fees, and tax consequences, should be completed. The Society's Replacement Questionnaire (RQ) provides a tool for the thorough analysis of replacement issues.

A1.1d.. Failing to note a preexisting medical condition on an insurance application is a form of concealment.

R1.2 A member shall respect the rights of others.

R1.3 A member shall disclose to the client all information material to the professional relationship, including, but not limited to, all actual or potential conflicts of interest. In a conflict of interest situation, the interest of the client must be paramount.

Applications for Rule 1.3

A1.3a. A potential conflict of interest is inherent in the relationship between the client and the financial service professional when the professional is compensated by commissions on the sale of financial products. In such circumstances, if asked by the client or prospect, the professional should disclose, to the best of his/her knowledge, all forms of compensation, including commissions, expense allowances, bonuses, and any other relevant items.

A1.3b. The potential for a conflict of interest exists when a financial service professional receives fees for referring business to another practitioner. The referring professional should disclose this information.

A1.3c. A member who serves as a director or trustee of an organization/business faces a conflict of interest when competing to provide product or services to this organization for compensation. For example, Jackie Jones, ChFC, a professional money manager, is on the board of XNet Corporation. XNet is currently interviewing candidates to manage its $10 million investment portfolio. If Jackie decides to seek XNet's account, she is in a conflict of interest situation. Under these circumstances, Jackie should disclose the conflict to all relevant parties and have the parties acknowledge and accept the conflict. Additionally, Jackie should consider recusing herself from all discussions and decision-making regarding the selection of XNet's money manager. She may also consider resigning from the board or taking her name out of consideration for the money manager position.

R1.4 A member shall give proper respect to any relationship that may exist between the member and the companies he or she represents.

Application for Rule 1.4

A1.4a. Society members frequently have contractual relationships with the company whose products they sell. Honoring the terms of these contracts and refraining from negative statements about such companies are examples of giving proper respect to the relationship. Note, however, the need to balance the requirements of Rule 1.4 with the duty to act in the best interest of the client.

R1.5 A member shall make and/or implement only recommendations that are appropriate for the client and consistent with the client's goals.

Applications for Rule 1.5

A1.5a. Compliance with Rule 1.5 requires the financial service professional to use his/her best efforts to (1) understand the client's/prospect's personal and financial background and experience; (2) understand the client's/prospect's risk tolerance; and (3) educate the client about the various options available to meet identified needs and goals. This may include utilizing a fact-finding and/or risk assessment tool, one-on-one educational/counseling sessions, sharing newspaper or magazine articles, etc. In these circumstances, the financial service professional is cautioned against providing advice if he or she is not properly licensed or authorized to do so. See also Rule 2.2 and the Application A2.2a.

A1.5b. Appropriateness of the recommendation to the client's needs must take precedence over any sales incentives available to the financial service professional, such as conventions, trips, bonuses, etc. For example, Bob Bucks needs to sell just one more policy to qualify for MDRT. He knows he can convince his best client to purchase additional insurance coverage even though Bob knows the current coverage is more than adequate. If Bob makes this sale, he has violated Rule 1.5.

R1.6 In the rendering of professional services to a client, a member has the duty to maintain the type and degree of professional independence that (a) is required of practitioners in the member's occupation, or (b) is otherwise in the public interest, given the specific nature of the service being rendered.

Application for Rule 1.6

A1.6a. The requirement of professional independence mandated by Rule 1.6 presents a special challenge for Society members who are contractually bound to sell the products of only one company, or a select group of companies. In such cases, the member must keep paramount his/her ethical duty to act in the best interest of the client, even if this means forgoing a sale.

CANON 2 *Competence*

A member shall continually improve his/her professional knowledge, skill, and competence.

Professionalism starts with technical competence. The knowledge and skills held by a professional are of a high level, difficult to attain, and, therefore, not held by the general public. Competence not only includes the initial acquisition of this specialized knowledge and skill, but also requires continued learning and practice.

RULES

R2.1 A member shall maintain and advance his/her knowledge in all areas of financial service in which he/she is engaged and shall participate in continuing education programs throughout his/her career.

Application for Rule 2.1

A. 2.1a. Compliance with Rule 2.1 requires, at a minimum, meeting the applicable continuing education standards set by state licensing authorities, the Society of Financial Service Professionals, the American College, the CFP Board of Standards, and any other entity with appropriate authority over the member's license(s) or other credentials. For example PACE, the joint CE program of the Society of and the American College requires 30 hours of CE every 2 years. The CFP Board of Standards also requires 30 hours of continuing education every 2 years for CFP™ licensees.

R2.2 A member shall refrain from giving advice in areas beyond the member's own expertise.

Applications for Rule 2.2

A2.2a. A member shall not give tax, legal, insurance, accounting, actuarial, investment, or other advice unless the member has professional training and is properly licensed in these areas. For example, to avoid the unauthorized practice of law, the financial service professional will clearly mark specimen documents, such as living or testamentary trusts or buy-sell agreements, as samples and inform the client that the documents must be reviewed by a licensed attorney.

A2.2b. Billy Burke, CFP, has a specialized financial planning practice that focuses on assisting clients with funding college for their children. When Billy's long-time client and friend, Margaret Hamilton, asks for help in managing the distribution of funds from her defined benefit plan, Billy knows this is beyond his area of expertise, but he doesn't want to let his friend down. Billy proceeds to recommend several investment options to Margaret, but neglects to mention the early withdrawal taxes and penalties. Billy has violated Rule 2.2.

CANON 3 *Confidentiality*

A member shall respect the confidentiality of any information entrusted to, or obtained in the course of, the member's business or professional activities.

A financial service professional often gains access to client records and company information of a sensitive nature. Each Society member must maintain the highest level of confidentiality with regard to this information.

RULES

R3.1 A member shall respect and safeguard the confidentiality of sensitive client information obtained in the course of professional activities. A member shall not divulge such information without specific consent of the client, unless disclosure of such information is required by law or necessary in order to discharge legitimate professional duties.

Application for Rule 3.1

A3.1a. Examples of sensitive client information include, but are not limited to, medical data, information about financial status, Social Security or credit card numbers, information about personal relationships, etc. In determining whether information is sensitive, the Society member should take a cautious approach, and if in doubt, discuss the issue with the client.

R3.2 A member shall respect and safeguard the confidentiality of sensitive company/employer information obtained in the course of professional activities. A member shall not divulge such information without specific consent, unless disclosure of such information is required by law or necessary in order to discharge legitimate professional duties.

R3.3 A member must ensure that confidentiality practices are established and maintained by staff members so that breaches of confidence are not the result of intentional or unintentional acts or omissions.

Application for Rule 3.3

A3.3a. A member who employs others who work with sensitive, confidential client information has the responsibility to train these employees in the handling of such information. These employees must be instructed that they will be held responsible for unauthorized disclosure of confidential data. For example, Judy Parker has set up detailed procedures for her staff to follow in safeguarding confidential client information. On three separate occasions, Judy overhead her office manager gossiping with friends about the size of Client X's investment portfolio. Judy has not taken any action in regard to the office manager's behavior. Judy has violated Rule 3.3.

CANON 4 *Integrity*

A member shall provide professional services with integrity and shall place the client's interest above his/her own.

Integrity involves honesty and trust. A professional's honesty and candor should not be subordinate to personal gain or advantage. To be dishonest with others is to use them for one's own purposes.

RULES

R4.1 A member shall avoid any conduct or activity that would cause unnecessary harm to others by:

- Any act or omission of a dishonest, deceitful, or fraudulent nature.
- Pursuit of financial gain or other personal benefits that would interfere with the exercise of sound professional judgments and skills.

R4.2 A member shall establish and maintain dignified and honorable relationships with those he/she serves, with fellow practitioners, and with members of other professions.

Application for Rule 4.2

A4.2a. A member needs to be respectful in all dealings with another financial service professional in competitive engagements and avoid at all costs defamatory remarks to the client or other professionals. This does not mean a member cannot provide impartial factual information about a competitor. For example, in trying to help a friend make a decision about which long-term care policy to purchase, Joe Carter, CLU, reviews the features of each contract and accurately notes that his competitor's policy fails to provide coverage for Home care. Joe recommends that his friend review this information with his agent.

R4.3 A member shall embrace and adhere to the spirit and letter of laws and regulations governing his/her business and professional activities. See also Rule 6.1.

R4.4 A member shall be truthful and candid in his/her professional communications with existing and prospective clients, and with the general public.

Applications for Rule 4.4

A4.4a. Financial service professionals will not use words or make statements in brochures or advertising materials or in any client communication that create false impressions or have the potential to mislead. For example, product salespersons should not refer to themselves as financial/estate planners/consultants, if they do not provide these services. Words such as deposits or contributions should not be used to describe life insurance premiums. Life insurance policies should not be referred to as retirement plans. Discussion of vanishing premiums and guaranteed performance should be avoided. Financial service professionals must avoid creating the impression that they represent a number of companies when they place business with only a few companies. (See also Rule 1.6.)

A4.4b. Candid communication is required when a client is acting or intends to act outside the law. In such cases, the member should terminate the professional relationship and seek the advice of appropriate advisors. For example, Lisa Long, CLU, CFP, an investment advisor, has been asked by her client to effect a transaction based on insider information. Lisa must immediately advise her client that insider trading is a violation of SEC rules and could result in criminal charges. Lisa should also document what has happened; and if, the client plans to proceed with the transaction, Lisa should terminate the relationship. Lisa should also consult her own legal and ethical advisors as to whether she has additional legal obligations under these circumstances. Lisa's legal obligations will impact her ethical obligations.

R4.5. A member shall refrain from using an approved Society designation, degree, or credential in a false or misleading manner.

Application for Rule 4.5

A4.5a. A member must not use Society-recognized professional designations in his/her company name, tagline, or brochures in a manner which would be misleading. For example, John Smith, ChFC, and Associates is acceptable. John Smith and Associates, Chartered Financial Consultants is not because it creates the impression that everyone associated with the firm is a Chartered Financial Consultant. (See Rule 7.7 also.)

CANON 5 *Diligence*

A member shall act with patience, timeliness, and consistency in the fulfillment of his/her professional duties.

A professional works diligently. Knowledge and skill alone are not adequate. A professional must apply these attributes in a prompt and thorough manner in the service of others.

RULES

R5.1 A member shall act with competence and consistency in promptly discharging his/her responsibilities to clients, employers, principals, purchasers, and other users of the member's services.

R5.2 A member shall make recommendations to clients, whether in writing or orally, only after sufficient professional evaluation and understanding of the client's needs and goals. A member shall support any such recommendations with appropriate research and documentation.

R5.3 A member shall properly supervise subordinates with regard to their role in the delivery of financial services, and shall not condone conduct in violation of the ethical standards set forth in this Code of Professional Responsibility.

CANON 6 *Professionalism*

A member shall assist in raising professional standards in the financial services industry.

A member's conduct in all matters shall reflect credit upon the financial services profession. A member has an obligation to cooperate with Society members, and other financial service professionals, to enhance and maintain the profession's public image and to work together to improve the quality of services rendered.

RULES

R6.1 A member has the duty to know and abide by the local, state, and national laws and regulations and all legal limitations pertaining to the member's professional activities.

Applications for Rule 6.1

A6.1a. The financial service profession is subject to state and federal laws and regulation in the areas of securities, insurance, banking, and unfair trade practices, among others. Society members must understand these laws and regulations and their applicability to their practices. For example, Susan Short, CLU, just earned her CFP license, and is planning on expanding her practice to include comprehensive financial planning services. Does Susan need to register as an investment advisor? Must she be licensed with the National Association of Securities Dealers? What about state insurance laws? Susan must answer these questions and comply with the appropriate requirements for her business activities.

A6.1b. Jon Planner receives equity commissions throughout the year. As part of a prearranged agreement, he transfers these commissions to the corporation for whom he works. Jon later learns that this is a violation of NASD rules and that commissions cannot be split with corporations. Jon is ethically obligated to correct this situation and to further educate himself on the rules and regulations applying to his business.

R6.2 A member shall support the development, improvement, and enforcement of such laws, regulations, and codes of ethical conduct that foster respect for the financial service professional and benefit the public.

Application for Rule 6.2

A6.2a. Suppose Congress is contemplating a measure that would increase the regulatory burden on financial service professionals by requiring increased documentation of specific client transactions. There is firm evidence that enactment of this measure would substantially reduce the likelihood of client's being misled or confused about such transactions. Rule 6.2 would require Society members to support such a measure.

R6.3 A member shall show respect for other financial service professionals and related occupational groups by engaging in fair and honorable competitive practices; collegiality among members shall not impede enforcement of this Code.

R6.4 A member shall cooperate with regulatory authorities regarding investigations of any alleged violation of laws or regulations by a financial service professional.

CANON 7 *Self-Regulation*

A member shall assist in maintaining the integrity of the Society's Code of Professional Responsibility and of the professional credentials held by all Society members.

Every professional has a responsibility to regulate themselves. As such, every Society member holds a duty of abiding by his/her professional code of ethics. In addition, Society members have a duty to facilitate the enforcement of this Code of Professional Responsibility.

QUESTION 62: How Does the Regulatory System Work?

This question deals with the Regulatory System overall and the following discusses the role of the State Insurance Departments. These questions are the entire FAQ (frequently asked questions) so the reader may locate any part relevant to them.

The regulation systems start with the National Association of Insurance Commissioners (NAIC) which serves as a vehicle for individual state regulators to coordinate their activities and share resources. Established in 1871, the NAIC functions as an advisory body and service provider for state insurance departments. Commissioners use the NAIC to pool scarce resources, to discuss issues of common concern and to align their oversight of the industry. Each state, however, ultimately determines what actions it will take.

The Purpose and Structure of Insurance Regulation

The fundamental reason for government regulation of insurance is to protect American consumers. State systems are accessible and accountable to the public and sensitive to local social and economic conditions. State regulation has proven that it effectively protects consumers and ensures that promises made by insurers are kept. Insurance regulation is structured around several key functions, including company licensing, producer licensing, product regulation, market conduct, and financial regulation and consumer services.

Company Licensing—State laws require insurers and insurance-related businesses to be licensed before selling their products or services. Currently, there are approximately 7,200 insurers in the United States. All U.S. insurers are subject to regulation in their state of domicile and in the other states where they are licensed to sell insurance.

Insurers who fail to comply with regulatory requirements are subject to license suspension or revocation, and states may exact fines for regulatory violations. In 2000, nearly 300 companies had their licenses suspended or revoked.

The NAIC's Uniform Certificate of Authority Application (UCAA) a company licensing systemhelps states expedite the review process of a new company license. In addition, an NAIC database has been developed to facilitate information sharing on acquisition and merger filings. Theses databases assist insurance regulators by creating a streamlined and more cost-efficient regulatory process.

Producer Licensing—. Insurance agents and brokers, also known as producers, must be licensed to sell insurance and must comply with various state laws and regulations governing their activities. Currently, more than 3.2 million individuals are licensed to provide insurance services in the United States. State insurance departments oversee producer activities in order to protect insurance consumer interests in insurance transactions.

The states administer continuing education programs to ensure that agents meet high professional standards. Producers who fail to comply with regulatory requirements are subject to fines and license suspension or revocation. In 2000, nearly 16,000 insurance producers had their licenses suspended or revoked.

When producers operate in multiple jurisdictions, states must coordinate their efforts to track producers and prevent violations. Special databases are maintained by the NAIC to assist the states in this effort. The National Insurance Producer Registry (NIPR)—a non-profit affiliate of the NAIC—was established to develop and operate a national repository for producer licensing information.

Product Regulation—State regulators protect consumers by ensuring that insurance policy provisions comply with state law, are reasonable and fair, and do not contain major gaps in coverage that might be misunderstood by consumers and leave them unprotected. The nature of the rate review, rating rules and forms varies somewhat among the states depending on their laws and regulations.

For personal property-casualty lines, about half of the states require insurers to file rates and to receive prior approval before they go into effect. With the exception of workers' compensation and medical malpractice, commercial property-casualty lines in many states are subject to a competitive rating approach. Under such a system, regulators typically retain authority to disapprove rates if they find that competition is not working.

Premiums for life insurance and annuity products generally are not subject to regulatory approval, although regulators may seek to ensure that policy benefits are commensurate with the premiums charged. Many states subject health insurance rates to prior approval—with all other lines using a "file and use" system or no provisions for review.

Financial Regulation—Financial regulation provides crucial safeguards for America's insurance consumers. The states maintain at the NAIC the world's largest insurance financial database, which provides a 15-year history of annual and quarterly filings on 5,200 insurance companies.

Periodic financial examinations occur on a scheduled basis. State financial examiners investigate a company's accounting methods, procedures and financial statement presentation. These exams verify and validate what is presented in the company's annual statement to ascertain whether the company is in good financial standing.

When an examination of financial records shows the company to be financially impaired, the state insurance department takes control of the company. Aggressively working with financially troubled companies is a critical part of the regulator's role. In the event the company must be liquidated or becomes insolvent, the states maintain a system of financial guaranty funds that cover consumers' personal losses.

Market Regulation—Market regulation attempts to ensure fair and reasonable insurance prices, products and trade practices in order to protect consumers. With improved cooperation among states and uniform market conduct examinations, regulators hope to ensure continued consumer protections at the state level.

Market conduct examinations occur on a routine basis, but also can be triggered by complaints against an insurer. These exams review agent-licensing issues, complaints, types of products sold by the company and agents, agent sales practices, proper rating, claims handling and other market-related aspects of an insurer's operation.

When violations are found, the insurance department makes recommendations to improve the company's operations and to bring the company into compliance with state law. In addition, a company may be subject to civil penalties or license suspension or revocation.

Consumer Services—The states' single most significant challenge is to be vigilant in the protection of consumers, especially in light of the changes taking place in the financial services marketplace. States have established toll-free hotlines, Internet Web sites and special consumer services units to receive and handle complaints against insurers and agents. The states also have launched an interactive tool to allow consumers to research company complaint and financial data using the NAIC Web site.

During 2000, state insurance departments handled 4.5 million consumer inquiries and complaints. As needed, state insurance departments worked together with policyholders and insurers to resolve disputes. In addition, many states sponsor educational seminars and provide consumer brochures on a variety of insurance topics. Some states publish rate comparison guides to help consumers get the best value when they purchase insurance.

The Purpose of Insurance Regulation—Government regulation of insurance companies and agents began in the states more than 100 years ago for one overriding reason—to protect consumers. State regulators' most important consumer protection is to assure that insurers remain solvent so they can meet their obligations to pay claims. States also supervise insurance sales and marketing practices and policy terms and conditions to ensure that consumers are treated fairly when they purchase insurance products and file claims.

The fundamental purpose for government regulation of insurers and agents—to protect American consumers. Effective consumer protection that focuses on local needs is the hallmark of state insurance regulation. State regulators understand local and regional markets and the needs of consumers in these markets. State policymakers recognize that consumer protection as their highest job priority. Meaningful evaluation of the existing state regulatory system or any Federal alternative must begin with a hard look at its impact on current protections that the public expects.

The difference between insurance and banking— Insurance is a commercial product based upon subjective business decisions: Will an insurance policy be offered to a consumer? At what price? What are the policy terms and conditions? Is a claim filed by a policyholder valid? If so, how much should the customer be paid under the policy's terms? Unlike most products, the purchaser of an insurance policy will not be able to fully determine the value of the product purchased until after a claim is presented—when it is too late to decide that a different insurer or a different product might make a better choice. All of these subjective aspects add up to one big certainty—insurance products can generate consumer backlash and dissatisfaction that require a high level of regulatory resources and responsiveness.

The cost of state insurance regulation—In 2000, state insurance departments employed 12,500 regulatory personnel nationwide and spent $880 million to be the watchful eyes and helping hands on consumer insurance problems. States also maintain a system of financial guarantee funds that cover personal losses of consumers in the event of insurer insolvency. The entire state insurance system is authorized, funded and operated at no cost to the federal government.

The **Financial Modernization Act of 1999**—also called Gramm-Leach-Bliley established a comprehensive framework to permit affiliations among banks, securities firms and insurance companies. Gramm-Leach-Bliley once again acknowledged that states should regulate the business of insurance. However, Congress also called for state reforms to allow insurance companies to compete more effectively in the newly integrated financial service marketplace and

to respond with innovation and flexibility to evermore demanding consumer needs.

States already have taken action to meet the specific requirements of Gramm-Leach-Bliley. Forty-six states have enacted a model law to establish a system of reciprocity to license out-of state insurance agents and brokers. This already exceeds the 29 states required by federal law to prevent establishment of the National Association of Registered Agents and Brokers—a quasigovernmental entity that would preempt state laws. In response to another provision that requires states to set minimum standards to keep insurance information private, the NAIC drafted model privacy regulations, and 49 states and the District of Columbia now meet or exceed the federal privacy requirement.

Modernizing insurance regulation—States are committed to streamline and simplify state insurance regulation while continuing to protect consumers. The nation's insurance commissioners announced their commitment to modernize the state system in specific areas by endorsing an action plan, the *Statement of Intent—The Future of Insurance Regulation*, which was adopted in March 2000. Working in their individual states and collectively through the NAIC, the commissioners have made tremendous progress on their goal of creating an efficient, market-oriented regulatory system for the business of insurance. The *Statement of Intent* set forth goals for improvement in producer licensing, product speed to market, privacy of consumer information and company licensing.

State legislatures working through the National Conference of State Legislatures (NCSL) and the National Conference of

Insurance Legislators (NCOIL) also are committed to reform state insurance regulation. In September 2001, the NCSL Executive Committee established the *Task Force to Streamline and Simplify Insurance Regulation*—co-chaired by Senator Kemp Hannon of New York and Representative David Counts of Texas—to lead state legislative efforts to modernize state insurance regulation. The Task Force is charged by the NCSL Executive Committee to explore the issues that confront state insurance regulation in the integrated financial marketplace and, if necessary, to recommend specific measures to the states for legislative consideration. Moreover, for many years, NCOIL has served as a forum for legislators to discuss the many issues confronting state insurance regulation and has recommended to states model laws to promote market-based regulatory structures.

The purpose of government supervision—is to make sure the critical personal interests of consumers are not lost in the arena of commercial competition. Once the consumer protection responsibilities of government insurance regulators are satisfied, it is fair to ask how the system of regulation can be made most compatible with the demands of commercial competition without sacrificing the needs of consumers. Regulators continue to give this matter our highest attention, as evidenced by our speed to market initiatives.

What are states doing to keep insurance markets competitive with other financial services products, especially with regards to life insurance and annuities?

Insurers, especially in the life insurance and annuities market, increasingly face direct competition from products offered by other financial services entities. State insurance regulators have worked diligently over the past two years to identify the issues in this area and come up with possible solutions to reflect the new market realities. Regulators now believe that a more efficient review process for these products is possible and could help insurers better compete in the marketplace while maintaining a high level of protection for insurance consumers. To accomplish this goal; regulators have endorsed the idea of an interstate insurance compact.

The NAIC has drafted an interstate compact proposal and currently is discussing it with state legislators and interested parties for possible legislative consideration during the 2003 legislative sessions.

The reason for the length of the states' modernization efforts—Insurance regulation is a complex matter and any change to the process should not be undertaken without thorough review and analysis of the impact of change to the business, companies and agents, and also to the consumers and policyholders the industry serves. However, the states have established aggressive timelines in order to meet their modernization objectives. They have come to a point where a number of the goals set out in the *Statement of Intent* have worked their way through the state legislative process. From the Producer Licensing Model Act to privacy regulations, the states have proven a commitment to modernizing insurance regulation and protecting consumers—as states have done for the past 130 years.

The purpose of modernization—is not just about the survival of the state system. It is about responding to change and, in turn, making the best insurance regulatory system in the world even better. State policymakers believe consumers are—and will continue to be—best served by the states. Regulators and legislators have accepted the challenge to make the state system of insurance regulation better, and they will continue to make progress in implementing this vision.

When state regulators say there is a need for more uniformity, aren't they making a case to get rid of the 50-regulator system?

Having similar processes with local control and application is really the best of both worlds. Consumers need to have the confidence that the people regulating their policies understand the area market. For example, Iowa consumers do not buy much hurricane insurance, and there is little need for crop insurance in New York City. However these types of insurance are very important in the regions in which they are sold.

Wouldn't it be better to create a federal agency like the SEC to oversee regulation?

Clearly—since the Gramm-Leach-Bliley Act passed—conglomerates are being formed and banks and insurance and securities firms that are converging. But there are still fundamental differences between banking, securities and insurance. Insurance is a product with which consumers have many issues and questions. State insurance regulators need to be there on a local basis to deal with them. The state system has the expertise and has demonstrated that it can be responsive to these situations.

When consumers have a problem with their insurance, it is often at a time of tragedy—when a child needs an operation and the insurance company won't pay for it, or a house just burned down and the insurance company is not coming through. So, insurance is very different from banking and securities products. Insurance also involves extremely complex contracts—so there is greater potential for consumer abuse.

The following is from the National Association of Insurance Commissioner's (NAIC) Web Site at www.naic.org. Copyright NAIC. Permission for this reprint granted by NAIC.

QUESTION 63: How Does State Insurance Regulation Work?

As in the preceding question, this question continues the discussion of regulation. This question reprints the National Association of Insurance Commissioners (NAIC)—Frequently Asked Questions about State Insurance Regulation.

Why is insurance regulated?

Government regulation of insurance companies and agents began in the states more than 100 years ago for one overriding reason—to protect consumers. State regulators' most important consumer protection is to assure that insurers remain solvent so they can meet their obligations to pay claims. States also supervise insurance sales and marketing practices and policy terms and conditions to ensure that consumers are treated fairly when they purchase insurance products and file claims.

What is the first priority of insurance regulators?

The fundamental purpose for government regulation of insurers and agents is to protect American consumers. Effective consumer protection that focuses on local needs is the hallmark of state insurance regulation. State regulators understand local and regional markets and the needs of consumers in these markets. State policymakers recognize that consumer protection as their highest job priority. Meaningful evaluation of the existing state regulatory system or any federal alternative must begin with a hard look at its impact on current protections that the public expects.

How is insurance different from banking?

Insurance is a commercial product based upon subjective business decisions: Will an insurance policy be offered to a consumer? At what price? What are the policy terms and conditions? Is a claim filed by a policyholder valid? If so, how much should the customer be paid under the policy's terms?

Unlike most products, the purchaser of an insurance policy will not be able to fully determine the value of the product purchased until after a claim is presented—when it is too late to decide that a different insurer or a different product might make a better choice. All of these subjective aspects add up to one big certainty—insurance products can generate consumer backlash and dissatisfaction that require a high level of regulatory resources and responsiveness.

What is the cost of state insurance regulation?

In 2000, state insurance departments employed 12,500 regulatory personnel nationwide and spent $880 million to be the watchful eyes and helping hands on consumer insurance problems. States also maintain a system of financial guarantee funds that cover personal losses of consumers in the event of insurer insolvency. The entire state insurance system is authorized, funded and operated at no cost to the federal government.

What is Gramm-Leach-Bliley?

The Financial Modernization Act of 1999—also called Gramm-Leach-Bliley—established a comprehensive framework to permit affiliations among banks, securities firms and insurance companies. Gramm-Leach-Bliley once again acknowledged that states should regulate the business of insurance. However, Congress also called for state reforms to allow insurance companies to compete more effectively in the newly integrated financial service marketplace and to respond with innovation and flexibility to evermore demanding consumer needs.

States already have taken action to meet the specific requirements of Gramm-Leach-Bliley. Forty-six states have enacted a model law to establish a system of reciprocity to license out-of-state insurance agents and brokers. This already exceeds the 29 states required by federal law to prevent establishment of the National Association of Registered Agents and Brokers—a quasi-governmental entity that would preempt state laws. In response to another provision that requires states to set minimum standards to keep insurance information private, the NAIC drafted model privacy regulations, and 49 states and the District of Columbia now meet or exceed the federal privacy requirement.

What are states doing to modernize insurance regulation?

States are committed to streamline and simplify state insurance regulation while continuing to protect consumers. The nation's insurance commissioners announced their commitment to modernize the state system in specific areas by endorsing an action plan, the *Statement of Intent—The Future of Insurance Regulation*, which was adopted in March 2000. Working in their individual states and collectively through the NAIC, the commissioners have made tremendous progress on their goal of creating an efficient, market-oriented regulatory system for the business of insurance. The *Statement of Intent* set forth goals for improvement in producer licensing, product speed to market, privacy of consumer information and company licensing.

State legislatures working through the National Conference of State Legislatures (NCSL) and the National Conference of Insurance Legislators (NCOIL) also are committed to reform state insurance regulation. In September 2001, the NCSL Executive Committee established the *Task Force to Streamline and Simplify Insurance Regulation*—co-chaired by Senator Kemp Hannon of New York and Representative David Counts of Texas—to lead state legislative efforts to modernize state insurance regulation. The Task Force is charged by the NCSL Executive Committee to explore the issues that confront state insurance regulation in the integrated financial marketplace and, if necessary, to recommend specific measures to the states for legislative consideration. Moreover, for many years, NCOIL has served as a forum for legislators to discuss the many issues confronting state insurance regulation and has recommended to states model laws to promote market-based regulatory structures.

How do regulators promote competitive markets?

The purpose of government supervision is to make sure the critical personal interests of consumers are not lost in the arena of commercial competition. Once the consumer protection responsibilities of government insurance regulators are satisfied, it is fair to ask how the system of regulation can be made most compatible with the demands of commercial competition without sacrificing the needs of consumers. Regulators continue to give this matter our highest attention, as evidenced by our speed to market initiatives.

What are states doing to keep insurance markets competitive with other financial services products, especially with regards to life insurance and annuities?

Insurers, especially in the life insurance and annuities market, increasingly face direct competition from products offered by other financial services entities. State insurance regulators have worked diligently over the past two years to identify the issues in this area and come up with possible solutions to reflect the new market realities. Regulators now believe that a more efficient review process for these products is possible and could help insurers better compete in the marketplace while maintaining a high level of protection for insurance consumers. To accomplish this goal, regulators have endorsed the idea of an interstate insurance compact. The NAIC has drafted an interstate compact proposal and currently is discussing it with state legislators and interested parties for possible legislative consideration during the 2003 legislative sessions.

Why are the states' modernization efforts taking so long?

Insurance regulation is a complex matter and any change to the process should not be undertaken without thorough review and analysis of the impact of change to the business, companies and agents, and also to the consumers and policyholders the industry serves.

However, the states have established aggressive timelines in order to meet their modernization objectives. They have come to a point where a number of the goals set out in the *Statement of Intent* have worked their way through the state legislative process. From the Producer Licensing Model Act to privacy regulations, the states have proven a commitment to modernizing insurance regulation and protecting consumers—as states have done for the past 130 years.

Isn't this really just about states protecting their turf?

Modernization efforts are not just about the survival of the state system. It is about responding to change and, in turn, making the best insurance regulatory system in the world even better. State policymakers believe consumers are—and will continue to be—best served by the states. Regulators and legislators have accepted the challenge to make the state system of insurance regulation better, and they will continue to make progress in implementing this vision.

When state regulators say there is a need for more uniformity, aren't they making a case to get rid of the 50-regulator system?

Having similar processes with local control and application is really the best of both worlds. Consumers need to have the confidence that the people regulating their policies understand the area market. For example, Iowa consumers do not buy much hurricane insurance, and there is little need for crop insurance in New York City. However these types of insurance are very important in the regions in which they are sold.

Wouldn't it be better to create a federal agency like the SEC to oversee regulation?

Clearly—since the Gramm-Leach-Bliley Act passed—conglomerates are being formed and banks and insurance and securities firms that are converging. But there are still fundamental differences between banking, securities and insurance. Insurance is a product with which consumers have many issues and questions. State insurance regulators need to be there on a local basis to deal with them. The state system has the expertise and has demonstrated that it can be responsive to these situations.

When consumers have a problem with their insurance, it is often at a time of tragedy—when a child needs an operation and the insurance company won't pay for it, or a house just burned down and the insurance company is not coming through. So, insurance is very different from banking and securities products. Insurance also involves extremely complex contracts—so there is greater potential for consumer abuse.

(The following is reprinted from the National Insurance of Commissioners (NAIC) Web Site—www.naic.org). Copyright NAIC. Permission for this reprint granted by NAIC.

CHAPTER 6: OTHER ISSUES BEFORE BUYING A POLICY

QUESTION 64: Okay, I'm ready to buy some life insurance, what should I expect?

The first step will be to complete a written application. This is necessary whether you apply through an advisor or directly to the company. There two newer methods at the time of the writing of this book. The first is called tele-underwriting which is where you are asked all the questions over the phone and then you sign an application at some later time. The second is similar; with this method the application is done over the internet, additional questions are asked over the telephone and then the paperwork (including an application) are signed when the policy is delivered. These methods are designed to reduce the processing time of applying for life insurance which can take several weeks under the traditional method.

An application is a form with a series of questions that will range from your identification information (address, phone number, drivers license, etc.), to personal financial information, as well as medical questions and avocation questionnaires (where appropriate). Avocations are hobbies (e.g.) such as rock climbing, scuba diving, etc.

QUESTION 65: How Will I Know That This Is the Right Policy for Me; In Other Words, Is It Suitable?

This question is complex and depends on whether or not you have an advisor; how knowledgeable they are on this subject, what state you live in, and how comfortable you feel with the methods in this book and with any other resources you may have consulted. Suitability is a term that basically means that a certain product is appropriate for a certain individual.

The difficult part of suitability with regard to life insurance is that there is no clear-cut answer for professional advisors either. Currently, there are suitability regulations for the sale of variable insurance products as these are under the purview of the NASD/SEC. In reviewing suitability regulations from the perspective of (non-variable) life insurance rather than securities regulation, there are significant differences. Existing suitability regulations for registered products are adaptations of the regulations for any/all investment products and are not always applicable to life insurance products. State suitability rules exist in only a small percentage of the states and vary in terms of requirements, terms and enforcement. The actual number of life insurance sales for non-registered products, that come under the purview of states that have suitability regulations, is probably well under 10 percent. This reflects the fact that the states with regulations are small (Iowa, Kansas, Minnesota, South Dakota, Vermont, Wisconsin, Arkansas, New Mexico, Ohio and Utah).

For years the mantra in the life insurance industry is that it is not bought, it is sold. It has also been taught by carriers and passed from agent to agent that life insurance is a unique product that can be a one-size-fits-all miracle tonic, that will cure whatever ails you. Life insurance, for the most part, has never been viewed as a part of an overall financial plan—rather it has been viewed as a financial plan in of itself. We need to recognize that life insurance is a financial asset rather than property and that, as a financial asset, needs to be measured on its own strength.

It is important to look at the history of how field representatives have determined life insurance needs. The word "agent" is important here since agents act on behalf of a principal, in this case, a life insurance company. Over the years, life insurance companies have been seeking to distance themselves from their agents (their distributors) and claim to bear no responsibility for the abuses carried out by some of their agents.

Suitability necessitates that agents and brokers fully understand their product. If sellers do not understand what they are selling, they cannot make a reasonable recommendation. For years, agents were asked to distribute products which were to some degree "black boxes" in other words, the agents had no idea what they were really distributing. The components of the products were a mystery in terms of the mortality costs, dividend determination and overhead expenses. This started to change with the introduction of universal life; however, until the American Society of CLU's and ChFC's (now the Society of Financial Service Professional's) introduced the Illustration Questionnaire (IQ)—the agents had neither knowledge nor ability to gain knowledge about the actual construction of the life insurance contracts. Added to that was the fact that agents and carriers were, until the introduction of the 1995—NAIC Life Insurance Illustrations Model Regulation, able to illustrate anything they wanted.

Another factor in determining suitability is the recognition that life insurance is indeed a financial asset and that it must stand up as such. A number of life insurance policies inherently do not. For example: In a case in which I was involved, the goal was to use life insurance to increase the future wealth of the beneficiaries. The clients' trust owned a $2 million, second-to-die (policy that pays a death benefit at the second death) life insurance and the insured's were, at the time a 72 year old couple. The policy had a planned annual premium of $50,000 for life. The rate of return at age 100 on death is only 2.4% (estate and income tax free) which is low considering there is a 20% chance that at least one person will live that long. Under NASD regulations, this would most likely not be a suitable investment, due to the low rate of return. However, based on the risk factor, there could always be an argument that, if the clients were to die early (soon), it would be a good investment. This illustrates how the mix of life insurance into the planning process can make it a complex topic.

There is no shortage of abuses—for example; a case reviewed by the author involved the sale of a Variable Universal Life policy with a face amount of $570,000 to a 33 year old woman who had no dependents or any other discernible reason for life insurance. This woman receives a significant annual income stream from the estate of her father, and will receive a significant distribution from the trust when she reaches age 40. The trust also provides her with a residence at no cost and pays for all medical bills and unforeseen circumstances. Her children will be treated similarly upon her death. The life insurance policy that was sold to this woman was sold as a cash accumulation vehicle, not as a life insurance policy.

Due in part to the history of abusive life insurance industry practices, a majority of households remain underinsured. For some of these people, it has been the author's experience that they are turned off by the thought of life insurance, due to prior negative experiences with life insurance salespeople. Another cause is the failure to provide a coherent basis for life insurance recommendations.

Following is a summary of the NASD Suitability Rules to Give a Sense of What Factors You Should Consider:

- Collect and document comprehensive information about the customer's background, financial assets, investment goals and risk tolerance. *(NASD Rule 2310(b), Recommendations to Customers (Suitability) (NASD Manual 2001).)*
- Only recommend policies that are appropriate for the customer's investment objectives and risk tolerance. *(The NASD reminds members of their responsibilities regarding the sale of variable life insurance NASD Notice to members 00-44 2000 [www.nasdr.com].)*
- Consider whether the customer wants and needs life insurance, and whether the investor has the financial wherewithal to make the necessary payments. *(The NASD reminds members of their responsibilities regarding the sale of variable life insurance,* supra.)
- Adopt procedures to ensure that replacement policies are suitable. *(The NASD reminds members of their responsibilities regarding the sale of variable life insurance,* supra.)
- Transactions whereby a customer finances a new variable life insurance policy or annuity through the use of cash values from an existing policy are presumed unsuitable. *(The NASD reminds members of their responsibilities regarding the sale of variable life insurance,* supra.)

One of the major issues in enforcing a suitability regulation is the long-term nature of life insurance. Often by the time a customer realizes he or she has been sold an unsuitable policy, many years have passed and the statute of limitations has expired. For this reason, it is essential that a life insurance suitability regulation contain a discovery rule to toll the statute of limitations. This ensures that customers will be protected from abuses that may take many years to unfold.

Under current state laws, life insurance agents and brokers have a duty of good faith and fair dealing. They do not currently have a duty to advise. It is time to recognize that, contrary to the mantra; life insurance is bought, and is bought as an investment product. Often customers do not understand what they are buying, and rely upon their brokers to recommend appropriate products. The representatives and insurers oftentimes either does not understand what they are selling, or recommend products for the primary benefit of themselves rather than for the benefit of their customers. The results are the abuses discussed earlier in this question.

Changing these approaches, will especially be difficult in an industry where the most respected agents/producers are those who sell the most life insurance. These are some of the individuals whose names and pictures are on the walls at the life insurance company and who qualify for special trips and recognition. There are no rewards or recognition for ethical issues. So consider your advisor's background. A majority of agents/producers do have their client's best interests at heart.

QUESTION 66: Is there a difference in how often I pay my premium?

Changing how often you pay your premium could save you money (it may be a lot!!) Almost always, you have a choice of whether to pay premiums monthly, quarterly, semi-annually or annually. Insurance companies typically charge extra when you pay other than annually.

This is a factor applied to the annual premium to arrive at the premium if you elect to pay on a semiannual, quarterly or monthly bank draft basis. The mode premium factor for semi-annual premiums ranges from 51% to 53%, which means that you pay an extra 2% to 6%, if you don't pay the premium annually. The mode factor for quarterly premiums ranges from 26% to 30%, which means that you pay an extra

4% to 20% by paying quarterly. The mode factor on monthly bank draft premiums ranges from 8.66% to 9%, meaning that you pay an extra 3.92% to 8%. The reason the monthly bank draft mode premium factor is more economical than the quarterly mode factor is because monthly bank draft persistency is better than quarterly mode persistency. (Companies charge these mode premium factors because when premiums are paid more often than annually, the company does not have the use of the premium dollars for the entire year. In addition, depending on the mode of payment selected, there is a higher probability that the policy will lapse)

However, that's not the whole story. The actual charge is higher as is illustrated by the calculation and usage of an "Annual Percentage Rate (APR)" as defined under the "Federal Truth In Lending" law. This calculation illustrates a higher percentage rate than shown in the paragraph above. This is due to the fact that the policy owner does not have usage of the entire annual premium for the entire year.

You can judge whether you are willing to pay the extra cost by calculating the annual percentage rate (APR). Unfortunately, insurance companies are not required to disclose the APR, so you have to calculate it yourself. You can produce a good approximation with one of the formulas below. The first is for monthly premiums, the second is for quarterly, and the third is for semi-annual.

For example, if the monthly premium is $95 and the annual premium is $1,000, the first of the formulas would produce an annual percentage rate of about 29.7 percent, and it would clearly be in your interest to pay it annually. The calculation is shown below; the factors are below the formulas.

Sample Calculation of APR—Monthly Premium is $95; Annual Premium is $1,000

$$APR = \frac{3{,}600((12*\$95)-\$1{,}000)}{(13*\$1{,}000) + (42*\$95)} = \frac{3{,}600\ (\$1{,}140-\$1{,}000)}{\$13{,}000+\$3{,}990} = \frac{3{,}600(\$140)}{\$16{,}990} = 29.7\%$$

Formulas for calculation APR

For Monthly
Premiums:

$$APR = \frac{3,600(12M-A)}{13A+42M}$$

For Quarterly
Premiums:

$$APR = \frac{1,200(4Q-A)}{5A-2Q}$$

For Monthly
Premiums:

$$APR = \frac{200(2S-A)}{A-S}$$

Where:

APR = Annual percentage rate, expressed as a percentage
M = Monthly Premium
Q = Quarterly Premium
S = Semi-Annual Premium
A = Annual Premium

The formulas and example are from The Insurance Forum published by Dr. Belth and appeared in the April 1997 Newsletter. On Dr. Belth's website you can find a calculator that will allow to solve for the Annual Percentage Rate as both a percentage and in dollar terms.

The reason the monthly bank draft mode premium factor is more economical than the quarterly mode factor is because monthly bank draft persistency is better than quarterly mode persistency. Companies charge these mode premium factors because when premiums are paid more often than annually, the company does not have the use of the premium dollars for the entire year. In addition, depending on the mode of payment selected, there is a higher probability that the policy will lapse. Also, this is oftentimes a profit center for the company.

It's important to keep in mind that the premiums on Universal Life policy's are designed to be flexible. As such, the policy owner has the option when of and when to pay. Therefore, the application of the "APR" concept may arguably not apply as life insurance premiums are not a debt (loan). Please note that as discussed in other parts of this book, missing premium payments can cause a policy to lapse, especially when they are non-scheduled, less than scheduled or the policy is under-funded.

There has been some litigation in this area as to whether companies should disclose "Annual Percentage Rate's (APR's). There are a few companies who have settled suits in this area and have added calculators to their web sites. They are not listed in this book as I feel that it would be inappropriate to send reader's to a specific company. An alternative calculator can be found at www.modalpremiumlitigation.com.

QUESTION 67: What is Insurable Interest?

Insurable interest is defined as that the person who is purchasing the policy has more to lose than to gain by insured's death and therefore may purchase a life insurance contract on somebody else's life. This is intended to prevent a person purchasing a policy unknowingly on another person for purposes of wagering, planned murder or any other reason.

An individual is deemed to have unlimited insurable interest in themselves and can purchase as much life insurance as they want (with no state restrictions); subject to the willingness of insurance companies to issue an applied for amount of coverage. Otherwise it as any instance where the insured carries an economic responsibility to a beneficiary.

Insurable interest is typically only required at the inception of the policy. After that, most States will allow that the beneficiary can be changed or the policy assigned without regard to insurable interest.

There are exceptions to these statements that vary on a State by State basis. Please contact your State Insurance Department (listed in Appendix A)

Recently there are concerns regarding questionable uses of life insurance and Insurable Interest has become a hot topic. Life insurance up until recently used for long accepted purpose of providing a beneficiary with a sum of money to replace some type of income loss. The usual needs on the personal side covered income protection for the family, mortgage, etc. and can used to pre-fund a potential estate tax liability. Other uses were for business purposes such as key-person indemnification, buy-sell funding, etc. There many different needs, though this covers the basics.

Over the last fifteen to twenty years, life insurance has entered into some very strange and complex uses. This is not altogether new. Some of these uses, had roots in sound principles while others did not. Stretching the limits of usage for life insurance is nothing new. As mentioned in the opening of the book (Question 1)—a concept known as the tontine annuity system was founded in Paris by the 17th-century Italian-born banker Lorenzo Tonti. Although essentially a form of gambling, this system has been regarded as an early attempt to use the law of averages and the principle of life expectancies in establishing annuities. Under the tontine system, associations of individuals were formed without any reference to age, and a fund was created by equal contributions from each member. The sum was invested, and, at the end of each year, the interest was divided among the survivors. The last remaining survivor received both the year's interest and the entire amount of the principal.

This eventually led to some not so desired ends resulting in the practice of taking out life insurance on strangers and having them murdered for profit. This was common in England in the 1700's and helped lead to the establishment of the "British Life Assurance Act of 1774, wherein a policy of life insurance can only be procured by a party that has an insurable interest in the life of the insured. Recently, however, a variety of situations has arisen in which the party seeking a life policy does not have an insurable interest, yet is not engaging in a wagering transaction of the kind the life assurance act and its progeny sought to forbid.

Understanding the concept of insurable interest will help in understanding some of the prevalent issues with the life insurance secondary marketplace and especially with a newer form generalized as Stranger Owned Life Insurance.

This marketplace has pros and cons (See Question 131). Those in favor state that it will give the elderly, and their advisors, an additional financial asset and additional leverage in terms of life insurance policy value. Those against the concept aside from just the fact that entire concept is considered "creepy" (my technical term) state that it could ultimately (though not realistically) lead to murder for hire as in old England though most likely result in financial havoc for the life insurance industry.

There are many issues of concern regarding the secondary life insurance marketplace. There are also the other uses of life insurance that stretch the intent of the tax rules and the meaning of "insurable interest". The only thing that is clear is that for now, it is here and will need to be considered in planning situations. However, the different types of transactions and risks need to be carefully considered.

The transactions range from the fairly benign to highly malignant and as often is the case, all might face the same treatment as they cannot be sorted apart. The "Insurable Interest" concept and the unintended usages of life insurance will have an impact, the questions is of what type and how much. Greed and abuse are fueling the debate and challenges brought on by the secondary marketplace. Remember that once a policy is sold, a third party gains a financial interest in the insured's early death and that the policy can be resold multiple times.

The future of the life insurance industry and a number of companies may be affected by the handling of the secondary marketplace. Despite all of the arguments, there are always facts and figures. Life insurance policies are priced based on mortality costs and expenses. The secondary marketplace and these other "concepts" introduce a new stress point on the pricing and there is no way that this cannot have an impact.

It's important to keep in mind that using life insurance for other purposes than intended paper could have dire consequences. Life insurance is for insuring lives rather than investing. The long term effects and the interpretation of insurable interest will have a significant impact on the future of the life insurance industry and will bear continued monitoring.

As an example of Insurable Interest, the following is how the State of California defines Insurable Interest (as mentioned above, each State's Insurance Code has it's own specific definition for Insurable Interest (please see Appendix A for a listing of State Insurance Departments). This is included as this provides a good representation of Insurable Interest rules. The State of California Insurance Code §10110 states that:

Every person has an insurable interest in the life and health of:

(a) Himself.

(b) Any person on whom he depends wholly or in part for education or support.

(c) Any person under a legal obligation to him for the payment of money or respecting property or services, of which death or illness might delay or prevent the performance.

(d) Any person upon whose life any estate or interest invested in him depends.

This is continued in Insurance Code § 10110.1:

(a) An insurable interest, with reference to life and disability insurance, is an interest based upon a reasonable expectation of pecuniary advantage through the continued life, health, or bodily safety of another person and consequent loss by reason of that person`s death or disability or a substantial interest engendered by love and affection in the case of individuals closely related by blood or law.

(b) An individual has an unlimited insurable interest in his or her own life, health, and bodily safety and may lawfully take out a policy of insurance on his or her own life, health, or bodily safety and have the policy made payable to whomsoever he or she pleases, regardless of whether the beneficiary designated has an insurable interest.

(c) Except as provided in Section 10110.4, an employer has an insurable interest, as referred to in subdivision (a), in the life or physical or mental ability of any of its directors, officers, or employees or the directors, officers, or employees of any of its subsidiaries or any other person whose death or physical or mental disability might cause financial loss to the employer; or, pursuant to any contractual arrangement with any shareholder concerning the reacquisition of shares owned by the shareholder at the time of his or her death or disability, on the life or physical or mental ability of that shareholder for the purpose of carrying out the contractual arrangement; or, pursuant to any contract obligating the employer as part of compensation arrangements or pursuant to a contract obligating the employer as guarantor or surety, on the life of the principal obligor. The trustee of an employer or trustee of a pension, welfare benefit plan, or trust established by an employer providing life, health, disability, retirement, or similar benefits to employees and retired employees of the employer or its affiliates and acting in a fiduciary capacity with respect to those employees, retired employees, or their dependents or beneficiaries has an insurable interest in the lives of employees and retired employees for whom those benefits are to be provided. The employer shall obtain the written consent of the individual being insured.

(d) An insurable interest shall be required to exist at the time the contract of life or disability insurance becomes effective, but need not exist at the time the loss occurs.

(e) Any contract of life or disability insurance procured or caused to be procured upon another individual is void unless the person applying for the insurance has an insurable interest in the individual insured at the time of the application.

(f) Notwithstanding subdivisions (a), (d), and (e), a charitable organization that meets the requirements of Section 214 or 23701d of the Revenue and Taxation Code may effectuate life or disability insurance on an insured who consents to the issuance of that insurance.

(g) This section shall not be interpreted to define all instances in which an insurable interest exists.

QUESTION 68: What Should I Consider in Choosing a Beneficiary?

This really will depend on your personal situation, as well as on the laws of your state. As I am not an attorney, I can only give you some basic guidance. A beneficiary is the person who will receive the funds in your policy when you die. You can name a primary and a contingent beneficiary, as well as naming multiple primary and contingent beneficiaries.

The proceeds from a life insurance policy usually go directly to the beneficiary, thus avoiding probate. Life Insurance proceeds are usually not subject to income tax. If there is still an estate tax and your estate is subject to this tax, then the life insurance proceeds may be subject to the estate tax. There are methods using a "trust" which can assist in this situation. It is advisable to work with an estate planning attorney and have a will drawn up and a trust, if the attorney feels that it a benefit to you. When you do meet with the estate planning attorney you should discuss your life insurance. If you already have drawn up a will or trust, you should call your attorney prior to applying for insurance. If you do not have either document, you can change the owner and beneficiary of your life insurance policy at any time.

If you have multiple beneficiaries, you can add one of the following definitions to further direct the distribution of the death benefit:

- Per Capita—this means that if a beneficiary dies before the insured, the remaining beneficiaries will equally divide that share of the proceeds in addition to receiving their own shares when the insured dies. (1) By head or by individual; (2) to share equally
- Per Stirpes—this means that if a beneficiary dies before the insured, that beneficiary's share of the proceed will pass upon that beneficiary's heirs rather going to the remaining beneficiaries when the insured dies. It means by family branches. A method of dividing benefits among living members of a class of beneficiaries and the descendants of deceased members.

It is very important matter to make sure that all documents are clear and concise because you will not be around to clarify them. Make sure that there are no spelling errors and full names are used. If you have a child under the age of 18 and you name them as a beneficiary whoever has physical guardianship will typically have financial guardianship. That may not be how you wish for it to be. Again, that's why it is a good idea to have estate planning done with an estate planning attorney.

In my opinion, only an estate planning attorney should handle estate planning. Beware of living trust seminars and non-attorneys peddling living trusts.

Another issue to consider is a simultaneous death, where the insured and primary beneficiary die together, such as in a car crash and it cannot be determined who died first. Some States have enacted the Uniform Simultaneous Death Act which provides that, in such a case, the proceeds are paid as if the primary beneficiary died first. Therefore, the proceeds would be received by the contingent beneficiary. If there were no contingent beneficiary, the insured's estate would receive the proceeds. Therefore, it's important to consider this in your estate planning and address it.

QUESTION 69: Who Should I Name as the Policy owner?

For the most part, the same issues that apply in choosing a beneficiary apply here as well. Typically, the insured is the owner (at least in community property states). I am not familiar as to whether or not this is the case in separate property states, since my practice has been limited to community property states. Separate property states have different estate planning practices. You may want to research this. A good place to start is with Nolo Press and their web site at www.nolo.com (phone # 1-800-728-3555). When the insured is not the owner it is generally for specific reasons, such as for estate planning purposes. As discussed in the previous question, you should strongly consider having at least a will drawn up. You may wish to discuss this with your attorney, if you have one.

It is not always necessary to engage an attorney if you wish to research the ownership and beneficiary issues yourself and are aware of the pros and cons.

QUESTION 70: What Are Life Insurance Survivor Options?

On fewer and fewer new policies and almost all older one, the insurer offers a variety of survivor options when the insurer passes away. The following is a list of the more common settlement options:

- Lump Sum Payment
- Income for a fixed period from 5 to 25 years. If you should die before the payments are complete, your beneficiary will get the remainder in the same time intervals.
- Life Income with a Guaranteed Payment. You collect a payment for the rest of your life at least equal to a guaranteed amount (calculated by the insurance company). If you should die before the guaranteed amount is paid, your beneficiary will receive the difference at your death.

- Joint and Survivor Life Income. Payments are made for your life and the life of your selected survivor. Your survivor does not have to get the same amount—it may be pre-selected at 33%, 66%, 100%, etc.
- Lifetime Income. This provides income for your life ONLY. When you die, payments cease altogether.
- Installment Refund with Life Income. You will receive income for life. Should you die before you have received total payments equal to your initial contribution, your beneficiary will receive the difference.
- Income of a specific amount. You can select an amount to be paid until the principal is exhausted.

The decision of which option to take is complicated. Keep in mind that the rate of return on the various options (except the lump sum) is low—so you may not be maximizing the rate of return). Another consideration is that, except for the lump sum option, access to the fund will be lost.

Currently, most carriers, upon presentation of a death certificate (and any required paperwork), deposit the proceeds into a money market account and send the beneficiary a checkbook. The checkbook can then be used to write checks up to the total amount of the death benefit (plus any interest).

CHAPTER 7: UNDERSTANDING UNDER-WRITING

QUESTION 71: What is underwriting and why is it important to me?

You've looked at various life insurance policies, you've compared companies, and now you're ready to apply for a policy. You may be about to embark on a long and winding path before that newly issued policy is in your hands. This is especially so if you have a significant health condition ranging from minor (e.g., height & weight, blood pressure) to major (e.g., cancer, heart disease). To get your policy issued, you must successfully pass the company's underwriting process. Choose your company with care: There are differences in underwriting philosophy from company to company.

QUESTION 72: How Do I Begin to Understand the Underwriting Process?

To understand the underwriting process, first recognize that insurance medicine differs from clinical medicine. The latter is about diagnosis and treatment; your doctor's job is to keep you well, and to make you well again if you get sick. That is clinical medicine. In contrast, insurance medicine seeks to determine the level of risk assumed by the insurance company if it issues a policy, and to set an appropriate premium to cover that risk.

Company A may react differently to a given medical condition than Company B. One company's "standard" risk is another carrier's rated (i.e., issued at a higher than standard premium rate) risk. While modern life underwriting is a sophisticated process, with elaborate point rating systems and complex underwriting manuals that vary from company to company, it is still more art than science.

Take the time to discuss the underwriting process with your insurance advisor so you will know what to expect. Make sure that your advisor is experienced enough to get you the best offer from a suitable company. A lot of agents will wait until the company makes an offer. Only at that point and sometimes only when the client persists, will the agent seek quotes from other companies. My philosophy is to do this ahead of time, in the hope and expectation that the company, with whom we start the process, will issue a policy. This involves an informal advance discussion of the case, with an underwriter, to reduce or eliminate any surprises.

In insurance medicine, the underwriter works with the company's medical director to make a mortality assessment (i.e., determine the applicant's life expectancy with reference to a mortality table), considering all relevant factors such as disease or medical problems present at the time of application. The underwriter considers all the available information and then renders an expert opinion of the applicant's insurability and the premium to be charged. Some weight may be given to the quality of care being received from a physician.

QUESTION 73: How Does The Underwriting Process Work?

At this point, you have selected the company to which you are going to apply for a policy, and also, your life insurance advisor. If your advisor is on the ball, he or she should have prepared a proposal based on the pre-underwriting issues described in the previous section. Caution—If you think there might be pre-underwriting issues and you have not disclosed them to your advisor, this could very well come back to haunt you.

The next step is completing the application. Answer the questions as completely, truthfully, and accurately as you can. Your advisor should be able to help you with any questions about the application. Your advisor is in most cases, an independent broker and not an employee of the insurance company. The advisor is not authorized to make or modify contracts, waive any requirements, or advise you to omit any information that may be requested by the insurance company. You must make a good faith full disclosure to the company of any and all information that may affect the underwriting of your application.

QUESTION 74: What Are Some Tips For My Life Insurance Examination?

Please note that I am not a physician, and I cannot guarantee the effectiveness of these tips. But they are a result of long experience and many discussions with home office underwriters and other involved people over the years:

- Insurance companies are looking for average people, not superman, so relax as much as possible during the examination. Underwriting is done on the basis of your medical history, as well as on the results of your current exam.
- It is better not to eat for eight hours prior to the examination and take little or no caffeine. Schedule a morning examination if at all possible, when you're more likely to be relaxed.
- Alcohol tends to elevate blood pressure for twelve to twenty-four hours. I suggest no alcohol for twenty-four hours prior to the examination.
- One key factor is a good night's rest before the exam.
- If possible, give a urine specimen before a blood pressure check, since the elimination of fluids tends to moderately lower blood pressure.
- If you are a smoker, we suggest that you do not smoke at all within thirty minutes of the exam. Smoking tends to elevate blood pressure by constricting the artery walls.
- Salt retains fluids. Avoid salt or use it very lightly for three or four days prior to the examination. This can have a beneficial effect on your blood pressure.
- To the best of your knowledge, give your complete medical history or important items. Be certain the examiner correctly lists the location of doctors and hospitals that you have seen in the

past, since the insurance company will most likely request their reports. Do not try to hide any of your medical history, since this tends to make it look worse than it probably is.

- You should discuss any potential problems with your advisor prior to the examination. This can affect your advisor's recommendations, such as which company or companies to apply to and how to prepare for the underwriting process. The advisor might want to discuss your case informally with the underwriter before you apply. In some cases, this can be beneficial.

- For the EKG (electrocardiogram) test, which is a graph of the electrical activity of the heart; be relaxed and comfortable prior to the EKG test. Do not use coffee or other stimulants. If you are aware of EKG changes that have been noted and evaluated in the past, then it is most helpful to bring those to the examiner's attention as well as to your advisor. Some people have an abnormal looking EKG but it is normal for them.

An employee of a third party firm (contracted by the company) may be contacting you, your advisors or acquaintances as part of a routine inspection regarding your preliminary insurance application. This is a traditional part of the application process. Usually, these questions are handled efficiently and in a professional manner. Please let your advisor know if there are any problems. This is known in the industry as an inspection report. It will seem as if you have been asked these questions before, and you probably have. Insurance companies try to corroborate information from different sources.

QUESTION 75: Who is The Medical Information Bureau (MIB)?

The Medical Information Bureau—known in the industry as MIB—was established in 1902. For most people, MIB remains a mysterious component in the life insurance underwriting process. If you have ever applied for life, health or disability insurance, chances are you're in the MIB database. MIB is a valuable asset to both the life insurance industry and the insurance buying public. MIB keeps premium costs low by helping to detect insurance fraud. Fraud runs up claim costs, which are borne by everyone who pays life insurance premiums.

According to the MIB website (located at www.mib.com)—"The vast majority of persons who apply for life, health, disability and long term care insurance are honest and forthright in their answers to questions on insurance applications and medical exam forms concerning any medical conditions they currently have as well as their health histories. That would additionally include information on any other hazards to which they may have been exposed at work or at play. Unfortunately a relatively few attempt to circumvent the process. In doing so, they increase the costs of the insurance company, which, in turn, may result in reduced dividends for existing policyholders and increased premiums for applicants."

MIB is nothing more than an information clearinghouse that stores information, gathered by over 600 insurers, in processing and underwriting cases. Member companies send an inquiry to MIB and receive a short, coded report with information on the applicant's medical history and other relevant underwriting information. MIB carefully guards the privacy of the information in its database, and only member companies may access it. All MIB member companies must agree to a strict set of standards for use of the data provided.

An MIB inquiry often guides insurers to information that is valuable in assessing risks. MIB is a taxpaying organization, supported by assessments from member insurance companies based on their total insurance in-force and business written in the previous year. Additional revenue comes from user fees based on the number of inquiries a member company submits to MIB. It is estimated that over 90% of the individual life insurance policies and 80% of the health and disability policies issued in the United States and Canada are subject to the MIB system. This is done through member companies and reinsurance treaties that nonmember companies have with member companies.

The MIB will also provide you with an annual record disclosure without charge. To request the free disclosure (according to the MIB website as of 8/22/2006), you must call MIB's toll-free phone number 866-692-6901. (TTY 866-346-3642 for hearing impaired).

Details from the web site http://www.mib.com/html/request_your_record.html:

A few things to bear in mind before you call—

If you have not applied for individually underwritten life, health, or disability insurance during the preceding seven year period, MIB will not have a record on you.

We will ask you for personal identification information to assist us in locating a record, if one exists. We may validate the identification information that you provided with other consumer reporting agencies.

You will be asked to certify under penalty of perjury that the information you provided about yourself to request MIB disclosure is accurate, complete and you represent that you are the person that is requesting disclosure.

Upon receipt of your (a) request for a Record Search and Disclosure, and (b) proper identification, MIB will initiate the disclosure process and provide you with:

- the nature and substance of information, if any, that MIB may have in its files pertaining to you;
- the name(s) of the MIB member companies, if any, that reported information to MIB; and,
- the name(s) of the MIB member companies, if any, that received a copy of your MIB record during the twelve (12) month period preceding your request for disclosure.

MIB is committed to the philosophy that every consumer should be entitled to know the contents of his or her record maintained by MIB and has the right to correct any inaccurate or incomplete information in the record.

QUESTION 76: What Is A Rated Premium (And/Or I Have a Known or Unknown Medical Condition)?

Once the insurance company receives your application, the underwriting department will begin the evaluation process—this is known as underwriting the case—to determine whether or not you qualify for the insurance and, if so, what is the appropriate rate classification (discussed previously). The company may determine that insurance coverage cannot be issued as applied for. In that case, the company is likely to offer you insurance on a modified (rated) basis.

Life insurance companies employ a medical director, who advises the underwriting department on difficult or borderline applications. The medical director will be an M.D., and may be a full time employee or a part time consultant.

If your application is a borderline case, chances are the medical director will have been consulted. In many cases you can negotiate with the company. This may call for furnishing additional detailed information about the condition or conditions that concern the underwriter. That is why it is important to find out the exact reason why your application was declined or rated. With that information in hand, you should then consult your personal physician. Always bear in mind that the insurance company is taking on a risk by offering you insurance, so that their view of your medical situation will necessarily be more conservative than your doctor's opinion. If your physician does not agree with the insurance carrier's decision, one of two things may be occurring.

First, your physician may not have been fully forthcoming with you regarding a health condition or you may have a new condition. Second is that the insurance carrier does not know the full details. This may be due to incomplete medical records or some other reason. This is where your choice of advisor can play a major role. Your advisor should act as your advocate in case your application is declined or modified, to see if furnishing additional information will allow the company to make a more favorable offer.

I have found that in about 50% of the cases where the initial offer is not favorable, this is due to poor communication. Your advisor will find out as much as possible about the company's reasoning for the declination or modified offer. Then you can discuss the situation with your own doctor. After assessing the situation in this way, your advisor may suggest further negotiations with the insurance company in an attempt to get a better offer. Alternatively, your advisor may suggest shopping around for a life insurance company with more experience in underwriting and issuing policies for cases similar to yours.

Underwriting departments tend to become specialists and to develop their own comfort levels with certain types of medical conditions. This is also true of life insurance companies, whose experience with different ailments will find its way into the company's underwriting criteria. After many years of working with these conditions, companies compile reliable statistics that may allow them to make a more favorable offer. Two very important underwriting variables are the company's risk tolerance for a given medical condition, and how it sets an appropriate rating and premium for that condition. These factors vary from company to company. Again, underwriting is more art than science, and different companies may view a given medical condition or lifestyle consideration differently.

Occasionally—perhaps 10% to 15% of the time—the applicant will be offered a rated policy. This means that the applicant does not meet the company's standard rating criteria and the company must therefore charge a higher premium to cover the increased risk. Ratings are assigned based on health history and lifestyle considerations. Here are some examples of situations that may result in a rated policy: (a) Family history of cancer or heart disease; (b) multiple moving traffic violations within a certain period of time; (c) hazardous avocation (e.g., deep scuba diving, parachute jumping, mountain climbing); (d) height and weight outside the company's standard criteria; (e) tobacco usage or any health issue that is not under control or otherwise being dealt with; (f) history of certain conditions, such as cancer or heart disease and many other conditions. The underwriter is looking for anything that might affect mortality.

Some companies offer an impaired risk program. These are designed to provide insurance to those who have health issues that caused them to be declined coverage elsewhere. There are a considerable number of such companies, and typically, it will be a large, respected company offering a full range of life insurance products. A few companies offer guaranteed issue or simplified underwriting programs. There are even some "impaired risk" products (i.e., for those with significant medical conditions) available with no extra premium over the company's standard rate. All rated and declined applications should at least be considered for impaired risk underwriting. It's worth a try in most cases. Appendix D has a list of a number of conditions and lifestyle considerations plus what to expect and assistance that can be given in underwriting. Your advisor is a valuable resource in determining options for your specific background.

Don't give up hope—there may be life insurance available to you at an affordable cost. The best way to find out is to check around. Your advisor can help you to do this.

Even with a rated premium, the applicant may have a life expectancy well into the 70s or 80s. Only about 5% to 6% of the time will the application be declined. Declined applications are comparatively rare and are reserved for the most serious medical conditions, such as cancer (currently under treatment) or advanced heart conditions.

Tobacco usage is another factor that can vary greatly from company to company. Smokers should take special care in selecting the right companies to apply to for coverage. (See Question 79).

Rate classifications: Since each applicant's circumstances are unique, the risk assessment process must be tailored to each applicant's situation. Underwriting requires good judgment, for there is no one magical solution to every underwriting problem. Here is where an independent life insurance advisor can pay off for you. Your advisor works with several different life insurance companies on a regular basis, and is therefore in a position to choose the company most likely to issue the sought after policy on the most favorable terms.

A life insurance policy is a financial asset, just like stocks and bonds. The key to successfully getting through the underwriting process is finding a company that will invest in your life. The company wants you to live long and prosper.

QUESTION 77: How Will My Build Affect My Insurance Premium?

This can often depend on the life insurance company. Your height and weight can have a significant impact on your life insurance premium. As your doctor probably reminds you each year is that the more you weigh, the greater your chances are of certain health conditions. And with life insurance companies; the more you weigh, the more you will pay. This extra amount of premium is incremental and increases as your weight increases over the desired weight. Even a slight amount of extra weight can change your rate class from an insurance company's best rate. The following question contains height and weight guidelines from one life insurance company.

Question 78: What Are Some Sample Guidelines to Qualify for Preferred Rates?

The following are samples from one life insurance company's underwriting guidelines as of October 2003. These guidelines are for this carriers best available rates and their next best rate category, so that you can see the difference. This is not a guarantee of any current guidelines.

	Best Available Rates:	Preferred Rates:
Impairments	No diseases, disorders or activities that would affect mortality.	No diseases, disorders or activities that would affect mortality.
Blood Pressure	No current, or history of, blood pressure treatment or medication. No current, or history of, blood pressure readings in excess of: 140/85 Age 60 or Younger 150/90 Age 61 or Older	Currently controlled and average reading in last 2 years (including treatment) does not exceed: 140/90 Age 60 or younger 150/90 Age 61 or Older
Family History	No cardiovascular or cancer disease (except basal cell carcinoma) in either parent or siblings on or before age 60.	For either parent, no cardiovascular death on or before age 60.
Driving History	No DWI, DUI, reckless driving, license revocation or suspension in last 5 years.	No DWI, DUI, reckless driving, license revocation or suspension in last 5 years.
Nicotine	No use of nicotine or nicotine substitutes in last 5 years. For cigar use, see statement for carrier	No use of nicotine or nicotine substitutes in last 3 years for Preferred No Nicotine Use. For cigar use, see statement for carrier
Cholesterol	Cholesterol 240 maximum.	Cholesterol 270 maximum.
CHOL/HDL Ratio	Cholesterol/HDL Ratio cannot exceed 5.0	Cholesterol/HDL Ratio cannot exceed 6.0
Alcohol/Substance Abuse	No history of, or treatment for, alcohol or substance abuse	No history of, or treatment for, alcohol or substance abuse in last 10 years
Cancer History	Preferred Best not available if any cancer history (except basal cell carcinoma)	Preferred not available if any cancer history (except basal cell carcinoma).
Aviation	Flat extra (available in most cases) or exclusion rider	Flat extra (available in most cases) or exclusion rider.
Hazardous Occupation or Avocation	Coverage available; however, may require flat extra	Coverage available; however, may require flat extra.

Build Chart	Male/Female, Height/Weight	Male/Female, Height/Weight
	5'0" 145 5'7" 176 6'2" 216	5'0" 154 5'7" 192 6'2" 234
	5'1" 149 5'8" 182 6'3" 222	5'1" 159 5'8" 197 6'3" 240
	5'2" 153 5'9" 188 6'4" 227	5'2" 164 5'9" 203 6'4" 246
	5'3" 158 5'10" 193 6'5" 233	5'3" 169 5'10" 209 6'5" 253
	5'4" 162 5'11" 199 6'6" 238	5'4" 175 5'11" 215 6'6" 260
	5'5" 166 6'0" 205 6'7" 243	5'5" 180 6'0" 221 6'7" 266
	5'6" 170 6'1" 211 6'8" 249	5'6" 186 6'1" 227 6'8" 273

QUESTION 79: How Will Tobacco Usage Affect My Premiums?

This will depend on the carrier. Carriers also treat the different forms of tobacco such as cigarettes, cigars and chewing tobacco in their own fashion. In any event, the usage of tobacco will increase your premium; the only question is how much. Rate classification for tobacco usage will depend on the type of tobacco. For non-tobacco classes, it will depend on the date of the last usage of tobacco. There is a wide range of how life insurance companies treat those who use tobacco. A couple of considerations are the type of tobacco used and, if no longer using tobacco, the last date of usage. This is an area that you need to have a representative who has access to a number of carriers and will get you quotes from multiple carriers.

If a carrier finds out, at any time, that an insured misrepresented information regarding tobacco usage, they will rescind the policy as a material misrepresentation. In other words, they will cancel the policy, thus defeating the entire purpose of obtaining coverage. Some carriers will pay the death benefit based on the amount of coverage that the premiums paid would have purchased on a smoker basis; however, the majority do not, as this is not fair to the truthful applicant.

QUESTION 80: How I Do I Find Out Why My Life Insurance Application Was Not Approved or Modified?

An option is to write a letter to the insurance company asking for the results of any exams and any other reasons for their decision. They will require the name and address of your physician and will send the information there. (NOTE: If your application was approved, you can also request the results of your exams).

This is required under the U.S. Fair Credit Reporting Act which states that life insurance companies must inform you why an "adverse decision" was made on your life insurance application (meaning why it rejected you or placed you in a higher-risk class).

Insurers are not required to go into great detail on exactly what medical condition led to an adverse decision. The concept is that insurers do not like to "intrude" on the relationship between applicants and their physicians, and insurers do not want to be in the position of giving an applicant a detailed diagnosis of his or her condition.

If the life insurance company has acquired medical information from your doctor, you can ask your doctor for the same information, along with an explanation of your condition.

Occasionally, in the exams performed for the insurance company; a new condition is found of which your physician is not aware of or chosen not to discuss with you. When this happens, you have to really press your physician to find out the truth.

QUESTION 81: What is Financial Underwriting?

An often overlooked but critical consideration is financial underwriting. This is especially important in larger cases and some business situations. You, as an individual applicant, may have to justify to the insurance company the amount of coverage applied for. Life insurance companies are sensitive to the over-insurance problem; where someone is insured for more than an insurable interest. When someone applies for a large amount of life insurance, there is reason why. Financial underwriting seeks to find out why, and to ensure that the amount of coverage can be justified. Therefore, the amount of coverage bears a definite relationship to the applicant's net worth and income. The underwriter needs to know the purpose of the coverage applied for. This helps the underwriter determine if the beneficiary's economic loss—in the event of the insured person's death—is in line with the total amount of insurance in-force.

Other factors, considered during the financial underwriting process, are a growth rate and duration variables. Forecasting the future value of financial and other assets is guesswork, and there is no reliable way to predict the future. Underwriters are trained to take future value into consideration. Future value is today's value plus compound interest and/or other growth in value over time, to a specific point in the future. It is calculated by using an assumed interest rate or rate of appreciation during the desired time horizon.

More sophisticated analyses of future value employ a very complex statistical technique, known as stochastic modeling. This takes variability of future possible outcomes into consideration. There is very little published information available to help in predicting how much net worth increases over time.

While medical underwriting is more art than science, the opposite is true of financial underwriting. Many tools and techniques have been developed over the years, such as income multiples, capitalization formulas, and the future value approach. The underwriter is looking for evidence of anti-selection (where the risks are not evened out; i.e. lopsided). This is also known as selection against the company. It means that the applicant and/or the intended beneficiary is especially claims conscious and thereby more likely to anticipate a death claim than the average insured risk. To help minimize the impact of financial antiselection, underwriters commonly apply four tests:

1) Vulnerability—Is insurance the best method for protecting the financial objective?
2) Attainability—Is the forecasted asset or value growth realistic?
3) Normalcy—Is the financial objective normal or speculative?

4) Desirability—How strongly motivated is the applicant to achieve the stated objective?

The risks considered during the financial underwriting process include:

- Inflation, which reduces purchasing power over time
- Family or partnership situations—Divorce or the possible breakup of a business partnership
- Financial uncertainty—e.g., job loss, disability or reduction of future profits/earnings
- Tax law changes, which affect future projections
- Market risks, which affect future values
- Interest rate changes, which affect asset valuations

QUESTION 82: How Does The Conditional Receipt Work?

The conditional receipt: In most cases, when your application is taken, you will tender the initial premium payment with the application and you receive a conditional receipt. The conditional receipt binds your life insurance coverage effective on the date of your application (the exact conditions vary a bit from company to company), provided that you are eligible for the coverage applied for. An example will help you understand how a conditional receipt works: Suppose you apply for a $1 million face amount life insurance policy, you are in excellent health on the date you applied for the coverage, and received a conditional receipt. Then suppose you are run over by a truck the next day in an unfortunate accident. Even though the insurance company has not even received your application, your beneficiary will receive the $1 million, once the company underwrites the case and determines that you were eligible for the coverage applied for. In this case, you paid just one premium payment and your beneficiary collects the proceeds.

Now suppose you have a serious heart condition, of which you are unaware. Otherwise, your situation is identical to that described above. You apply for the coverage, get your conditional receipt and take a medical examination the next day. On the way home, the truck runs over you and you are killed. Since you were not eligible for the coverage as applied for, the company underwrites the case, discovers your heart condition, declines the claim and returns your premium payment to your beneficiary. That's how a conditional receipt works. It is, in effect, a limited life insurance agreement, good until the company can underwrite the case and make a final determination of your eligibility for the coverage you applied for.

QUESTION 83: Why is Honesty is the Best Policy and or what the Insurance Company Doesn't Know Can Hurt You?

Keep in mind that a life insurance policy is a unilateral contract. One party makes an offer and the other party accepts it "as is." This differs from most contracts, which are bilateral.

Most policies are issued with a two year "incontestability" clause. A typical such clause reads: "Except for non-payment of premium, we will not contest this contract after it has been in-force during the insured's lifetime for two years from the date of issue." During the first two years, the company can challenge (contest) the policy if there is any reason to do so, such as suspicion that the applicant lied.

One commonly asked question is what if I smoke and don't admit it? Most likely the application will not make it through the underwriting process, because nicotine will show up in the urinalysis or in the medical records. Even if a smoker makes it through the underwriting process and gets a policy issued without disclosing tobacco use, if he or she dies during the contestable period, the company can rescind the policy (cancel it retroactively) and deny the claim. In that case, the company's sole obligation to the beneficiary would be to return the premium payments that have been made, with interest. In case of outright fraud, a company may choose to contest a claim for longer than the two year contestable period.

QUESTION 84: Is There Anything Else That I Need to Know About Underwriting?

This section is an overview of the life insurance underwriting process. Each company has its own individual procedure and requirements. Most companies will look at the state Department of Motor Vehicle reports. You may be asked to fill out a supplementary questionnaire, such as a travel or aviation form.

The life insurance company retains (keeps or underwrites) the risk, up to the company's specified retention level. For example, a life insurance company might retain up to $1 million on any one insured life. Above the retention level, the case is reinsured with one or more other companies. The reinsurance process is invisible to the insured person, and the original writing company is solely responsible for paying the death benefit in the event of a claim. If yours is a very large case, your advisor will help coordinate the underwriting and reinsurance process and this can smooth the issuance of your policy.

Your advisor and your approach to and attitude towards the underwriting process can have a significant impact on a favorable outcome. Life insurance companies are in business to serve the public and make money. They are vitally interested in a deal that amounts to a win-win situation for both parties to the contract.

CHAPTER 8: MONITORING YOUR IN-FORCE LIFE INSURANCE POLICY

QUESTION 85: How Do I Monitor and Evaluate an In-force Policy?

As we've seen, there are many components that can affect the performance of a life insurance policy. The key in monitoring and evaluating a life insurance policy is determining how and if these components have changed and are affecting its performance. There are differences if you are monitoring a policy purchased recently and monitoring (or evaluating) an older policy. I will make that distinction where it is possible.

QUESTION 86: What Areas Should I Review For Potential Changes?

Life insurance is an asset that must be purchased and monitored with care. The following questions cover areas where attention to detail can add value for the beneficiaries and prevent trouble in the future. The focus is on existing policies, however many of these items also apply to new policies.

- Face amount—Every two to three years, you should review your term life insurance needs
- Policy type (discussed in Chapter 2, Questions 4 through 19)—such as whether the policy is term, whole life, universal life, variable life, etc.
- Riders—are they still needed?

The following is a summary that I prepare annually, for each client to ensure that all information is updated and the owner and/or trustee is fully informed. The summaries are based on information provided by the insurance carriers. It does not cover every potential issue; it is designed for policy owners to have the basics of their policy and it is always used in conjunction with the carrier's most recent annual statement and the following guide. Not all of the categories are applicable in every instance. This may be useful to you in reviewing some of the more important factors of your policy.

Term Policy Information:

- Insured:
- Carrier:
- Policy Number:
- Type of Coverage:
- Face Amount:
- Issue Date:
- Premium Mode:
- Modal Premium:
- Premium (if switched to Annually):
- Annualized Current Premium:
- Annual Savings if Switched to Annual:
- Re-Entry Date:
- Last Conversion Date:
- Primary Beneficiary:
- Contingent Beneficiary:
- Owner:
- Riders:
- Notes/Comments:
- Outstanding Items:

The following is a guide to the terms used above. Other terms specific to your term policy may be found in the glossary section:

- **Type of Coverage**: This is the type of term life insurance coverage insuring your life.

- **Face Amount:** This is the amount your beneficiaries would receive in the event of your death (less any policy loans outstanding).

- **Premium:** This is your premium and how it is paid.

- **Issue Date:** The date your policy became effective and was issued by the insurance company.

- **Re-Entry Year:** If applicable, this is the year that you will need to re-qualify for preferred rates. Please read your policy for further information or contact my office.

- **Last Conversion Year:** This is the last year that you can convert your term life insurance to permanent life insurance without evidence of insurability.

- **Primary Beneficiary:** This is your primary beneficiary.

- **Contingent Beneficiary:** If applicable, this is your contingent (or secondary) beneficiary who would receive the proceeds of your policy should your primary beneficiary predecease you.

- **Riders**: If applicable, what riders you have elected on this policy.

QUESTION 87: Is My Current Permanent Life Insurance Policy In Good Health?

If you have a life insurance advisor, then they should have been reviewing the policy with you. You should have also been presented with an in-force illustration, which will tell you how the policy is projected to perform into the future, based on current values and assumptions. These in-force illustrations are critical to you as a policy owner.

However, before we discuss in-force illustrations, you may wish to use the following list to help gather information about your policy.

Whole Life Policy Information:

- Insured:
- Carrier:
- Policy Number:
- Type of Coverage:
- Face Amount:
- Issue Date:
- Premium Mode:
- Modal Premium:
- Premium (if switched to Annually):
- Annualized Current Premium:
- Annual Savings if Switched to Annual:
- Primary Beneficiary
- Contingent Beneficiary
- Policy owner:
- Premium Payer:
- Riders:
- In-force Illustration Dates: Last: Next:
- Gross Cash Value
- Surrender Charge
- Policy Loan
- Net Cash Value
- Participating or Non-Participating:
- Paid Up Additions:
- Crediting rate, loan rates, etc.
- Notes/Comments: This Section would include notes about the results of the most recent in-force illustration, which is typically requested from the carrier every 3 years or upon request from the policy owner.
- Outstanding Items:

The following is guide to terms for whole life insurance (further terms are found in the glossary):

Your Guide to Your Whole Life Insurance Summary

This brief guide may be helpful to you in understanding your whole life insurance annual statement. This guide covers only the most commonly used terms and is generic in the sense that it is not specific to any particular whole life policy or issuing company. Some terms will not apply to your policy and your policy may contain terms not listed here. Please consult your policy or policies for definitions and terms specific to each policy, and please call or email me with any questions.

- **Death Benefit:** This is the amount—minus any outstanding policy loan(s)—that your beneficiary or beneficiaries would receive in the event of your death.

- **Interest Rate:** The interest rate credited on your policy by the insurance company, which is applied to the accumulation value less any policy loans. Interest is compounded monthly. The more frequently interest is compounded, the higher the effective annual rate, but the difference between, for example, monthly and quarterly compounding is small.

- **Interest credited/Charge on Loan Account:** The net interest credited or charged by the company on any loan debt for the specified period.

- **Issue Date:** The effective date of your policy and the date it was issued by the insurance company.

- **Loan or Loan Debt:** An amount borrowed against the Accumulated Value.

- **Loanable Value:** The amount you may borrow against your Accumulated Value, as of the report date.

- **Loan Repay:** A payment applied to reduce your loan debt.

- **Net Cash Surrender Value:** This is the amount payable if you surrender your policy as of the report date.

- **Paid-up Insurance:** Insurance on which all required premiums have been paid and no further premiums will ever become due and payable. This term is frequently used to mean the reduced paid-up insurance that is available as a non-forfeiture option on most whole life policies.

- **Premium Payment:** The sum of all premiums received on your policy during the period covered by the statement.

- **Surrender Charge:** The charge for early surrender of the policy. This is the difference between the accumulation (or account) value and the net cash surrender value. The surrender charge typically decreases each year and disappears after a certain number of years.

Universal Life Policy Information:

- Insured:
- Carrier:
- Policy Number:
- Type of Coverage:
- Face Amount:
- Issue Date:
- Premium Mode:
- Modal Premium:
- Premium (if switched to Annually):
- Annualized Current Premium:
- Annual Savings if Switched to Annual:
- Primary Beneficiary
- Contingent Beneficiary

- Policy owner:
- Premium Payer:
- Riders:
- In-force Illustration Dates (next and last):
- Gross Cash Value
- Surrender Charge
- Policy Loan
- Net Cash Value
- Crediting rate, loan rates, etc.
- Notes/Comments: This Section would include notes about the results of the most recent in-force illustration, which is typically requested from the carrier every 3 years or upon request from the policy owner.
- Outstanding Items:

The following is a guide to terms for universal life insurance (further terms are found in the glossary)

Your guide to your universal life insurance summary

This is a guide to your universal life insurance annual statement. Please note that this is a generic guide and is for the most commonly used terms. Some terms will not apply to your policy and your policy may contain terms not listed here. Please consult your policy(ies) for definitions and terms specific to your policy(ies). Please call or email me with any questions.

- **Policy Issue Date**—The date your policy became effective and was issued by the insurance company.

- **Current Specified Amount/Death Benefit**—This is the amount your beneficiaries would receive in the event of your death (less any policy loans outstanding).

- **Premium Payment**—The sum of all premiums received on your policy during the summary period.

- **Premium Expense, Fees & Other Expenses**—Policy fees and other costs associated with the set-up and administration of your policy.

- **Cost of Insurance/Mortality Costs**—the amount deducted each month from the Accumulated Value to cover charges for the cost of insurance.

- **Interest Credited**—The amount of interest credited on your policy.

- **Interest Rate**—The interest rate credited on your policy, applied to the accumulation value, minus any policy loans. Interest is compounded monthly.

- **Withdrawals**—A full or partial withdrawal of the Net Cash Surrender Value.

- **Loan or Loan Debt**—An amount borrowed against the Accumulated Value.

- **Loanable Value**—The amount you may borrow against your Accumulated Value as of the date reported.

- **Loan Repay**—A payment applied to reduce your loan debt.

- **Interest credited/Charge on Loan Account**—The net interest credited/charge on any loan debt for the specified period.

- **Accumulation/Account Value**—Your account balance; this is the amount upon which interest is credited and will generally include any amount set aside, in the loan account, to secure any loan debt.

- **Surrender Charge**—The charge for early surrender of the policy. This is the difference between accumulation/account value and the net cash surrender value. This value will typically decrease each year and will disappear entirely after a certain number of years.

- **Net Cash Surrender Value**—This is the amount payable if you surrender your policy on the date reported.

QUESTION 88: What Is an In-force Illustration?

An in-force illustration is the only way to gauge the potential future performance of a policy. An in-force illustration/ledger is an illustration produced from a certain point (as current as possible) using the actual values and using current assumptions (the actual interest rate the company is crediting and the current mortality and expense factors. It allows you to compare past (actual) performance with anticipated performance. In other words, you are using actual performance as a measure rather than the original projections in the sales illustration generated at the time of issue. This applies to all permanent (cash value) life insurance policies, where the policy and its values are not fully guaranteed.

QUESTION 89: How Do I Order an In-force Illustration?

These can be requested from the life insurance company; it can take anywhere from a couple of days to a few weeks to receive them.

The following is a sample request form for an in-force ledger illustration:

-----------------------------------START LETTER------------------------------------

Date

Attn: Policy owner Services
Carrier Name & Address

Re: Policy Number, Insured Name, Owner Name

Dear Sir or Madam:

My life insurance policy number is listed above. Please provide three in-force proposals *(Note: depending on your situation, you may not need all three)*:

1. Illustrate to maturity with current premiums, based on current interest rate and mortality assumptions
2. Illustrate to maturity the minimum premium required to endow the policy at maturity based on current interest rate and mortality assumptions

Please also indicate the current surrender value, loan value and the cost basis in the policy to date. Please call me if you have any questions and thank you for your prompt attention to this matter.

Sincerely,

Policy owner's name & signature

-----------------------------------END LETTER------------------------------------

QUESTION 90: What Will the In-force Illustration Tell Me?

An In-force illustration will tell you if your policy will continue to its maturity (the longest it can continue to). You can always use the original sales illustration as your benchmark.

The first illustration requested in the letter above will show you for how many years the policy will continue, using the current cash value, death benefit, premium payment, mortality costs, expenses and interest rates. If the policy will terminate before the maturity age, the second illustration will show you what the minimum premium is that needs to be paid in order to continue the policy to the maturity of the contract.

Depending on your situation, you can ask for other in-force illustrations. For example, if the policy was originally designed on a limited premium payment schedule, you can request the company to furnish an in-force illustration to determine how many more years the premium will actually need to be paid.

As discussed in the policy loan chapter (10, questions 106-109) a loan will most likely cause your policy to implode over the long run depending on its size and all the components that affect a life insurance policy.

For the purposes of this book, we will take a look at how a universal life policy issued in 1971 by a large well rated (see questions 44-48 #) life insurance company, has performed. Each company's format is different. Also, over the last few years, due to many abuses and to provide a greater degree of consumer protection, an illustration is lengthier and provides significantly more detail (See Question 40) than in prior years. Please keep in mind that for the most part, every company's illustration is different, and as each of their products by necessity.

On this, the original illustration, the proposed insured's name would be in the upper left hand corner along with his or her personal information. The company's name (blanked out) is at the top. The basic design information is at the top right hand corner—a death benefit of $750,000 with a proposed annual premium payment of $5,661. The first two columns; A—is at the end of year and B is the policy age at the end of that year. Policy (Insurance) age changes six months and one day before one's actual birthday, for most companies. I have yet to find a logical reason for this, except that it benefits the life insurance companies. Column 3 shows the annualized premium and/or withdrawals. Columns 4, 5 and 6 show the values at the assumed interest rate (8.25%), which, as we now know, a very optimistic interest rate. Column 4 shows the assumed cash value (surrender value), column 5 shows the assumed accumulation value and column 6 shows the assumed death benefit. Columns 7, 8 and 9 show the guaranteed values, based on the guaranteed interest rate of 5.5% and guaranteed mortality and expense charges. Please note that, at the time when this illustration was created how buried the guaranteed rates are; on page 4, second paragraph, third line. Today, the company has to show guarantees in an easy to find fashion. Columns 7, 8 and 9 are the same as columns 4, 5 and 6 except for being based on guaranteed values rather than current values.

Once you have this, you can gauge how the policy is actually performing. For our case study, we will use a client of mine who was policy age 47 at issue. At the time in-force illustrations were run, he was age 56. So only nine years had elapsed since he purchased a $750,000 universal life insurance policy with XYZ Life. Due to the assumptions at that, time he was projected to pay a premium of $5,661 annually which would endow the policy at his age 95. We ran an in-force proposal (A) and found that, to still have the policy endow at his age 95, and based on the now current assumptions, he would need to increase his premium to $10,800 annually. XYZ has not given him any indication that the policy is so far off the original marks and they are not alone in their failure to do so. Only a few carriers now have added a line on the annual report, stating the client age at which the policy will lapse or mail in-force illustrations on their own volition.

Original Sales Illustration

6-A

```
CLIENT:                                    ...LIFE INSURANCE COMPANY        INITIAL FACE AMOUNT: $750,000
MALE AGE: 47 NON-SMOKER                                                     1ST YR. ANN. PREM.  $5,661
                                                                           PAYABLE: ANNUALLY

CASH VALUE ACCUMULATION TEST 30 (KIND 1881)
```

END OF POLICY YR AGE	ANNUALIZED PREMIUM AND/OR WITHDRAWALS	ASSUMED INTEREST RATE (8.25%) CURRENT MONTHLY DEDUCTIONS **			GUARANTEED INTEREST RATE * GUARANTEED MONTHLY DEDUCTIONS		
		CASH VALUE	ACCUM VALUE	DEATH BENEFIT	CASH VALUE	ACCUM VALUE	DEATH BENEFIT
1 48	5,661	0	3,493	750,000	0	3,312	750,000
2 49	5,661	0	7,162	750,000	0	4,981	750,000
3 50	5,661	0	11,211	750,000	0	6,384	750,000
4 51	5,661	0	15,607	750,000	0	7,507	750,000
5 52	5,661	881	20,381	750,000	0	8,244	750,000
SUBTOTAL	28,305						
6 53	5,661	6,815	25,565	750,000	0	8,479	750,000
7 54	5,661	12,444	31,194	750,000	0	8,180	750,000
8 55	5,661	18,596	37,306	750,000	0	7,224	750,000
9 56	5,661	25,943	43,943	750,000	0	5,478	750,000
10 57	5,661	33,150	51,150	750,000	0	2,879	750,000
SUBTOTAL	56,610						
11 58	5,661	43,627	58,627	750,000			
12 59	5,661	53,742	66,692	750,000			
13 60	5,661	64,199	74,699	750,000			
14 61	5,661	75,035	83,285	750,000			
15 62	5,661	85,625	92,375	750,000			
SUBTOTAL	84,915						
16 63	5,661	97,439	101,939	750,000			
17 64	5,661	109,026	112,026	750,000			
18 65	5,661	120,525	122,775	750,000			
19 66	5,661	133,423	134,173	750,000			
20 67	5,661	146,289	146,289	750,000			
SUBTOTAL	113,220						

30 THIS ILLUSTRATION ASSUMES THAT THE DEFINITIONAL REQUIREMENTS FOR A LIFE INSURANCE CONTRACT UNDER I.R.C. SECTION 7702 HAVE BEEN SATISFIED BY COMPLYING WITH THE CASH VALUE ACCUMULATION TEST.

THIS IS AN ILLUSTRATION NOT A CONTRACT. PRESENTED BY ANTHONY STEUER   ON JANUARY 17, 1991. CA.   VERSION 9.00 PAGE 1 OF 5

6 - B

.. LIFE INSURANCE COMPANY
(R)

CLIENT: .
'ALE AGE: 47 NON-SMOKER

INITIAL FACE AMOUNT: $750,000
1ST YR. ANN. PREM. $5,661
PAYABLE: ANNUALLY

CASH VALUE ACCUMULATION TEST @@ (KIND 1881)

END OF POLICY YR AGE	ANNUALIZED PREMIUM AND/OR WITHDRAWALS	ASSUMED INTEREST RATE (8.25%) CURRENT MONTHLY DEDUCTIONS **			GUARANTEED INTEREST RATE * GUARANTEED MONTHLY DEDUCTIONS		
		CASH VALUE	ACCUM VALUE	DEATH BENEFIT	CASH VALUE	ACCUM VALUE	DEATH BENEFIT
21 68	5,661	158,025	158,025	750,000			
22 69	5,661	171,772	171,772	750,000			
23 70	5,661	185,058	185,058	750,000			
24 71	5,661	198,963	198,963	750,000			
25 72	5,661	213,373	213,373	750,000			
SUBTOTAL	141,525						
26 73	5,661	228,243	228,243	750,000			
27 74	5,661	243,477	243,477	750,000			
28 75	5,661	259,111	259,111	750,000			
29 76	5,661	274,705	274,705	750,000			
30 77	5,661	290,262	290,242	750,000			
SUBTOTAL	169,830						
31 78	0	299,708	299,708	750,000			
32 79	0	308,346	308,346	750,000			
33 80	0	316,078	316,078	750,000			
34 81	0	322,867	322,867	750,000			
35 82	0	328,548	328,548	750,000			
SUBTOTAL	169,830						
36 83	0	333,034	333,034	750,000			
37 84	0	336,157	336,157	750,000			
38 85	0	337,607	337,607	750,000			
39 86	0	337,112	337,112	750,000			
40 87	0	334,227	334,227	750,000			
SUBTOTAL	169,830						

@@ THIS ILLUSTRATION ASSUMES THAT THE DEFINITIONAL REQUIREMENTS FOR A LIFE INSURANCE CONTRACT UNDER I.R.C. SECTION 7702 HAVE BEEN SATISFIED BY COMPLYING WITH THE CASH VALUE ACCUMULATION TEST.

THIS IS AN ILLUSTRATION NOT A CONTRACT. PRESENTED BY ANTHONY STEUER   ON JANUARY 17, 1991. CA.   VERSION 9.00 PAGE 2 OF 5

6-K

CLIENT:
MALE AGE: 47 NON-SMOKER

LIFE INSURANCE COMPANY
(SM)

INITIAL FACE AMOUNT: $750,000
1ST YR. ANN. PREM. $5,667
PAYABLE: ANNUALLY

CASH VALUE ACCUMULATION TEST @@ (KIND 1881)

END OF POLICY YR AGE	ANNUALIZED PREMIUM AND/OR WITHDRAWALS	ASSUMED INTEREST RATE (8.25%) CURRENT MONTHLY DEDUCTIONS **			GUARANTEED INTEREST RATE * GUARANTEED MONTHLY DEDUCTIONS		
		CASH VALUE	ACCUM VALUE	DEATH BENEFIT	CASH VALUE	ACCUM VALUE	DEATH BENEFIT
41 88	0	328,354	328,354	750,000			
42 89	0	318,794	318,794	750,000			
43 90	0	306,662	306,662	750,000			
44 91	0	284,658	284,658	750,000			
45 92	0	257,153	257,153	750,000			
SUBTOTAL	169,830						
46 93	0	219,520	219,520	750,000			
47 94	0	169,008	169,008	750,000			
48 95	0	101,794	101,794	750,000			
SUBTOTAL	169,830						

@@ THIS ILLUSTRATION ASSUMES THAT THE DEFINITIONAL REQUIREMENTS FOR A LIFE INSURANCE CONTRACT UNDER I.R.C. SECTION 7702 HAVE BEEN SATISFIED BY COMPLYING WITH THE CASH VALUE ACCUMULATION TEST.

THIS IS AN ILLUSTRATION NOT A CONTRACT. PRESENTED BY ANTHONY STEUER   ON JANUARY 17, 1991. CA.   VERSION 9.00 PAGE 3 OF 5

CLIENT:
MALE AGE: 47 NON-SMOKER

... LIFE INSURANCE COMPANY
(SM)

INITIAL FACE AMOUNT: $750,000
1ST YR. ANN. PREM. $5,661
PAYABLE: ANNUALLY

THE FOLLOWING EXPLANATORY NOTES APPLY TO THIS LIFE INSURANCE ILLUSTRATION

THIS ILLUSTRATION ASSUMES THAT THE ASSUMED INTEREST RATE (AS SHOWN) IS CREDITED AND CURRENT MONTHLY DEDUCTIONS ARE WITHDRAWN FOR THE LIFE OF THE POLICY. CHANGES OF THE CURRENT INTEREST RATE OR MONTHLY DEDUCTIONS MAY REQUIRE ADDITIONAL PREMIUM PAYMENTS TO KEEP THE POLICY IN FORCE.

THE CURRENT INTEREST RATE IS 8.250%. IT IS NOT GUARANTEED.
THE COMPANY MAY DECLARE A HIGHER OR LOWER CURRENT INTEREST RATE BUT IT WILL NEVER BE LESS THAN THE GUARANTEED RATE.
* THE CUMULATIVE GUARANTEED INTEREST RATE IS 5.50%, DETERMINED ON POLICY ANNIVERSARIES. THE ACCUMULATION VALUE WILL NOT BE LOWER THAN THE VALUE THAT WOULD HAVE ACCRUED IF THE INTEREST RATE HAD ALWAYS BEEN 5.50%.
** CURRENT MORTALITY DEDUCTIONS ARE NOT GUARANTEED AFTER THE FIRST YEAR.

IN ADDITION TO THE DEATH BENEFIT ILLUSTRATED THE COMPANY WILL PAY THE BENEFICIARY AT THE DEATH OF THE INSURED THAT AMOUNT BY WHICH THE ACCUMULATION VALUE INCREASED SINCE THE LAST POLICY ANNIVERSARY. THIS CONTRACTUAL PROVISION APPLIES REGARDLESS OF INTEREST RATE. THE DEATH BENEFIT WILL BE REDUCED BY THE AMOUNT OF ANY LOAN.

ANNUALIZED PREMIUMS ARE THE SUM OF THE PERIODIC PAYMENTS YOU PLAN TO MAKE EACH YEAR.

WITHDRAWALS (-) ARE THE AMOUNTS TAKEN FROM THE POLICY'S CASH VALUE AND PAYABLE TO YOU. APPLICABLE SURRENDER CHARGES HAVE BEEN DEDUCTED FROM THE POLICY'S VALUES. CERTAIN TYPES OF WITHDRAWALS MAY BE SUBJECT TO TAX. YOU SHOULD CONSULT YOUR TAX ADVISOR AS TO THE TAXABILITY OF ANY PLANNED WITHDRAWAL. A PENALTY FREE WITHDRAWAL CAN BE REQUESTED IN POLICY YEARS TWO AND AFTER FOR AN AMOUNT NOT TO EXCEED 10% OF THE CURRENT ACCUMULATION VALUE OR 100% OF THE CASH VALUE, WHICHEVER IS LESS. WITHDRAWALS IN EXCESS OF THE PENALTY FREE WITHDRAWAL WILL BE CHARGED APPLICABLE SURRENDER CHARGES.

THE ACCUMULATION VALUE IS THE POLICY VALUE BEFORE THE APPLICATION OF SURRENDER CHARGES. THE CASH VALUE IS THE ACCUMULATION VALUE LESS ANY APPLICABLE SURRENDER CHARGES, AND IS THE AMOUNT ACTUALLY AVAILABLE TO YOU UPON SURRENDER (LESS ANY OUTSTANDING POLICY LOANS).
UNDER THE TECHNICAL AND MISCELLANEOUS REVENUE ACT OF 1988 (TAMRA), A LIFE INSURANCE CONTRACT BECOMES A MODIFIED ENDOWMENT CONTRACT (MEC) WHEN ACTUAL PREMIUMS PAID EXCEED A SPECIFIED 7-PAY PREMIUM LIMIT OR WHEN CERTAIN CHANGES ARE MADE TO POLICY BENEFITS. IT IS OUR UNDERSTANDING THAT THE 7-PAY LIMIT FOR EACH OF THE FIRST SEVEN YEARS OF THIS ILLUSTRATION IS $54,443. AMOUNTS RECEIVED FROM A MEC PRIOR TO THE DEATH OF THE INSURED MAY BE FULLY TAXABLE AND, BEFORE THE OWNER IS AGE 59-1/2, SUBJECT TO A 10% PENALTY TAX. NOTE THAT ALL MEC'S ISSUED BY THE TRANSAMERICA LIFE COMPANIES TO THE SAME OWNER DURING ANY 12-MONTH PERIOD SHALL BE TREATED AS ONE MEC. FOR ADDITIONAL INFORMATION, CONSULT YOUR TAX ADVISOR.

THE BASIC UNDERWRITING REQUIREMENTS ARE: PARAMEDICAL, HOS, BLOOD PROFILE, ECG, INSPECTION REPORT

ESA 002833   TARGET = 8302.50
THIS IS AN ILLUSTRATION NOT A CONTRACT. PRESENTED BY ANTHONY STEUER ON JANUARY 17, 1991. CA. VERSION 9.00 PAGE 4 of 5

6-1E

TOTAL P.06

CLIENT:
MALE AGE: 47 NON-SMOKER

THE INSURANCE COMPANY
(SH)

INITIAL FACE AMOUNT: $750,000
1ST YR. ANN. PREM. $5,661
PAYABLE: ANNUALLY

COST INDEXES

PERIOD OF YEARS	AT THE ASSUMED ILLUSTRATIVE RATE		AT THE MINIMUM GUARANTEED INTEREST RATE	
	SURRENDER*	PAYMENT*	SURRENDER*	PAYMENT*
10	6.20	7.55	7.55	7.55
20	1.03	7.55	##	##

* THE SURRENDER AND PAYMENT COST INDEX FACTORS ARE FOR $1000 EQUIVALENT LEVEL DEATH BENEFIT ON THE INDICATED PREMIUM PAYMENT BASIS FOR THE PERIOD OF TIME SHOWN. ALL OTHER THINGS BEING EQUAL, A LOWER INDEX INDICATES A LOWER COST POLICY.

NO COST INDEX IS SHOWN BECAUSE THE PLANNED PREMIUM PAYING PERIOD IS LESS THAN 20 YEARS.
MORE INFORMATION ABOUT CONSUMER COST INDICES CAN BE FOUND IN THE LIFE INSURANCE BUYER'S GUIDE PROVIDED TO YOU BY YOUR AGENT.

THIS IS AN ILLUSTRATION NOT A CONTRACT. PRESENTED BY ANTHONY STEUER ON JANUARY 17, 1991. CA. VERSION 9.00 PAGE 5 of 5

In-Force Illustration—Current Assumptions

This excerpt from an in-force illustration shows the current premium and current assumptions—the policy will lapse without value at the insured's age 81. At the bottom of the first page in the circled section, we can see where the policy's cash value annual increase starts to slow down and then starts decreasing rapidly.

(E-A1)

CA   CO. 01   JC-00000   KIND 21881   JANUARY 7, 1999

ISSUED APRIL 16, 1992

POLICY NO

NTTIW FACE AMOUNT- $755,000
URRENT ACCUM VALUE BALANCE: $32,449.42
AACCUM VALUE BALANCE PROJECTION TO:
PRIL 16, 1999 $32,044.58
URRENT WEIGHTED INTEREST RATE, 05.68%
ASH VALUE ACCUMULATION TEST 98.01881

MALE   ISSUE AGE 47
NON SMOKER
PREMIUMS PAYABLE, ANNUALLY
TABLE RATING NONE

PREMIUMS PAID TO DATE: 45,280.00

* * * * * * * * * END OF YEAR POLICY VALUES * * * * * * *

		ANNUALIZED	PROJECTED VALUES AT GUARANTEED INTEREST RATE AND GUARANTEED MONTHLY DEDUCTIONS			NON-GUARANTEED PROJECTED VALUES AT ILLUSTRATED INTEREST RATES AND MONTHLY DEDUCTIONS		
POLICY YEAR NO & AGE	NON-GUAR. INTEREST RATE	PREMIUM OUTLAY AND/OR WITHDRAWALS	CASH VALUE	ACCUM VALUE	DEATH BENEFIT	CASH VALUE	ACCUM VALUE	DEATH BENEFIT
9	56	05.50	5,661	13,452	31,452	750,000	18,987	36,987	750,000
2	57	05.50	5,661	12,148	30,148	750,000	24,219	42,219	750,000
1	58	05.50	5,661	12,974	27,974	750,000	32,366	47,366	750,000
2	59	05.50	5,661	12,142	24,892	750,000	39,781	52,531	750,000
3	60	05.50	5,661	10,258	20,758	750,000	47,118	57,818	750,000
1	61	05.50	5,661	7,166	15,416	750,000	54,385	62,635	750,000
2	62	05.50	5,661	1,945	8,695	750,000	62,938	67,688	750,000
5	63	05.50	5,661	0	609	750,000	65,121	72,631	750,000
7	64	05.50	5,661	0	0	0	74,533	27,533	750,000
3	65	05.50	5,661	0	0	0	80,707	82,457	750,000
9	86	05.50	5,661	0	0	0	86,577	87,327	750,000
3	67	05.50	5,661	0	0	0	92,439	92,380	750,000
1	68	05.50	5,661	0	0	0	96,442	96,442	750,000
2	69	05.50	5,661	0	0	0	100,170	100,120	750,000
3	70	05.50	5,661	0	0	0	102,970	102,970	750,000
1	71	05.50	5,661	0	0	0	105,212	105,212	750,000
5	72	05.50	5,661	0	0	0	106,544	106,544	750,000
3	73	05.50	5,661	0	0	0	106,731	106,731	750,000
7	74	05.50	5,661	0	0	0	105,422	105,422	750,000
3	75	05.50	5,661	0	0	0	102,367	102,367	750,000

4,870
3,678 inc
2,850 inc
2,242 inc
1,332 inc
187 inc
1,308 Decrease
3,055 Decrease

ACCUM VALUE PROJECTED TO 04/16/99 ASSUMES THAT POLICYOWNER WILL PAY PREMIUMS TOTALING   IN ADDITION TO PREMIUMS PAID TO
IF SHOWN ABOVE RIGHT CORNER. THIS PROJECTED VALUE IS BASED ON THE CURRENT WEIGHTED INTEREST RATE AS DESCRIBED IN EXPLANATORY NOTES

YOU'VE MADE A RECENT PAYMENT. IT MAY NOT BE REFLECTED ON THIS ILLUSTRATION.

LEASE REFER TO THE ATTACHED EXPLANATORY NOTES.

HIS IS AN ILLUSTRATION, NOT A CONTRACT.

THE COMPANIES
NOT COMPLETE WITHOUT ALL PAGES PAGE 1 OF 3

E-A-8

CO. 01   10-80000   KING DHARL   JANUARY 7, 1999

POLICY NO.

ISSUED APRIL 16, 1991

MALE   ISSUE AGE 47
NON-SMOKER
PREMIUMS PAYABLE: ANNUALLY
TABLE RATING: NONE

INITIAL FACE AMOUNT: $750,000
CURRENT ACCUM VALUE BALANCE $32,144.42
ACCOUN VALUE BALANCE PROJECTED TO:
APRIL 16, 1999 $32,044.98
CURRENT WEIGHED INTEREST RATE: 05.68%
CASH VALUE ACCUMULATION TEST NO 0188%

PREMIUMS PAID TO DATE: 45,289.00

* * * * * * * * * END OF YEAR POLICY VALUES * * * * * * * *

POLICY YEAR END & AGE	NON-GUAR. INTEREST RATE	ANNUALIZED PREMIUM OUTLAY AND/OR WITHDRAWALS	PROJECTED VALUES AT GUARANTEED INTEREST RATE AND GUARANTEED MONTHLY DEDUCTIONS			NON-GUARANTEED PROJECTED VALUES AT ILLUSTRATED INTEREST RATES AND MONTHLY DEDUCTIONS		
			CASH VALUE	ACCUM. VALUE	DEATH BENEFIT	CASH VALUE	ACCUM VALUE	DEATH BENEFIT
9	56	05.50	5.661	13,462	31,462	750,000	18,98/	36,907	750,000
10	57	05.50	5,661	12,148	30,148	750,000	24,219	42,219	750,000
11	58	05.50	5,661	12,074	27,974	750,000	32,366	47,366	750,000
12	59	05.50	5,661	12,142	24,892	750,000	39,781	52,531	750,000
13	60	05.50	5,661	10,258	20,758	750,000	47,118	57,618	750,000
14	61	05.50	5,661	7,166	15,616	750,000	54,385	62,635	750,000
15	62	05.50	5,661	1,945	8,695	750,000	60,920	67,668	750,000
16	63	05.50	5.661	0	409	750,000	68,131	72,631	750,000
17	64	05.50	5.661	0	0	0	74,533	77,533	750,000
18	65	05.50	5.661	0	0	0	80,207	82,457	750,000
19	66	05.50	5,661	0	0	0	86,577	87,327	750,000
20	67	05.50	5.661	0	0	0	92,139	92,139	750,000
21	68	05.50	5,661	0	0	0	96,442	96,442	750,000
22	69	05.50	5,661	0	0	0	100,120	100,120	750,000
23	70	05.50	5,661	0	0	0	102,970	102,970	750,000
24	71	05.50	5.661	0	0	0	105,212	105,212	750,000
25	72	05.50	5.661	0	0	0	106,544	106,544	750,000
26	73	05.50	5.661	0	0	0	106,731	106,731	750,000
27	74	05.50	5.661	0	0	0	105,422	105,422	750,000
28	75	05.50	5.661	0	0	0	102,367	102,367	750,000

1: ACCUM VALUE PROJECTED TO 04/16/99 ASSUMES THAT POLICYOWNER WILL PAY PREMIUMS TOTALING $0 IN ADDITION TO PREMIUMS PAID TO
DATE SHOWN ABOVE RIGHT CORNER. THIS PROJECTED VALUE IS BASED ON THE CURRENT WEIGHTED INTEREST RATE AS DESCRIBED IN EXPLANATORY NOTES.

IF YOU'VE MADE A RECENT PAYMENT, IT MAY NOT BE REFLECTED ON THIS ILLUSTRATION.

PLEASE REFER TO THE ATTACHED EXPLANATORY NOTES.

LIFE INSURANCE COMPANY
- LIFE COMPANIES
NOT COMPLETE WITHOUT ALL PAGES PAGE 1 OF 3

THIS IS AN ILLUSTRATION, NOT A CONTRACT.

E-A-3

`·CA`   `CO. OC`   `ID-00000    KIND 61881        JANUARY 7. 1999`

                                              (SM)   POLICY NO
                                     ISSUED APRIL 16. 1991

TTAL FACE AMOUNT: $750,000   MALE   ISSUE AGE 47
RRENT ACCUM VALUE BALANCE: $32,449.42   NON-SMOKER
ACCUM VALUE BALANCE PROJECTED TO: PREMIUMS PAYABLE: ANNUALLY
RIL 16. 1999 $32,044.98   TABLE RATING: NONE
RRENT WEIGHTED INTEREST RATE: 06.68%
SH VALUE ACCUMULATION TEST @@ 0.881   PREMIUMS PAID TO DATE: 45,298.80

```
* * * * * * * * *END OF YEAR POLICY VALUES* * * * * * * * *
```

		ANNUAL 1790	PROJECTED VALUES AT GUARANTEED INTEREST RATE AND GUARANTEED MONTHLY DEDUCTIONS			NON-GUARANTEED PROJECTED VALUES AT ILLUSTRATED INTEREST RATES AND MONTHLY DEDUCTIONS		
POLICY YEAR ID & AGE	NON-GUAR. INTEREST RATE	PREMIUM OUTLAY AND/OR WITHDRAWALS	CASH VALUE	ACCUM VALUE	DEATH BENEFIT	CASH VALUE	ACCUM VALUE	DEATH BENEFIT
76	05.53	5.661	0	0	0	96,671	96,671	750,000
77	06.53	5.661	0	0	0	87,899	87,899	750,000
78	05.50	5.661	0	0	0	75,548	75,548	750,000
79	05.50	5.661	0	0	0	58,928	58,928	750,000
80	05.50	5.661	0	0	0	37,409	37,409	750,000
81	05.50	5.661	0	0	0	20,315	20,315	750,000

ACCUM VALUE PROJECTED TO 04/16/99 ASSUMES THAT POLICYOWNER WILL PAY PREMIUMS TOTALING   10 IN ADDITION TO PREMIUMS PAID TO
JE SHOWN ABOVE RIGHT CORNER. THIS PROJECTED VALUE IS BASED ON THE CURRENT WEIGHTED INTEREST RATE AS DESCRIBED IN EXPLANATORY NOTES

YOU'VE MADE A RECENT PAYMENT. IT MAY NOT BE REFLECTED ON THIS ILLUSTRATION.

EASE REFER TO THE ATTACHED EXPLANATORY NOTES.

                                                      .. LIFE INSURANCE COMPANY
                                                         LIFE DYNAMICS
IS IS AN ILLUSTRATION. NOT A CONTRACT.   NOT COMPLETE WITHIN ALL PAGES PAGE 2 OF 3

In-Force Illustration—Assumptions to Endow Policy

This in-force illustration shows that to continue the policy and have it endow (cash value equal the death benefit at age 100), would now require an annual premium of $10,711 based on the interest rate and mortality charges at the time this illustration was run.

POLICY YEAR ID & AGE	NON-GUAR. INTEREST RATE	ANNUALIZED PREMIUM OUTLAY AND/OR WITHDRAWALS	CASH VALUE	ACCUM VALUE	DEATH BENEFIT	CASH VALUE	ACCUM VALUE	DEATH BENEFIT
56	05.50	10,711	18,605	36,675	750,000	34,208	42,258	750,000
57	05.50	10,711	22,707	41,707	750,000	34,967	52,567	750,000
58	05.50	10,711	29,237	44,237	750,000	48,973	63,573	750,000
59	05.50	10,711	34,426	47,176	750,000	62,600	75,350	750,000
60	05.50	10,711	38,935	49,035	750,000	76,532	87,032	750,000
61	05.50	10,711	42,586	50,836	750,000	90,808	99,058	750,000
62	05.50	10,711	44,561	51,311	750,000	104,791	111,541	750,000
63	05.50	10,711	46,204	50,704	750,000	117,935	124,435	750,000
64	05.50	10,711	46,510	49,510	750,000	134,785	141,785	750,000
65	05.50	10,711	44,515	46,765	750,000	149,450	151,703	750,000
66	05.50	10,711	41,405	42,155	750,000	165,432	166,182	750,000
67	05.50	10,711	35,338	35,338	750,000	181,245	181,245	750,000
68	05.50	10,711	26,111	26,111	750,000	196,667	196,667	750,000
69	05.50	10,711	14,041	14,041	750,000	212,119	212,119	750,000
70	05.50	10,711	0	0	0	227,815	227,815	750,000
71	05.50	10,711	0	0	0	243,934	243,934	750,000
72	05.50	10,711	0	0	0	260,334	260,334	750,000
73	05.50	10,711	0	0	0	276,954	276,954	750,000
74	05.50	10,711	0	0	0	293,676	293,676	750,000
75	05.50	10,711	0	0	0	310,476	310,476	750,000

ACCUM VALUE PROJECTED TO 04/16/99 ASSUMES THAT POLICYOWNER WILL PAY PREMIUMS TOTALING   SO IN ADDITION TO PREMIUMS PAID TO THE SHOWN ABOVE RIGHT CORNER. THIS PROJECTED VALUE IS BASED ON THE CURRENT WEIGHTED INTEREST RATE AS DESCRIBED IN EXPLANATORY NOTES.

YOU'VE MADE A RECENT PAYMENT. IT MAY NOT BE REFLECTED ON THIS ILLUSTRATION.

PLEASE REFER TO THE ATTACHED EXPLANATORY NOTES.

                                    LIFE INSURANCE COMPANY
                                    LIFE COMPANIES
IS IS AN ILLUSTRATION, NOT A CONTRACT.   NOT COMPLETE WITHOUT ALL PAGES. PAGE 1 OF 4

E-B-2

.. CA   CO. 01   TO-53000   KIND 01081   JANUARY 7, 1999

                                                              POLICY NO.
                          ISSUED APRIL 16, 1991

INITIAL FACE AMOUNT: $750,000   MALE   ISSUE AGE 47
CURRENT ACCUM VALUE BALANCE: $32,419.42   NON-SMOKER
ACCUM VALUE BALANCE PROJECTED TO: PREMIUMS PAYABLE: ANNUALLY
APRIL 16, 1999 $32,044.90   TABLE RATING: NONE
CURRENT WEIGHTED INTEREST RATE: 05.59%
CASH VALUE ACCUMULATION TEST @@ 01081   PREMIUMS PAID TO DATE: 45,286.00

* * * * * * * * * *END OF YEAR POLICY VALUES* * * * * * * * *

| | | ANNUALIZED | PROJECTED VALUES AT GUARANTEED INTEREST RATE AND GUARANTEED MONTHLY DEDUCTIONS | | | NON-GUARANTEED PROJECTED VALUES AT ILLUSTRATED INTEREST RATES AND MONTHLY DEDUCTIONS | | |
POLICY YEAR END & AGE	NON-GUAR. INTEREST RATE	PREMIUM OUTLAY AND/OR WITHDRAWALS	CASH VALUE	ACCUM VALUE	DEATH BENEFIT	CASH VALUE	ACCUM VALUE	DEATH BENEFIT
9	76	05.59	10,711	0	0	0	326,951	326,951	750,000
10	77	05.59	10,711	0	0	0	343,077	343,077	750,000
11	78	05.59	10,711	0	0	0	358,841	358,841	750,000
12	79	05.59	10,711	0	0	0	374,187	374,187	750,000
13	80	05.59	10,711	0	0	0	389,170	389,170	750,000
4	81	05.59	10,711	0	0	0	403,898	403,898	750,000
5	82	05.59	10,711	0	0	0	418,395	418,395	750,000
6	83	05.59	10,711	0	0	0	432,785	432,785	750,000
7	84	05.59	10,711	0	0	0	447,157	447,157	750,000
8	85	05.59	10,711	0	0	0	461,536	461,536	750,000
9	86	05.59	10,711	0	5	0	476,046	476,046	750,000
9	87	05.59	10,711	0	0	0	490,756	490,756	750,000
1	88	05.59	10,711	0	5	0	505,732	505,732	750,000
2	89	05.59	10,711	0	0	0	521,112	521,112	750,000
3	90	05.59	10,711	0	0	0	537,001	537,001	750,000
4	91	05.59	10,711	0	0	0	553,793	553,793	750,000
5	92	05.59	10,711	0	0	0	571,511	571,511	750,000
6	93	05.59	10,711	0	0	0	590,407	590,407	750,000
7	94	05.59	10,711	0	0	0	611,078	611,078	750,000
8	95	05.59	10,711	0	0	0	634,264	634,264	750,000

1 ACCUM VALUE PROJECTED TO 04/16/99 ASSUMES THAT POLICYOWNER WILL PAY PREMIUMS TOTALING $0 IN ADDITION TO PREMIUMS PAID TO DATE SHOWN ABOVE RIGHT CORNER. THIS PROJECTED VALUE IS BASED ON THE CURRENT WEIGHTED INTEREST RATE AS DESCRIBED IN EXPLANATORY NOTES.

IF YOU'VE MADE A RECENT PAYMENT, IT MAY NOT BE REFLECTED ON THIS ILLUSTRATION.

PLEASE REFER TO THE ATTACHED EXPLANATORY NOTES.

                                                    LIFE INSURANCE COMPANY
                                                    LIFE COMPANIES
THIS IS AN ILLUSTRATION, NOT A CONTRACT.   NOT COMPLETE WITHOUT ALL PAGES PAGE 2 OF 4

E-B-3

The policy's performance was affected not only by the decreased interest rate but also by an increase in the mortality costs. The increase in the mortality costs was not shown anywhere in the in-force illustration. If you see a dramatic difference in the potential performance of your policy as shown here with the close to doubling of the premium, there may be more than meets the eye. Your agent may not always know as well as the front line customer service representative not knowing. So either press your agent or someone at the company. For me, it took using a software package designed for this purpose and ultimately a letter by an attorney involved with the case to a Vice-President of the company to confirm that they had raised the mortality costs. This is not always an easy matter when there is a large discrepancy. If you're hitting a brick wall with your agent and/or the insurance company, use one of the resources discussed through this book such as a life insurance analyst/consultant or the Department of Insurance (in your State).

QUESTION 91: Are There Other Issues If I Purchased A Limited Premium Payment Policy?

Limited Premium Payment Period policies almost always have not lived up to their promises. These were referred to, at one time, as Vanishing Premium Policies (this term is now not allowed by the insurance code, due to its misleading nature. At one point, agents and carriers could formulate an illustration (within some parameters) to make a policy attractive to a potential policy owner. Especially (in most cases) for these policies, an in-force illustration will show a much longer anticipated premium payment period.

These policies were sold under the concept of a vanishing premium, using illustrations and based on current assumptions at the time. When this was popular, the illustrated interest rates or dividend scales (perhaps coupled with a surrender of dividend additions) showed that the premium would "vanish" after a certain number of years. In other words, no further premiums would be due. At that time, there was no emphasis on guaranteed assumptions by either the carrier or the agent. In fact, the agent could generate an illustration using their own format that did not show the guarantees.

A distinction to be made is that this misleading term of "Vanishing Premium" is actually a non-guaranteed projection of a limited premium payment period. One of the problems with the term vanishing premium is the ease of confusing it with paid-up life insurance, a similar concept but featuring a guaranty. Once a policy is paid up, continuation of coverage is guaranteed regardless of future dividends. The truth is that a limited premium payment design can be useful, as long as it is understood that premium payments may be due for a longer period or may need to start again at some point, if this is indicated. A good of number of companies and agents have not taken any action to warn their clients. Again, this is where an in-force illustration is extremely useful.

Another sign of these policies is that they will almost always have a significant amount of term insurance mixed into them, and the non-guaranteed returns from the policy are required to replace the term portions of the policy with permanent insurance. When this does not happen because of declining interest rates and perhaps other unmet projections, three related developments threaten the future of the policy. Reduced non-guaranteed returns leave fewer investment dollars inside the policy to generate additional dividends and cash value growth. With poorer investment results and lower dividends, additional permanent insurance, which must be acquired with these dividends, is not purchased at a fast enough rate to replace the term insurance on the planned schedule. In turn, the continuing presence of too much term insurance, as the insured ages, increases the policy's mortality charges and leaves less money left over to accumulate as the cash value reserve inside the policy. As that reserve fails to build fast enough because of reduced investment returns and is, at the same time, depleted with higher than projected insurance costs, there is a good chance that the policy will fall apart before the insured dies.

Some policies, from what are generally regarded as reputable companies, have gone so far as to offer step-rated or "graded" premiums, which depend on dividends to avoid an additional out-of-pocket cost to the policyholder when the future premium increase occurs. In some cases, the premiums do not increase for the first ten years. However, when interest or dividend rates fall or insurance costs go up, dividends will be insufficient to pay the increased premium, and the risk of policy lapse is especially high. This is just an example of the lengths to which life insurers will go to try to appear competitive price-wise.

The danger with a good number of these policies is that they can terminate very quickly. The other type of policy that can be worse is a "lowball" premium policy. These policies have premiums that are too low to support the policy if there are any changes from the current assumptions at time of purchase. The chance of this occurring is less than winning the lottery.

If you are considering a policy with a limited premium payment period, you should request an illustration with a dividend scale reduced by 200 basis points or an interest rate 2% below the current projected rate respectively. Considering the last few years, this still may not be sufficient. Keep in mind that you can continue to pay the premium or increase it to meet the originally planned payment period, if you would like to.

QUESTION 92: How Do I Measure a Life Insurance Policy's Internal Performance As Well As Compare it with another Policy?

There are many ways to compare life insurance policies and also measuring their internal performance. We will take a look at a few of the various methods. Each has its pros and cons; also, some are easier to use than others. It can be difficult to compare similar types of policies, let alone different types of policies.

There are many different methods of determining the performance of a policy and to use these methods in a replacement situation. Please note that these are applicable to permanent (cash value) life insurance policies only and not to term life insurance.

For the most part, comparing term insurance is comparing premiums. Another consideration, with term life insurance, is the conversion factor (are the policies that you can convert to limited or can you convert to any of the company's permanent policies?). *(Ben Baldwin—Life Insurance Investment Advisor, Probus Publishing Company, c 1988)*

INTEREST ADJUSTED INDICES—

These indices were adopted by the National Association of Insurance Commissioners (NAIC), in 1976, as a life insurance solicitation model regulation, they were then recommended to each state for their adoption. This regulation has been adopted in almost every state. This regulation requires that insurers provide buyers with an interest-adjusted surrender cost index and an interest-adjusted net payment cost index for the 10th and 20th policy years, using a 5% interest assumption.

Keep in mind that this is automatically calculated on a proposal for a new policy. However, if you wish to calculate it yourself for any reason or understand the numbers better than shown on the initial illustration. The inputs required for the interest-adjusted methods are:

1. The annual level premiums accumulated at 5%.
2. The face amount
3. The time period over which the analysis is to be made (the model regulation requires it for 10 and 20 years.
4. The interest rate. The NAIC chose 5% net after-tax as an acceptable long-term interest rate, from personal investments of comparable security and stability as a life insurance policy.
5. Dividends are to be accumulated at 5% interest, if dividends are available in the contract.
6. The cash surrender value.

The NAIC require the use of two indices. The interest-adjusted net payment cost index assumes that the policy is continuing in-force, and therefore only the dividend values plus 5 percent interest earnings (if the policy in question pays dividends) are available to the policy owner to reduce cost. The cash surrender value is not available and, therefore not included in the interest-adjusted net payment cost index. The interest-adjusted surrender cost index assumes the policy is terminated; thus the cash value is available to reduce cost and is included in the calculation of the surrender cost index. *(Ben Baldwin—Life Insurance Investment Advisor, Probus Publishing Company, c 1988)*

INTEREST-ADJUSTED NET PAYMENT COST INDEX—

This index is based upon the continuation of the policy. Since the policy is continuing in-force, it assumes that the cash value of the policy is not available to the policy owner. Dividends and 5 percent interest on those dividends are assumed to be available to the policy owner in participating policies.

This index is calculated by accumulating the annual dividends, if available, plus the five percent interest earnings on those dividends for the period of time in question. In order to convert those dividend credits and their interest earnings to a level amount for the period of time in question, the amount is divided by the future value of $1 at 5 percent for the period. The payment of $1 per year, assuming a percent interest rate and a 20 year time period, results in a future value of $34.72 in 20 years. By dividing the insurance company provided future dividend income value by this 20 year divisor, you will find out what number of dollars would have had to have been deposited annually to arrive at this amount. The ten year divisor is $13.21; that is $1 per year, deposited at the beginning of the year into an account earning 5 percent, and would accumulate $13.21 in 10 years. If you do not have a calculator, use these factors to change the total value of the dividends, available at the end of the period of time, to the level annual equivalent credit that can be used to offset the adjusted premium.

The adjusted premium is the level annual premium accumulated at five percent. For example a $1,000 annual premium accumulated at 5 percent for 20 years would be $34,719.30. If the 20th year accumulation of dividends was $12,000, you would calculate the 5 percent interest adjusted dividend value by dividing the $12,000 by 20 years, ($600) then calculating the future value of that average annual dividend of $600 compounded at 5 percent for 20 years for 20 years and arrive at an adjusted dividend value of $20,831.60. The difference between the adjusted dividend premium ($34,719.30), and the interest adjusted dividend ($20,831.60), $13,887.70 is the interest adjusted cost for this $100,000 policy. To calculate what this $13,887.70 total cost is as an equivalent to a 20-year interest adjusted annual premium you can use your calculator or the 20 year factor of 34.72 described above. $13,887.70 divided by 34.72 is $400. Dividing this amount by 100 gives us the per $1,000 interest adjusted net payment cost index of $4.00. (Ben Baldwin— Life Insurance Investment Advisor, Probus Publishing Company, c 1988)

INTEREST-ADJUSTED SURRENDER COST INDEX

The interest-adjusted surrender cost index assumes that the cash surrender value of the policy, and any termination dividend available at the termination of a policy, will be available, as well as the dividends and their interest earnings.

If, in the example above, the total cash available upon surrender amounted to $10,000 you would then subtract the $10,000, from the $13,887.70 insurance cost determined without considering the cash surrender value, and arrive at $3,887.70 for the $100,000 policy. Dividing that amount by the 20-year 5-percent factor of 34.72 results in the amount of $112. Dividing this amount by 100 gives you the per $1,000 interest adjusted surrender cost index of $1.12. This can then be used to compare this policy to others of comparable size and type.

According to the Report of the Joint Special Committee on Life Insurance Costs, (Footnote—*Report to American Life Convention, Institute of Life Insurance and Life Insurance Association of America (New York: Institute of Life Insurance, May 4, 1970), page 6)* the advantages of these two interest adjusted methods are as follows:

1) They take the time value of money into account.
2) They are easy to understand.
3) They do not require recourse to advanced mathematics.
4) They do not suggest a degree of accuracy that is beyond that justified by the circumstances.
5) They are significantly similar to the traditional methods, so that transition could be accomplished with a minimum of confusion.

Although these indices do take the time value of money into consideration, neither the public nor insurance agents have found them easy to understand or communicate. The public does regard these devices as having a degree of accuracy beyond that which is justified. This is due to the facts that are on each illustration and, as such, are given a high degree of credibility.

As with a lot of things in life, the lowest price may not always be the best. Life insurance companies can manipulate the internal design of their policies to wind up with a low index. The interest-adjusted indices then, although they do take the time value of money into consideration, fail because you cannot rely on assumed policy values 10 and 20 years hence. Strict reliance on the indices, and the potential misuses of indices, can mislead rather than help the consumer.

The ledger statements from which the indices are derived are becoming less and less accurate due to the degree of complexity and types of products, the volatility of the economy and the many changes in the life insurance industry. Due to these factors, the indices will become less and less useful as an appropriate tool for comparing life insurance products. *(Ben Baldwin—Life Insurance Investment Advisor, Probus Publishing Company, c 1988)*

LINTON YIELD METHOD

This is most likely the oldest method, named after Mr. Albert Linton (President of Provident Mutual, with a background as an actuary) who, in the 1930's, demonstrated that a whole life insurance policy or an endowment life insurance policy could be analyzed as equivalent to a combination of decreasing term insurance and a savings fund. Basically, it derives estimated investment returns on cash value policies and can be used to determine policy returns on a year by year basis; so-called one year ROR's (rates of return). There are many slight variations on this method. There are many variations of the Linton Yield to assist with different tasks.

This is the basic method and is the method used by *Mr. James Hunter at the Consumer Federation of America.* As he describes it the starting point is the next policy anniversary; the numbers come from a current illustration (either new for a proposed policy or an in-force illustration for an existing policy). Assume that a person surrenders their policy for the year end surrender value (not accumulation/cash value prior to the surrender charge), and then changes their mind and asks to reinstate immediately. The cost to reinstate is the surrender value plus the next annual premium. (Rider costs not providing insurance on the insured must be excluded.)

Here is how to calculate an annual Rate of Return (ROR). You may wish to do this for several future years to see any trends.

DBt = Death Benefit, policy year t. Use the average death benefit during the year, if changing.

Pt = Annual premium for year t; divide other premium frequencies by appropriate factors from VII above to convert non-annual premiums to annual premiums.

CSVt = Cash surrender value end of year t, including cash value of any paid-up additional insurance (PUA's). (If dividends are held at interest, exclude them from the calculation; but, in this case add the year-end dividend, but not interest, to CSVt. If the dividend option is cash or "reduce premium", do not use the prior year dividend; add the year-end dividend to CSVt.)

TCt = Term Cost for risk amount in year t.

TRt = assumed market term rate for alternative policy.

PFt = any annual term policy fee.

Basic Concept: $BVt * (1 + RORt/100) = EVt$. Solve for RORt.

> where, BVt = Beginning-of-year policy value = CSVt-1 (prior year surrender value) + Pt - TCt;
> EVt = End-of-year surrender value, including Dt for any dividend not used for PUA's.

$TCt = (DBt - BVt) * TRt + PFt$, or $TCt = (DBt - (CSVt-1 + Pt - TCt)) * TRt + PFt$

or $TCt = [(DBt - CSVt-1 - Pt) * PR + PF]/(1-TR)$, from 8th grade algebra.

Finally, $RORt = [(EVt / BVt) - 1] * 100$.

Example—Suppose you want the 11th policy year ROR for a policy whose 10th year surrender value is $8,938, whose 11th year surrender value is $10,538, and whose annual premium is $1,159. (Dividends buy PUA's.) The death benefit during the next year averages $107,600. The cost of one-year term insurance for this person in his or her risk class and age is $1.22 per $1,000 per year plus $50. (It is not appropriate, at least not without an "apples to apples" warning, to use 10-year or 20-year term rates because these policies may not be renewed without evidence of insurability.) We have:

TC11 = [(107,600 - 8,938 - 1,159) * 1.22/1,000 + 50] / (1 - .00122) = 169

RORt = [(10,538 / (8,938 + 1,159 - 169)) - 1] * 100   **RORt = 6.1%.**

This section taken from notes from a talk by Mr. James hunter, FSA on September 28, 2001

THE JOSEPH M. BELTH METHOD

Joseph M. Belth, Ph.D., Professor of Insurance at Indiana University is the publisher of *The Insurance Forum*. This publication is provocative and features his work on getting at the truth from life insurance companies. Part of that work is determining the true costs of life insurance policies.

The method he came up with is a level price approach, and is based on the premise that the protection, provided by an insurance policy was not the full face amount of the policy, but is the face amount of the policy minus its cash surrender value. As discussed previously this would be the amount at risk to the carrier; in other words the protection.

Professor Belth used the level cost method to attempt to measure the average cost to policy owners of this amount at risk. Professor Belth also developed a price per thousand dollars, for each age, for this net amount of protection. These were then converted, as yearly prices, into amounts that represented a level price per thousand, for each age, for this net amount of protection, provided by the policy for a particular time period. Professor Belth has referred to them as benchmark life insurance costs that represent a base value of the protection provided by a policy.

In June and October of 1982 issues of *The Insurance Forum*, Professor Belth published an updated method of determining costs and/or rates of return within life insurance policies that was more easily adapted by the individual in determining the cost efficiency of his individual policy.

His formula is as follows, with the following inputs:

1) Death benefit (F)
2) Policy cash surrender value as of the last previous anniversary date (CVP)
3) Policy cash surrender value as of the current anniversary date (CSV)
4) Most recent annual premium (P)
5) Most recent annual dividend or credited interest or a combination—whichever is applicable (D)
6) Insured's insurance age (six months and one day prior to next actual birthday)
7) Assumed alternative use of funds interest rate (i). This is the rate of interest that the policy owner (or whoever is doing the calculation) feels could be earned in an investment with liquidity equivalent to that within the life insurance policy.
8) Benchmark rates per $1,000 of life insurance (Net Amount at Risk)

The table used by Dr. Belth for the cost of term insurance for the policy owner is derived as he describes it in *The Insurance Forum"* of June 1982, *Volume 9, Number 6.* Due to the time elapsed since then, we are using more current figures.

The term costs that we will use are from *the 2003 edition of Tax Facts (published by the National Underwriter Company).* The table is for one year term rates, used in the calculation of the "cost" of pure life insurance protection, which may be taxable to an employee in certain situations.

What we are saying is that, if the price of your life insurance protection per $1,000 is in the vicinity of the 'raw material cost' (that is the amount needed just to pay death claims based on population rates), your life insurance protection is reasonably priced".

One Year Term Premiums for $1,000 of Life Insurance Protection- One Life					
Age	Premium	Age	Premium	Age	Premium
0	$0.70	34	$0.98	67	$15.20
1	0.41	35	0.99	68	16.92
2	0.27	36	1.01	69	18.70
3	0.19	37	1.04	70	20.62
4/5	0.13	38	1.06	71	22.72
6	0.14	39	1.07	72	25.07
7	0.15	40	1.10	73	27.57
8	0.16	41	1.13	74	30.18
9	0.16	42	1.20	75	33.05
10	0.16	43	1.29	76	36.33
11	0.19	44	1.40	77	40.17
12	0.24	45	1.53	78	44.33
13	0.28	46	1.67	79	49.23
14	0.33	47	1.83	80	54.56
15	0.38	48	1.98	81	60.51
16	0.52	49	2.13	82	66.74
17	0.57	50	2.30	83	73.07
18	0.59	51	2.52	84	80.35
19	0.61	52	2.81	85	88.76
20	0.62	53	3.20	86	99.16
21	0.62	54	3.65	87	110.40
22	0.64	55	4.15	88	121.85
23	0.66	56	4.68	89	133.40
24	0.68	57	5.20	90	144.30
25	0.71	58	5.66	91	155.80
26	0.73	59	6.06	92	168.75
27	0.76	60	6.51	93	186.44
28	0.80	61	7.11	94	206.70
29	0.83	62	7.96	95	228.35
30	0.87	63	9.08	96	250.01
31	0.90	64	10.41	97	265.09
32	0.93	65	11.90	98	270.11
33	0.96	66	13.51	99	281.06

Professor Belth's Formula:

$$\frac{(P + CVP)\,(1 + i) - (CSV + D)}{(F - CSV)\,(.001)}$$

P = Premium
CVP = Cash Value Previous Year
i = Alternate use of Funds Interest Rate (Net after Taxes)
CSV = Cash Surrender Value this year
D = Dividend or Interest Credited
F = Death Benefit

This method is suitable for comparing policies specifically for a replacement situation. *(Ben Baldwin—Life Insurance Investment Advisor, Probus Publishing Company, c 1988)*

THE BEN BALDWIN SYSTEM

This is an alternative system devised by Ben Baldwin: An Alternative Method-The Baldwin System for the financial analysis of life insurance on an individual basis. It seeks to cure the previously stated defects in all of the previously discussed systems.

According to Mr. Baldwin—in testing and evaluating this system on the financial evaluation of life insurance, a computer program was developed. This has been used to test the system with all types of life insurance: term, whole life, single premium life, universal life, variable life and universal variable life. The program gives simultaneous results of Professor Belth's system of evaluating the cost effectiveness of life insurance policies, the cash-on-cash rate of return and cash and life insurance value rate of return. The Baldwin System has proved to be valuable in making individual decisions regarding existing life insurance and potential purchases. Although it takes a bit of effort to understand, you should be able to understand the data that is used in coming up with the conclusions and then you are in a good position to evaluate the results.

The step-by-step procedure follows:

STEP 1

Determine how much life insurance is provided by the policy.

Total Death Benefit		_____
Less Total Current Asset Value	-	_____
Equals "Life Insurance"		_____

Total Death Benefit

Total death benefit is the face amount of the policy plus any policy provisions which increase the death benefit in the event of a natural death, i.e., term insurance riders or paid up additional life insurance as a result of dividends being left in your policy.

Total Current Asset Value

Total current asset value is what you would get for your policy if you went to the insurance company and cashed it in today. It includes the amount of any loans which you would not have to pay back as a result of cashing in the policy. The objective of this calculation is to determine how much of the total death benefit is your money and how much is life insurance company money, "life insurance."

STEP 2

Determine what you have paid to maintain the life insurance in force this year.

Premium	_____
Plus Net After-tax Loan Interest Cost	_____
Plus Net After-tax Cost of Cash Left in the Policy	_____
Equals Total Current Year's Cost	_____

Premium

The premium portion of what you have paid to maintain the life insurance is the billed gross premium for the policy or what you have chosen to pay if the policy is a universal life type of contract without a stated premium.

Loan Interest Costs

The net after-tax loan interest cost is calculated first by determining the gross loan interest paid for the year. For example, if the policy had an outstanding loan of $ 1,000 at a 5 percent interest rate, the gross loan interest would be $ 50. For tax year 1987, assuming this is considered consumer interest, this interest would be 65 percent deductible (40 percent in 1988, 20 percent in 1989, 10 percent in 1990 and zero percent deductible thereafter). Assuming this is a 1987 calculation, 65 percent of the $ 50 interest charge is deductible, or $ 32.50 ($ 50 x 65 percent = $ 32.50). We will assume that you are in the 28 percent federal tax bracket, and that the state income tax bracket adds percent to that, bringing your total marginal tax bracket to 30 percent. Thus, the $ 32.50 income tax deduction would reduce your tax liability by $ 9.75 tax reduction = $ 40.25).

Personal life insurance policy loans are becoming more expensive as a result of the provisions of the Tax Reform Act of 1986. Life insurance policy loans are more expensive for lower-bracket taxpayers than they are for high-bracket taxpayers.

There are further unseen costs for life insurance policy loans. In the last few years, most life insurance companies have offered enhancements to their participating whole life insurance policies. If the policy-owner accepts a higher interest charge on policy loans, he will be rewarded with high dividends. Conversely, if the policy-owner refuses the enhancement in order to maintain his low policy loan interest rate, he will receive lower dividends. See Chapter 10, Questions 106-109 for more information on policy loans.

This dividend credit differential between borrowers and non-borrows is effectively an increase in the cost of life insurance policy loans. The precise dividend differential and loan interest rate alternatives offered to an individual policy owner in an enhancement or upgrade offer, can be used to determine the impact on a specific policy.

The wisdom of leveraging life insurance-borrowing to pay premium, the so called "minimum deposit plans"-are questionable at best today. What loan interest has to be paid? What effect does it have on dividends? What are the loan proceeds to be used for? For example, if the money is to be used to finance investments, you would expect the interest expense to deductible up to an amount equal to the annual portfolio investment income. However, if it is used to make consumer purchases (such as an automobile) or to carry life insurance, it will be subject to the phase out of deductibility which will make it a less economical strategy. As stated in Forbes, June 29, 1987, "if you own a minimum deposit life insurance policy, condolences are in order"

Opportunity Costs

The net after-tax cost of cash left within an insurance policy may be considered an "opportunity" cost. If you are able to borrow on your life insurance policy at 5 percent and are able to invest that money at an amount more than 5 percent, it makes no sense to borrow on the policy and reinvest. If you choose not to do that, and leave the cash within your life insurance policy, you are sacrificing the opportunity.

That lost opportunity is a cost that could be added to your cost of holding a life insurance policy.

Economic conditions in 1987 have made it difficult to borrow from a policy, pay loan interest, and profitably reinvest the money to earn an easy profit. The increase costs for policy loan interest, and reduced dividends for policies that retained their low interest rate on policy loans, combined with the lower interest rates available on alternative safe investments, provided little opportunity for gain.

For example, we have just established that if you as an individual in the 30 percent combined marginal tax bracket borrowed from your policy at 5 percent, the net after tax deduction cost of the loan would be as follows:

Interest charge on $1,000 loan	$	50.00
Amount of loan interest deductible		65%
Deductible interest (65% x 50):	$	32.50
Amount of deduction in 30 percent tax bracket		
(30% x $ 32.50) equals:	$	9.75
Net cost of $ 50 interest charge ($ 50—$ 9.75)	$	40.25

If you were then to reinvest the $ 1,000 at 5.5 percent taxable outside of the policy, the following would be the result:

Interest earnings	$	55.00
Income tax on interest earnings (30 % x $ 55)	-	16.50
Net after tax gain	$	38.50

Net benefit realized by borrowing and reinvesting:

Cost	$	40.25
Benefit		38.25
Gain (Loss)		($1.75)

In addition to this loss, you may also have lost the opportunity to receive higher dividends.

The situation in the early 1980s was far different. You would have found that if you had $ 1,000 at a 5 percent interest cost, and pay a total of $ 50 in interest for the year, your net after-tax cost for that $ 50-a-year deductible loan interest was $ 25, assuming the 50 percent tax bracket. You could then have put those funds in a money market account, earn 10 percent on the $ 1,000, (gross interest return of $ 100 per year), pay 50 percent tax on those earnings, and net $ 50 per year. You could, therefore, earn a 100 percent profit on the net $ 25 after-tax cost of your policy loan. Had you not borrowed on his policy and left the $ 1,000 within the policy during that period of time, you would be sacrificing these earnings. This lost opportunity cost may be considered an additional cost for maintaining your life insurance policy.

STEP 3

What cash benefits did you receive as a result of maintaining the policy in force for the current year?

Current Year's Increase in Cash Value,
Account Value, or Asset Value   _____
Plus Current Year's Dividend, if any   _____
Equals Total Policy-owner Credit   _____

Critics will find weaknesses and advocates will find strengths in this particular section of this system for the financial analysis of life insurance. The critics will say that you are looking at the policy for only one particular year. They will question whether the financial results for any particular year are an accurate report on what has happened in the past, or a predictor of what will happen in the future. The criticism is valid because the policy under analysis could be a variable life insurance policy with its investment in a common stock account in a year when the common stock fund has taken a substantial beating. If that were the case, current year return could easily be negative. If you concluded that one year's negative return meant that you should get rid of the policy, that may certainly be an erroneous conclusion. You should perform further evaluation by re-entering your numbers in the formula using the average annual increase in account value and the average annual dividend received since the policy's inception as the credits received as a result of maintaining the policy in force. For inputing into the policy, you could use average annual premium, average policy loan costs, and the average net after-tax costs for maintaining cash within the policy. This would give you an indication of average return from policy inception. From the standpoint that each policy owner is trying to make a "Where do we go from here?" decision, the current year's actual return will be far more important than such averages.

If you are considering an upgrade or enhancement offer, you can use the formula by entering the assumptions such as the elimination of the policy loan and the acceptance of the higher dividend yields to determine the impact of the offer.

Advocates of this system of financial analysis of life insurance will appreciate the fact that it can tell them what is going on within a life insurance policy in the current year and, by using other inputs, what has gone on since policy inception. It can also be used to evaluate the financial result of accepting upgrade offers and increasing, decreasing or eliminating policy loans.

STEP 4

Determine your investment in the contract.

> Total Asset Value _____
> Less (Subtract: Loan Outstanding) _____
> Equals Investment Remaining in Contract _____

The investment capital in the contract is extremely important, as it is the investment upon which you are going to calculate your investment return. It is the investment at the moment of your evaluation. Some users of this system will wish to refine this figure to make it closer to the policy-owner's average investment in the contract during the year in question. That is, you could calculate your investment in the contract at the beginning and at the end of the year and then add the two together, subtract any policy loan, and divide by two to come up with the average investment in the contract for that year.

Others may wish to decrease the investment in the contract by the amount of ordinary income tax they would have to pay on the gain within the policy if they surrendered it and/or any back-end load. The gain in the contract is total policy value less the policy-owner's basis. This is subject to ordinary income tax upon policy surrender. This is valid if the policy is to be dropped and the income tax paid; however, it is invalid if this tax liability is to be avoided by using a 1035 tax-free exchange into either another life insurance policy or an annuity contract or continue the policy.

For our purposes, it is better that you understand the logic in the procedure using the current existing investment in the contract.

When entering the figure for the outstanding policy loan, the unpaid outstanding interest on the policy loan at the time of the evaluation should be added to the policy loan amount.

STEP 5

Determine the dollar amount of return you have earned in the current policy year.

From step 3 above, take your increased value for the current policy year and subtract step 2, your current input into the contract for the current year.

Policy-owner Credit (Step 3)	_____
Minus Policy-owner Costs (Step 2)	_____
Equals Policy-owner Net Gain (Loss)	_____

STEP 6

Determine your cash on cash return for the current year.

In order to determine your cash-on-cash annual percentage rate of return for the current year, take the amount of the credit from step 5, and divide it by your investment remaining in the contract from step 4.

Amount of Credit (Step 5)   _____
÷ Amount Invested (Step 4)   _____
Equals % Cash on Cash Return   _____

STEP 7

Determine your policy-owner's equivalent taxable return.

The cash-on-cash return varies in value for high—and low-bracket taxpayers. This is easier to communicate if you have the number that represents the pre-tax rate of return that you would have to obtain on a taxable investment outside of the life insurance contract in order to match that non-taxable return within the policy. In order to accomplish this, take your tax-free rate of return as calculated in step 6 above and divide it by one minus your tax bracket.

Policy-owner's Untaxed Cash on Cash (Step 6)
Rate of Return (Step 6)
÷ (1 minus Tax Bracket)   _____
Equals Equivalent Taxable Return: %

STEP 8

Determine the value of your life insurance.

This is a very important question these days, when life insurance policies are being touted as competitive investments regardless of the life insurance protection they provide. If you are not in need of life insurance protection and place no value on the life insurance protection provided by the contract, then you need go no further in the financial evaluation of the life insurance contract. Step 7, the cash-on-cash return, is all that is the value, and the viability of the life insurance contract as an investment depends upon the competitiveness of this cash-on-cash return with other investment alternatives available.

Other individuals will place varying values on the life insurance protection provided by the contract. The young non-smoker who has an opportunity to purchase term insurance at discounted rates through his association, his employer or some other advantageous source would put one value on the life insurance that he could obtain in his preferred status. An individual who is older, has a great personal need for life insurance and has just had a heart attack—so that existing life insurance could not be replaced—would place a much higher value on the net amount at risk. In some cases the insurance protection will have so much value to the policy-owner that the cash-on-cash return or investment return of the policy would be irrelevant.

"Life insurance" does have value, and that value has to be individually determined. The most accurate cost per thousand to be entered in this section of the formula would be the figure you obtained as a result of applying to an insurance company for an equivalent amount of term life insurance, submitting to medical examination, and receiving an offer for term insurance at a contractually guaranteed rate. All other entries are estimates and the financial analysis is only as good as that estimate is accurate.

Once the equivalent retail value of term life insurance is determined, it is multiplied by the amount of life insurance protection provided by the contract (face amount of the policy minus asset value of the policy as determined in step 1) to determine the value of the life insurance within the contract.

Some would argue that your retail cost of the term insurance divided by one minus your current marginal tax bracket is the figure that should be entered. This figure would represent the amount that you would have to earn in total to service a retail term insurance policy. For example, for every $ 100 a policy-owner in the 30-percent marginal state and federal tax bracket must pay for term insurance, that policy-owner must earn $ 142.86 (100 ÷ (1—.30) = $ 142.857). This communicates that in order to send a check to an insurance company for $ 100, you must earn $ 142.86, pay the 30 percent tax ($ 42.86 [$ 142.06 x .30 = $ 42.86]) and send the balance, $ 100, to the insurance company.

This method of valuing the cost of retail term insurance would be accurate if the untaxed earnings on an investment within the life insurance policy were entirely sufficient to cover all mortality and expense charges within the policy. We have taken the more conservative approach using just the equivalent retail cost of term insurance for the policy-owner.

Value of "Life Insurance":

Life Insurance in Thousands (Step 1) x Policy-owner's Cost

Per $1000 of Life Insurance   _____
Equals Value of Life Insurance: _____

STEP 9

Determine the total value you receive as a result of continuing this life insurance contract.

The total value you receive as a result of continuing the life insurance contract is the cash-on-cash return plus the value of the life insurance protection. Add the life insurance value determined in step 8 to the cash return of step 5 to come up with the total dollar amount of benefit you receive from the contract.

Policy-owner Net Gain (Loss) (Step 5)   _____
+ Life Insurance Value (Step 8)   _____
Equals Total Benefit Received: _____

STEP 10

Determine the percentage return on the contract when the cash-on-cash return is added to the life insurance value.

Value Received ÷ Amount Invested = _____ % Rate of Return
(Step 9)   (Step 10)

STEP 11

Determine the equivalent taxable return that you must earn to match this tax-deferred/tax-free return from the life insurance contract.

Percent Rate of Return (Step 10) ÷ (1 Minus Tax Bracket) = _____ %

(Ben Baldwin—Life Insurance Investment Advisor, Probus Publishing Company, c 1988)

CHAPTER 9: WHAT SHOULD I KNOW ABOUT LIFE INSURANCE REPLACE-MENTS?

QUESTION 93: Why Would I Consider a Life Insurance Replacement?

A life insurance policy is a financial asset. It is a good idea to review it on a regular basis to make sure you are getting the value you expected, in exchange for the premium dollars you pay the life insurance company. Things change in the real world, and your life insurance policy can be affected by such things as changes in the issuing company's financial condition and by competition.

Life insurance is also a financial tool, a complex tool that provides you with financial leverage. There is no substitute for life insurance, for it is unique in its ability to provide a self-completing financial plan, should the insured person die unexpectedly. Life insurance can be used to replace lost income, pay the federal estate tax and provide money for many other worthwhile purposes.

Replacing an in-force life insurance policy can be a very good idea or a very bad one. It depends on many factors. Traditionally, the viewpoint within the life insurance industry is that replacing an existing life insurance policy with a new one is generally not in the policy owner's best interest. This statement is ambiguous in the sense that it can be both true and false at the same time. Dealing with the complexities of the life insurance replacement issue is like peeling away the layers of an onion. Remove several layers and there are still many layers remaining.

This report is intended to aid you in the replacement decision-making process. It is not an exhaustive treatment of the subject, because your individual situation is unique and there is no one-size-fits-all solution. Our purpose here is to help you evaluate the pertinent facts and circumstances, when considering whether or not to replace an existing life insurance policy. A replacement may be internal (i.e., replacing it with a new policy from the same company) or external (i.e., replacing it with a policy from a different company).

QUESTION 94: How Is Replacement Defined?

Simply stated, replacement means discontinuing one life insurance policy to purchase another. A very fine line divides replacement (which is permissible under state insurance law) from twisting (which is prohibited by state law). Twisting is like churning—replacing a life insurance policy primarily for the agent's benefit, to earn a new agent commission. Twisting is defined as the practice wherein an agent induces a policy owner through misrepresentation to discontinue an existing life insurance policy and purchase a new one with the proceeds.

State law determines the legal meaning of the word "replacement" and it varies substantially by state. It is a good idea to become familiar with your own state's definition of the term. To locate your state's insurance code and replacement regulations a good place to start is with the National Association of Insurance Commissioners website, (www.naic.org) and follow the link to your state's insurance department.

You will quickly find that your state has some fairly strict insurance regulations, but enforcement varies by state. Some state insurance departments are better funded and hence better staffed than others. In general, the larger state insurance departments are better equipped to enforce the replacement regulations, but this is not always the case.

QUESTION 95: What Issues Favor Replacement?

Has the insured's insurability and/or health improved since the existing policy was issued? If the existing policy was issued in a substandard rating class (i.e., with an extra premium charge), will the company replace/remove the rating? If the insured person was formerly a smoker but is now a non-smoker, will the current company change the premium to a non-smoker rate? If the current company will not assist the policy owner in these circumstances, replacement might well be justified.

What is the current company's financial condition compared to the proposed carrier? Has either company's financial condition significantly deteriorated? A justified replacement may be needed in order to rectify an unjustified replacement. Policy ownership problems may trigger replacement. For example, if an ex-spouse or business partner claims partial or full ownership, a replacement might be indicated. The current policy may no longer suit your current life insurance needs. The policy may be an old non-participating policy (i.e., it does not pay dividends) which has not been updated by the company to give you the benefit of potentially more favorable current interest and mortality experience.

QUESTION 96: What Issues favor retention of an old policy?

- If you replace the existing policy, you will incur new first year expense charges for agent compensation, issue and underwriting.
- The suicide clause and contestable period (where the company can challenge the policy) start anew, unless the replacing insurer is willing to waive them (be sure to ask).
- If your health has deteriorated since the issue of the original policy, or if the original policy was issued with no premium difference between smokers and non-smokers and you are a smoker.
- If the existing policy has especially favorable policy provisions such as an attractive guaranteed interest rate on policy loans. Keep in mind that recent tax law changes may have diminished the benefits of a policy loan.
- If the existing policy does not qualify for an Internal Revenue Code Section 1035 tax-free exchange (there is more information on this in a separate section of this report). For example, if there is a policy loan outstanding, it may be difficult to affect a tax-free exchange. The taxable income generated by an exchange that does not qualify for tax-free treatment could be significant.

Different considerations apply to the decision making process for term life insurance vs. permanent policies. You will find worksheets in Questions 98 and 99 that will help you do a replacement self-evaluation of both permanent and term life insurance.

Replacing an existing life insurance policy may not be in the policy owner's best interest. Buying a new policy most likely means a new sales load for commissions and other charges assessed by the company, along with a new suicide clause. The latter is the company's right to challenge a death claim during the first two years the policy is in force, if suicide is the cause of death. Two years is typical, but some policies have a one year suicide exclusion. Existence of the suicide and contestability periods, advancing age or health concerns and the loss of important grandfathered rights are some of the obvious reasons that most replacements cannot be justified. Before replacing policies, discuss it with the carrier. As carriers continually enhance their policies, they recognize that their policies may become obsolete and will consider upgrade and exchange programs.

On the other hand, there may be circumstances where replacement is indicated by the facts and circumstances. The ethical agent will provide the client with the facts and objective information needed to make an informed decision. These should include the reasons why the current policy should not be replaced and—when appropriate—how the existing policy might be modified to accomplish the goals. The need for additional coverage is not, by itself, a justification for replacement. A better approach is purchasing a new policy to cover the additional amount needed.

QUESTION 97: What Are Some Questions to Consider Before Replacing?

- What do you wish a new policy to achieve that your existing policy does not?
- Have you contacted the current company to see if the policy can be modified to meet the desired objectives? Policy performance may actually be quite competitive, if the factors adversely affecting this performance have been experienced by all insurers. In

particular, the dramatic fall in interest rates over the last 20 years has lowered the returns of all traditional whole life and universal life policies to one degree or another. Rather than replace the competitive policy of a well-rated insurer, whose returns have only gone down to some extent with the broad decline in interest rates, it may be more appropriate to make any necessary adjustments to assure the continuation of the policy by raising the premium, paying it for a longer time, reducing the policy's death benefit, or seeking an adjustment with an updated policy from the same insurer.

- Compare the benefits of each policy. Differences in the underlying investments of the old and new policies may make rate of return comparisons difficult or misleading, especially if the proposed new policy is variable and equity investments are contemplated in place of the old insurer's fixed income-oriented investment portfolio. Investment returns obviously need to be adjusted for risk for comparisons to be meaningful, and the other factors affecting product performance—mortality, expenses, and lapse rates—need to be considered as well.

- Be aware that a new policy will have new suicide and incontestable provisions, unless the company is willing to waive them.

- Will the replacement (if it is a permanent life insurance policy with a cash value) qualify as a tax-free exchange under Internal Revenue Code Section 1035? (see Question 101)

- Will you be able to qualify both financially and health-wise for the new coverage?

- Have you been urged to borrow from a current policy or policies to finance the new coverage? <u>This is not a good idea</u>.

- Is this a replacement proposal that attempts to increase the death benefit for an existing premium or to lower the premium for an existing death benefit, by guaranteeing a death benefit—but only to a certain advanced age, such as age 95 or 100. Purchasers of "permanent" insurance want their policies to be "permanent" and not to expire before they do, if they happen to live an especially long time.

Term life insurance is less complicated than permanent, cash-value life insurance, so we will consider term life insurance first.

QUESTION 98: What Type of Worksheet Can I Use With A Proposed Term Life Insurance Replacement?

This worksheet summarizes some important factors to consider. Not all of these factors necessarily apply to your situation. This is not an exhaustive list but it covers the most likely scenarios. The worksheet is a good base on which to build in deciding whether or not to replace an in-force term policy. If you are familiar with spreadsheet computer programs such as Excel, Lotus 1-2-3 or Quattro Pro, you can build a spreadsheet that will give you a side-by-side comparison of your present term policy and the proposed policy.

Term insurance generally does not pay dividends and does not accumulate cash values. Term insurance runs for a specified period of time, and it expires without value at the end of that term. During the term it provides pure life insurance protection in the amount for which you contract for with the life insurance company. A good example is a $1 million 10-year term policy. If the insured person dies during the 10-year term period, the policy pays $1 million to the designated beneficiary. If the insured person dies after the 10 years is up, the policy pays nothing. Many term policies are renewable at a higher premium rate, and many are convertible to permanent life insurance at any time during the policy term.

Term policies come in many forms. The most common are annual renewable term, decreasing term (e.g., mortgage cancellation insurance) and level premium term. Some policies offer guarantees and others do not. It pays to shop around. You may also want to record the comparison information you are given, the source and the date. Try to verify that the information is current because you will making a decision based on that information.

	Present Policy	Proposed Policy
Company Name		
AM Best Rating and Ranking (15 Ratings from A++ to F)		
Standard & Poor's Rating & Ranking (20 Ratings from AAA to CC)		
Moody's Rating & Ranking (21 Ratings from Aaa to C)		
Fitch Rating & Ranking (24 Ratings from AAA to D)		
Weiss Rating and Ranking (16 Ratings from A+ to F)		
Type of Coverage: Annual Renewable Term (ART), Level Premium, Decreasing Term, Mortgage Insurance, Etc.		
Date of Issue		
Face Amount (Death Benefit)		
Annualized Premium		
Premium Detail– Will the Premium Increase? • If yes, By How Much? • If it is level, then how much longer will it remain at the current level? • What will happen to it at the end of the level premium period?		
What are the Premium Guarantees, if any?		
Is it Group or Individual Coverage - If Group, do you plan to stay with the group, employers, association, union, etc.?		
Policy Expiration Date		
Conversion and/or Exchange Option? • If Yes, until what date? • Is there a conversion premium credit?		
Is there a Re-Entry Provision, and if so what are the details?		
Are there any riders on the policy such as- Waiver of Premium, Accidental Death Benefit, Family Rider, Spouse Rider, Child Rider, Etc.?		
Cost of Rider(s)		

QUESTION 99: What Type of Worksheet Can I Use With A Proposed Permanent Life Insurance Replacement?

Because of the cash value element and its complexities, it is much more difficult to analyze a permanent life insurance policy in a potential replacement situation. There are many types of different permanent life insurance policies. For the purpose of this worksheet, we will use the generic term "permanent life insurance" to mean any type of life insurance that builds up a cash value, including whole life, universal life, variable life, variable universal life and all variations on each of these policy types.

Please note that the use of the word "illustrated" in this worksheet means that results are not guaranteed. An illustration is nothing more than a projection based on a bundle of assumptions which are almost certainly not going to occur in real life. That does not mean that life insurance companies are guilty of a sinister conspiracy against the consumer. Quite the contrary, the truth is that neither the insurance company nor any person knows the future, so we have to make intelligent guesses. The result is a so-called linear or deterministic projection.

Perhaps the key assumption in a linear projection is the future interest rate that will be credited by the company to the policy. This is usually expressed as a level interest rate. For example, an illustration might assume an interest credited rate of 6%. In the real world, interest rates fluctuate, so in practice, that 6% illustrated rate is not realistic, even if it is a perfectly reasonable assumption. A truly realistic illustration would have to assume a constantly variable interest rate, which is virtually impossible. Since we don't know the future, how does one come up with a variable interest rate?

Keep in mind that different companies use different assumptions in preparing illustrations. Illustrations alone should never be used to compare policies. State insurance regulations require—for your protection—that both the proposed replacing company and your existing company prepare current illustrations for your consideration in making an intelligent replacement decision.

These illustrations will show the effects of the surrender charge on the existing and proposed policies. In situations where the current policy will be modified, but not terminated, comparisons should include in-force ledgers of the policy before and after the change, if available. The terms "ledger" and "illustration" mean the same. Some companies use the term ledger illustration instead.

Reduced scale illustrations—illustrations showing lower interest rate crediting assumptions—should be provided on both existing and proposed policies to demonstrate the effects of volatility on the performance of non-guaranteed policy elements under varying circumstances. This is a reasonable substitute for the stochastic modeling described above. In other words, if an illustration with a lower interest rate than is reasonably thought will be achieved shows that the plan will work, there is every indication that it will work in the real world, as long as things don't go completely awry.

The reduced scale illustrations should be consistent with those required by NAIC model illustration regulations, when applicable in your state. This worksheet is intended for evaluation purposes only and is not a substitute for state replacement requirements. Also, for variable life insurance, you will need to look at the sub-accounts and most likely will need the use of an investment analyst.

The term "sub-account" means the funds within a variable life or variable universal life policy in which the money is invested. A sub-account is similar to a mutual fund, except that it comes under the umbrella of a life insurance policy. It is, however, highly misleading to think of a variable life or variable universal life policy as a mutual fund with a thin layer of life insurance on top. We mention this because that terminology is sometimes used by well meaning but misguided agents to describe a variable life policy. A better way to think of a variable life or variable universal life policy is as a permanent life policy which uses mutual funds (sub-accounts) to manage the cash value element within the policy.

Illustrations should never be the sole criteria for evaluating a replacement. Illustrated cash values and illustrated death benefits are never reliable predictions of future results. More information is needed. As a minimum, you should attempt to find out what the underlying assumptions are for the in-force illustration on the current policy, and for the sales illustration for the proposed policy. You should be aware that there might be differences in the assumptions used by each company, which may render a comparison based upon such illustrations invalid. Make sure you are comparing apples to apples. Also keep in mind that replacement of an existing policy generally results in the reduction of cash surrender value as a result of new acquisition costs.

A valuable tool to assist you in replacement situations is a current "in-force illustration". In-force illustrations allow you to gauge past performance against anticipated future performance. These are for simple situations that do not include a policy loan and for some of the other more complex situations listed throughout this book.

	Present Policy	Proposed Policy
Company Name		
AM Best Rating and Ranking (15 Ratings from A++ to F)		
Standard & Poor's Rating & Ranking (20 Ratings from AAA to CC)		
Moody's Rating & Ranking (21 Ratings from Aaa to C)		
Fitch Rating & Ranking (24 Ratings from AAA to D)		
Weiss Rating and Ranking (16 Ratings from A+ to F)		
Type of Coverage: Whole Life, Universal Life, Variable Life, Variable Universal Life, Joint/Survivor Life, Etc.		
Date of Issue		
Current Face Amount (Death Benefit)		
Is the Death Benefit- • Level or Increasing • How many years is it guaranteed for? • How many years will it last for based on current/illustrated assumptions?		
Annualized Premium-the mode by which the premium is paid will affect the performance of the policy.		
How will the Premium payment mode affect the policy- • Premium necessary to guarantee coverage at initial/current levels for duration of policy? • If the Premium is to be payable for a certain number of years? • Number of years based on current assumptions? • Number of years based on guaranteed assumptions?		
Cash/Surrender Value—current policy? Compare current policies projected values (based on current assumptions) with new policies first year value (note surrender charges may significantly if not completely reduce early values in any new policy)		
Policy Maturity/Termination Date		
Term Rider (if applicable)- • If yes, what is the ratio the initial term amount to the total death benefit? • Does the term rider convert to permanent insurance? • If so, when does it do so and is it guaranteed? • Is the term rider guaranteed in any other fashion?		
Are there any riders on the policy? If so, which ones?		
Cost of Rider(s)		

QUESTION 100: Are There Any Special Situations To Consider?

Is there a policy loan? If there is, then the situation has just become even more complicated. You should consult the section (Chapter 10, Questions 106-109) in this book on policy loans. For example, will the new company assume the loan from the old company? Most companies will not. The simplest solution is to repay the loan on the old policy before exchanging it. Otherwise you might wind up with taxable income as a result of the replacement.

Issues for policy Loans for both the current policy and if applicable—the proposed policy:

- Gross Interest Rate:
- Fixed or Variable Rate:
- Direct Recognition:
- Universal Life: What is the current spread between the loan rate and interest credited on the borrowed amount? Is this spread guaranteed?

Does the policy qualify as life insurance under Internal Revenue Code Section 7702?

Section 7702 states that a life insurance policy issued after 1984 will be treated as life insurance for tax purposes only if it is:

1) Considered a life insurance contract under applicable (state) law; and
2) It meets either the cash value accumulation test or a combination guideline premium—cash corridor test.

Issue dates—Depending on the issue date on which the current policy was issued, the following "grandfathered features will be lost if the policy is replaced:

- August 8, 1963—The current policy was purchased on or before 8/6/63, so IRC Section 264(a)(3) which limits deductions for interest indebtedness does not apply. If the current policy has met the "four out of seven" test of IRC Section 264(c)(1), interest on indebtedness is deductible to the extent otherwise allowed by law. Personal interest deductions are generally denied for tax years beginning after 1990, regardless of when the policy was purchased. IRC Sec. 163(h)(1).

- June 20, 1986—The current policy was purchased on or before June 20, 1986. Certain policies purchased for business purposes after this date have a $50,000 ceiling on the aggregate amount of indebtedness for which an interest deduction is allowed. IRC Sec. 264(a)(4).

- June 20, 1988—Policy was issued on or before 6/20/88 and is not subject to Modified Endowment Contract rules. IRC Sec. 7702A. Substantial increases in the death benefits of grandfathered contracts after 10/20/88 may cause the imposition of the MEC rules. H.R. Conference Report No. 1104, 100th Cong., 2d Sess. (TAMRA '88) reprinted in 1988-3 CB 595—596.

- October 21, 1979—Variable annuity contracts purchased before 10/21/79 are eligible for a step-up in basis, if the owner dies before the annuity starting date. IRC Sec. 72; Rev. Rul. 79-335, 1979-2 CB 292.

- August 14, 1982—An annuity issued prior to 8/14/82 is subject to more favorable (basis out first) cost recovery rules for withdrawals. IRC Sec. 72(e). Such policies are not subject to the 10% penalty on withdrawals made prior to age 59 ½. IRC Sec. 72(q)(2).

- February 28, 1986—To the extent contributions are made after 2/28/86 to a deferred annuity held by a non-natural person (such as a business entity), the contract will not be entitled to tax treatment as an annuity. IRC Sec. 72(u).

- September 14, 1989—A survivorship life policy, issued prior to 9/14/89, is not subject to the 7-pay MEC test if there is a reduction in benefits. IRC Sec. 7702A(C)(6).

You should seek competent legal counsel before applying these factors to any specific situation.

QUESTION 101: Are There Any Tax Issues to Consider with a Replacement and what is Internal Revenue Code Section 1035?

Please note that this section is not intended as tax advice and should not be construed in such a manner. Please consult your tax advisor for advice in your specific situation.

Overview of Internal Revenue Code Section 1035—Typically, upon the surrender of a life insurance contract, gain is immediately recognized by the policy owner, to the extent the value of the policy received exceeds the policy owner's adjusted basis in the transferred policy.

Section 1035 allows certain exchanges of life insurance to be made without the immediate recognition of gain. Section 1035 allows the tax, that otherwise would be imposed on lump-sum disposition of certain life insurance policies (and annuities), to be postponed. The following are the types of exchanges allowed, through Section 1035 that would result in no gain (or loss) to be recognized:

- An ordinary life insurance contract for another ordinary life insurance contract (one for which the face amount (i.e., the death benefit) is not ordinarily payable in full during the insured's life).
- An ordinary life insurance contract for an endowment contract (one that depends in part on the life expectancy of the insured but that may be payable in full in a single payment during the insured's lifetime).
- An ordinary life insurance contract for an annuity (one payable during the life of the annuitant only in installments).
- An endowment contract for another endowment contract that provides for regular payments beginning at a date not later than the date payments would have begun under the contract exchanged.
- An endowment contract for an annuity contract.
- An annuity contract for an annuity contract.

Generally, a contract received in a 1035 exchange carries over elements of the original contract, in addition to basis. Please note that there are a number of Internal Revenue Service Private Letter Rulings, Revenue Rulings and modifications. These are the basic rules, however, as previously stated; they may not apply in your specific situation.

QUESTION 102: What Are Some Myths About Replacement?

Myth: Your Policy is on the old mortality table and therefore your current insurance company is taking advantage of you by failure to recognize that people are living longer today than when the older mortality table was developed.

Fact: The non-forfeiture values and reserves are based on the older table, but that alone is not a problem. The real issue is whether current mortality experience is being reflected in the dividend, if the policy is participating, or in the mortality charge, if the policy is interest-sensitive.

Myth: Your policy is out of date. A claim like this implies that periodic policy recycling is "normal" and an accepted and desirable business practice.

Fact: If current mortality and interest experience is being credited, the age of the policy should not be of concern. If not, you may have a valid case for replacement. Another valid replacement indicator: the policy owner has an old policy in which the company made no distinction between smokers and non-smokers (some companies refer to this as a unismoker policy). If this is the case and the client is a non-smoker, replacement should be considered on the merits. Another situation is one in which the policy owner would like one or more features that are not available on the present policy.

Myth: The company that wrote your policy is out business (or has been taken over). The real myth is that such a situation always has negative implications for the policy owners. It may be that the company has simply changed its name, which happens quite often in today's fast-paced business climate.

Fact: You need more information before reaching any conclusions. The company may have changed its name, been merged into another company or been purchased by a stronger company—which could make retention of the existing policy that much more desirable.

Myth: You should buy cheap term life insurance and invest the difference in premium between term and permanent life insurance. The myth here is that there is never a need for permanent life insurance.
Fact: Sometimes there are permanent needs that require permanent life insurance, although in the majority of cases term life insurance will meet the need at a much more attractive cost. It depends on the situation and circumstances. When it comes to life insurance, one size definitely does not fit all.

Myth: The agent portrays state insurance department mandated replacement forms and procedures in a way that implies that the state endorses replacements. The agent might, for example, say that this is the state approved procedure for helping people in your situation.
Fact: The real intent of insurance department replacement forms and procedures is to assist the consumer in making an intelligent decision about whether or not a replacement is desirable, under the particular circumstances.

QUESTION 103: What Are Some Reasons For Replacing?

Survey Results: Showing Why Policy-Owners Replaced Their Policies:

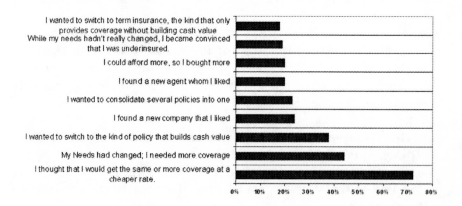

Chart Note: Multiple Responses were permitted.

(Source: Life Insurance Marketing and Research Association (LIMRA)— "Replacement Now", April 17, 1985, P.5)

QUESTION 104: What are Some Areas to Use Caution in Making a Replacement?

Generally, the exchange or replacement of insurance or annuity contracts is a good idea, except for a very few reasons:

- The "bonus" credit can be offset by the insurance company's adding additional contract charges.
- Other contract provisions, like surrender charges, eventually expire with an existing contract. However, new charges may be imposed with a new contact or may increase the period of time for which the surrender charge applies.

- Higher charges, such as annual fees for the new contract, may apply.
- Costly new contract features may not be needed. Since the initial costs of a life insurance policy or annuity contract are charged against early cash value increases or may result in substantial surrender charges, the contract owner or policy owner that exchanges an existing policy or contract is undergoing this a second time.
- In a life insurance policy incontestable and suicide clauses generally begin anew on the new contract.
- An existing life insurance policy or annuity contract may have more favorable provisions than a new life insurance policy or annuity contract, especially in areas such as loan interest rates, settlement options, disability benefits and tax treatment which may be lost.

No exchange or purchase of an annuity or life insurance policy should be made until all of the options have been carefully studied and any questions answered. The decision to exchange a policy or contract should be made only on the basis of the net improvement in the position of the client. It has been proven 1035 Exchanges can accomplish that.

QUESTION 105: How Have The Replacement Regulations Evolved To Provide More Protections For Consumer?

Buying a life insurance policy—while usually a fairly simple transaction—can involve a complex array of financial data. An agent can easily mislead the purchaser, intentionally or unintentionally. Because replacement is such a troublesome issue and a big problem, the National Association of Insurance Commissioners (NAIC) has formulated model replacement regulations, which require the disclosure of certain information considered pertinent to the proposed replacement decision. Here is a history of the replacement regulations:

- 1970—The NAIC adopted its first Model Replacement Regulation. This Regulation requires an insurer (or agent) to provide the consumer contemplating a replacement with (1) a notice and (2) a Comparison Statement. The notice states that "as a general rule, it is not advantageous to drop or change existing life insurance in favor of a new policy". The Comparison Statement is to be completed by the replacing agent. It is to provide the consumer with comparative data on the existing and proposed policies, in order to assist the consumer in his or her replacement decision.

- 1978—The NAIC adopted a revised, strengthened replacement regulation at its December 1978 meeting. Several states still pattern their replacement regulations on this version. The agent who proposes a replacement must provide the insured with a Replacement Notice and a completed Comparative Information Form. The agent is required to leave with the applicant copies of all sales materials used, and to send the replacing insurer signed copies of the Notice and the Comparative Information Form, plus a copy of the sales proposal(s). An agent attempting to conserve the in-force policy (i.e., persuade the policy owner to change his or her mind about replacement) must leave with the consumer a copy of all materials used in connection with that effort, and must submit to his or her own company a copy of such materials.

  The replacing insurer must mail the existing insurer a verified copy of the Comparative Information Form within three days of receiving the insurance application. In turn, the replacing insurer must delay issuance of the new policy for twenty days or provide a 20-day unconditional refund offer with the replacing policy. If the existing insurer undertakes a conservation effort, it must either complete, correct, and send to the consumer the Comparative Information Form it received from the replacing insurer or send the consumer a Policy Summary completed in compliance with the solicitation regulation (if the state has adopted one). Cost comparison information need not be included in the Policy Summary. The existing insurer is, in turn, to provide the replacing insurer with a copy of the materials it sent the consumer in its efforts to conserve the policy.

- 1984—The 1984 NAIC Model Replacement Regulation was adopted. This model is patterned in key parts, after the replacement regulation adopted by Virginia in 1982. Several states have regulations similar to this model. The new regulation retains much of the previous version, but it eliminates the requirement that a comparison form be used. The notice that must be given to the applicant is far simpler than earlier versions and it puts more of the burden on the consumer to protect his or her own interests. Other differences in procedure are mandated. Although the newer version is generally acknowledged to be an improvement over earlier model regulations, it still leaves much to be desired.

The NAIC continues to work on the replacement issue and further evolutionary changes can be expected in replacement regulations. The summer, 2000 issue of the NAIC's official publication, Journal of Insurance Regulation, featured an article about replacement. An abstract of that article follows. You may purchase a copy of that issue through the NAIC website: www.naic.org. *(Journal of Insurance Regulation, summer 2000, Vol. 18(4): 427-447)*

CHAPTER 10: WHAT YOU NEED TO KNOW ABOUT POLICY LOANS

QUESTION 106: What Is A Policy Loan and Why You May Not Want One?

Life insurance policies have evolved from a simple method of sharing risk to complex financial instruments. Policy loans are one of the most complex, misunderstood and misused components of a life insurance policy. They are like termites, and if left to their own devices, they eventually will cause an insurance policy to collapse on itself. This could result in the insured having no coverage and, possibly, a huge tax penalty.

The term "policy loan" is a misnomer, according to *Law and the Life Insurance Contract by Muriel Crawford and William Beadles*. A loan is defined as the transfer of money by one person-the creditor to another person-the debtor-upon agreement that the debtor will return to the creditor an equivalent sum at a later date, usually plus interest. A policy loan is not truly a loan, because the policy owner does not agree to repay the money transferred to him or her by the insurer, although interest is still charged. It is an advance of money that the insurer eventually must pay out under terms of the policy. Thus, a policy loan does not create a creditor-debtor relationship between the insurer and the policy owner.

U.S. Supreme Court Justice Oliver Wendell Holmes came to the same conclusion in Board of Assessors vs. New York Life Insurance Company, one of the leading court decisions involving policy loans. "The so-called liability of the policyholder never exists as a personal liability, it is never a debt, but is merely a deduction in account from the sum the plaintiffs (the insurer) ultimately must pay," the justice wrote in 1910.

Policy loans are more complicated than agents sometimes purport them to be, with promises of premium-free life insurance. In reality, borrowing to pay premiums reduces the death benefit. Some companies today even suggest to clients with underperforming policies that a policy loan could support their faltering policy. But this robs Peter to pay Paul, and the policy owner eventually must make up the difference.

Out-of-control policy loans can erode a life insurance policy over time, eventually draining all the death benefits as well as saddling the policy owner with a substantial tax bill.

The basic calculation for the potential taxable income impact would be to add the net cash (surrender) value plus any dividends received (either prior or accumulated) and the loan balance at the time of surrender. From that sum, subtract the basis (sum of premiums) paid into the policy and that will be the gain in the policy that is subject to income tax. Please note that this is a rule of thumb and may not apply in all cases depending on ownership, transfers, if it is held inside a qualified plan, etc. However, this should give you a starting point. A carrier will usually be able to provide you with the basis and the other necessary figures as well as the potential gain typically reported to the Internal Revenue Service on a 1099. Please note that this is not tax advice; for tax advice; please consult your tax advisor.

QUESTION 107: Are Policy Loans Tax-Free?

The Tax Reform Act of 1986 magnified the tax ramifications of policy loans and added new penalties, making this area even more complex. Consider the so-called minimum deposit life insurance plans. Before the passage of TRA '86, interest due on loans to finance these types of life insurance policies, sold after March 1, 1954, was not tax deductible. This was further expanded under Internal Revenue Code Section 264(a)(3), which states, "a deduction is denied for interest paid on an indebtedness incurred or continued to purchase or carry a life insurance, endowment or annuity contract...pursuant to a plan of purchase which contemplates the systematic direct or indirect borrowing of (sic) part of or all of the increases in the cash value of such contract either from the insurer or otherwise."

This rule (also referred to as the plan-of-purchase rule) applies only to contracts issued between Aug. 6, 1963, and the implementation of TRA '86. It contains four exceptions. If a financed plan met at least one of these exceptions, interest was deductible. A simplified explanation of these exceptions follows. For more detailed information, check the full version of the Internal Revenue Code.

- The four-out-of-seven rule. This provides that interest on a financed plan is tax deductible if no part of (at least) four of the first seven annual premiums of a policy is paid through borrowing, either from the policy or elsewhere. A new seven-year period begins if a "substantial increase in borrowing occurs." If borrowing in any year exceeds the premium for that year, the excess is considered to be borrowings used to finance the previous year's premium. If the policy owner borrows an amount that exceeds the total of three years' premiums, then the four-out-of-seven rule has been violated, irrespective of when the borrowing occurred during the period. Once the seven years have passed, it appears that borrowing beyond that period could be at any level. This was the most commonly used exception.
- The $100 exception. The interest deduction will be allowed for any taxable year in which the interest in connection with any systematic plan of borrowing does not exceed $100. Where such interest exceeds $100, the entire amount of interest (not just the amount in excess of $100) is nondeductible under Internal Revenue Code Section 264(a)(3).
- The unforeseen-events exception. If the indebtedness is incurred because of an unforeseen substantial loss of income or unforeseen substantial increase in the taxpayer's financial obligations, the deduction will be allowed under this rule, even though the loan is used to pay premiums on the contract. An event is not "unforeseen," however, if at the time the contract was purchased it could have been foreseen.
- The trade-or-business exception. If the indebtedness is incurred in connection with the taxpayer's trade or business, the interest deduction will not be denied. Thus, if an insurance policy is pledged as part of the collateral for a loan, the interest deductions will come within this exception if the taxpayer can show that the amounts borrowed were actually used to finance the expansion of inventory or other similar business needs.

QUESTION 108: How Does A Policy Loan Become Harmful?

Let's look at a case study. As part of a divorce settlement, a woman owned a life insurance policy that had been issued to her ex-husband in 1967. At the time of issue, the insured was 38. The policy was a whole life paid up at age 90 with a death benefit of $100,000. But, before the policy had been transferred to the woman, a policy loan had been taken out on the policy.

In 1999, the policy had an outstanding loan of $62,098.42, with an interest rate of 5%. The policy's basis (the sum of premiums paid minus the sum of any dividends received in cash or credited against the premiums) at the time was $59,018, and the net surrender value was $947.43. The policy had reached a point at which it was "over-loaned," which means the woman could no longer borrow against the policy to pay the premiums and loan interest. The policy owner had received a bill of $2,949.67 for loan interest due, and the annual premium due was $2,152. This meant that there was an annual cost of $5,101.67 to carry a policy with a net death benefit of $37,901.58 (original death benefit of $100,000, less the outstanding loan balance of $62,098.42).

The policy owner had few options. She could pay the $5,101.67 to keep the policy in-force. Surrendering the policy and collecting the $947.43 would have resulted in a taxable gain of $4,027.85. This taxable gain is calculated by taking the gross proceeds (the net surrender value of $947.43, plus the outstanding loan of $62,098.47) and subtracting the basis of $59,018. In this scenario, the policy owner would have had to pay $1,611.14 in income taxes (in the 40% total tax bracket), and she no longer would have the benefit of the life insurance policy.

Another option was to take extended term life insurance in the amount of the original policy's current net benefit ($37,901.58) for about 12 months or to take a reduced paid-up policy with a death benefit of $3,399. She chose to take the reduced paid-up death benefit, which means there are no further premiums or interest due.

The situation above is quite common. The tax ramifications for this woman were minimal. Others do not fare as well.

QUESTION 109: How Can A Policy Loan Be A Pitfall?

Law and the Life Insurance Contract addresses the potential tax pitfalls for which life insurance policyholders must be on the lookout. The book specifically mentions minimum deposit insurance plans, which are financed through payments-either out-of-pocket or with a policy loan. "Minimum deposit insurance plans can constitute an unexpected `tax trap' for the ill-informed or just unlucky," the book states. "These potential pitfalls suggest that financing life insurance should be approached only with the greatest of care. Even then, it is risky and subject to factors beyond the insurer's and policy owner's control."*(Law and the Life Insurance Contract; Muriel T. Crawford and William T. Beadles; Irwin, 1989, 6th Edition).*

An example that illustrates this "tax pitfall"; is that of a 31-year-old man whose father had bought him a financed (minimum deposit) policy, with a death benefit of $150,000, when the insured was 4 years old. The man's father was the original owner, and ownership was transferred to the insured on his 21st birthday. The man's father remembered that the agent who sold the policy had told him that, after the initial payment, the policy could be put on automatic premium loan. There would be no further premiums or other costs to be paid, the agent had said, and there always would be a fully paid-up death benefit of $150,000. This was simply not true, even though the policy had been sold on the basis of its being a fully guaranteed policy.

The situation was dire. The policy loan was up to $70,327.83, and, with dividend additions, the gross death benefit had grown to $184,300.17. The problem was revealed when it was discovered that the net cash value was $74,600.61. This was the maximum allowable loan on the policy. But, at the next renewal, the loan would increase to $75,414.72, so no further loan value was available. The insured received a bill for loan interest of $3,348.94, and because the premium was $1,515, his total annual out-of-pocket cost would be $4,863.94 for $185,000 of coverage. This was not an affordable premium for this insured. If he let the policy lapse, he would have a taxable gain of $39,247.41. There would have been a net surrender value of $5,352.98. Assuming that the insured was in a combined 35% tax bracket, he

would have had to pay $8,383.61 for a supposedly paid-up-for-life pol-
icy. The only way have prevented the policy from exploding was to
surrender paid-up additions, which the carrier said would not lower
the basis. This was a short term solution.

The carrier did not give the policyholder any indication that the policy was so far off the original marks. This is not unusual. Only a few
carriers have added a line to their annual reports stating the client age
at which policies will lapse, making it important for policyholders to
monitor policy performance regularly. Often, the agent who sold the
policy has no further contact with the insured after the original sale, so
the policy is not re-viewed. Policy loans present a similar issue. A policy with a large loan and loan interest can eventually crash, creating an
issue of no coverage and a significant phantom income-tax gain. This is
because the IRS considers any policy value over basis to be taxable
income. For example, a 35-year-old man owned a policy that his father
had purchased for him when he was 4 years old for a single premium
of $10,000. The policy contract was designed to default to an automatic
premium loan, which means the son was borrowing his annual premium payments against the value of the policy.

He, therefore, has never made a premium payment out of his own
pocket. Recently, however, the automatic loan program reached its
limit—that is, the total value of the policy had been borrowed against.
As a result, the insurer notified the insured man that annual payments
of $4,000 would be required to keep the policy in-force. If he let the pol-
icy lapse, he would have had a phantom taxable gain of more than
$70,000—the value of the policy, less the $10,000 initial payment. This
was a significant problem for the man, since his annual income was
about $45,000. He decided to keep the policy in-force until a better
solution could be found.

How long will companies continue to lure life policyholders with
the promise of something for nothing? As these examples demonstrate,
a policy loan can be a time bomb in a life insurance policy. And as with
any type of bomb, if not defused correctly, it can be disastrous. That
ticking sound you hear is all the policy loans out there just waiting to
explode.

CHAPTER 11: LIFE INSURANCE AND QUALIFIED RETIREMENT PLANS

QUESTION 110: Should I Have A Life Insurance Policy Inside Of A Qualified Retirement Plan?

Qualified retirement plans are designed to encourage employees to save money now, so that they will have enough to sustain them when they are no longer working. Employer contributions are deductible for the employer and tax deferred for employees, within certain limits. The money that employees authorize their employers to divert into these savings plans—called elective deferral contributions-are tax deferred. Earnings on these monies also are tax deferred. Participants pay income tax when they receive distributions from their plans.

Simply stated, a qualified plan is a tax-favored accumulation vehicle. Permanent (cash value) life insurance can also be used as an accumulation vehicle. In these cases, premiums are paid with after-tax dollars, and the death benefit is income-tax free.

Paying life-insurance and annuity premiums with qualified-plan dollars is controversial. Why put an accumulation vehicle that enjoys tax-deferred treatment inside a plan that, by definition, is tax deferred? Life insurance and annuities are relatively expensive, in part because the vast majority of them are sold by agents on commission. This leaves producers open to allegations that their sales pitches may be aimed more at filling their own wallets, rather than helping customers choose their best investment tool.

When asked why he targeted banks, bank robber Willie Sutton, as the legend goes, replied, "Because that's where the money is." Miners headed to California in 1849 because they heard that gold was there. Some producers recommend paying life-insurance and annuity premiums with qualified-plan dollars, in part, because the plans are a ready source of otherwise scarce premium dollars.

Selling life insurance is a tough but financially rewarding job for the producers who master the art and climb to the top of their field. Selling annuities is easier, but the temptation is there to sell high-commission life policies. The truth is, commission payouts are life and annuity producers' bread and butter. The fact that this business is highly commission-driven draws the attention of regulators who are increasingly focused on market conduct.

The plaintiffs' bar (attorneys) already has noticed that life insurance and annuities are being sold within qualified plans. Complaints have been filed and cases are pending. There will probably be more.

QUESTION 111: Why Can It Be A Good Idea To Have Life Insurance Inside Of A Qualified Retirement Program?

To understand why, a good starting place to look is at 403(b) plans, which are tax-deferred retirement plans for employees of schools and other nonprofit organizations. These plans are also known as tax-sheltered annuities, even though the term includes mutual funds and "incidental" life insurance. The rules for selling life insurance inside a 403(b) plan are fairly loose. A participant can use up to 50% of the aggregate contributions made to a 403(b) plan to purchase whole life insurance. In the case of universal life insurance, only 25% of the aggregate contributions can be used to purchase a policy.

Consider, for example, that a tax-sheltered annuity participant has accumulated $100,000. Now suppose a producer persuades the participant to use $49,000 to pay for a whole life insurance policy. The result: life insurance sales charges and other expenses eat up a lot of participant dollars, which otherwise could be growing toward a retirement nest egg. There is no question that this sale earned the producer a nice commission. But there are arguments in favor of such a purchase:

- The life insurance is purchased with pretax dollars.
- The life insurance provides a self-completing financial and/or estate plan.
- The participant may keep the policy after retirement (by paying income tax on the cash value).
- Premiums can be paid from previously accumulated contributions.
- If no longer needed, the life insurance cash value can be transferred to an annuity contract.
- The participant can borrow the cash value subject to Internal Revenue Service Code Sec. 72(p) rules.
- The life insurance company calculates the annual cost of insurance that must be included in the participant's taxable income. This amount is based on so-called "P.S. 58" one-year term rates described in Revenue Ruling 55-747, 1955-2 CB 228.

QUESTION 112: Why is having Life Insurance inside a Qualified Retirement Program Not a Good Idea?

The arguments against buying life insurance with qualified-plan dollars are as follows:

- It is more of a commission-driven than a needs-oriented sale.
- The mortality charges introduce an additional cost element when compared with an annuity or mutual fund. (Annuities on which the surrender charge is waived upon death contain a mortality element, but it is small enough to ignore for our purposes.)
- It is an attempt to fill a permanent need with temporary coverage. The life insurance policy must be distributed by the plan at retirement and income tax paid on it, or it must be converted to an annuity payout or surrendered.
- Income tax must be paid each year on the current cost of the "incidental" life insurance element.
- It uses up the participant's 403(b) contribution limit-called the exclusion allowance.
- All other things being equal, a lot less money will be accumulated when life insurance is used as the accumulation vehicle.

QUESTION 113: What Else Do I Need To Know About Life Insurance Inside a Qualified Plan?

Qualified plans, including employee stock-ownership plans, can offer life insurance to plan participants as long as the U.S. Treasury's "incidental benefit" rule is met. That is, the life insurance must be secondary to the plan's mission of providing retirement income. In general, the incidental rule is satisfied if the cost of the life insurance is less than 25% of the cost of benefits under the plan. In addition to the 25% rule, another test applies: The initial amount of life insurance protection cannot exceed 100 times the monthly annuity payable upon retirement. The so-called "100 to 1" test does not limit the death benefit, but instead it provides a safe harbor for plan trustees.

On or before retirement, the plan must surrender the life insurance and use the cash value to provide retirement benefits or distribute the policy to the participant. In general, the cash value of the life insurance policy must be included as taxable income in the year the distribution is made. A better measure of the value of the life insurance policy, however, may be the policy reserve maintained by the life insurance company.

Only recently have annuities inside qualified retirement plans become controversial. In some cases, annuities are the traditional funding vehicle. For example, two of the three permissible investment vehicles for most 403(b) participants are annuities-fixed annuities, variable annuities and mutual funds. The controversy focuses on variable annuities, which typically have considerably higher expense charges than mutual funds.

Again, the argument centers on funding a tax-deferred plan with a high-expense investment vehicle—a variable annuity. This is a fair concern, since there are several alternative investment vehicles that have lower expense charges than variable annuities.

Solving this problem is theoretically easy. If you must fund a qualified plan with variable annuities, make sure the cost is comparable to the mutual fund alternative. Several companies offer low-cost variable annuities, but they don't pay any agent commission. Therein lays the problem. We have come full circle back to the fact that this is a commission-driven business. Logically, variable-annuity sales should be a tiny fraction of what they are. A fee-only financial advisor usually will recommend a variable annuity, only when the client has a maximized qualified pension plan and individual retirement account contributions-and has cash left to invest. Quite simply, the public does not seek out variable annuities; agents sell them to the public. The same is true of life insurance.

Producers often urge affluent clients to allocate some of their qualified retirement funds to life insurance and annuity contracts. The sales pitch inevitably stresses the tax benefits of purchasing these products within a qualified plan. Keep in mind that most tax professionals will say that letting tax considerations drive the decision-making process is a bad idea. It always seems to come back to haunt you.

Including life insurance inside a qualified plan is fraught with complexity. Absent careful planning, the ability to avoid estate taxes and some income taxes on the death benefit will be lost. The combined effect could mean loss of 70% to 80% of the death benefit and/or the accumulated value.

QUESTION 114: Are There Any Government Regulation Issues and Concerns (Insurance Industry as well) regarding Life Insurance in A Qualified Plan?

We must also consider the Employee Retirement Income Security Act of 1974, when life insurance or annuities are included in a qualified plan. The U.S. Department of Labor oversees ERISA. The Department of Labor has contended that funding death benefits, in qualified plans with permanent life insurance, is a breach of fiduciary duty. To date, the majority of cases involving the Department of Labor have dealt with highly abusive practices in plans covering large numbers of employees. Sooner or later, the department will focus its attention on smaller plans, too.

The life insurance industry has a big public-relations job ahead. It cannot fall back on the ancient standard of caveat emptor-let the buyer bewares. The industry must proactively set market-conduct standards and enforce them rigorously.

The Insurance Marketplace Standards Association is an important step in the right direction. Mandatory commission disclosure at the point of sale would be helpful in exposing commission-driven products. As experience in the United Kingdom demonstrates, mandatory commission disclosure need not put agents out of business. In the mid-1990s, British financial-services regulators began requiring life companies to reveal expenses, commissions, lapse rates and surrender values to consumers at the point of sale. This transparency led to a more professional sales force and improved persistency. It also demonstrated that consumers don't mind if agents receive commissions, but they will object to big commission numbers.

It is not always inappropriate to employ life insurance inside qualified plans, but many of these sales are inappropriate. In the right situation, with good legal and tax advice and a competent insurance advisor, it can all work out just fine.

That, unfortunately, describes a small percentage of such sales, but word is getting out. At the time of the writing of this book, two well-known life insurers recently acknowledged that they no longer allow the use of their life insurance products inside qualified plans. The wisdom of that decision will become apparent; as yet another round of class-action litigation rocks the industry in the foreseeable future.

Despite all the issues discussed above, life insurance sales to pension plans were on the rise again in 2001. The justification is that the 2001 tax law increased the amount that individuals could contribute to their pension and profit sharing plans. Before the tax changes, high net worth individuals were limited in their contribution level and there was not enough capacity to commit premium dollars to a retirement plan.

In 2002, the defined benefit commenced to increase and, combined with the elimination of the actuarial reductions in benefits at age 62, meant a further increase for many. This increase allows for potentially increased life insurance inside the plan.

The issues discussed above still apply. And thus, the use of life insurance inside a qualified plan usually will lead to more problems than benefits.

CHAPTER 12: TAXES AND LIFE INSURANCE

NOTES: The information discussed in the following questions (#115-121) is based on certain life insurance policy, tax and legal assumptions, but is not meant as legal or tax advice and is, also, subject to change. Only your own attorney, accountant or other tax professional can give you such advice.

QUESTION 115: Does The Cash Value of My Permanent Life Insurance Policy Grow on a Tax-Deferred Basis?

The Tax Court has held, in a case involving a cash basis taxpayer, that the cash values were not constructively received by the taxpayer where he could not reach them without surrendering the life insurance policy. The necessity of surrendering the life insurance policy constituted a substantial "limitation or restriction" on their receipt. (Theodore Cohen, 39 TC 1055 (1963), 1964-1 CB 4.)

QUESTION 116: How are Withdrawals from a Permanent Life Insurance Policy Typically Taxed?

Living proceeds received under life insurance contracts which satisfy the conditions of the seven pay test of IRC Sec. 7702A (b) (i.e., not modified endowment contracts) are taxed according to the FIFO method of accounting. They are taxed under the "cost recovery rule" no matter when the contract was entered into or when premiums were paid. In other words, such amounts are included in gross income only to the extent they exceed the investment in the contract. However, distributions taken in the first fifteen policy years which reduce the benefits of the contract may be, to a limited extent, taxable. (Internal Revenue Code sec. 77022)

QUESTION 117: Are Policy Loans Income Tax Free?

Policy loans under life insurance policies are not treated as distributions, assuming the policy qualifies as life insurance under IRC Sec. 7702 and is not considered a modified endowment contract. Upon lapse or surrender, the outstanding loan balance is automatically repaid from policy values held as collateral (death benefit is reduced by the amount of the policy loan). However, this use of collateralized policy values to repay a loan during a lapse or surrender may cause the recognition of taxable income. (IRC Sec. 7702).

QUESTION 118: What Are the Income Tax Consequences of the inside Interest during the Policy's Lifetime and at Surrender/Termination

The value of a life insurance policy can impact a number of situations. Often omitted in sales presentations, is the possibility of a taxable gain, if the policy is surrendered. The inside interest is typically income tax deferred. The inside interest is either income tax exempt or partially income tax exempt, depending upon how the policy terminates and the circumstances surrounding termination. There are four possibilities:

1. The policy terminates upon the insured's death. The death benefit is generally received income tax free by the beneficiary, so the inside interest is income tax exempt.
2. The policy is surrendered and the sum of the cash value and the total dividends is smaller than the total premiums; that is, there is a "loss" on surrender. The cash value is generally received income tax free by the policyholder so the inside interest is income tax exempt. The "loss" is not deductible because the price of the protection exceeds the inside interest, and the price of the protection is not deductible, except to the extent it offsets what otherwise would be taxable as inside interest.

3. The policy is surrendered and the sum of the cash value and the total dividends is equal to the total premiums; that is, there is no "gain" or "loss" on surrender. The cash value is generally received income tax free by the policyholder, so the inside interest is income tax exempt. In this instance, the price of the protection and the inside interest are equal, so that the otherwise nondeductible price of the protection offsets the otherwise taxable inside interest.

4. The policy is surrendered and the sum of the cash value and the total dividends is larger than the total premiums; that is, there is a "gain" on surrender. The "gain" generally is ordinary income to the policyholder in the year the policy is surrendered, so that the inside interest is partially income tax exempt and partially taxable. The inside interest, which in this instance exceeds the price of the protection, is income tax exempt to the extent of the price of the protection and taxable to the extent the inside interest exceeds the price of the protection.

(Source: *The Insurance Forum; November 2001 issue; article excerpt; Dr. Joseph Belth*)

QUESTION 119: Are There Any Taxes On A Life Insurance Death Benefit?

The common conception is that life insurance is not subject to taxation. This is half-true and half-false. Life Insurance is almost always not subject to income taxation, however under current tax law (2003); it is still subject to estate taxation.

As a general rule, life insurance death proceeds are excludable from the beneficiary's gross income. IRC Sec. 101(a)(1). Death proceeds from single premium, term life insurance, periodic premium or flexible premium life insurance policies are received income tax free by the beneficiary regardless of whether the beneficiary is an individual, a corporation, a partnership, a trustee, or the insured's estate. (Treasury Regulation 1.101-1). However, the death benefits may be subject to estate taxes, gift taxes and any other inheritance tax. This is a good reason to visit with an estate planning professional; somebody who is appropriately licensed and qualified.

How to roughly calculate your potential estate tax:

1. Total your gross estate. Include anything of value in which you have an ownership interest: Home and other real estate, retirement plan balances, stocks, mutual funds, other investments, businesses, life insurance proceeds (not held outside your estate), etc.
2. Subtract all allowable deductions, such as funeral and administrative expenses, mortgages, loans, credit card debt, charitable deductions, Adjustable Taxable gifts (post-1976 lifetime taxable transfers not included in gross estate), gift taxes paid on post-1976 taxable gifts, and applicable tax credits (e.g., unified tax credit, state death tax credit, foreign tax credit, tax on prior transfers credit, marital deduction, other applicable expenses).
3. If you have a positive net estate, this is your net taxable estate.
4. Use the table below to calculate your tentative estate tax.

Notes:

Your unified credit is subtracted from your tentative tax, if unused during your lifetime. The unified tax credit means that no federal estate tax is payable on a taxable estate equal to your exemption equivalent. Estate taxes are due when your tentative tax is greater than your unified credit.

Your estate may be valued at death or six months later, whichever is more beneficial. If you own a farm or closely held business, your method of paying tax will be different.

Use this information to generate a rough idea of your potential estate tax. Be sure to check that this is the current tax table by visiting the IRS web site at or consult with a properly certified estate planning advisor.

Estate Tax Table:

The Economic Growth and Tax Relief Reconciliation Act of 2001 have changed the federal estate tax numbers. Below are the non-guaranteed changes:

Year	Exemption	Maximum Tax Bracket	Unified Credit
2003	$ 1 Million	49 percent	$ 345,800
2004	$ 1.5 Million	48 percent	$ 555,800
2005	$ 1.5 Million	47 percent	$ 555,800
2006	$ 2 Million	46 percent	$ 780,800
2007	$ 2 Million	45 percent	$ 780,800
2008	$ 2 Million	45 percent	$ 780,800
2009	$ 3.5 Million	45 percent	$1,455,800
2010	N/A	N/A	N/A
2011 **	$ 1 Million**	55 percent**	$ 345,800**

**The Taxpayer Relief Act of 1997 numbers will be reinstated provided that The Economic Growth and Tax Relief Reconciliation Act of 2001 are not extended. Under current law, the federal estate tax is cancelled for only year 2010.

Please note that I am not an attorney and this is not legal advice. You should consider consulting an attorney or at the minimum purchasing an appropriate book for Nolo Press. This applies for any tax related question.

QUESTION 120: How Could The Estate Tax Affect My Estate?

This table shows that the estate tax (as long as it is around) affects everyone including the most rich and famous. The table is an overview of the gross estates, settlement costs and percent their estate shrunk due to settlement costs. Please note this table is based upon publicly available information and may not be accurate in all cases. Please also note that this is based upon the estate tax rates at the time of each person's death. The bottom line is that proper planning is an important part of life for everyone.

Name:	Gross Estate:	Settlement Costs:	Percent Shrinkage:
Marilyn Monroe	$818,176	$450,327	55%
Franklin Roosevelt	1,940,999	574,867	30%
Herbert Hoover	2,162,479	827,634	38%
Clark Gable	2,806,525	1,108,038	30%
Dwight D. Eisenhower	2,905,857	671,429	23%
Russell Firestone	3,739,969	1,187,546	32%
Cecil B. DeMille	4,043,607	1,396,064	35%
Al Jolsen	4,385,143	1,349,066	31%
Gary Cooper	4,984,985	1,530,454	31%
Marion Davies	5,519,009	3,311,781	60%
Henry J. Kaiser, Sr.	5,597,772	2,488,364	44%
Alfred Pillsbury	6,346,498	2,269,707	36%
Dean Witter	7,451,055	1,830,717	26%
Stanley Field	8,447,719	4,678,657	55%
Harry M. Warner	8,946,618	2,308,444	55%
William Skelly	9,735,075	4,264,891	54%
Elvis Presley	10,165,434	7,374,635	73%
Alwin C. Ernst, CPA	12,642,431	7,124,112	56%
Thomas Slick	14,594,650	2,093,328	14%
Charles Woolworth	16,788,702	10,391,303	62%
J.P. Morgan	17,121,482	11,893,691	73%
Sewell Avery	19,100,000	14,083,959	74%
A.H. Wiggin	20,493,999	14,847,333	72%
Mrs. Andrew Carnegie	20,620,340	13,163,899	64%
Sen. Robert Kerr	20,800,000	9,500,000	46%
William Boeing	22,386,158	10,589,748	47%
Walt Disney	23,004,851	6,811,943	30%
John D. Rockefeller	26,905,182	17,125,988	64%
Bill Graham	30,000,000 + (Estimated)	$16,000,000+ (Estimated)	53%
Frederick Vanderbilt	76,838,530	42,846,112	56%
Malcolm Forbes	1,000,000,000 (Estimated)	550,000,000 (Estimated)	55% (Estimated)

QUESTION 121: How Is A Monetary Settlement Received From An Insurance Company Class Action Settlement Taxed?

Policyholders eligible for compensation are usually given several options, depending on the life insurance company. The tax ramifications will depend on the method you choose. You will need to discuss this with your tax advisor. On most life insurance policies (except for

Modified Endowment Contracts (MEC's), discussed in Question 12), any amount taken from a policy, up the amount of premiums paid in (your basis), is received income tax free; any amount received after that is subject to income tax (treated as gain).

Policyholders, eligible for compensation in a class action lawsuit may be offered several options. Most of the carriers involved have offered two to three "relief choices" to policyholders eligible for class action settlements. The choices included a refund of premiums (with interest) and two types of "basic claim relief." There could be taxable money involved in each choice.

If you opt for a return of premium with interest, the premium is not subject to taxes, but the interest would be. For other settlement options, distributions from a life insurance policy are not taxable until you've received more money than you paid in premiums. Any amount above that is taxed at the ordinary income rate.

If you take a settlement from a life insurance company due to a lawsuit, the company will send you an Internal Revenue Service (IRS) form 1099. This form shows who you received income from and how much. Therefore, the IRS will know that you received this money, and will match it up with your tax return. This form shows gross earned income, which is fully taxable. The insurance company should also provide you with a document showing how the amount of the settlement breaks down. This allows you to pay taxes only on the amount above the sums of your premium paid; if applicable. These forms are required to be sent by the insurance company by January 31st of the year your tax is due.

Either, the Form 1099MISC, which applies to miscellaneous income; this form shows the total amount you received. Or you will receive a Form 1099INT, which lists the interest payment of your premium that you received.

This can be confusing, so you should seek a qualified tax advisor.

CHAPTER 13: LIFE INSURANCE TRUSTS

QUESTION 122: What Is An Irrevocable Life Insurance Trust And Why Should I Consider It?

One of the main reasons to have set up these trusts historically has been to avoid or minimize any potential estate tax. Currently, there are other planning purposes for these trusts. An advantage of the life insurance trust is that it removes the life insurance from the estate of the insured. **Please note that I am not an attorney and this is not to be used as legal advice.**

Despite the advantages of an irrevocable life insurance trust (ILIT), it is important for anyone thinking about setting one up to keep these points in mind:

- If you transfer an existing life insurance policy into the ILIT and die within three years of the transfer, then the policy will revert back to your estate and will be subject to estate taxes.
- The trust is irrevocable. If it is your trust and you are funding it with a life insurance policy, you are considered the Grantor. You must give up complete control over the trust and will not have any rights including: changing the beneficiary, making policy loans, withdrawing funds and terminating the policy.
- Once a payment is made to the trust, the trustee will send out a letter; under the gift-tax exclusion rules under what's known as the Crummey provision (named after a legal case regarding this issue). This letter allows beneficiaries a 30 day period (typically) wherein they have the opportunity to withdraw their share.
- Enables the grantor to leverage the annual gift tax exclusion to a much larger sum of money, through the purchase of life insurance.

- Provides the insured's heirs estate liquidity on a transfer tax-free basis.
- Replaces estate assets used to pay estate taxes or to provide a charitable bequest.
- Gives the grantor the opportunity to control the distribution of the death proceeds through the trust provisions in a manner consistent with overall estate objectives
- Protects the trust assets from the trust beneficiaries' creditors.
- The heirs are not obligated to use the proceeds to pay the estate taxes
- Trusts can cost approximately $500 to $2,000 and should be drawn up by an attorney. The more complex the situation, the higher the fee can be.

You should carefully consider who the trustee is and discuss the ramifications with your attorney.

Special Considerations of Life Insurance-

An example is: If the owner resides in a community property state and the policy is purchased with community property funds, one-half the proceeds are owned by the surviving spouse, no matter who the policy names as the beneficiary. This result can be varied by a written agreement between the spouses in which one spouse transfers all interest in a particular insurance policy to the other spouse. Insurance Companies should supply this form upon request. *(Plan Your Estate, NOLO Press)*

QUESTION 123: How Does An Irrevocable Life Insurance Trust Work?

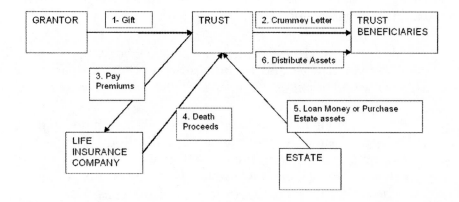

1. Grantor/insured annually makes a gift to the irrevocable trust in an amount sufficient to pay the premiums on a life insurance policy.

2. The trustee of the trust annually makes the gifts available to the trust beneficiaries for a limited number of days pursuant to the Crummey withdrawal provisions in the trust document. This qualifies the gift for the gift tax annual exclusion treatment.

3. If the trust beneficiaries fail to exercise the withdrawal right over the cash gift, the trustee may use the gift to pay premiums for the life insurance policy. The trustee is the owner and beneficiary of the policy.

4. At the death of the grantor/insured, the life insurance death proceeds pass transfer tax-free to the trust.

5. The trustee may loan money to purchase assets from the estate, thus providing liquidity to the estate to help pay estate taxes.

6. The trust assets are distributed to the beneficiaries of the trust as directed by the terms of the trust document

QUESTION 124: What Is My Basic Role If I'm Named Trustee?

The first thing to realize is the importance of fully understanding your role and responsibility as a trustee. As a trustee you also become a fiduciary. Both are defined here:

- Fiduciary: A fiduciary is defined as a person who occupies a position of special trust and confidence in handling the affairs or funds of another person (*Law and the Life Insurance Contract*).

- Trustee: A person to whom property is legally committed in trust, to be applied either for the benefit of specified individuals, or for public uses; one who is in trusted with property for the benefit of another; also, a person in whose hands the effects of another are attached in a trustee process. (*Source*: *Webster's Revised Unabridged Dictionary*)

Fiduciaries of an irrevocable life insurance trust have a duty to act in the best interest of beneficiaries. Most fiduciary breaches are the result of a lack of prudence. Basically, the fiduciaries do not understand their responsibilities.

QUESTION 125: What Are Some Tools To Assist Me As A Trustee And Fiduciary?

This book provides some tools in performing your duties. If you wish an external resource; find a knowledgeable advisor to assist yourself or seek out a professional trustee or learn about more about life insurance policies and trusts. Be advised that a significant percentage of advisors and professional trustees do not possess sufficient knowledge to be of significant assistance.

Issues to keep in mind are:

- Are the policy type, face amount, planned premium, riders, underwriting class, insured, ownership and beneficiary designations correct?
- Is the policy performing according to the original illustrations, sales letters and materials?
- Are there are any surprises—such as unexpected loans, required premiums or change in modified endowment contract status?
- Do you have a current in-force illustration? This is the only way to evaluate the policy, so it is important to examine the carrier's illustration questionnaire. My recommendation is to do this every 2-3 years.
- Review the rate of return as discussed in question 19.
- Is the policy providing good value?
- Should it be replaced (see the replacement chapter 9, question numbers 93-105)

CHAPTER 14: MISCELLANEOUS ISSUES

QUESTION 126: What Happens When It Is Time For A Claim To Be Paid?

It is a good idea for a policy to be in an easily accessible place for the beneficiary. A safe deposit box may not be advisable as some states will seal the safe deposit box upon the death of the owner. The next step is to either call your life insurance agent or call the life insurance company to request the form. The life insurance company will require a death certificate. It is advisable for the person handling the affairs of the deceased to obtain several death certificates.

If your policy is part of a group employee benefits program (as an insured), you should make sure that it is noted somewhere for your beneficiary. You may be able to call the insurance company, or your employer's human resources department may need to be contacted.

Other types of life insurance are with credit card companies or other financial institutions, travel life insurance, mortgage life insurance, accidental death insurance, credit life insurance and with the Social Security Administration. Finding these policies may require research and phone calls to lenders, etc regarding any life insurance benefits.

When submitting a claim, the insured may have chosen a payment plan. If you are not aware of the option, the insurance company will inform you about the option and how it works. If the policy owner has not chosen the settlement option, it will need to be chosen at the time the claim is filed. There is no income tax on the death benefit. You control all the options except for the Lump Sum cost. However, if the beneficiary, for any reason, cannot manage money, then the other settlements should be considered, unless there someone who can manage the money for them.

The more commonly found settlement options are:

- **Lump sum**—The life insurance company pays the entire death benefit in one lump sum, which allows you to do what you wish with it. The company typically will open a money market account and issue a check book. That way, you do not need to make any decisions until you are ready. There are no restrictions on this account of any type.
- **Specific income provision**—You receive from the company both principal and interest on a predetermined schedule.
- **Life income option**—You receive a guaranteed income for life. The amount of income depends on the death benefit, your gender, and your age at the time of the insured's death.
- **Interest income option**—The company holds the proceeds and pays you interest on them. The death benefit remains intact and goes to a secondary beneficiary upon your death

This is an area where life insurance companies do act quickly. If all the paperwork is in order and a death certificate is received, a beneficiary usually receives the death benefit within a week when the life insurance carrier does act quickly.

If an insured passes away within two years of the life insurance policy's issue date, the incontestability and suicide clauses can come into play. The suicide clause is self-explanatory. The incontestability clause allows the insurer to challenge a policy for suspected mistruths, such as concealing a condition such as heart trouble and/or passing away from something heart related. This would be grounds for denying a claim. A common occurrence is when someone is a smoker and claims not to be. In this event, the insurer will either completely deny the claim or pay the death benefit, based on the amount of coverage that the premiums paid would have purchased on a smoker basis. If an insurer does decide to investigate, it can take between a month to a month and a half in most cases. Therefore, be truthful and honest; otherwise, you can negate the whole reason for getting life insurance in the first place.

QUESTION 127: What Happens When You Need to Track down a Missing and/or Unknown Life Insurance Policy

Depending on the life insurance company, they may require the life insurance policy at the death of the insured. Alternatively, you may know that the insured had a life insurance policy(ies); but you do not know who the carrier was.

Even if you find the life insurance policy (ies), there may be a question as to whether or not you will actually receive the death benefit due. You will need to find out if the policy is still in-force. This will depend on the type of policy, and sometimes, on the carrier:

- Term life insurance is very simple. If the insured passes away at or after the policy has passed the grace period, the premium has not been paid and the carrier will not accept payment, then there is no death benefit. If the insured passes away before this point, then the death benefit will be paid.
- Whole Life should continue if there is an automatic premium loan provision which will borrow money from the policy's cash value to pay premiums. Once the cash value is exhausted, the policy will lapse.
- Universal Life—each month the company will deduct from the cash value the cost of insurance (mortality cost), expense charges and any other costs. Once the cash value is exhausted, the policy will lapse.
- Other policies such as variable life, variable universal life, and survivorship life policies of each type will stay in-force, depending on whether they are a type whole life or universal life.
- Typically, with a permanent life policy, you will receive the money, if the death occurred while the policy was "in-force," meaning all premium payments were made up until the time of death. If a certain amount of time since the death occurs, the carrier will pay the benefit *with interest* from the date of death; the amount of time varies by carrier.

Please note that there may exist certain modifications on each type of policy; so it is always a good idea to check with the insurance company. Older policies can have different methods those discussed above.

If the policy lapsed—meaning the insured stopped making premium payments before he died—there is a chance that you might get nothing. When a permanent life insurance policy lapses, most insurance companies switch its status from permanent insurance to one of two options:

- **"Extended term"**—The insurance company uses the cash value of the policy to buy a short-term life insurance policy using the cash value of the policy.
- **"Reduced paid up"**—The insurance company will keep the policy in-force, but reduces the death benefit.

If the policy lapses, and the extended-term period expires before the insured dies, the policy is worthless and the beneficiary will get nothing. If the insured dies *before* the extended-term period is up, the beneficiary will receive the death benefit. If the policy lapsed *because* the insured died (thus ending premium payments), the beneficiary will still collect the full death benefit, regardless of when the extended term was up. In any case as before, a death certificate is still required.

The following is a checklist of tips for keeping life insurance policies where beneficiaries may find them as well as for other places where beneficiaries can look:

- **Keep all your financial records (especially your life insurance policy) in one place**—Don't force your beneficiaries to search your house from top to bottom when you're gone.
- **Your safety deposit box**
- **Your file cabinets, address books, etc.**
- **Your computer**
- **Your beneficiary should go through canceled checks and contact your bank for copies of old checks**—Look for checks made out to insurance companies.

- **Check credit card statements**—Credit card companies also issue life insurance.
- **If you are a beneficiary ask those who may have known about your relative's finances**—Contact the deceased's family, friends and advisors, i.e. lawyer, accountant, banker, financial advisor, insurance agent(s) and trustee. The insurance agent(s) would be the most likely to know about life insurance policies.
- **The beneficiary should check probate court records**—for details of your relative's estate. If the estate has gone through or is in probate court, a life insurance policy could show up as an asset.
- **The beneficiary should contact the deceased's current and prior employers**—The Human Resources person should know of any group insurance as well as any supplement life insurance or if applicable with the Union Welfare office.
- **Contact the Medical Information Bureau**—They offer a "policy locator service". The service offers a way to help locate lost life insurance policies by submitting a decedent's name for a search against their Policy Locator database. This database contains information processed over the last eleven years (as of 2006) consisting of over 140 million records representing inquiries submitted on individually underwritten life insurance applications. Application activity often leads to policies and matches against this database are identified. As of August 2006, the cost for this service is $75 U.S. The web site address is: http://www.mib.com/html/lost-life-insurance.html.
- **Contact every insurance company with which you had a policy**—even if you're not sure it is still in-force. There are over 2000 life insurance companies in the United States, a list of most of their web sites can be found on my web site www.tonysteuer.com in the resources section.
- **Check the mail for a year after death for premium notices**—if a policy has been paid up, there will not be any notice of premium payments due. Typically the company may still send an annual notice regarding the status of the policy or it may pay or send notice of a dividend.
- **Review your loved one's income tax returns for the past two years**—Look for interest income from and interest expenses paid to life insurance companies. Life insurance companies pay interest on accumulations on permanent policies and charge interest on policy loans.

- **Check to see if the insurance company has changed names—**this can be done through your state's insurance department (see listing in Appendix A). Another resource is online at A.M. Best's web site—www.ambest.com or their annual reference Best's Key Ratings Guide (life/health edition) which should be available in the reference section of many larger libraries. This annually updated reference contains a list of insurance company names and addresses, as well as insurers' name changes, mergers and other information.

- **Check with the state's unclaimed property office—**After a number of years (typically 3 years and can be dictated by the state), an insurance company holding the unclaimed money cannot find the rightful owner, it must turn over either the full death benefit or the cash value to the state's comptroller's department (only if the insurance company knows that the insured has passed away). The state where the insured last lived is usually the state where the funds are turned over to. The department maintains a database that lists the names and addresses of lost beneficiaries. There are millions of insurance policies that are "lost" and you are not alone in trying to track down a "lost" policy. Many states will try to contact beneficiaries. See Appendix C for a listing of each State's Unclaimed Property Office's contact information.

QUESTION 128: What If A Life Insurance Company Goes Bankrupt?

In the early 1980s the issue of a life insurance company becoming bankrupt or insolvent was a relative rarity. By the early 1990s, however there were some well-known insurance companies which were placed into receivership.

Because insurance companies are regulated by the states, federal bankruptcy law is not applicable to insurance receivership proceedings. In fact, insurance companies cannot declare bankruptcy; instead, they are placed into insolvency receivership or liquidation by the state's insurance department. State liquidation courts then rule on the many complex issues involved in an insurance company insolvency, including what becomes of the insurance policies and cash values.

Oftentimes, the policies can be bought by other insurers with the death benefits remaining the same, but this may involve a lowering of cash values and/or an increase in premiums.

Insurance companies are regulated by individual states, and it is ultimately the responsibility of the states to safeguard the solvency of insurers licensed to do business in their state. When states determine that an insurer is insolvent, the mechanism used to protect policyholders is the guaranty association system. All 50 states, the District of Columbia, and Puerto Rico have guaranty associations to which licensed life and health insurers must belong.

The best resource for information on this issue is the National Organization of Life and Health Insurance Guaranty Associations (www.nolhga.com). The following information is from their website.[1]

> The National Organization of Life and Health Insurance Guaranty Associations (NOLHGA) is a voluntary association composed of the life and health insurance guaranty associations of all 50 states, the District of Columbia, and Puerto Rico. When an insolvency involves multiple states, NOLHGA assists its state guaranty association members in quickly and cost-effectively fulfilling their statutory obligations to policyholders.

> NOLHGA was founded in 1983 after the state guaranty associations determined that there was a need for a coordinating mechanism to assist affected guaranty associations in efficiently meeting their statutory obligations in the face of the often-complex issues resulting from the insolvency of an insurer licensed to do business in multiple states.

> State guaranty associations provide coverage, up to certain statutory limits, for resident policyholders of insolvent member insurers. NOLHGA provides its member state guaranty associations with a method for quickly and cost-effectively fulfilling their statutory obligations to policyholders in the event of a multi-state life and health insurer insolvency.

> When an insurer licensed in multiple states is declared insolvent, NOLHGA, on behalf of affected member state guaranty associa-

tions, assembles a task force of guaranty association officials. This task force—with the support of NOLHGA staff, legal experts, actuaries, and financial experts—develops a plan for meeting member association obligations. Typically, the task force analyzes the company's commitments; ensures that covered claims are paid; and, where appropriate, arranges for covered policies to be transferred to a healthy insurer.

The task force may also support the efforts of the receiver to dispose of the company's assets in a way that maximizes their value. When there is a shortfall of estate assets needed to fulfill all of the covered policyholder obligations of the insolvent insurer, guaranty associations assess the licensed insurers in their states a proportional share of the funds needed.

At all steps in the process, the affected state guaranty associations, working together through NOLHGA, cooperate with the receiver and other interested parties to build consensus on the steps needed to resolve an insolvency equitably and efficiently.

There are several key benefits that the state guaranty associations seek to achieve by working together through NOLHGA. The first is to decrease costs to the member insurers that fund state guaranty associations. Rather than each state association hiring its own legal and financial experts, the associations work together through NOLHGA and use one team of experts, significantly reducing costs to guaranty associations. This coordination of effort also helps reduce the length of time a receiver may require to develop a plan of rehabilitation or otherwise resolve a multi-state insolvency.

Since its creation in 1983, NOLHGA has assisted its member guaranty associations in guaranteeing more than $20.1 billion in coverage benefits for policyholders and annuitants of insolvent companies.

---

[1] The language from NOLHGA's web site is reprinted with the permission of NOLHGA, all rights reserved. Information on NOLHGA's web site is not intended as legal advice; no liability is assumed in connec-

tion with its use. Consumers should seek advice from a qualified attorney when considering any questions relating to guaranty association coverage.

QUESTION 129: As a Business Owner, Are There Any Special Planning Concepts?

This question is designed to serve as an overview of some of the most commonly used business planning concepts funded with life insurance. For each of these concepts we have listed, where applicable, description, plan objective, advantages, disadvantages, income tax position, gift tax position, estate tax position, ownership, premium payor, beneficiary, disability benefit, control of policy values, loss of use of money, cost recovery, deductible contribution of premium, corporate resolution, plan document or agreement and discrimination available.

CAVEAT: The information contained herein is to serve as an overview only. Consideration of the usage of any concepts requires an analysis of all the facts surrounding the case. Further amplification of concept features would have resulted in a voluminous and cumbersome amount of material. Feature descriptions are based on current interpretations of existing tax laws which are subject to change. Legal opinions are to be secured from the client's attorney/tax advisors as the concepts are applied.

BUY-SELL CROSS-PURCHASE

DESCRIPTION: Exchange stock or business interest for cash and/or notes among business owners or third party buyers.

PLAN OBJECTIVE: Convert non-liquid business interest to cash.

ADVANTAGES: Fair market value guaranteed and imme-
                             diate; keep heirs out of business.

DISADVANTAGES: Ties up personal discretionary income.

INCOME TAX POSITION: Gain, if any, upon sale of appreciated
                             stock subject to income tax.

GIFT TAX POSITION: None.

ESTATE POSITION: Value of business interest, as established
                             in buy-out agreement, includible in
                             owner's estate.

OWNER OF POLICY: Business purchasers, if not trusted.

PREMIUM PAYOR: Business purchasers or trustee.

BENEFICIARY: Business purchasers, if not trusted.

DISABILITY BENEFIT: Yes, if waiver of premium is included.

CONTROL OF
POLICY VALUES: Business purchasers or trustee.

LOSS OF USE OF MONEY: Yes.

COST RECOVERY: No.

DEDUCTIBLE CONTRIBUTION
OF PREMIUM: No.

CORPORATE RESOLUTION,
PLAN DOCUMENT OR
AGREEMENT: Agreement only.

DISCRIMINATION
AVAILABLE: Not applicable.

BUY-SELL ENTITY STOCK REDEMPTION

DESCRIPTION: Corporation redeems deceased's stock for cash and/or notes.

PLAN OBJECTIVE: Creates market for stock at a fair value and liquidity for stockholders.

ADVANTAGES: Fair market value guaranteed and immediate; keep heirs out of business.

DISADVANTAGES: No improved cost basis for surviving stockholder; life insurance cash value or proceeds may be subject to alternate minimum tax.

INCOME TAX POSITION: Gain, if any, upon sale of appreciated stock subject to income tax.

GIFT TAX POSITION: None.

ESTATE POSITION: Value of business interest, as established in buy-out agreement, includible in owner's estate.

OWNER OF POLICY: Corporation, if not trusted.

PREMIUM PAYOR: Corporation.

BENEFICIARY: Corporation, if not trusted.

DISABILITY BENEFIT: Yes, if waiver of premium is included.

CONTROL OF
POLICY VALUES: Corporation.

LOSS OF USE OF MONEY: Yes.

COST RECOVERY: No.

DEDUCTIBLE CONTRIBUTION
OF PREMIUM: No.

CORPORATE RESOLUTION,
PLAN DOCUMENT OR
AGREEMENT: Yes.

DISCRIMINATION
AVAILABLE: Not applicable.

SECTION 303—PARTIAL REDEMPTION

DESCRIPTION: Partial redemption of stock without being treated as a dividend.

PLAN OBJECTIVE: Provide liquidity for estate settlement costs and business continuation for surviving family members.

ADVANTAGES: Conversion of non-marketable stock to cash for liquidity.

DISADVANTAGES: No improved cost basis for surviving stockholder; life insurance cash value or proceeds may be subject to alternate minimum tax.

INCOME TAX POSITION: Gain, if any, upon sale of appreciated stock subject to income tax.

GIFT TAX POSITION: None.

ESTATE POSITION: Fair market value of stock includible in shareholder's estate.

OWNER OF POLICY: Corporation.

PREMIUM PAYOR: Corporation.

BENEFICIARY: Corporation.

DISABILITY BENEFIT: Yes, if waiver of premium is included.

CONTROL OF
POLICY VALUES: Corporation.

LOSS OF USE OF MONEY: Yes.

COST RECOVERY: No.

DEDUCTIBLE CONTRIBUTION
OF PREMIUM: No.

CORPORATE RESOLUTION,
PLAN DOCUMENT OR
AGREEMENT: Yes.

DISCRIMINATION
AVAILABLE: Not applicable.

EXECUTIVE BONUS (SECTION 162) ARRANGEMENT

DESCRIPTION: Employer payment of premiums to pro-
                        vide additional personal life insurance
                        coverage to key employees and owners.

PLAN OBJECTIVE: Help owner and key employee buy addi-
                        tional life insurance protection.

ADVANTAGES: Discriminatory.

DISADVANTAGES: Can place dollars received in higher
                        individual income tax bracket (assuming
                        corporation has taxable income less than
                        $75,000)

INCOME TAX POSITION:	Bonus considered income to employee.
GIFT TAX POSITION:	Upon assignment, three-year time limit must be met to remove from employee's estate.
ESTATE POSITION:	Includible if incidence of ownership by insured is involved.
OWNER OF POLICY:	Insured or third party.
PREMIUM PAYOR:	Employee using premium bonus.
BENEFICIARY:	Named by owner.
DISABILITY BENEFIT:	Yes, if waiver of premium is included.
CONTROL OF POLICY VALUES:	Insured or third party owner.
LOSS OF USE OF MONEY:	Yes, on after-tax cost of bonus.
COST RECOVERY:	No.
DEDUCTIBLE CONTRIBUTION OF PREMIUM:	Bonus deductible to corporation when paid to employee (if not considered unreasonable compensation).
CORPORATE RESOLUTION, PLAN DOCUMENT OR AGREEMENT:	No.
DISCRIMINATION AVAILABLE:	Yes.

GROUP CARVE OUT

DESCRIPTION:

Replace excess group term life insurance (over $50,000) with individual life insurance contracts for employees.

PLAN OBJECTIVE:

Provide permanent insurance protection for employees on a more attractive basis than group term. (May also reduce employer cost.)

ADVANTAGES:

Life insurance protection for employees on a more attractive economic basis than excess group term.

DISADVANTAGES:

Can place dollars received in higher individual income tax bracket (assuming corporation has taxable income less than $75,000); guaranteed issue may be unavailable.

INCOME TAX POSITION:

Income tax free to beneficiary, but premium or P.S. 58 economic benefit currently taxable to employee if bonus plan or split dollar is used.

GIFT TAX POSITION:

Upon assignment, three-year time limit must be met to remove from employee's estate.

ESTATE POSITION:

Included if not assigned to a third party; three-year rule applies.

OWNER OF POLICY:

Insured or third party.

PREMIUM PAYOR:

Employer (employee may contribute to some plans).

BENEFICIARY: Named by insured employee or third
                               party owner.

DISABILITY BENEFIT: Yes, if waiver of premium is included.

CONTROL OF
POLICY VALUES: Insured or third party owner.

LOSS OF USE OF MONEY: Yes.

COST RECOVERY: No.

DEDUCTIBLE CONTRIBUTION
OF PREMIUM: Yes, to employer if Section 162 Bonus
                               Plan is used.

CORPORATE RESOLUTION,
PLAN DOCUMENT OR
AGREEMENT: No.

DISCRIMINATION
AVAILABLE: Yes.

GROUP TERM LIFE

DESCRIPTION: Provides insurance coverage at reasonable
                               rates to employee and/or dependant.

PLAN OBJECTIVE: Provide personal insurance for employ-
                               ees and/or dependents.

ADVANTAGES: Life insurance protection for employees
                               at reasonable rates.

DISADVANTAGES: The irretrievable cost of the program;
                               non-discriminatory.

INCOME TAX POSITION:	First $50,000 of coverage tax free; excess taxed at Table 1 rates (unless plan is discriminatory). Premiums deductible by employer on all employees except partners and sole proprietors.
GIFT TAX POSITION:	Upon assignment, three-year time limit must be met to remove from employee's estate.
ESTATE POSITION:	Included if not assigned to a third party; three-year rule applies.
OWNER OF POLICY:	Employer owns master policy with employee receiving certificate.
PREMIUM PAYOR:	Employer (employee may contribute to some plans).
BENEFICIARY:	Named by insured employee or third party owner.
DISABILITY BENEFIT:	Yes, if waiver of premium is included.
CONTROL OF POLICY VALUES:	Generally, no policy values, as term is used.
LOSS OF USE OF MONEY:	Yes.
COST RECOVERY:	No.
DEDUCTIBLE CONTRIBUTION OF PREMIUM:	Yes, to employer for employees.
CORPORATE RESOLUTION, PLAN DOCUMENT OR AGREEMENT:	Yes.

DISCRIMINATION
AVAILABLE: No, see Internal Revenue Code Section 79.

KEY PERSON

DESCRIPTION: Plan to indemnify business for death of a
                                    key person and loss of his/her skill and
                                    experience.

PLAN OBJECTIVE: Provide tax-free dollars to recruit, hire,
                                    train or replace skills and profits of
                                    deceased key personnel.

ADVANTAGES: Guarantee flow of tax-free dollars to
                                    replace lost profits; recruit, hire and train
                                    replacement; assure business continuity.

DISADVANTAGES: Premiums paid with after-tax employer
                                    dollars; life insurance cash value or pro-
                                    ceeds may be subject to alternate mini-
                                    mum tax.

INCOME TAX POSITION: Premium payments nondeductible by
                                    employer; insurance proceeds received
                                    tax-free by employer.

GIFT TAX POSITION: None.

ESTATE POSITION: May increase value of business interest
                                    includible   in   deceased   key
                                    employee/owner's estate.

OWNER OF POLICY: Employer (corporation).

PREMIUM PAYOR: Employer (corporation).

BENEFICIARY: Employer (corporation).

DISABILITY BENEFIT: Yes, if waiver of premium is included.

CONTROL OF
POLICY VALUES: Employer (corporation).

LOSS OF USE OF MONEY: Use of money may be recovered when
                           plan is funded by life insurance.

COST RECOVERY: Premiums recovered through tax-free
                           life insurance proceeds.

DEDUCTIBLE CONTRIBUTION
OF PREMIUM: No.

CORPORATE RESOLUTION,
PLAN DOCUMENT OR
AGREEMENT: Yes.

DISCRIMINATION
AVAILABLE: Yes.

PAYROLL DEDUCTION LIFE

DESCRIPTION: Mass marketed individual life insurance
                           paid by salary deductions.

PLAN OBJECTIVE: Help wage earners pay for personal life
                           insurance coverage conveniently.

ADVANTAGES: Guaranteed issue available; convenient,
                           portable coverage.

DISADVANTAGES: Benefits provided by after-tax employee
                           dollars.

INCOME TAX POSITION: Premium payments using after tax dollars.

GIFT TAX POSITION:	Upon assignment, three-year time limit must be met to remove from employee's estate.
ESTATE POSITION:	Included if not assigned to a third party; three-year rule applies.
OWNER OF POLICY:	Insured or third party.
PREMIUM PAYOR:	Employee.
BENEFICIARY:	Named by insured employee or third party owner.
DISABILITY BENEFIT:	Yes, if waiver of premium is included.
CONTROL OF POLICY VALUES:	Insured or third party owner.
LOSS OF USE OF MONEY:	Yes.
COST RECOVERY:	No.
DEDUCTIBLE CONTRIBUTION OF PREMIUM:	No.
CORPORATE RESOLUTION, PLAN DOCUMENT OR AGREEMENT:	Yes (salary deduction authorization forms).
DISCRIMINATION AVAILABLE:	Yes.

SALARY CONTINUATION—DEATH BENEFIT ONLY

DESCRIPTION:

Provides death benefits only to employee's beneficiaries.

PLAN OBJECTIVE:

Lock in key personnel and provide additional benefits for owners.

ADVANTAGES:

Discriminatory; locks in key employees; legal way to use corporate dollars for personal benefits.

DISADVANTAGES:

Benefits provided by agreement subject to continuation of business; employer deduction delayed until benefits paid.

INCOME TAX POSITION:

Annual death benefit fully deductible by corporation, taxable as ordinary income to beneficiary in excess of first $5,000 (assuming death benefit was forfeitable before employee's death).

GIFT TAX POSITION:

May be completed gift at employee's death.

ESTATE POSITION:

No, unless employee retains any right in the plan.

OWNER OF POLICY:

Employer (corporation).

PREMIUM PAYOR:

Employer (corporation).

BENEFICIARY:

Employer (corporation).

DISABILITY BENEFIT:

Yes, if waiver of premium is included.

CONTROL OF
POLICY VALUES:

Employer (corporation).

LOSS OF USE OF MONEY: Use of money may be recoverable when plan is funded by life insurance.

COST RECOVERY: Possible when plan is funded of life insurance.

DEDUCTIBLE CONTRIBUTION
OF PREMIUM: No.

CORPORATE RESOLUTION,
PLAN DOCUMENT OR
AGREEMENT: Yes.

DISCRIMINATION
AVAILABLE: Yes.

KEY EMPLOYEE COVERAGE WORKSHEET

Key Employee—is an important coverage as are all the others. To give you an idea of the value of these concepts, here is a sample worksheet for Key Person coverage:

	EXAMPLE	YOUR COMPANY
Key Executive's Salary	$ 100,000	$
Total Salary Compensation for Management Group	$ 500,000	$
Executive's Salary as % of Total Management Compensation	20%	%
Transition Period (Years)	2	

REPLACEMENT COST (TRANSITION AND TRAINING)—(A)

Replacement Executive's Salary **	$ 150,000	$
Current Executive's Salary	- 100,000	-
Additional Salary	50,000	
Transition Period (Years)	x 2	x
Total Additional Salary	$ 100,000	$
Fee to Executive Recruiter		

(_20% of Salary)	30,000	_____
Replacement Cost (Additional		
Salary Plus Recruiter's Fee)	$ 130,000	$ _____

POTENTIAL IMPACT ON SALES—(B)

Anticipated Sales for ____2 Years	$ 5,000,000	$ _____
% Attributed to Current Executive	20%	_____ %
Sales Attributed to Current Executive	1,000,000	_____
Sales Potentially Lost	$ 500,000	$ _____

POTENTIAL IMPACT ON CREDIT LINES—(C)

Anticipated Line of Credit	$ 1,000,000	$ _____
% Attributed to Current Executive	20%	_____ %
Credit Line Potentially Lost	200,000	_____

OTHER POTENTIAL IMPACT—(D)_____   _____

TOTAL KEY EXECUTIVE VALUATION
(A)+(B)+(C)+(D) $ 830,000 $ _____

* This may indicate the executive's relative importance and may be useful in determining the impact on sales and credit lines.
** Replacement executive's compensation may have to be substantially higher if he does not have an equity ownership position.

Appropriate worksheets are available for some of the other methods either through the internet, books, etc. However for buy-sell planning and most of the others, it is important to meet with your advisors (especially your attorney; tax attorney preferable for planning and agreements).

QUESTION 130: Can I Donate My Life Insurance Policy To a Non-Profit/Charitable Organization?

Donating life insurance policies to a Non-Profit/Charitable organization is a fairly common event. A main reason is that it amplifies the gift. If a gift of premiums, of let's say $1,000 a year were given to the organization for 20 years, that would be substantially less than a death benefit of $100,000 at that time.

However, some development professionals are not familiar with the concept or do not wish to accept life insurance as a gift. Be advised that the policies can present potential hazards for the organizations. The other issue is that life insurance is not often understood and as such is refused as a gift.

This does not mean that a life insurance policy will not be accepted. It simply means that either the planned giving officer at the organization will need to be educated by a life insurance agent or other advisor who can assist them in feeling comfortable. If the planned giving officer is knowledgeable about life insurance or has an advisor whom they can call, then the policy can typically then be gifted.

The issues that will typically be addressed by a non-profit/charity in accepting a policy would be:

- An appraisal of a life insurance policy and a determination of its fair market value
- Valuations in special circumstances
- An assessment of the danger of accepting an encumbered policy (with a policy loan outstanding)
- Completion of Internal Revenue Service Form 8283
- A review of any other risks in accepting a life insurance policy

The value of the gift can depend on a number of variables and, for this; you would need to consult a properly qualified appraiser for life insurance policies.

As mentioned, using life insurance in conjunction with charitable gift planning has also been around for quite some time and for the most part is generally accepted. An outright gift of a life insurance policy to charity works out well for both the donor and for the recipient charity. Typically, such a gift will result in an income tax deduction for the donor to the extent of his or her basis in the policy (or the policy value if less). No income tax deduction is available if the donor merely designates the charity as policy beneficiary, whether revocable or irrevocable, for failure to satisfy the partial interest rule.

There is generally no insurable interest on the donor's life on the part of the charity. Thus, the gift could be made, but is potentially voidable under a traditional concept of insurable interest. The unwelcome tax consequence is that because the charity's interest is voidable under the state's insurable-interest law, and a challenge to such interest would likely cause ownership of the policy to revert to the donor or his heirs, the gift is only a partial interest which does not qualify for the income tax or gift tax charitable contribution deductions.

Virtually every state has enacted provisions allowing charities to own life insurance policies where the insured is a donor in whose life the charity does not otherwise have an insurable interest. They typically require the consent of the insured. Some define "charitable organization" with reference to I.R.C. §501(c)(3) (e.g. Fla. Stat. Ch. 27.404); others refer to their own law (e.g. N.Y. Ins. Law §3205(b)(3).These variations means that although insurable interest should not present a real problem to charitable giving of life insurance policies, the planner should (as always) be sure to consult applicable state law.

There are some new additional tax risks due to Investor Initiated Life Insurance (see Question 132: What is Investor Initiated Life Insurance (IILI))? Investors are involving charities in their efforts to acquire life insurance policies that would not otherwise be available because the investors lack an insurable interest in the insured's. One variation of non-recourse premium financing transactions involves promising modest benefits to a charity or university in order to market to its list of wealthy older donors and alumni. [In North Carolina and Texas, for example, legislators changed the definition of "insurable interest" to allow charities and other tax-exempt entities to participate in IILI transactions. In other states, lobbying continues with key legislators to change the insurable interest law and allow IILI transactions for their favorite charity or university.]

This allows the promoters to identify clusters of potential insureds through a single source. The promoters typically convince the donors to allow the investors to use their "excess insurability" by promising the charity an expected payment estimated at 2% to 5% of the eventual death benefit after payment of all expenses and a guaranteed profit to the investors. In essence, the charity is paid a modest finder's fee. Meanwhile, the charity may not be aware of its potential exposure under the securities laws, the potential 100% excise tax on money going into one of these schemes, the potential harm to its reputation, or the risk to its tax-exempt status.

The two preceding paragraphs are from: "Free Life Insurance: Risks and Costs of Non-Recourse Premium Financing" by R. Marshall Jones, Stephan R. Leimberg, and Lawrence J. Rybka, Attorneys.

QUESTION 131: What Are Some Tips on Understanding Viatical and Life Settlements to Sell A Life Insurance Policy?

People living with a terminal illness often face very tough financial choices. A life settlement or viatical settlement is one option that can give you cash to help with expenses. A life or viatical settlement is the sale of a life insurance policy to a third party. The owner of the policy sells it for a percent of the death benefit. The buyer becomes the new owner and/or beneficiary of the life insurance policy, pays all future premiums and collects the entire death benefit when the insured dies.

Initially, back in 1989, the viatical business began with good intentions, as a method to allow terminally ill AIDS patients early access to a portion (or all) of their life insurance policy's death benefits. Viaticals eventually expanded to include other conditions such as cancer, heart disease and any other life threatening illness.

The industry has been troubled by a high number of unethical, illegitimate operations. These operations have gone after potentials Viators in an aggressive manner. These companies have given the industry a bad name and led to more regulation and scrutiny.

The main difference between life settlements and viatical settlements is that with a viatical settlement is that the insured must be terminally ill. Life settlements do not require the insured to be terminally ill, however, they must be a maximum age and the amount of settlement will depend on their age and health.

Defining common terms:

- The person selling the life insurance policy is the viator. He or she will get money from the settlement. This person gives up ownership of the policy in return for cash now. The viator generally has a terminal illness.
- A life or viatical *settlement provider* is the person or company that buys the life insurance policy. The buyer becomes the policy owner, and must pay any premiums that are due, and eventually collects the entire death benefit from the insurance company.
- The person or company who represents the seller and can "shop" for offers is a *settlement broker*. The buyer pays the broker a commission if the sale is completed.
- An *Accelerated Death Benefit* (ADB) is a feature of a life insurance policy that typically pays some or all of the policy's death benefit before the insured dies. It may be another way to get cash from a policy without selling it to a third party.

Issues to consider with Viatical Settlements:

- To sell your life insurance policy, you must have a terminal disease and an estimated life expectancy of 36 months in most cases, or less, although there are companies that will buy policies from people with greater life expectancies, such as 60 months.
- There is no requirement that you have to be an AIDS patient. More and more companies are expanding to terminally ill cancer and heart patients or to those suffering from other fatal diseases. Up until recently AIDS patients have been the main source because the disease's course is fairly predictable, but that could change as new treatments and drugs that prolong life are used by more AIDS patients.
- Many different types of policies can be sold, including whole life, term and universal. In many cases, group policies also can be sold—for instance, if a disability waiver locks in coverage and the policy is assignable or convertible. You will need to check specifics with the company. In addition, policies need to have

been in-force beyond any contestability period, usually two years. Group policies that are converted must not require a new contestability period.

- To sell the policy, your financial advisor may be able to assist you; keep in mind that he or she will receive a fee (commission) on the sale of a percentage (5% to 7%) of either the cash value or death benefit. You may also choose to approach viatical funding companies directly. Make sure you get offers from more than one and do not be afraid to negotiate. If you do not have any advisors, there usually are brokers and providers who advertise in magazines and newspapers for the gay community. Community organizations and health, financial or legal professionals may provide a referral. In some states, it is not legal for doctors or lawyers to collect a fee from a company for steering clients their way.

- Check whether or not your state insurance department has licensing and other requirements for funding or brokerage companies to conduct business in that state; currently only a few states do. The number of states that do however is growing quickly. It's important to check to see whether your company is properly licensed. Otherwise, you might get hit with unnecessary taxes. Recent changes in federal tax laws allow an exemption from federal taxes on proceeds from viatical settlements only when you do business with a company that is properly licensed. If your state doesn't have licensing requirements, then the company must comply with the National Association of Insurance Commissioner's Model Act and Regulations on viatical settlements (see above).

- The company must be licensed in the state where it is making the transaction, not where it is located. For example, if a company is based in California but doing business in New York, it must be licensed in New York. If the company is doing business in Nevada, there is no law there. That means you should do business only with companies that comply with the National Association of Insurance Commissioner's Model Act and Regulations on viatical settlements. Ask any broker or funding company with which you deal whether they are licensed and, if so, in which states. Call those state's insurance divisions to verify and see if there are any complaints. See Appendix A for contact information on the various State Insurance Departments. You should also check with your own state insurance regulators to see if new regulations are imminent.

- Keep in mind that you do not need to sell the entire policy. You can sell whatever percentage you would like (the company may have a minimum as a purchase requirement).

- The amount you receive will depend on a variety of factors, such as anticipated life expectancy (unfortunately the shorter it is, the higher the pay out); the anticipated premiums the company will have to pay, if there are any loans outstanding against the policy, whether there is a premium waiver in case of disability, the insurance company's ratings, prevailing interest rates, and the company's targeted rate of return. A life expectancy of 6 months or less typically brings about 80 percent of the policy's death benefit, although sometimes it can be as high as 85 percent. Conversely, a life expectancy of 60 months would bring 25 to 30 percent.

- If you have cash value in the policy, you can usually withdraw it.

- The process typically takes four to eight weeks to viaticate a policy, although it can take longer, especially with some group policies. You can help speed things up by notifying your physician and insurance company to expect the inquiries from the viatical company.

- After Dec. 31, 1996, the proceeds from a viatical settlement will no longer be subject to federal tax under some circumstances. The person selling the policy must have a life expectancy of two years or less. Also, the company buying the policy must be properly licensed in states that require that and/or the company has to comply with the National Association of Insurance Commissioner's Model Act and Regulations on viatical settlements.

- The lump sum payout could result in the loss of state and federal need-based aid such as Medicaid, food stamps or SSI.

- Depending on your financial situation, specifically, if you owe a lot of money to hospitals, doctors or other creditors, they may seek payment from the proceeds you receive. Also, if you have filed bankruptcy, the creditors lay claim.

- The viatical company normally will not contact you after settlement, but it will track your status so it knows when the policy "matures"—that is, when the viator dies and the policy becomes payable. It can do this in a number of ways, for example by as keeping in touch with your primary physician. You should check how a company you are considering handles this sensitive issue.

- Viatical contracts are required by some states to have a period when the contract can be canceled for a period of 30 days from the time it is signed, and 15 days after the viator receives the proceeds. Companies in states where there is no such regulation almost always offer a similar clause.
- If you live past your anticipated life expectancy, there are no repercussions for you. That is part of the risk for the company.
- As with anything and as the song goes—"You Better Shop Around"—to make sure that you are getting a fair price. This is a type of transaction that you can negotiate with the companies. There is usually no set price.

Life Settlements:

A life settlement allows a person to sell a life insurance policy and receive a cash amount higher than the cash surrender value. The policy ownership is transferred to an unrelated investor in exchange for a cash payment in excess of the policy's cash surrender value. The investor makes required premium payments and collects the death benefit when the insured person dies. Life settlements are identical in form to viatical settlements, except for the expected remaining lifetime of the insured, which is less than two years for viaticals.

The following are some facts about Life Settlements to keep in mind:

- Most companies require that the insured be a minimum age of at least 65 or older
- The policy usually has to have a minimum death benefit of $250,000
- May be useful where a policy is not performing up to expectations
- The Life Insurance is not needed
  - o In a business insurance situation such as a "key person" or a "buy-sell" agreement where an insured leaves and the policy is no longer necessary
  - o A loan secured by life insurance has been paid in full
- The proceeds from the life settlement can be used to:

- o   Provide cash gifts to family members
- o   Provide funds for charitable giving or to establish a charitable remainder trust
- The policy is beyond the two-year contestable period
- Useful when an insured person's health has substantially worsened since policy's issue date and/or when current life expectancy is between 2 and 12 years.
- Returns to investors are above average sometimes reaching 12% or more, the shorter the life span, the greater the return.
- The investor incurs significant transaction expenses, including underwriting, commissions, reinsurance, administration and taxes on the gain at death
- Commissions to financial advisors, brokers and independent agents with a life insurance license generally range from 4% to 6% of the amount paid for the settlement.
- The policy may be resold multiple times
- Lack of privacy—ongoing tracking of the insured person's health and medical records until death.

What are the Current Tax Considerations for Life Settlements?

- On the sale of a life policy, the owner normally owes income tax on the excess of the life settlement proceeds over the tax basis in the contract.
- At the insured's death, the life settlement investor normally owes income tax on the excess of the death benefit over the investor's investment in the contract.
- If the life policy were retained rather than sold, the entire death benefit would pass income tax free to the insured's estate or named beneficiary.

Recent Statistics on Life Settlements:

- Policies with face amounts (death benefits) totaling an estimated $3.3 billion were transferred in 2004. That number is expected to have reached $5.5 billion for 2005.
- $1.5 million is the current average face amount of policies involved in life settlements.

- The target group for life settlement providers is about 2%, or $188 billion, of the $9.4 trillion in-force life insurance policies.

Source: "Life Settlements, The Concept Catches On, 2006, Conning Research & Consulting, Inc.—Financial Advisor Magazine—April 2006

Life settlements are generally accepted as legal. Thirty-seven states in the U.S. have created laws around the practice of life settlements.

What are some tips to consider prior to selling a life insurance policy through a Viatical Settlement or a Life Settlement (Non-Investor Initiated Life Insurance—See Question 132: What Is Investor Initiated Life Insurance (IILI):

- Is there still a need for life insurance?
- If you're interested in selling your policy, you should visit your State Insurance department for more information and to review the appropriate State Insurance Department laws. The California Department of Insurance website is www.insurance.ca.gov. The National Association of Insurance Commissioners (with links to other State Insurance Departments) is www.naic.org.
- Consider all your options
- Find out if the policy has any cash value. This cash value may be used to meet immediate needs and keep the policy in-force for beneficiaries. The cash value may also be able to be used as security for a loan from a financial institution
- Find out if the life insurance policy has an accelerated death benefits provision. It could pay a substantial portion of the policy's death benefit and then the policy would not need to be sold to a third party. A greater number of companies and policies are including this type of provision than in the past.
- If I sell my policy, how do they decide how much cash I get?
- Is this an employer or other group policy? If so, do I need their permission to sell it?
- If I sell my policy, who will be the legal owner?
- Do I need the advice of a tax or estate planning advisor before I decide to sell my policy?
- Find out the tax implications. Not all proceeds are tax-free

- Know that the proceeds are subject to the claims of any creditors
- Understand what information a buyer must know about you to buy your policy, and who else might get that information. Know that you must provide certain medical and personal information and that this may be disclosed to investors.
- Understand how the process works and when the phases will happen
- Decide whether to sell the policy directly to a life or viatical settlement provider or go through a settlement broker who will do the comparison shopping
- If you don't use a settlement broker, comparison shop on your own
- Any life or viatical settlement offer is just that, an offer that does not need to be accepted.
- Check all application forms for accuracy, especially information about medical history
- You must be truthful in your answers to application questions
- Make sure the settlement provider agrees to put your settlement proceeds in escrow with an independent party or financial institution to make sure your funds are safe during the transfer
- Find out if you have the right to change your mind about the settlement after you get the proceeds. If you have that right, you'll have to return the money you were paid and the premiums the buyer paid. In many states you have a certain period of time to change your mind
- Can the policy be resold?

QUESTION 132: What Is Investor Initiated Life Insurance (IILI))?

Investor Initiated Life Insurance (IILI) is the latest attempt to twist life insurance into a speculative financial instrument to take advantage of the unique tax features of life insurance (i.e. income tax-free death benefit and cash value accumulation). Using life insurance as a commodity to speculate in human lives threatens the survival of life insurance companies. The difference between IILI and Life Settlements is that Life Settlements are supposedly for purchasing in-force policies that were purchased when there was a "real" insurable need and which no longer exists rather than IILI which involves no "real" insurable need. IILI also combines Premium Financing (see Question 133: What Is Premium Financing?) into the mix.

The concept includes the bribing of wealthy, elderly individuals to apply for large policies destined for purchase by investors. Basically, the insured is provided with life insurance for two years with no out-of-pocket cost—"free insurance". These prospective insured's, generally between age 72 and 85 with a net worth of at least $5 million, are approached with the concept that they "own" an asset in the form of their insurability and that they can monetize this wasting asset by consenting to be insured under a IILI policy.

This concept of selling an individual's unused insurance capacity through a structured life settlement may appear advantageous to all parties involved, however, combining the use of premium financing with the future planned life settlement may be contrary to one of the basic principles upon which the insurance industry is founded, which is the insurable interest doctrine.

IILI is not a type of life insurance product, it is a particular use of a life insurance policy such as key person, buy-sell, etc; however it is a potentially "malignant" concept and is un-established in many areas as we will look at. The concept combines the premium-financed purchase of a life insurance contract with the future sale of that contract in a life settlement.

The Parties to a IILI transaction:

- Insured—person whose life the insurance is on
- Life insurance agent/broker—person who "sells" the life insurance
- Life insurance company
- Investor group—the viator or life settlement market maker
- Special purpose lender—see premium financing section
- Internal Revenue Service—possibly depending on how the policies are set up and the future interpretation of these types of policies.

How it works (an example of a basic IILI arrangement, please note there are many types):

1) An agent/broker proposes to a prospective insured that they own a "wasting asset" in the form of their insurability and that this can be monetized by consenting to be insured under a IILI policy. There is no traditional life insurance need and they are acquiring the life insurance strictly for monetary purposes. They are generally offered one (or a combination) of the following if they qualify for the program: two years of free life insurance; an up-front cash distribution of 1-1/2% to 3% of the death benefit (or a free luxury car); a portion of the net profits from the expected sale of the policy to a life settlement company after two years or, in some instances, another 1-1/2% to 3% of the insurance benefit when the insured dies. The insured will generally not put up any money themselves.

2) The client secures a non-recourse premium financing loan from the lender to finance a life insurance policy.

3) The proposed insured qualifies for the issuance of a $2 million or larger permanent life insurance policy.

4) The third-party investor group makes or guarantees a non-recourse loan to the non-grantor irrevocable trust created to purchase the policy.

5) As part of the policy purchase, the trust collaterally assigns the policy to the lender.

6) After 24 months or longer, in order to satisfy both the policy's incontestability provision and state insurance laws regulating the sale of newly issued policies, the insured`s trustee chooses from the following options, if available:

   - Repay the loaned premiums with interest along with any cash advances, origination fees, termination fees or other charges; pay all future premiums and keep the policy; or
   - Sell the policy to a life settlement company; or
   - Transfer ownership of the policy to the lenders in full satisfaction of the loan.

There are many issues to be concerned about when reviewing/considering a IILI transaction and the discussion of which for the most part, are beyond scope of this book. The following is a partial list of potential issues that appeared in articled titled "Free" Life Insurance: Risks and Costs of Non-Recourse Premium Financing. By: R. Marshall Jones, Stephan R. Leimberg, and Lawrence J. Rybka, attorneys.

- Future insurability—if the maximum amount of life insurance (capacity) is purchased on a single life, then that insured would probably not be able to ever purchase life insurance again in the future. This would be of concern if a true need were to surface. This is an especially important factor as the capacity for life insurance is shrinking both in the U.S. and around the world, it is becoming difficult if not impossible to write large amounts of life insurance (partially due to IILI)

- Ethical/Moral Issues—As mentioned in the introduction, there are some ethical and moral concerns with selling your life insurance and/or insurability (unused life insurance capacity) to an investor group or stranger. A review of these issues is beyond the scope of this research paper.

- Appropriate Disclosures—there are no standard disclosures at this time

- Policy resale—the original purchaser is not obligated to keep the policy, they can resell it

- Privacy—life settlement contracts have little protection for personal and health information

- Violations of state "insurable interest" insurance laws and regulations—third-party investors offer the insureds two years of "free" insurance because it is illegal for them to purchase insurance on the life of an individual unless the original applicant-owner has an insurable interest at the time the policy is purchased. Without an insurable interest, the policy would be void from inception and the death benefit will not be paid to the investors. To protect the public, all states have insurable interest statutes designed to discourage speculation on an insured's life. Generally, the initial owner and beneficiary must have a strong economic interest in, and benefit from, the continued life of the insured. For example, family members are generally presumed to have an insurable interest in their spouses and parents. These laws vary from State to State

- Litigation risk—if a State Insurance Department rules that an insurance interest law is violated, the insured`s trust and estate, and their agents and advisors may become embroiled in unexpected litigation. This could occur either during the insured`s lifetime or after death.

- Premium Financing Issues—(See Question #133: What Is Premium Financing and How Does It Work?) Special issues to IILI—The cost of repaying the loan and keeping the policy: It is very unusual for an insured to participate in a "free insurance" premium financing program with the primary intent of repaying the loan after two years and keeping the insurance for the originally stated "insurable interest" purpose. In general, the purpose of the repayment option is to give apparent legitimacy to the insurance transaction and not to encourage repayment. In fact, the insured usually has lower-cost private or commercial recourse financing available as an alternative. The decision to use higher-cost non-recourse financing is yet another indication that the insured never intended to pay premiums after the second policy year. Even the most compliant and professional non-recourse premium financing programs generally expect to earn at least a compounded 15% return on equity for the investors. Many programs impose a much higher actual cost of repayment through a combination of exit fees and other charges to dramatically discourage repayment.

- Fraud and misrepresentation by the insured—The standard life insurance application requires insureds to sign written statements regarding their health, financial circumstances, policy ownership, and the purpose of the insurance. Companies rely on this information as part of their consideration for issuing coverage. The answers to most of these questions become part of the contract. Most life insurance contracts provide that the policy may not be contested by the insurance company after two policy years. A standard part of "free insurance" premium financing transactions is an indemnification provision whereby the insured agrees to indemnify the lenders and investors for any loss resulting from a material misrepresentation or omission. The insured, or the insured's family, may be liable for the investors' loss-potentially the multi-million dollar death benefit that was not paid to the investors-if any misrepresentation of these items is discovered during the contestable period. If the misrepresentation is intentional and material, it may give rise to fraud that extends beyond the contestable period.

- Rebating—Another area of risk to insured's is the use of cash incentives to purchase the policy. The New York State Insurance Department General Counsel Opinion, citing lack of insurable interest for one of these transactions, also made the point that free insurance might constitute an illegal rebate. Most state insurance regulations either prohibit or severely restrict the offer of rebates to clients who buy insurance. The few states that allow this practice require that any rebates fit within specific parameters established by the state. (California does allow rebates under certain specific conditions).

- Violations of state insurance statutes on "wet ink" viaticals- Many states have enacted model statutes prohibiting the sale of life insurance as an investment for the benefit of a disinterested third party. Furthermore, to guard against so-called wet ink viatical transactions (i.e., the sale of a newly-issued policy to a life settlement company "almost before the ink is dry"), the National Association of Insurance Commissioners' ("NAIC") Viatical Settlements Model Regulation has been adopted by a number of states to prohibit the sale of insurance policies within 24 months of the policy issue date. This restriction applies to both policy owners and licensed life insurance agents and brokers.

- Potential violations of federal or state securities law—in addition to insurance law issues, advisors must consider these programs as possible securities transactions. Insureds, their advisors, and insurance agents/brokers may face significant, long-term financial exposure if the non-recourse premium financing transaction is a security but not structured to be fully compliant with federal and state securities laws. One of the more serious and often overlooked transaction risks is the possibility that the insured, the trustee, and the advisors are participating in the issuance, sale, or solicitation of unregistered securities in violation of sections 5(a) and 5(c) of the Securities Act of 1933. This risk should cause great pause because transactions falling under securities law may require very specific disclosure in the transaction and many additional statutory remedies.

- The risk of failure to comply with the Patriot Act—Some countries have more favorable tax laws regarding investor-owned life insurance that make U.S.-issued life insurance policies particularly attractive. Consequently, foreign investors have entered both the non-recourse premium financing market and the life settlement arena.

- The unknown tax cost of the unpaid loan—There does not appear to be any clear or certain guidance regarding the tax consequences related to non-payment of the loan. .An argument can be made that any "free" insurance benefit should be taxed as ordinary income and that income tax may be due on 100% of any forgiven loan balance, including all accrued interest and any waived fees or charges. The tax opinions will vary from advisor to advisor and from transaction to transaction.

- The risk of estate tax on the death benefit—because the investors are looking for insured's with a projected life expectancy of 120 months (ten years) or less, advisors must evaluate the risk that the death benefit will be included in the insured`s taxable estate if he or she dies during this period.

What is the impact on life insurance carriers of Investor Initiated Life Insurance?

There is some debate as to what the bottom line impact will be to life insurance companies. There will be some impact due to the way that life insurance companies price their policies. The pricing of a life insurance policy is dependent upon a number of actuarial-based assumptions, one of which is expected lapse rates.

The majority of life insurance policies in force today, were sold, and priced, prior to the secondary life insurance marketplace. Therefore, when the products were designed, companies took into historical lapse rates (this includes surrenders). Lapse rates impact the premiums since life insurers insurance companies assume that a certain number of policyholders will lapse (discontinue paying premiums) rather than retaining the policy until death.

Life insurance product pricing is a function of 3 pricing factors: cost of insurance charges (COI's), policy expenses and policy interest earnings.

This is a delicate balance for companies to be both competitive and profitable. Well, some companies try harder to be profitable than others, that's another story.

Life settlements make estimating lapse assumptions more difficult because policyholders are opting to sell their policies rather than allowing them to lapse. If insurers price policies based on significantly lower lapse assumptions than are realized, insurers lose. Furthermore, the insurer cannot raise rates on guaranteed premium policies to make up the shortfall. Consequently, they could be compelled to hoard more reserves to pay claims. This will impact profitability and could upset the delicate balance.

QUESTION 133: What Is Premium Financing and How Does It Work?

Premium financing has been around for years in the life insurance industry and has been heavily promoted especially among wealthier clients. It occurs when an outside (third party) lending source such as a bank or hedge fund pays premiums on a life insurance contract.

The unique characteristics in these premium financing arrangements are that the loan is assumed to be renewed until death and the insurance proceeds are relied upon to be sufficient to repay the loan at death and to provide your client's family with the insurance coverage they need. Conceptually, this is a great idea: you use borrowed funds to pay for the insurance program which will ultimately pay off the loan and provide the family with the needed funds at their death.

Premium financing is especially attractive in low interest rate environments when it is likely that the death benefit will exceed the loan and accrued interest. This can also be an attractive method of buying more life insurance if a trust is unable to purchase additional insurance due to taxable gift limitations.

Interest is generally compounded in a premium finance arrangement with an optimal loan period of less than 10 years. Therefore, the best prospects for premium financing are insureds who are age 70 or older, with a life expectancy of from 10 to 15 years.

Unfortunately, there are significant risks that you assume which could derail the entire program. In addition to determining product suitability, purchasers should be wary of loan terms and implied interest rate assumptions when considering premium financing. Purchasers need to understand the life insurance contract, including the future yield assumptions, death benefit structure, cost assumptions and, of course, the appropriate amount of the death benefit.

Most loans for premium are variable; the interest rate depends on the type of contract and the personal guarantee of either the insured or the purchaser. Financing for premiums is generally based on LIBOR (the London interbank offered rate) plus an additional percentage cost, assuming sufficient collateral. Banks will usually lend up to 70% of the cash value of a universal life contract or below 50% when lending against the cash value of a variable universal life contract.

How does Premium Financing Work:

The premium financing loan works similarly to other loans and has these three components:

1) Interest Rate—is usually a variable one year rate but can sometimes be fixed up to 10 years.
2) Loan Term is usually for one year, but can sometimes be as high as 10 years. Each year during the loan term, the lender will review the loan to make sure everything is in order. If the numbers don't match up, adjustments will have to be made to bring everything in line. At the end of the loan term, you must either repay the loan or reapply for a new loan which will be subject to new financial underwriting. There is no guarantee the lender will renew the loan either due to a change in financial situation or a change in the lender's willingness to offer this type of loan.
3) Collateral has to be posted for the loan. The policy's cash surrender value is usually acceptable as collateral and, to the extent it is not sufficient to cover the loan, additional collateral will have to be posted—usually in the form of marketable

securities. There may be an indefinite number of collateral calls should the value of the collateral fall at any time.

How does a Premium Financing Loan tie-in with a life insurance policy—some carriers have recently developed death benefit riders which are intended to grow the death benefit by the amount of the loan and, in some cases, also the interest. Today's riders fall into one of three categories:

1) Return of Premium Rider—increases the death benefit each year by the premiums paid in that year. The death benefit is intended to keep pace with the loan's principal so the loan principal can be repaid at death while still providing the insurance coverage needed. This rider is used when the goal is to pay the loan interest each year.

2) Return of Premium with Interest Rider—increases the death benefit each year by that year's premiums and interest. This death benefit is intended to keep pace with the loan's principal plus accrued interest so the entire loan can be repaid at death while providing the needed insurance coverage. This rider would be used to accrue loan interest.

3) No Rider—leaving the only option as the choice of type of death benefit—either the Level Death Benefit Option or the Increasing Death Benefit Option—neither of which are designed to work in the premium financing sale. The best option would most likely be the Increasing Death Benefit option to have some death benefit growth to at least keep pace with part of the growing loan balance.

While the life insurance purchase and the loan are two separate transactions, attempts have been made to combine them. In recent years, lenders have become more willing to provide the necessary capital for clients to fund their insurance programs and carriers have become more receptive to designing their products to work in the premium financing markets. Since the insurance policy and the loan operate independently of each other, there are no built in mechanisms or guarantees that they will work in sync. In other words, should changes to one occur without a corresponding change in the other, the entire premium financing arrangement could fail to perform as projected resulting in a precarious situation.

What are the risk factors affiliated with using premium financing:

The following risk factors both alone or in combination, would result in a significant burden and could cause the entire program to fail:

- Interest Rate Risk—If the loan interest rates increase more than projected, more money may need to be paid into the program and/or more collateral may need to be provided than originally anticipated. If there is not sufficient funds and/or collateral to make up this shortfall, the entire loan could be called—forcing the loan be repaid prior to the original planned on date which could be an inopportune time.
- Collateral Risk—If the value of collateral falls below the level required by the lender to satisfy the loan, additional collateral could be required. If there is not sufficient collateral to make up this shortfall, the entire loan could be called—forcing the repayment before originally planned. This also could occur at an inopportune time and put collateral at risk.
- Asset Risk:
    o While Alive—Should the loan be called and the collateral posted not be sufficient to repay the loan, other asets, whether cash or otherwise, may be at risk of being forfeited to satisfy the outstanding loan balance.
    o At Death—Should the total death benefit be less than expected:
        ▪ The *net* death benefit available after repaying the loan, could be less than needed to satisfy estate liquidity needs, thus, putting other assets at risk of having to be sold to satisfy this need.
        ▪ ii. If the *total* death benefit is less than the outstanding loan balance, not only would there not be any death benefit available for the family, but the family would owe the remaining loan balance—without neither the funds to satisfy this loan obligation nor those to satisfy the estate liquidity need.
- Earnings Risk:
    o If the policy's cash surrender value does not perform as projected, there may be a requirement of more collateral than originally anticipated. If the policy's death benefit

does not, or can not, grow sufficiently to keep pace with the outstanding loan, then there is at risk of either not getting as much coverage as expected, after the loan is paid off, or, worse yet, getting no insurance coverage at all *and* having to come up with additional funds to repay the balance of the loan. There is no guarantee that the insurance policy will be able to repay the entire loan *and* provide the needed insurance protection.

If a Side Fund is used to accumulate assets to later offset the loan, the growth of this side fund could be lower than projected. This could require that additional funds be paid off the loan as scheduled and/or require a longer time than expected to repay the loan from the Side Fund.

- Policy Design Risk:
  - o Policy Pricing—the cost of an increasing death benefit, especially in the later years, can have an enormous effect on the policy's premium requirements. With premium financing programs, higher premiums means larger loans since a larger loan is needed to pay the policy's higher premium. However, a larger loan means even higher death benefits are needed which in turn mean higher premiums. This circular dependency can require significantly more insurance just to satisfy the ultimate loan. While this may be nice for commission purposes, it poses a particular problem if the cost to maintain the entire program becomes either more expensive than just purchasing the insurance outright or becomes cost prohibitive.
  - o Lack of Guarantees—there is no guarantee the policy will keep pace with the outstanding loan balance. Since the loan is repaid from the insurance proceeds first, if the loan is larger than projected, the additional amount would be paid from the death benefit originally intended to be available for the beneficiary. Therefore, there would be insufficient coverage, or possibly no coverage.
- Loan Underwriting Risk—loans can be made for a fixed term of years, but can not be made in perpetuity. Premium financing programs assume the loan continuously gets renewed at the end of each term until the insured's death when the insurance proceeds are intended to repay the loan. Since each loan renewal is subject

to the lender's underwriting guidelines, the lender's desire to continue to fund insurance premiums and the individual's financial situation, there is no guarantee the lender will renew the loan nor that any lender will offer a new loan to continue the program. In this event, the loan could be required to be repaid at a time other than death and from funds other than the insurance policy.

- Reinsurance Risk—depending on the design of the insurer's policy, if an increasing death benefit is used to keep pace with the outstanding loan balance, the *ultimate* death benefit may have to be underwritten *up-front*. The following could be issues in these situations:
  - o The insured not qualify, due to medical or other reasons, for the required amount of reinsurance, thereby, limiting the amount of coverage available to repay the loan.
  - o Even if the insured can qualify, there may not be sufficient reinsurance available in the marketplace to satisfy the ultimate need—thereby limiting the amount of insurance that can be purchased up-front.

Since worldwide reinsurance capacity is limited, if the insured is able to secure all the reinsurance they need, these committed amounts would not be available to satisfy any of their other insurance needs, such as Key Person, increased Estate Liquidity needs, etc.

QUESTION 134: What Is Private Placement Life Insurance?

Private Placement Life Insurance Products (PPIP) are non-registered Variable Universal (VUL) policies and Variable Annuity (VA) contracts that are offered exclusively to high net worth individuals. These products are filed with and approved by State Insurance Departments and are designed to comply with the current Internal Revenue Service (IRS) tax code. They have been referred to as a "hedge fund in a life insurance wrapper".

A Private Placement Variable Universal Life (PPVUL) Policy is a non-registered tax U.S. tax compliant Internal Revenue Code (IRC) Section

7702, flexible premium life insurance policy that provides the same income-tax exempt death benefits as other variable life policies. Premiums less charges and fees are invested into the various investment options inside the insurer's separate account. PPVUL provides flexible investment options (with some non-registered investments within asset classes that are not available in other life insurance policies), flexible premium payments and flexible compensation to brokers. PPVUL purportedly provides transparency to the buyer and seller.

What are the similarities between PPVUL and VUL?

- Under current U.S. Tax Law, the tax benefits include:
    - o tax deferral of any current policy investment earnings and gains;
    - o tax-free exchanges between the underlying investment options;
    - o tax-free withdrawals (up to basis) and loans from the policy cash value free of income tax (provided the policy is a non-MEC (modified endowment contract) under IRC Section 7702A);
    - o ncome tax-free death benefit to the policy's beneficiaries.

How does a PPVUL differ from Variable Universal Life insurance (VUL)?

- Higher face amounts are required to maintain IRC Section 7702 compliance. Financial underwriting can be stringent and the reinsurance marketplace can be restrictive. Underwriting requirements are the same.
- Investment Flexibility—
    - o access to alternative investment styles and managers
    - o ability to use hedge fund strategies aimed at reducing volatility
    - o can add/customize options without a lengthy filing and SEC registration subject to minimum deposit requirements of $5 million within total life of the policy
- Load and charge structure:
    - o State regulators mostly allow charges to be negotiated including insurance product charges, distribution expenses

and front end loads which are all generally more competitive than retail products.

  o No surrender charges—retail life insurance policies generally have significant back-end surrender charges (on a decreasing scale lasting through fifteen and up to twenty years)

  o Compensation is usually asset based and is relatively low as a percentage of premiums

- The funds can have liquidity issues, for example, where the money is "locked up" for five years
- Can only be purchased by an "Accredited Investor" who is a "Qualified Purchaser", as defined by Regulation D of the Securities Act of 1933.

Insurance companies requires the investment manager to comply with IRC Section 817 and related rules with respect to "diversification requirements and investor control". A prospective policy owner must relinquish control and ownership with respect to the investment options available within a policy.

CONCLUSION: WHAT SHOULD I MAKE OF ALL OF THIS?

Life Insurance is a very valuable component of financial planning. Life Insurance is also a very complex financial instrument and needs to be treated as such. Every day life insurance companies introduce new products and marketing concepts. As you've seen in this book, selecting and maintaining the "right" life insurance policy is a challenge.

The human mind seeks simple answers, but very often the simple answer is not the right answer. Proper selection of a life insurance product requires more than simply choosing the lowest priced policy. Many other factors must be considered in making an intelligent choice. For most people, consulting a qualified and objective life insurance specialist is the best way to ensure that an appropriate recommendation is made in the circumstances.

The problem, from a consumer perspective, is making sure that the advice given is professionally objective. There are many fine people who make their living selling life insurance, but they depend for a living on making sales. This tends to affect their recommendations. For example, very often inexpensive term life insurance will do the job effectively for the least cost.

Yet even when term insurance will suffice, a great deal of permanent coverage is aggressively sold in these circumstances. The fact is that commissions on term insurance are much lower than on permanent coverage. Therefore, the incentive is there to sell permanent over term.

This is the reality and that is one reason why I decided to seek a life insurance analyst's license as well as to write this book.

The other purpose of this book is that oftentimes the life insurance salesperson does not service/review the life insurance coverage. As we've seen with the permanent (cash value) life insurance policies this can lead to some bad situations.

The tools in this book are designed to assist in making you in understanding life insurance and monitoring your portfolio easier.

Please keep in mind there is no substitute for the value that life insurance can bring into play for providing discounted dollars and protection that you need.

The more informed you are the better choices you can make.

The man who questions opinion is wise; the man who quarrels with facts is a fool—Frank A. Garbutt

APPENDIX A: CONTACT INFORMATION FOR ALL STATE INSURANCE DEPARTMENTS

Alabama Department of Insurance
201 Monroe Street, Suite 1700
Montgomery, Alabama 36104

Phone: 334-269-3550
Fax: 334-241-4192
Web: www.aldoi.gov

Alaska Division of Insurance
550 West 7th Avenue, Suite 1560
Anchorage, Alaska 99501-3561

Phone: 907-269-7900
Fax: 907-269-7912
Web: http://www.dced.state.ak.us/insurance/

American Samoa Government
Office of the Governor
Pago Pago, American Samoa 96799

Phone: 684-633-4116
Fax: 684-633-2269
Web: http://www.samoanet.com/asg/

Arizona Department of Insurance
2910 North 44th Street, Suite 210
Phoenix, Arizona 85018-7256

Phone: 602-912-8400
Fax: 602-912-8452
Web: http://www.state.as.us/id/

Arkansas Department of Insurance
1200 West 3rd Street
Little Rock, Arkansas 72201-1904

Phone: 501-371-2600
Fax: 501-371-2629
Web: http://www.state.az.us/id/

California Department of Insurance
300 Capitol Mall, Suite 1700
Sacramento, California 95814

Phone: 916-492-3500
Fax: 916-445-5280
Web: http://www.insurance.ca.gov/docs/index.html

State of California
45 Fremont Street, 23rd Floor
San Francisco, California 94102

Phone: 415-538-4040
Fax: 415-904-5889
Web: http://www.insurance.ca.gov/docs/index.html

State of California
300 South Spring Street
Los Angeles, California 90013

Phone: 213-346-6400
Fax: 213-897-6771
Web: http://www.insurance.ca.gov/docs/index.html

Colorado Division of Insurance
1560 Broadway, Suite 850
Denver, Colorado 80202

Phone: 303-894-7499
Fax: 303-894-7455
Web: http://www.dora.state.co.us/insurance

Connecticut Department of Insurance
P.O. Box 816
Hartford, Connecticut 06142-0816

Phone: 860-297-3800
Fax: 860-566-7410
Web: http://www.state.ct.us/cid/

Delaware Department of Insurance
Rodney Building
841 Silver Lake Boulevard

Phone: 302-739-4251
Fax: 302-739-5280
Web: http://www.state.de.us/inscom

Dept. of Insurance & Securities Reg.
Government of the District of Columbia
810 First Street, N.E., Suite 701
Washington, DC 20002

Phone: 202-727-8000
Fax: 202-535-1196
Web: http://disr.washingtondc.gov/

Florida Department of Financial Services
State Capitol
Plaza Level Eleven
Tallahassee, Florida 32399-0300

Phone: 850-413-2806
Fax: 805-413-2950
Web: http://www.doi.state.fl.us/

Georgia Department of Insurance
2 Martin Luther King, Jr Drive
Floyd Memorial Bldg., 704 West Tower
Atlanta, Georgia 30334

Phone: 404-656-2056
Fax: 404-657-7493
Web: http://www.inscomm.state.ga.us/

Dept. Of Revenue & Taxation
Insurance Branch
Government of Guam
Building 13-3, 1st Floor
Mariner Avenue
Tivan, Barrigada, Guam 96913

Phone: 671-475-1843
Fax: 671-472-2643
Web: http://www.gov.gu/

Hawaii Insurance Division   Phone: 808-586-2790
Dept. of Commerce & Consumer Affairs Fax: 808-586-2806
250 S. King Street, 5th Floor   Web: http://www.state.hi.us/dcca/ins
Honolulu, Hawaii 96813

Idaho Department of Insurance   Phone: 208-334-4250
700 West State Street, 3rd Floor   Fax: 208-334-4398
Boise, Idaho 83720-0043   Web: http://www.doi.state.id.us/

Division of Insurance   Phone: 515-281-5705
State of Iowa   Fax: 515-281-3059
330 E. Maple Street   Web: http://www.iid.state.ia.us/
Des Moines, Iowa 50319

Illinois Department of Insurance   Phone: 312-814-2427
100 West Randolph Street, Suite 5-570   Fax: 312-814-5435
Chicago, Illinois 60601-3251   Web: http://www.state.il.us/ins/default.htm

Indiana Department of Insurance   Phone: 317-232-2385
311 W. Washington Street, Suite 300   Fax: 317-232-5251
Indianapolis, Indiana 46204-2787   Web: http://www.ai.org/idoi/index.html

Kansas Department of Insurance   Phone: 785-296-7801
420 S.W. 9th Street   Fax: 785-296-2283
Topeka, Kansas 66612-1678   Web: http://www.ksinsurance.org/

Kentucky Department of Insurance   Phone: 502-564-6027
P.O. Box 517   Fax: 502-564-1453
Frankfort, Kentucky 40602-0517   Web: http://www.doi.state.ky.us/

Louisiana Department of Insurance   Phone: 225-342-5423
1702 N 3rd Street   Fax: 225-342-8622
Baton Rouge, Louisiana 70802   Web: http://www.ldi.la.gov/

Maine Bureau of Insurance   Phone: 207-624-8475
Dept. of Professional & Financial Reg.   Fax: 207-624-8599
State Office Building, Station 34   Web: http://www.maineinsurancereg.org/
Augusta, Maine 04333-0034

Maryland Insurance Administration
525 St. Paul Place
Baltimore, Maryland 21202-2272

Phone: 410-468-2090
Fax: 410-468-2020
Web: http://www.mdinsurance.state.md.us/

Division of Insurance
Commonwealth of Massachusetts
One South Station, 4th Floor
Boston, Massachusetts 02110

Phone: 617-521-7301
Fax: 617-521-7758
Web: http://www.state.ma.us/doi/

Office of Financial and Insurance Services
State of Michigan
611 W. Ottawa St., 2nd Floor North
Lansing, Michigan 48933-1020

Phone: 517-373-0220
Fax: 517-373-4870
Web: http://www.cis.state.mi.us/ofis/

Minnesota Department of Commerce
85 7th Place East, Suite 500
St. Paul, Minnesota 55101-2198

Phone: 651-296-6025
Fax: 651-282-2588
Web: http://www.commerce.state.mn.us/

Mississippi Insurance Department
501 Northwest Street
Woolfolk State Office Bldg, 10th Fl

Phone: 601-359-3569
Fax: 601-359-2474
Web: http://www.doi.state.ms.us/

Missouri Department of Insurance
301 West High Street, Suite 530
Jefferson City, Missouri 65101

Phone: 573-751-4126
Fax: 573-571-1165
Web: http://www.insurance.state.mo.us/

Montana Department of Insurance
840 Helena Avenue
Helena, Montana 59601

Phone: 406-444-2040
Fax: 406-444-3497
Web: http://www.state.mt.us/sao

Nebraska Department of Insurance
Terminal Building, Suite 400
941 'O' Street

Phone: 402-471-2201
Fax: 402-471-4610
Web: http://www.nol.org/home/NDOI/

Nevada Division of Insurance
788 Fairview Drive, Suite 300
Carson City, Nevada 89701-5753

Phone: 775-687-4270
Fax: 775-687-3937
Web: http://www.doi.state.nv.us/

New Hampshire Insurance Department Phone: 603-271-2261
56 Old Suncook Road   Fax: 603-271-1406
Concord, New Hampshire 03301   Web: http://www.state.nj.us/dobi/index.html

New Jersey Department of Insurance Phone: 609-292-5360
20 West State Street CN325   Fax: 609-984-5273
Trenton, New Jersey 08625   Web: http://www.state.nj.us/dobi/index.html

New Mexico Department of Insurance Phone: 505-827-4601
PO Drawer 1269   Fax: 505-476-0326
Santa Fe, New Mexico 87504-1269   Web: http://www.nmprc.state.nm.us/inshm.htm

New York Department of Insurance   Phone: 212-480-2289
25 Beaver Street   Fax: 212-480-2310
New York, New York 10004-2319   Web: http://www.ins.state.ny.us/

North Carolina Dept. of Insurance   Phone: 919-733-3058
PO Box 26387   Fax: 919-733-6495
Raleigh, North Carolina 27611   Web: http://www.ncdoi.com/

North Dakota Dept. of Insurance   Phone: 701-328-2440
600 E. Boulevard   Fax: 701-328-4880
Bismarck, North Dakota 58505-0320   Web: http://www.state.nd.us/ndins/

Ohio Department of Insurance   Phone: 614-644-2658
2100 Stella Court   Fax: 614-644-3743
Columbus, Ohio 43215-1067   Web: http://www.ohioinsurance.gov/

Oklahoma Department of Insurance   Phone: 405-522-4969
2401 NW 23rd St., Suite 28   Fax: 405-521-6635
Oklahoma City, Oklahoma 73107   Web: http://www.oid.state.ok.us/

Oregon Insurance Division   Phone: 503-947-7980
350 Winter Street NE, Room 440   Fax: 503-378-4351
Salem, Oregon 97310-3883
Web: http://www.cbs.state.or.us/external/ins/index.html

Pennsylvania Insurance Department   Phone: 717-783-0442
1326 Strawberry Square, 13th Floor Fax: 717-772-1969
Harrisburg, Pennsylvania 17120   Web: http://www.insurance.state.pa.us/

Puerto Rico Dept of Insurance   Phone: 787-722-8686
Cobian's Plaza Building   Fax: 787-722-4400
1607 Ponce de Leon Avenue   Web: http://www.ocs.gobierno.pr/
Santurce, Puerto Rico 00909

Rhode Island Insurance Division   Phone: 401-222-5466
Dept. Of Business Regulation   Fax: 401-222-5475
233 Richmond Street, Suite 233   Web: http://www.dbr.state.ri.us/
Providence, Rhode Island 02903-4233

South Carolina Dept. of Insurance Phone: 803-737-6212
300 Arbor Lake Drive   Fax: 803-737-6229
Suite 1200   Web: http://www.state.sc.us/doi/
Columbia, South Carolina 29223

South Dakota Division of Insurance Phone: 605-773-4104
Dept. of Commerce & Regulation   Fax: 605-773-5369
118 West Capitol Avenue
Pierre, South Dakota 57501-2000
Web: http://www.state.sd.us/state/executive/dcr/insurance/

Tennessee Dept. of Commerce & Ins. Phone: 615-741-6007
Davy Crockett Tower, Fifth Floor   Fax: 615-532-6934
500 James Robertson Parkway   Web: http://www.state.tn.us/commerce/
Nashville, Tennessee 37243-0565

Texas Department of Insurance   Phone: 512-463-6464
333 Guadalupe Stree   Fax: 512-475-2005
Austin, Texas 78701   Web: http://www.tdi.state.tx.us/

Utah Department of Insurance   Phone: 801-538-3800
3110 State Office Building   Fax: 801-538-3829
Salt Lake City, Utah 94114-1201   Web: http://www.insurance.utah.gov/

State Corporation Commission   Phone: 804-371-9694
Bureau of Insurance   Fax: 804-371-9873
Commonwealth of Virginia, PO Box 1157
Richmond, Virginia 23218
Web: http://www.state.va.us/scc/division/boi/index.htm

Division of Banking & Insurance   Phone: 340-773-6449
1131 King Street, Suite 101   Fax: 340-773-4052
Christiansted   Web: http://www.usvi.org/
St. Croix, Virgin Islands 00820

Vermont Division of Insurance   Phone: 802-828-3301
Dept. of Banking, Ins. & Securities Fax: 802-828-3306
89 Main Street, Drawer 20   Web: http://www.bishca.state.vt.us/
Montpelier, Vermont 05620-3101

Washington State Office of the InsurancePhone 360-725-7100
Commissioner   Fax: 360-586-3109
PO Box 40255   Web: http://www.insurance.wa.gov/
Olympia, Washington 98504-0255

Office of the Commissioner of Insurance Phone: 608-267-1233
State of Wisconsin   Fax: 608-261-8579
125 South Webster Street
GEF III – 2nd Floor
Madison, Wisconsin 53707-7873
Web: http://badger.state.wi.us/agencies/oci/oci_home.htm

West Virginia Dept. of Insurance   Phone: 304-558-3354
PO Box 50540   Fax: 304-558-0412
Charleston, West Virginia 25305-0540 Web: http://www.state.wv.us/insurance/

Wyoming Department of Insurance   Phone: 307-777-7401
Herschler Building   Fax: 307-777-5895
122 West 25th Street, 3rd East   Web: http://insurance.state.wy.us/
Cheyenne, Wyoming 82002-0440

Please note that this information was current as of the time of the
writing of this book and may have changed. If you are unable to
locate your State Insurance Department, you may wish to try the
National Association of Insurance Commissioners at 816.842.3600 or
www.naic.org. Their mailing address is 2301 McGee Street, Suite
800, Kansas City, Missouri, 64018-2262.

Appendix B: Contact Information for Each State Guaranty Associations

In the unlikely event your insurance company should become insolvent; the following is the contact information for the individual state guaranty associations together with statutory references where benefit limits can be found. State codes are frequently available on the internet or in most libraries. Additional information can be found on the National Organization of Life and Health Insurance Guaranty Associations (NOLHGA) website www.nolhga.com.

Alabama Life & Disability Insurance Guaranty Association

6 Office Park Circle, Suite 200	Phone:	205-879-2202
Birmingham, AL 35223	Fax:	205-879-2292

Code of Alabama §§ 27-44-1 to –21

Alaska Life & Health Insurance Guaranty Association

PO Box 103415	Phone:	907-243-2311
Anchorage, AK 99510-3415	Fax:	907-279-1545

Alaska Statutes §§ 21.79.010 to .990

Arizona Life & Disability Insurance Guaranty Fund

1110 W. Washington Suite 270	Phone:	602-364-3863
Phoenix, AZ 85007	Fax:	602-364-3872

Arizona Revised Statutes §§ 20-681 to –695

Arkansas Life & Health Insurance Guaranty Association

425 West Capitol, Suite 3700	Phone:	501-375-9151
Little Rock, AR 72201-2181	Fax:	501-375-6484

Arkansas Code §§ 23-96-101 to –121

California Life & Health Insurance Guarantee Association

8383 Wilshire Boulevard, Suite 815   Phone: 323-782-0182

Beverly Hills, CA 90211   Fax: 323-782-8108

Web: http://www.califega.org

California Insurance Code §§ 1067.01 to .18

Colorado Life & Health Insurance Protection Association

PO Box 36009   Phone: 303-292-5022

Denver, CO 80236   Fax: 303-292-4663

Web: http://www.lhipa.org

Colorado Revised Statutes §§ 10-20-101 to –120

Connecticut Life and Health Insurance Guaranty Association

130 Maple Street   Phone: 860-647-1054

Wethersfield, CT 06109   Fax: 860-647-1054

Web: http://www.ctlifega.org

General Statutes of Connecticut §§ 38a-858 to –879

Delaware Life & Health Insurance Guaranty Association

Christiana Executive Campus   Phone: 302-456-3656

220 Continental Drive, Suite 309   Fax: 302-456-3680

Newark, DE 19713

Web: http://www.delifega.org

Delaware Code Annotated §§ 18-4401 to –4420

District of Columbia Life & Health Insurance Guaranty Association

1200-G Street, NW Suite 800   Phone: 202-434-8771

Washington, DC 20005   Fax: 202-347-2990

District of Columbia Code Annotated §§ 31-5401 to –5416

Florida Life & Health Insurance Guaranty Association

3740 Beach Boulevard, Suite 201-A   Phone: 904-398-3644

Jacksonville, FL 32207-3877   Fax: 904-398-4474

Florida Statutes Annotated §§ 631.711 to .737

Georgia Life & Health Insurance Guaranty Association

2177 Flinstone Drive, Suite R   Phone: 770-621-9835

Tucker, GA 30084   Fax: 770-938-3296

Code of Georgia Annotated §§ 33-38-1 to –22

Hawaii Life & Disability Insurance Guaranty Association

1132 Bishop Street, Suite 1590	Phone:	808-528-5400
Honolulu, HI 96813	Fax:	808-528-5279

Web: http://www.hilifega.org

Hawaii Revised Statutes §§ 431:16-201 to –219

Idaho Life & Health Insurance Guaranty Association

8324 Northview, Suite 104	Phone:	208-378-9510
Boise, ID 93704	Fax:	208-378-7683

Web: http://www.idlifega.org

Idaho Official Code §§ 41-4301 to –4319

Illinois Life & Health Insurance Guaranty Association

8420 W. Bryn Mawr Avenue, Suite 550	Phone:	773-714-8050
Chicago, IL 60631-3404	Fax:	773-714-8052

Illinois Compiled Statutes §§ 215 5/531.01 to .19

Indiana Life & Health Insurance Guaranty Association

251 E. Ohio Street, Suite 1070	Phone:	317-636-8204
Indianapolis, IN 46204-2143	Fax:	317-264-2395

Web: http://www.inlifega.org

Indiana Code §§ 27-8-8-1 to –18

Iowa Life & Health Insurance Guaranty Association

700 Walnut Street, Suite 1600	Phone:	515-248-5712
Des Moines, IA 50309-3899	Fax:	515-283-8018

Web: http://www.ialifega.org

Code of Iowa §§ 508C.1 to .19

Kansas Life & Health Insurance Guaranty Association

2909 S.W. Maupin Lane	Phone:	785-271-1199
Topeka, KS 66614-5335	Fax:	785-272-0242

Web: http://www.kslifega.org

Kansas Statutes Annotated §§ 40-3001 to –3018

Kentucky Life & Health Insurance Guaranty Association

4010 Dupont Circle, Suite 232	Phone:	502-895-5915
Louisville, KY 40207	Fax:	502-895-6543

Web: http://www.kylifega.org

Kentucky Revised Statutes Annotated §§ 304.42-010 to –190

Louisiana Life & Health Insurance Guaranty Association

451 Florida Street, North Tower Suite 1400   Phone: 225-381-0656

Baton Rouge, LA 70801   Fax: 225-344-1132

Louisiana Revised Statutes Annotated §§ 22:1395.1 to .19

Maine Life & Health Insurance Guaranty Association

PO Box 881   Phone: 207-633-1090

Boothbay Harbor, ME 04538   Fax: 207-633-1088

Maine Revised Statutes Annotated §§ 24A 4601 to 4619

Maryland Life & Health Insurance Guaranty Corporation

PO Box 671   Phone: 410-998-3907

Owings Mills, MD 21117-6071   Fax: 410-998-3909

Annotated Code of Maryland, Insurance §§ 9-401 to –419

Massachusetts Life & Health Insurance Guaranty Association

PO Box 3171   Phone: 413-744-8483

Springfield, MA 01101-3171   Fax: 413-744-4949

General Laws of the Commonwealth of Massachusetts §§ 175 146B

Michigan Life & Health Insurance Guaranty Association

1640 Haslett Road, Suite 160   Phone: 517-339-1755

Haslett, MI 48840-8683   Fax: 517-339-5500

Web: http://www.milifega.org

Michigan Compiled Laws §§ 500.7701 to .7780

Minnesota Life & Health Insurance Guaranty Association

4760 White Bear Parkway, Suite 101   Phone: 651-407-3149

White Bear Lake, MN 55110   Fax: 651-407-3150

Web: http://www.mnlifega.org

Minnesota Statutes §§ 61B.18 to .32

Mississippi Life & Health Insurance Guaranty Association

PO Box 4562   Phone: 601-981-0755

Jackson, MS 39296   Fax: 601-362-9544

Mississippi Code Annotated §§ 83-23.201 to –235

Missouri Life & Health Insurance Guaranty Association

994 Diamond Ridge, Suite 102   Phone: 573-634-8455

Jefferson City, MO 65109   Fax: 573-634-8488

Web: http://www.mo-iga.org

Missouri Revised Statutes §§ 376.715 to .758

Montana Life & Health Insurance Guaranty Association

PO Box 951   Phone: 262-965-5761

Oconomowoc, WI 53066-0951   Fax: 262-965-5200

Web: http://www.mtlifega.org

Montana Code Annotated §§ 33-10-201 to –236

Nebraska Life & Health Insurance Guaranty Association

1900 U.S. Bank Bldg.   Phone: 402-474-6900

233 South 13th Street   Fax: 402-474-5393

Lincoln, NE 68508

Web: http://www.nelifega.org

Revised Statutes of Nebraska §§ 44-2701 to –2720

Nevada Life & Health Insurance Guaranty Association

One East First Street Suite 1211   Phone: 775-329-8387

Reno, NV 89501   Fax: 775-323-4997

Web: http://www.nvlifega.org

Nevada Revised Statutes §§ 686C.010 to .390

New Hampshire Life & Health Insurance Guaranty Association

47 Hall Street, Suite 2   Phone: 603-226-9114

Concord, NH 03301   Fax: 603-224-6713

New Hampshire Revised Statutes Annotated §§ 408-B:1 to :20

New Jersey Life & Health Insurance Guaranty Association

One Gateway Center, 9th Floor   Phone: 973-623-3989

Newark, NJ 07102   Fax: 973-623-1861

New Jersey Statutes Annotated §§ 17B:32A-1 to –19

New Mexico Life Insurance Guaranty Association

PO Box 13449   Phone: 505-237-9397

Albuquerque, NM 87192-3449   Fax: 505-237-9496

New Mexico Statutes Annotated §§ 59A-42-1 to –16

Life Insurance Company Guaranty Corporation of New York

919 Third Avenue	Phone:	212-909-6813
New York, NY 10022	Fax:	212-521-7813

Web: http://www.nylifega.org

Consolidated Laws of New York Annotated, Insurance §§ 28 7701 to 7718

North Carolina Life & Health Insurance Guaranty Association

PO Box 10218	Phone:	919-833-6838
Raleigh, NC 27605-0218	Fax:	919-833-9576

Web: http://www.nclifega.org

General Statutes of North Carolina §§ 58-62-2 to –95

North Dakota Life & Health Insurance Guaranty Association

PO Box 8875	Phone:	701-235-4108
Fargo, ND 58109-8875	Fax:	701-492-2844

Web: http://www.ndlifega.org

North Dakota Century Code §§ 26.1-38.1-01 to –16

Ohio Life & Health Insurance Guaranty Association

1840 Mackenzie Drive	Phone:	614-442-6601
Columbus, OH 43220	Fax:	614-442-0004

Ohio Revised Code Annotated §§ 3956.01 to .20

Oklahoma Life & Health Insurance Guaranty Association

201 Robert S. Kerr Avenue, Suite 600	Phone:	405-272-9221
Oklahoma City, OK 73102	Fax:	405-236-3121

Web: http://www.oklife.org

Oklahoma Statutes §§ 36-2021 to –2043

Oregon Life & Health Insurance Guaranty Association

3541 Elderberry Drive, South	Phone:	503-588-1974
PO Box 4520	Fax:	503-588-2029
Salem, OR 97302-8520		

Web: http://www.orlifega.org

Oregon Revised Statutes §§ 734.750 to .890

Pennsylvania Life & Health Insurance Guaranty Association

290 King of Prussia Road, Suite 218	Phone:	610-975-0572
Radnor Station Building, No. 2	Fax:	610-975-9348
Radnor, PA 19087		

Pennsylvania Consolidated Statutes §§ 40-991.1701 to .1718

Asociación de Garantia de Seguros de Vida e Incapacidad de Puerto Rico

Union Plaza Building, Suite 240	Phone:	787-765-2095
416 Ponce de Leon Avenue	Fax:	787-758-7087
Hato Rey, PR 00918		

Laws of Puerto Rico Annotated §§ 26-3901 to –3918

Rhode Island Life & Health Insurance Guaranty Association

The Foundry, Suite 426	Phone:	401-273-2921
235 Promenade Street	Fax:	401-273-4933
Providence, RI 02908		
Web: http://www.rilifega.org		

General Laws of Rhode Island §§ 27.34.3-1 to –20

South Carolina Life, Accident & Health Insurance Guaranty Association

PO Box 706	Phone:	803-536-9874
Orangeburg, SC 29116-0706	Fax:	803-536-2636
Web: http://www.sclifega.org		

Code of Laws of South Carolina §§ 38-29-10 to -200

South Dakota Life & Health Insurance Guaranty Association

PO Box 1030	Phone:	605-336-0177
Sioux Falls, SD 57101-1030	Fax:	605-335-3639
Web: http://www.sdlifega.org		

South Dakota Codified Laws §§ 58-29C-1 to –62

Tennessee Life & Health Insurance Guaranty Association

1200 One Nashville Place	Phone:	615-242-8758
150 4th Avenue North	Fax:	615-256-8197
Nashville, TN 37219		
Web: http://www.tnlifega.org		

Tennessee Code Annotated §§ 56-12-201 to –220

Texas Life, Accident, Health & Hospital Service Insurance Guaranty Association

6504 Bridge Point Parkway, Suite 450   Phone: 512-476-5101

Austin, TX 78730   Fax: 512-472-1470

Web: http://www.txlifega.org

Texas Codes Annotated, Insurance § 21.28D

Utah Life & Health Insurance Guaranty Association

955 E. Pioneer Road   Phone: 801-572-1218

Draper, UT 84020   Fax: 801-572-5067

Utah Code Annotated §§ 31A-28-101 to –120

Vermont Life & Health Insurance Guaranty Association

c/o National Life Insurance Company, M-230   Phone: 802-229-3553

One National Life Drive   Fax: 802-229-3762

Montpelier, VT 05604

Web: http://www.vtlifega.org

Vermont Statutes Annotated §§ 8—4151 to 4185

Virginia Life, Accident & Sickness Insurance Guaranty Association

c/o APM Management Services, Inc.

8001 Franklin Farms Drive, Suite 238   Phone: 804-282-2240

Richmond, VA 23229   Fax: 804-282-1816

Web: http://www.valifega.org

Code of Virginia Annotated §§ 38.2-1700 to –1721

Washington Life & Disability Insurance Guaranty Association

12514 S.E. 16th Street   Phone: 425-562-3128

Bellevue, WA 98005   Fax: 425-746-1861

Web: http://www.walifega.org

Revised Code of Washington §§ 48.32A.005 to .902

West Virginia Life & Health Insurance Guaranty Association

PO Box 816   Phone: 304-733-6904

Huntington, WV 25712   Fax: 304-733-6905

West Virginia Code §§ 33-26A-1 to –19

Wisconsin Insurance Security Fund

2445 Darwin Road, Suite 101   Phone: 608-242-9473

Madison, WI 53704-3116   Fax: 608-242-9472

Web: http://www.wilifega.org

Wisconsin Statutes §§ 646.01 to .73

Wyoming Life & Health Insurance Guaranty Association

PO Box 36009   Phone: 303-292-5022

Denver, CO 80236   Fax: 303-292-4663

Web: http://www.wlhiga.org

Wyoming Statutes Annotated §§ 26-42-101 to –118

This information is from the NOHLGA'S website www.nolhga.com. The site contains a substantial amount of other information and resources on this subject.

APPENDIX C: TRACKING DOWN A MISSING LIFE INSURANCE POLICY

ALABAMA
State Treasury
Unclaimed Property Division
PO Cox 302520
Montgomery, AL 36130-2520
Web: http://www.treasury.state.al.us

ALASKA
Department of Revenue
Treasury Division
Unclaimed Property Section
PO Box 110405
Juneau, AK 99811-0405
Web: http://www.revenue.state.ak.us/treasury/ucp/index.htm

ARIZONA
Department of Revenue
Unclaimed Property Unit
PO Box 29026
Site Code 9026
Phoenix, AZ 85038-902
Web: http://www.revenue.state.az.us/unclm/index.htm

ARKANSAS
Unclaimed Property Division
Auditor of State
1400 W. 3rd St., Suite 100
Little Rock, AR 72201-1811
Web: http://www.state.ar.us/auditor

CALIFORNIA
State Controller
Division of Collections – Bureau of
Unclaimed Property
3301 C Street, Suite 712
PO Box 942850
Sacramento, CA 94250-5873
Web: http://www.sco.ca.gov/

COLORADO
Colorado Unclaimed Property Division
1120 Lincoln Street, Suite 1004
Denver, CO 80203-2136
Web: http://www.treasurer.state.co.us

CONNECTICUT
Unclaimed Property Division
Office of State Treasurer
55 Elm Street
Hartford, CT 06106
Web: http://www.state.ct.us/ott/

DELAWARE
Bureau of Abandoned Property
PO Box 8931
Wilmington, DC 19899
Web: http://www.state.de.us/revenue/escheat/escheat.htm

DISTRICT OF COLUMBIA
Office of Finance & Treasury
Unclaimed Property Unit
810 First Street NE, Room 401
Washington, DC 20002
Web: http://cfo.washingtondc.gov/services/financial/unclaimed_property/index.shtm

FLORIDA
Chief Financial Officer's Office
Bureau of Unclaimed Property
PO Box 1910
Tallahassee, FL 32302-1910
Web: http://up.dbf.state.fl.us

GEORGIA
Georgia Department of Revenue
Property Tax Division
4245 International Pkwy, Suite A
Hapeville, GA 30354-3918
Web: http://www2.state.ga.us/departments/dor/ptd

GUAM
Treasurer of Guam
PO Box 884
Agana, GU 96910

HAWAII
Department of Budget and Finance
Unclaimed Property Program
PO Box 150
Honolulu, HI 96810-0150
Web: http://www.ehawaiigov.org/bf/ucp/html

IDAHO
Idaho State Tax Commission
Unclaimed Property Section
PO Box 36
Boise, ID 93722-0410
Web: http://www2.state.id.us/tax/ucp_search_idaho.htm

ILLINOIS
Office of State Treasurer
Unclaimed Property Division
PO Box 19495
Springfield, IL 62794-9495
Web: http://www.state.il.us/treas

INDIANA
Attorney General's Office
Unclaimed Property Division
402 W. Washington, Suite C-531
Indianapolis, IN 46204
Web: http://www.state.in.us/attorneygeneral/

IOWA
The Great Iowa Treasure Hunt
Ola Babcock Miller Building
1112 E. Grand Avenue
3rd Floor West
Des Moines, IA 50319
Web: http://www.greatiowatreasurehunt.com

KANSAS
Unclaimed Property Division
900 Jackson, Suite 201
Topeka, KS 66612-1235
Web: http://www/kansascash.com/cgi-win/index.kst

KENTUCKY
Unclaimed Property Division
Kentucky Department of Treasury
Suite 183, Capitol Annex
Frankfort, KY 40601
Web: http://www.kytreasury.com

LOUISIANA
State Treasurer
Unclaimed Property Division
PO Box 91010
Baton Rouge, LA 70821
Web: http://www.treasury.state.la.us/

MAINE
State Treasurer's Office
Abandoned Property Division
39 State House Station
111 Sewall Street, 3rd Fl
Burton M. Cross Building
Augusta, ME 04333-0039
Web: http://www.state.me.us/treasurer/property.htm

MARYLAND
Unclaimed Property Unit
301 We. Preston Street
Baltimore, MD 21201-2385
Web: http://www.marylandtaxes.com/default.asp

MASSACHUSETTS
Abandoned Property Division
1 Ashburton Place, 12th Floor
Boston, MA 02108
Web: http://www.state.ma.us/treasury/

MICHIGAN
Department of Treasury
Unclaimed Property Division
Lansing, MI 48922
Web: http://www.michigan.gov/treasury/0,1607,7-121-1748_1876
1912—-,00.html

MINNESOTA
Minnesota Department of Commerce
Unclaimed Property Division
85 7th Place East, Suite 600
St. Paul, MN 55101-3165
Web: http://www.state.mn.us/cgi-bin/portal/mn/jsp/content.do?
id=-536881373&agency=Commerce

MISSISSIPPI
Treasury Department
Unclaimed Property Division
PO Box 138
Jackson, MS 39205-0138
Web: http://www.treasury.state.ms.us/

MISSOURI
State Treasurer's Office
PO Box 1004
Jefferson City, MO 65102
Web: http://www.sto.state.mo.us

MONTANA
Department of Revenue
Unclaimed Property Division
Sam W. Mitchell Bldg
125 N. Roberts, 3rd Floor
PO Box 5805
Helena, MT 59604-5805
Web:http://www.discoveringmontana.com/revenue/css/2forindividuals
/08unclaimedproperty.asp

NEVADA
Office of the State Treasurer
Unclaimed Property Division
555 E Washington Avenue, Suite 4200
Las Vegas, NV 89101-1070
Web: http://nevadatreasurer.com/

NEW HAMPSHIRE
Treasury Department
Unclaimed Property Division
25 Capitol Street, Room 205
Concord, NH 03301
Web: http://www.state.nh.us/treasury/

NEW JERSEY
Department of the Treasury
Unclaimed Property
PO Box 214
Trenton, NJ 08695-0214
Web: http://webdb.state.nj.us/treasury/taxation/unclaimsrch.htm

NEW MEXICO
Taxation & Revenue Department
Unclaimed Property Division
PO Box 25123
Santa Fe, NM 87504-5123
Web: http://ec3.state.nm.us/ucp/

NEW YORK
State Comptroller
New York State Office of Unclaimed Funds
110 State Street, 8th Floor
Albany, NY 12236
Web: http://www.osc.state.ny.us/

NORTH CAROLINA
Department of State Treasurer
Esheat & Unclaimed Property
325 North Salisbury Street
Raleigh, NC 27603-1385
Web: http://www.treasurer.state.nc.us/

NORTH DAKOTA
State Land Department
Unclaimed Property Division
PO Box 5523
Bismarck, ND 58506-5523
Web: http://www.land.state.nd.us/

OHIO
Department of Commerce
Division of Unclaimed Funds
77 South High Street – 20th Fl
Columbus, OH 43266-0545
Web: http://www.com.state.oh.us/

OKLAHOMA
Oklahoma State Treasurer's Office
Unclaimed Property Division
4545 North Lincoln Boulevard, Suite 106
Oklahoma City, OK 73105-3413
Web: http://www.unclaimed.state.ok.us/

OREGON
Division of State Lands
Unclaimed Property Division
775 Summer Street NE, Suite 100
Salem, OR 97301-1279
Web: http://www.oregonstatelands.us/

PENNSYLANIA
State Treasurer
Unclaimed Property Division
PO Box 1837
Harrisburg, PA 17105-1837
Web: http://wwwtreasury.state.pa.us/

PUERTO RICO
Office of the Commissioner of Financial Institutions
Commissioner
PO Box 11855
San Juan, PR 00910-3855
Web: http://www.cif.gov.pr

QUEBEC
Quebec Public Curator
600 Rene-Levesque West
Montreal, PQ H3B 4W9
Web: http://www.curateur.gouv.qc.ca/cura/html/anglais/unclaimed/
provis.html

RHODE ISLAND
Department of Treasury
Unclaimed Property Division
PO Box 1435
Providence, RI 02901-1435
Web: http://www.state.ri.us/treas/treas.htm

SOUTH CAROLINA
Office of the State Treasurer
Unclaimed Property Division
PO Box 11778
Columbia, SC 29211-1778
Web: http://www.state.sc.us/treas

SOUTH DAKOTA
State Treasurer's Office
500 East Capitol Ave.
Pierre, SD 57501-5070
Web: http://wwwstate.sd.us/state/executive/treasurer/prop.htm

TENNESSEE
Treasury Department
Unclaimed Property Division
Andrew Jackson Bldg., 10th Floor
500 Deaderick Street
Nashville, TN 37243-0242
Web: http://www.treasury.state.tn.us/unclaim/

TEXAS
Texas Comptroller of Public Accounts
Unclaimed Property Division
PO Box 12019
Austin, TX 78711-2019
Web: http://wwwwindow.state.tx.us/up/

UTAH
State Treasurer's Office
Unclaimed Property Division
341 South Main St., 5th Floor
Salt Lake City, UT 84111
Web: http://www.treasurer.state.ut.us/

VERMONT
State Treasurer's Office
Unclaimed Property Division
133 State Street
Montpelier, VT 05633-0001
Web: http://www.tre.state.vt.us/AbanProp/index.htm

VIRGIN ISLANDS
US Virgin Islands
Office of the Lieutenant Governor
Division of Banking
18 Kongens Gade
Simon K. Mohammed, Examiner
St. Thomas, USVI, VI 00802

VIRGINIA
Department of Treasury
Unclaimed Property Division
PO Box 2478
Richmond, VA 23218-2478
Web: http://www.trs.state.va.us/

WASHINGTON
Department of Revenue
Unclaimed Property Division
PO Box 448
Olympia, WA 98507-0448
Web: http://ucp.dor.wa.gov

WEST VIRGINIA
Office of State Treasurer
One Players Club Drive
Charleston, WV 25311
Web: http://www.wvtreasury.com/

WISCONSIN
State Treasurer's Office
Unclaimed Property Division
PO Box 2114
Madison, WI 53701-2114
Web: http://www.ost.state.wi.us

WYOMING
Office of the State Treasurer
Unclaimed Property Division
2515 Warren Avenue, Suite 502
Cheyenne, WY 82002
Web: http://treasurer.state.wy.us/unclaimed.asp

Please note that this information was current as of the time of the writing of this book and may have changed. If you are unable to locate your State's web page from these links, try your State's Home Web Page.

APPENDIX D: ADDITIONAL FACTORS THAT MAY IMPACT UNDERWRITING AND WHAT YOU NEED TO KNOW

Any underwriting will include exam requirements which will depend on the company, your age, the amount applied for and specific medical conditions. Both medical and non-medical factors can affect an underwriter's decision. The following is a list of the most common medical and non-medical factors and information that the underwriter will usually be looking at, and a general idea of what decision to expect. Please keep in mind that is to give you a sense of what to expect and is not a guarantee of a specific outcome. You will find that the decisions can vary from company to company.

As a reminder and as we discussed in Question 76, a Substandard Table Rating/Flat Extra is an extra premium imposed by a life insurance company based on certain health conditions and other areas such as avocation, travel, etc. These are applied against a company's standard rates rather than the preferred rates. A flat extra is a flat dollar amount of premium in addition to the initial premium amount. A table rating is an additional percentile of premium multiplied by the cost per $1,000 of coverage; each table is an additional 25% of premium. These may drop off or reduce automatically after a certain number of years. If you feel that the reason for this extra premium no longer exists, you can petition the company to have it removed (at no cost to you)

PLEASE NOTE THAT THE FOLLOWING INFORMATION IS NOT MEDICAL ADVICE NOR IS ANY OF IT GUARANTEED. IT IS SUBJECT TO CHANGE AND IS PRESENTED HERE TO GIVE YOU A GENERAL IDEA.

Avocation or Hobbies & Aviation Risk Factors—Non-medical factors, such as avocations or hobbies can frequently affect the underwriter's decision. The rate class will depend on a number of issues and can range from preferred to highly rated.

Alcohol—If use is socially, then it should not be a problem. If recovering, then the premium will be rated for first few years and will be more favorable the longer the time period eventually to a possible preferred.

Aortic Valve Disorder—Very mild cases of aortic valve regurgitation are usually approved at Standard, sometimes better. More severe cases where fatigue, chest pain, atrial fibrillation, edema, enlarged heart (cardiomegaly) or heart failure is present will be rated to a decline. Case will also be table rated to a decline depending on how many valves have had to be replaced.

Asthma—Bronchial Asthma: Mild, Lungs clear = standard with possibility of preferred;

Moderate, Chronic with Acute episodes, treated by injection or spray, slight wheezing = Standard to Table 2 range; Severe episodes treated by hospitalization, chronic steroid use = Table 2 to Table 6 range

Atrial Fibrillation—Approval depends on the severity of the arrhythmia, what treatment has been utilized, if another cardiac condition is present and how many episodes client has had. Many underwriters will issue credits for a recent, well done, stress and/or echo or a cardiac catheterization which is normal. A history of heart attack, angioplasty or bypass surgery combined with an arrhythmia usually results in a decline from the carrier. Simple arrhythmias can be Standard. Others are usually table 2 and up depending on the findings of the cardiac work-up and period of stability.

Bladder Cancer—The underwriting offer will depend on the grade and invasiveness of the tumor. Low grade tumors that did not invade beyond the mucosa can usually be approved at Standard. More invasive, severe tumors may have a postponement period of 1-5 years with a flat extra then added on.

Breast Cancer—The offer depends on tumor size, invasiveness and stage. Most breast cancers carry a 1-5 year postponement depending on the factors listed above. Afterward a flat extra is added along with a possible table rating for more severe cancers. Depending on the type and severity of the cancer, the flat extra/rating can be lifted after 5-10 disease free years.

Bundle Branch Block (BBB)—A left BBB is a medium rating at minimum. Right BBB without any complications is usually standard. Approval will depend on the severity of the BBB, age at diagnosis and any related complications or diseases.

Cancer—Many cancers can be standard after a 5 to 7 year period from the date of the last treatment. Prior to that expect flat extra ratings of anywhere from $5.00 to $15.00 per thousand.

Cardiac Catheterization—Underwriting offer depends on the severity of the disease in conjunction with family history and/or any contributing factors (hypertension, diabetes, obesity, etc). Mild disease under good control can be Standard. Moderate to severe disease can be anywhere from a low rating to decline depending on control, compliance and contributing factors.

Cholesterol Levels—Carriers usually put the most emphasis on HDL ratio, but they also factor in total cholesterol. If both of these are within normal limits (ratio of 5.0-5.5 or below and total of 200-220 or below for most companies), carrier will offer their best rates if all other criteria are met. As both of these numbers increase, the offer will be closer to Standard. Most carriers will apply table ratings to total cholesterol that exceeds 300 and a ratio that exceeds 10.0.

Chronic Bronchitis—Mild disease with minimal reduction in lung function can be standard. Others will be moderate substandard rating up to decline for severe diseases.

Chronic Lymphocytic Leukemia—The offer will depend on the age of onset and the number of symptoms you experience. If leukemia was acquired before the age of 50, white blood count is under relative control and no anemia or enlargement of the organs is present, the best offer will be a mid-range rating. Persons diagnosed at an earlier age or with a more progressive form of the disease can expect a very high rating to decline.

Colorectal Cancer—The offer will depend on how invasive the tumor is and the Duke's score. Depending on these two factors, there will be a postponement period of 1-5 years depending on severity, then a flat extra. Standard is available after a certain period (anywhere from 3-10 years) again, depending on severity of tumor.

Coronary Artery Bypass Graft (CABG)—Applicants are typically insurable 6 months after a bypass. May be insurable after 3 months with negative stress test performed after the bypass. Most often will receive a mid to low table rating 3-6 months after the procedure.

Coronary Artery Disease—There are many factors to consider when underwriting CAD including: age, smoking status, cholesterol, LV function and ejection fraction (both of which can be found on the stress test), whether or not you had a heart attack, if an angioplasty or bypass graft(s) was done, and any information from your physician(s) regarding current cardiac condition. Because so many factors are involved, it is probably best to consult with a life insurance advisor so they can contact an underwriter with case specifics in order to obtain a tentative quote. However, good cases are generally in the table 2-4 range. Best cases can be Standard after 10 years.

Crohn's Disease—Crohn's Disease in the most mildest of cases, last attack over 5 years ago, duration less than 2 weeks, and no maintenance medications could possibly be Standard. Most common underwriting for Crohn's Disease is a low table rating. Very severe Crohn's Disease, frequent attacks, need corticosteroids for maintenance and will most probably be a decline.

Depression—Some situational Depression = Preferred. Mild and controlled with medications = Standard to low table rating, Manic Depression and/or Bipolar = mid-table rating and up and

Suicidal thoughts and attempts = Postpone for 2 years.

Diabetes—The rating for DM depends upon the age at onset and the duration of the disease.

Good control and not requiring insulin will reduce the rating. Sometimes an offer to Standard can be obtained if the DM is well controlled for at least 1 year and current blood sugar is within normal limits. Will not do better than Standard. Insulin using diabetics are usually a low table rating at the very best. Evidence of Neurological, Kidney, or Vision problems will add greatly to any rating. Coronary Artery Disease with diabetics is a very poor risk.

Driving Under the Influence—DUI may be standard after 3 years. Sometimes a single episode violation can be standard sooner. This will require adequate explanation. Multiple DUI's are usually a decline.

Drugs—Marijuana use is a possible smoker. Drug abuse: Postpone for 2 years, 2—4 years = high table rating. 4—6 years = low to mid table rating; 6+ years = Standard and some carriers will go preferred with 10+ years out of rehabilitation.

Emphysema—If still smoking, high substandard to a decline. Mild emphysema may be standard if diagnosed early and lung function is close to normal. Others will be moderate to high table rating.

Hepatitis A, B, C—Approval depends on type of hepatitis (A, B, C, alcoholic, etc.), if it is chronic or acute, the cause of the hepatitis (virus, parasite, etc.), the results of current tests and labs, age and treatment. If the case is mild, in remission and all lab results are normal, Standard is usually available. More severe cases that are chronic with elevated labs and current flare up are table rated. If you are currently drinking alcohol, the case is usually a decline.

Hypertension (High Blood Pressure)—Well-controlled hypertension can expect a possible preferred rating with some of the carriers. Uncontrolled hypertension will require several table ratings added to a standard rate, depending on the blood pressure readings.

Irregular Heart Beat—Approval depends on the severity of the arrhythmia, what treatment has been utilized, if another cardiac condition is present and how many episodes client has had. Many underwriters will issue credits for a recent, well done, stress and/or echo or a cardiac catheterization which is normal. A history of heart attack, angioplasty or bypass surgery combined with an arrhythmia usually results in a decline from the carrier. Simple arrhythmias can be

Standard. Others are usually a low table rating and up depending on the findings of the cardiac work-up and period of stability.

Mitral Valve Prolapse—MVP is probably the most common of the heart valve lesions. Many individuals w/MVP are asymptomatic. Usually an individual with a negative echo and no complications or family history of heart disease can get Standard. Some carriers will even go Preferred with an especially good history.

Multiple Sclerosis—Assuming diagnosis has been made—Typically postpone within 1st year of diagnosis. Age 35 and over at onset—slowly progressive with infrequent episodes mid-table rating. More Progressive disease with frequent episodes (more than 2 per year) = high table rating. Rapidly Progressive disease = Decline

Myocardial Infarction (Heart Attack)—Most carriers will wait 3-6 months after the incident before making an offer. The extent of table ratings and/or flat extras depends on the severity of the MI, your age at the time of underwriting, your current smoking status and the results of recent cardiac tests. The best way to gauge how you will be underwritten is to consult your Life Insurance Advisor with the specific details so that they can discuss it with an underwriter.

Ovarian Cancer—The offer will depend on the stage of the tumor and how far the cancer spread. Most ovarian cancers will have a 1-5 year postponement period followed by a flat extra of anywhere from $7 to $15 per thousand for 5 or more years.

Pacemaker—Approval is dependent primarily on the underlying impairment that precipitated the pacemaker installation. In other words, you are usually not rated solely on the fact that the pacemaker was installed, but rather based on the disease or event that caused the pacemaker to be needed. Most pacemaker cases will be rated following a rather lengthy postponement period to determine stability. It is probably best to discuss the specific details of the case with your life insurance advisor so they can discuss it with an underwriter.

Parkinson's Disease—Those Parkinson's disease individuals who have later onset disease without the problems of depression or dementia can usually be offered policies at very mild ratings such as low table ratings. Disease more severe than mild will be in the mid-table ratings.

Percutaneous Translumitnal Angioplasty (PTCA)—The best case scenario is a low table rating with select cases becoming standard after 10 years.

Pneumonia—Preferred is possible with a single episode completely healed. Multiple episodes usually indicate an underlying disorder and the rating will be for the underlying disease.

Prostate Cancer—Offer depends on the age at diagnosis, Gleason score, method of treatment, and pre-operative PSA level. If client had a radical prostatectomy or radiation treatment, case will be postponed for 3-6 months. If you are younger than age 50, your case will be postponed at least 5 years. After the postponement period, the case will be approved with a table rating which usually remains for the life of the policy.

Prostate Specific Antigen (PSA)—A PSA of approximately 0-4 is normal for males to age 60. After age 60 the normal PSA may increase to 4.5-6.5. "Free PSA" should be above 20%. If the elevated PSA is a new finding on the carrier's lab tests, carrier will usually postpone the case until you have gone to your doctor for a work up. Some carriers may offer a table rating depending on the degree of elevation. If you have a history of elevated PSA due to enlarged prostate or infection, the carrier will usually not rate the file (can get Standard or Preferred) as long as you have recently had follow up with your doctor and cancer has been ruled out.

Proteinuria—The offer will depend on the type of proteinuria. Transient and orthostatic proteinuria is of no medical concern and carries no extra rating. You can usually be approved at what he otherwise qualifies for medically. Proteinuria related to diabetes, hypertension or other known kidney disorders can be standard to table rated depending on your age (older people-above 50-normally have a larger amount of protein in their urine) and the amount of protein found in the specimen. However, even a small amount of protein with diabetes is not a good sign and can cause a case to be highly rated or even declined.

Pulmonary Disease (COPD)—COPD is usually underwritten based on several factors including: the results of pulmonary function tests, frequency of attacks, frequency of hospitalization, and current smoking history. A mild case of COPD with little obstruction and few attacks may be Standard to a low table rating depending on whether or not you are a smoker. Moderate to severe cases of COPD are usually in the middle table rating to decline range, again depending on whether or not you currently smoke.

Pulmonary Function Testing (PFT)—Entirely dependent on the results of the test. When there is a history of pulmonary disease, normal PFTs can result in a standard rating.

Renal (Kidney) Disease—Anywhere from standard on up to decline. Much will depend on the kidney's ability to act as a filter and this will be assessed by the BUN and creatinine levels. If these are normal and stable then standard is possible.

Rheumatoid Arthritis—If uncomplicated most of these cases will be standard and mild cases even preferred. If any of the stronger medicines are required for control, i.e. gold salts, prednisone, or methotrexate, then the case may be rated slightly.

Sarcoidosis—After complete recovery, standard is not usual. Prior to that table ratings or flat extra ratings may be applied. A low to mid-range table rating may be appropriate for disease that is stable but not yet resolved.

Skin Cancer—The offer depends on the type of skin cancer, invasiveness, tumor size and stage. Basal cell carcinoma is the least serious type of skin cancer and many carriers will offer Preferred if you are medically healthy otherwise. Skin cancers confined to the dermis or outer layers of skin and removed completely can usually be approved at Standard. Persons with the most severe forms of skin cancer will be postponed from 1-5 years and then a flat extra will be added.

Sleep Apnea—If the apnea is mild, it can usually be treated with lifestyle change and may resolve itself. Most carriers will offer Standard in these cases. More serious apneas may require a CPAP (Continuous Positive Airway Pressure) machine or even surgery. More severe cases will be table rated and non compliance with treatment will usually result in a declination.

Systemic Lupus Erthematosas (SLE)—If Lupus involves the skin only then standard may be expected. Lupus that involves the kidneys, heart, or lungs is often highly rated to decline.

Testicular Cancer—The offer will depend on how invasive the tumor is as well as the stage and type. A non invasive tumor (Stage 0), can often be considered at Standard. For more severe tumors, there could be a postponement period of 1-5 years followed by a flat extra. However, testicular cancer responds very well to current treatment and many testicular cancers, even those that are metastic, can be approved Standard in a relatively short period of time.

Tobacco usage—Underwriting approvals vary widely from carrier to carrier. Some carriers will accept occasional cigar smokers (usually < or = 12/year) as a nonsmoker. Others consider any tobacco use as "smoker" class. Some have separate classifications for "smoker" and "tobacco". However, most carriers will consider an applicant with >.5 nicotine in the urine as a smoker. A value of .5 or < nicotine in the urine is usually considered as "second hand smoke" and many applicants, if they do not admit to any tobacco use on the application, will be considered nonsmokers with this value (please see question 79 for information on how this can void a life insurance policy). The best way to gauge how you will be underwritten is to consult your advisor with the specific smoking details. The rates for smokers are significantly higher than those for non-smokers.

Transient Ischemic Attack (TIA)—Underwriting offer will depend on age at time of attack and number of attacks. Over age 40, will be a postpone until 3 months after last attack. After the postponement, file will be approved with a low table rating. Possible Standard after 5 or more years without any further episodes. Some TIA cases will fit into a special table low-middle table range to Standard underwriting programs. Please check with your advisor for details.

Ulcerative Colitis—Mild Ulcerative Colitis—less than 1 attack per year, no maintenance medications or have been surgically corrected can possibly be Standard. Generally, ulcerative colitis is underwritten with low to mid-range tables added to a standard rate. Severe ulcerative colitis will be declined until surgically corrected.

Valvular Heart Surgery—Most cases will be postponed for 6 months after valve surgery. After this time the approval usually depends on how many valves have been replaced and the current assessment of the valve disorder. Mild cases with one valve replaced are about a low to middle table rating. More severe cases with up to three valves replaced are very highly rated to a decline.

(This section reprinted with permission of BISYS)

GLOSSARY: KEY LIFE INSURANCE TERMS

Absolute Assignment: The irrevocable transfer of all the policy owner's rights in a life insurance policy.

Accelerated Death Benefit Rider—Rider that allows payment of a portion of the face amount prior to the death of the insured, if the insured is diagnosed with a terminal illness or injury.

Acceptance—Assent by an offeree to the terms of an offer.

Accidental Death Benefit—A feature of a life insurance policy providing an additional benefit if the insured dies in an accident. Because the face amount of the policy is often doubled under this provision, it is also called a double indemnity.

Accident: An event or occurrence which is unforeseen and unintended.

Accident and Health Insurance: A type of coverage that pays benefits, sometimes including reimbursement for loss of income, in case of sickness, accidental injury, or accidental death.

Accidental Death Benefit: A benefit in addition to the face amount of a life insurance policy, payable if the insured dies as the result of an accident. Sometimes referred to as "double indemnity."

Acquisition Costs: The insurer's cost of putting new business in-force, including the agent's commission, the cost of clerical work, fees for medical examinations and inspection reports, sales promotion expense, etc.

Actual Authority: The authority to act on the principal's behalf that n agent reasonably believes he or she has been given by the principal. Actual authority can be express or implied.

Actuarially Fair: The price for insurance which exactly represents the expected losses

Actuary—Mathematician employed by an insurance company to calculate premiums, reserves, dividends and insurance, pension and annuity rates, using risk factors obtained from experience tables. These tables are based on both the company's history of insurance claims and other industry and general statistical data.

Additional insured: an assured party specifically named under an insurance policy

Adhesion, Contract of: A contract that is drafted by one party and accepted or rejected by the other, with no opportunity to bargain with respect to its terms.

Adjustable Life Insurance: A type of insurance that allows the policyholder to change the plan of insurance, raise or lower the face amount of the policy, increase or decrease the premium and lengthen or shorten the protection period.

Adjusted gross estate: Approximately the net worth of the deceased— the beginning point for the computation of estate taxes.

Adjuster: A person who investigates and settles losses for an insurance carrier.

Adjusting: The process of investigating and settling losses with or by an insurance carrier.

Adjustment Bureau: Organization for adjusting insurance claims that is supported by insurers using the bureau's services.

Adverse Selection: The tendency of persons who present a poorer-than-average risk to apply for, or continue, insurance to a greater extent than do persons with average or better-than-average expectations of loss.

Admitted Assets: Assets allowed by state regulatory authorities and by the National Association of Insurance Commissioner for statutory accounting statements. Only the value of the admitted assets may be shown on the statutory balance sheet. (See also Non-admitted Assets).

Age Last: Age based on the individual's current age or their age on of their last birthday.

Age Limits: Stipulated minimum and maximum ages below and above which the company will not accept applications or may not renew policies.

Age Nearest: Age based on the individuals nearest birthday. If the individual is more than 6 months or 182 days into their birthday year, the birthday would be treated as if it had already occurred that year (also referred to as Insurance Age).

Agent: An insurance company representative licensed by the state, who solicits, negotiates or effects contracts of insurance, and provides service to the policyholder for the insurer.

Alien Insurer: An insurance company domiciled in another country.

Amendment: A formal document changing the provisions of an insurance policy signed jointly by the insurance company officer and the policy holder or his authorized representative.

Annual Statement: The annual report, as of December 31, of an insurer to a state insurance department, showing assets and liabilities, receipts and disbursements, and other financial data.

Anti-selection: The tendency of persons who present a poorer-than-average risk to apply for, or continue, insurance to a greater extent than do persons with average or better-than-average expectations of loss.

Apparent Authority: Agency authority a person has because a principal has created the appearance of authority to a third person.

Application: A signed statement of facts made by a person applying for life insurance and then used by the insurance company to decide whether or not to issue a policy. The application becomes part of the insurance contract when the policy is issued.

Assets: All funds, property, goods, securities, rights of action, or resources of any kind owned by an insurance company. Statutory accounting, however, excludes non-admitted assets, such as deferred or overdue premiums, that would be considered assets under generally accepted accounting principles (GAAP).

Assignment—The passing of beneficial rights from one party to another. A policy or certificate of insurance cannot be assigned after interest has passed unless an agreement to assign was made or implied prior to the passing of interest. An assignee acquires no greater rights than were held by the assignor and a breach of good faith by the assignor is deemed to be breach on the part of the assignee

Assumption certificate: an endorsement to an insurance contract stating that reinsurance proceeds will be paid directly to the named payee in the event of an insurer's insolvency.

Assumption of Risk Doctrine: Defense against a negligence claim that bars recovery for damages if a person understands and recognizes the danger inherent in a particular activity or occupation.

Attained Age: The age of the insured at the time of renewal (current age)

Automatic Premium Loan: Cash borrowed from a life insurance policy's cash value to pay an overdue premium after the grace period for paying the premium has expired.

Automatic Reinsurance: An agreement that the insurer must cede and the reinsurer must accept all risks within certain explicitly defined limits. The reinsurer undertakes in advance to grant reinsurance to the extent specified in the agreement in every case where the ceding company accepts the application and retains its own limit.

Bad faith: the allegation that insurers have failed to act in good faith, i.e., that they have acted in a manner inconsistent with what a reasonable policyholder would have expected

Basis: An amount attributed to an asset for income tax purposes; used to determine gain or loss on sale or transfer; used to determine the value of a gift.

Beneficiary—The person named in the policy to receive the insurance proceeds at the death of the insured. A secondary or contingent beneficiary will receive the proceeds if the primary beneficiary cannot collect.

Benefits: The amount payable by the insurance company to a claimant, assignee or beneficiary under each coverage.

Binder: A written or oral contract issued temporarily to place insurance in-force when it is not possible to issue a new policy or endorse the existing policy immediately. A binder is subject to the premium and all the terms of the policy to be issued.

Binding Receipt: A receipt given for a premium payment accompanying the application for insurance. If the policy is approved, this binds the company to make the policy effective from the date of the receipt.

Branch Office System: Type of life insurance marketing system under which branch offices are established in various areas. Salaried branch managers, who are employees of the company, are responsible for hiring and training new agents.

Breach of contract: The failure of a party to perform a promise according to its terms, without a legal excuse

Business Insurance: A policy which primarily provides coverage of benefits to a business as contrasted to an individual. It is issued to indemnify a business for the loss of services of a key employee or a partner who becomes disabled.

Business Life Insurance: Life insurance purchased by a business enterprise on the life of a member of the firm. It is often bought by partnerships to protect the surviving partners against loss caused by the death of a partner, or by a corporation to reimburse it for loss caused by the death of a key employee.

Buy-Sell Agreement: An agreement made by the owners of a business to purchase the share of a disabled or deceased owner. The value of each owner's share of the business and the exact terms of the buying-and-selling process are established before death or the beginning of disability.

Cancellation: The discontinuance of an insurance policy before its normal expiration date, either by the insured or the company.

Capacity: The amount of capital available to an insurance company or to the industry as a whole for underwriting general insurance coverage or coverage for specific perils.

Capital Retention Approach: A method used to estimate the amount of life insurance to own. Under this method, the insurance proceeds are retained and are not liquidated.

Capital Stock and Surplus: Represents the excess of a company's assets over its liabilities as reported in its financial statements. Stock companies have capital stock and surplus. Capital stock represents funds paid into the company by stockholders. Surplus represents the remaining excess of assets over liabilities. Mutual companies only have surplus since there are no stockholders in a mutual company.

Captive agent—Representative of a single insurer or fleet of insurers who is obliged to submit business only to that company, or at the very minimum, give that company first refusal rights on a sale. In exchange, that insurer usually provides its captive agents with an allowance for office expenses as well as an extensive range of employee benefits such as pensions, life insurance, health insurance and credit unions.

Cash Surrender Value—The amount payable if a life insurance policy is canceled by the insured before it either matures or is payable on death. Cede—To transfer risk from a direct insurer to his re-insurer.

Ceding insurer—One who cedes a risk to his re-insurers or retrocessionaires.

Cession: Amount of the insurance ceded to a re-insurer by the original insuring company in a reinsurance operation.

Chartered Life Underwriter (CLU): An individual who has attained a high degree of technical competency in the fields of life and health insurance and who is expected to abide by a code of ethics. Must have minimum of three years of experience in life or health insurance sales and have passed ten professional examinations administered by The American College.

Child Rider: Rider which provides insurance to the insured's child (ren)

Claim: A request for payment of a loss which may come under the terms of an insurance contract.

Claimant—The first or third party. That is any person who asserts right of recovery.

CLU: See Chartered Life Underwriter.

Collateral Assignment: A temporary transfer of some, but not all, policy rights to a lender to provide security for a loan.

Combined Ratio: Basically, a measure of the relationship between dollars spent for claims and expenses and premium dollars taken in; more specifically, the sum of the ratio of losses incurred to premiums earned and the ratio of commissions and expenses incurred to premiums written. A ratio above 100 means that for every premium dollar taken in, more than a dollar went for losses, expenses, and commissions.

Commission: The part of an insurance premium paid by the insurer to an agent or broker for his services in procuring and servicing the insurance.

Commissioner: A state officer who administers the state's insurance laws and regulations. In some states, this regulator is called the director or superintendent of insurance.

Concealment: Deliberate failure of an applicant for insurance to reveal a material fact to the insurer.

Conditional Receipt: A receipt given for premium payments accompanying an application for insurance. If the application is approved as applied for, the coverage is effective as of the date of the prepayment or the date on which the last of the underwriting requirements, such as a medical examination, has been fulfilled.

Conservation: The attempt by the insurer to prevent the lapse of a policy.

Consideration: One of the elements for a binding contract. Consideration is acceptance by the insurance company of the payment of the premium and the statement made by the prospective policyholder in the application.

Contest, policy: A court action challenging the validity of a policy.

Contingent Owner: The person to succeed as owner of a life insurance policy if the original owner dies.

Contract: A binding agreement between two or more parties for the doing or not doing of certain things. A contract of insurance is embodied in a written document called the policy.

Contract law: the portion of civil law that interprets written agreements between parties and resolves disputes between them.

Contribution Principle: The principle under which divisible surplus is distributed among policies in the same proportion as the policies are considered to have contributed to that surplus.

Conversion Privilege: A privilege granted in an insurance policy to convert to a different plan of insurance without providing evidence of insurability.

Convertible Term Insurance: Term insurance which can be exchanged, at the option of the policyholder and without evidence of insurability, for another plan of insurance. Credit life insurance. Term life insurance issued through a lender or lending agency to cover payment of a loan, installment purchase, or other obligation, in case of death.

Cost Basis: An amount attributed to an asset for income tax purposes; used to determine gain or loss on a life insurance contract to determine the value of a gift

Cost-of-Living Rider: Benefit that can be added to a life insurance policy under which the policy owner can purchase one-year term insurance equal to the percentage change in the consumer price index with no evidence of insurability.

Cost of pure risk: all costs related to pure risk which includes, from the perspective of shareholders, retained risk, loss prevention costs, insurance costs, and more.

Coverage: The scope of protection provided under a contract of insurance; any of several risks covered by a policy.

Cross liability clause: obligates an insurer to protect each insured separately.

Cross Purchase Agreement: specifies the terms for the surviving partners or shareholders to buy a deceased's share of the business's ownership.

CSR: Customer service representatives support the work of insurance agents with a variety of tasks that must be done within a company or agency to deliver services to and handle requests from clients.

Cumulative Premium—The total amount paid over the course of a specified amount of years.

Current Assumption Whole Life Insurance: Nonparticipating whole life policy in which the cash values are based on the insurer's current mortality, investment, and expense experience. An accumulation account is credited with a current interest rate that changes over time. Also called interest-sensitive whole life insurance.

Current with Reentry Premiums—Applicable to certain term life insurance policies—Non-Guaranteed premiums at the time of re-entry.

Death Benefit: A payment made to a designated beneficiary upon the death of the employee annuitant.

Declarations: Statements in an insurance contract that provide information about the property or life to be insured and used for underwriting and rating purposes and identification of the property or life to be insured.

Declination: The insurer's refusal to insure an individual after careful evaluation of the application for insurance and any other pertinent factors.

Deferred Compensation: Arrangements by which compensation to employees for past or current services is postponed until some future date.

Demutualization: the process of changing the legal structure of an insurance company from a mutual form of ownership to a stock form of ownership.

Deposit Premium: The premium deposit paid by a prospective policy holder when an application is made for an insurance policy. It is usually equal, at least, to the first month's estimate premium and is applied toward the actual premium when billed.

Deposit Term Insurance: A form of term insurance, not really involving a "deposit," in which the first-year premium is larger than subsequent premiums. Typically, a partial endowment is paid at the end of the term period. In many cases the partial endowment can be applied toward the purchase of a new term policy, or, perhaps, a whole life policy.

Direct Recognition: A procedure under a policy's dividends which directly reflects earnings on borrowed and non-borrowed values of that policy.

Direct Response System: A marketing method where insurance is sold without the services of an agent. Potential customers are solicited by advertising in the mail, newspapers, magazines, television, radio, and other media.

Direct writer—Method of selling insurance directly to insureds through a company's own employees, through the mail, the Internet, or at airport booths.

Disability: a physical or a mental impairment that substantially limits one or more major life activities of an individual. It may be partial or total. (See Partial Disability; Total Disability.)

Disability Benefit: A feature added to some life insurance policies providing for waiver of premium, and sometimes payment of monthly income, if the policy holder becomes totally and permanently disabled.

Disclosure—The duty of the insured and his broker to tell the underwriter every material fact before acceptance of the risk.

Dismemberment: Loss of body members (limbs), or use thereof, or loss of sight due to injury.

Dividend: A policy holder's share in the insurer's divisible surplus fund apportioned for distribution, which may take the form of a refund of part of the premium on a participating policy.

Dividend Addition: An amount of paid-up insurance purchased with a policy dividend and added to the face amount of the policy.

Divisible Surplus: Represents that portion of a company's earnings for the year that have been designated for distribution as dividends to policy owners.

Doctrine of reasonable expectations: a legal doctrine that holds policies will be interpreted according to how a reasonable person who is not trained in the law would expect

Domestic Insurer: An insurance company is a domestic company in the state in which it is incorporated.

Donor: The person making a gift.

Double Indemnity: A policy provision usually associated with death, which doubles payment of a designated benefit when certain kinds of accidents occur.

Earned Premium: That portion of a policy's premium payment for which the protection of the policy has already been given. For example, an insurance company is considered to have earned 75 percent of an annual premium after a period of nine months of an annual term has elapsed.

Economic Policy: Special type of participating whole life insurance in which the dividends are used to buy term insurance or paid-up additions equal to the difference between the face amount of the policy and some guaranteed amount.

Effective Date: The date on which the insurance under a policy begins.

Embedded Value: the sum of these two elements: (1) shareholders' equity considering the assets at market value and (2) in-force life insurance business valued at the present value of future after-tax statutory profits

Endorsement: An additional piece of paper, not a part of the original contract, which cites certain terms and which, when attached to the original contract, becomes a legal part of that contract.

Endowment: Life insurance payable to the policyholder if living, on the maturity date stated in the policy, or to a beneficiary if the insured dies prior to that date.

Entire Contract Clause: Provision in life insurance policies stating that the life insurance policy and attached application constitute the entire contract between the parties.

Entity Purchase Agreement: specifies the terms for the business to buy back a deceased's share of the business's ownership.

Equity in the Unearned Premium Reserve: Amount by which an unearned premium reserve is overstated because it is established on the basis of gross premium rather than net premium.

Estate: The assets and liabilities of a person left at death.

Estate Planning: Developing a plan to transfer all of your property from one generation to the next or within a generation.

Evidence of Insurability: Any statement of proof of a person's physical condition and/or other factual information affecting his/her acceptance for insurance.

Exclusive Agent: An agent who is employed by one and only one insurance company and who solicits business exclusively for that company.

Expense Loading: See Loading.

Expense Ratio: The ratio of a company's operating expenses to premiums.

Exposure Unit: Unit of measurement used in insurance pricing.

Extended Term Insurance: A form of insurance available as a non-forfeiture option. It provides the original amount of insurance for a limited period of time.

Face Amount—The amount stated on the policy that will be paid at death or maturity. It does not include additional amounts payable under accidental death or other special provisions, or acquired through the use of policy dividends.

Fair premium: the premium level that is just sufficient to fund an insurer's expected costs and provide insurance company owners with a fair return on their invested capital.

Family Income Policy: Special life insurance policy combining decreasing term and whole life insurance that pays a monthly income of $10 for each $1000 of life insurance if the insured dies within the specified period. The monthly income is paid to the end of the period, at which time the face amount of insurance is paid.

Family Policy: A life insurance policy providing insurance on all or several family members in one contract, generally whole life insurance on the principal breadwinner and small amounts of term insurance on the other spouse and children, including those born after the policy is issued.

Fiduciary: A person who holds something in trust for another.

Fixed Amount Option: Life insurance settlement option in which the policy proceeds are paid out in fixed amounts.

Fixed Expenses: Fixed expenses are those not directly related to a policy (a premium tax, for example is a direct expense, as is the payment of a commission associated with the sale of a policy). Includes: advertising, accounting, planning, rent, computer facilities, etc. These expenses must be allocated to each "block" of policies sold and the distribution is discretionary and can be critical. Some insurers assume too many (or too few) policies will be sold, thereby reducing (or increasing) the fixed expense factor assumed in the pricing of the policy. This may lead to lower credits or increased policy charges.

Fixed Period Option: Life insurance settlement option in which the policy proceeds are paid out in fixed amounts.

Flexible Premium Policy or Annuity: A life accident policy or annuity under which the policyholder or contract holder may vary the amounts or timing of premium payments.

Flexible Premium Variable Life Insurance: A life insurance policy that combines the premium flexibility feature of universal life insurance with the equity-based benefit feature of variable life insurance.

Foreign Insurer: An insurer is a foreign company in any state other than the one in which it is incorporated.

Fortuitous Loss: Unforeseen and unexpected loss that occurs as a result of chance.

Franchise Insurance: Insurance under individual contracts issued to the employees of a common employer or the members of an association under an arrangement by which the employer or association agrees to collect the premiums and remit them to the insurer. The insurer usually agrees to waive its right to discontinue or modify any individual policy, unless it's simultaneously discontinues or modifies all other policies in the same group.

Fraternal Life Insurance: Life insurance provided by fraternal orders or societies to their members.

Fraternal Society: A social organization that provides insurance for its members.

Free-Look Period—Time during which the policyholder may return the policy if he/she is not completely satisfied and receive a complete refund. The customary length of time for a "free look" is 30 days

Fronting Company: A domestic insurance company that provides claims or administrative services to a captive

Future Increase Option: A provision found in some policies that allows the insured to purchase additional disability income insurance at specified future dates regardless of the insured's physical condition.

General Agency System: Type of life insurance marketing system in which the general agent is an independent businessperson who represents only one insurer, is in charge of a territory, and is responsible for hiring, training, and motivating new agents.

Generation skipping tax: a transfer tax imposed on gift or inheritance to those at least two generations younger than the person making the transfer

Gift: A voluntary transfer of property to another person, made without receiving consideration in return.

Grace Period—A period of time after a premium due date, usually 30 or 31 days, during which an insurance policy remains in-force and the overdue premium may be paid without penalty.

Gross premium—The full amount of premium, ignoring taxes or deductions.

Graded Commission Scale: A commission scale providing for payment of a high first-year commission and lower renewal commissions.

Gross estate: All of the assets and liabilities owned at death.

Guaranteed insurability—An option that permits the policyholder to buy additional stated amounts of life insurance at stated times in the future without evidence of insurability.

Gross Rate: The sum of the pure premium and a loading element.

Group Contract: A contract of insurance made with an employer or other entity that covers a group of persons identified as individuals by reference to their relationship to the entity.

Group Creditor Life Insurance: Life insurance provided to debtors by a lending institution to provide for the cancellation of any outstanding debt should the borrower die. Normally term insurance limited to the amount of the loan.

Group Life Insurance: Life insurance usually without medical examination, on a group of people under a master policy. It is typically issued to an employer for the benefit of employees or to members of an association, for example a professional membership group. The individual members of the group hold certificates as evidence of their insurance.

Group Ordinary Life Insurance: Group insurance plan providing life insurance for employees. Traditional whole life policy is split into decreasing insurance protection and increasing cash values.

Group Paid-Up Life Insurance: Accumulating units of single premium whole life insurance and decreasing term insurance, which together equal the face amount of the policy. Provided through a group life insurance plan.

Group Permanent Plan: Type of pension plan in which cash value life insurance is issued on a group basis and cash values in each policy are used to pay retirement benefits when a worker retires.

Group Term Life Insurance: Most common form of group life insurance. Yearly renewable term insurance on employees during their working careers.

Group Universal Life Products (GULP): Universal life insurance plans sold to members of a group, such as individual employees of an employer. There are some differences between GULP plans and individual universal life plans; for instance, GULP expense charges generally are lower than those assessed against individual policies.

Guaranteed Insurability Option: (see "Future Increase Option")

Guaranteed Investment Contract GIC): An investment contract with an insurer in which the insurer guarantees both principal and interest on a pension contribution.

Guaranteed Premiums: The guaranteed maximum payment for the purchased policy.

Guaranteed Purchase Option: Benefit that can be added to a life insurance policy permitting the insured to purchase additional amounts of life insurance at specified times in the future without requiring evidence of insurability.

Guaranteed Renewable: A contract that the insured has the right to continue in-force by the timely payment of premiums (1) until at least age 50 or (2) in the case of a policy issued after age 44 for at least five years from its date of issue, during which period the insurer has no right to make unilaterally any change in any provision of the contract while the contract is in-force, except that the insurer may make changes in premium rate by classes.

Guaranteed Renewable Contract: A contract that the insured person or entity has the right to continue in-force by the timely payment of premiums for a substantial period of time, during which period the insurer has no right to make unilaterally any change in any provision of the contract, while the contract is in-force, other than a change in the premium rate for classes of policyholders.

Guaranteed Renewable Contract: A health policy which the company guarantees to renew for life or until the insured reaches a specified age, usually 65.

Guaranty Fund: A fund, derived from assessments against solvent insurance companies, to absorb losses of claimants against insolvent insurance companies.

Home Service Life Insurance: Industrial life insurance and monthly debit ordinary life insurance contracts that are serviced by agents who call on the policy owners at their homes to collect the premiums. The amount of life insurance per policy generally is larger than $1000.

Human Life Value: For purposes of life insurance, the present value of the family's share of the deceased breadwinner's future earnings.

Incontestability: Life policies provide that, except for non-payment of premiums and certain other circumstances, the policy shall be incontestable after the policy has been in-force for two years during the lifetime of the insured.

Incontestable clause—A policy provision in which the company agrees not to contest the validity of the contract after it has been in-force for a certain period of time, usually two years.

Incurred Claims: Incurred claims equal the claims paid during the policy year plus the claim reserves as of the end of the policy year, minus the corresponding reserves as of the beginning of the policy year. The difference between the year end and beginning of the year claim reserves is called the increase in reserves and may be added directly to the paid claims to produce the incurred claims.

Incurred-but-not-reported (IBNR) reserves: liability account on an insurer's balance sheet reflecting claims that are expected based upon statistical projections but which have not yet been reported to the insurer

Indemnification: Compensation to the victim of a loss, in whole or in part, by payment, repair, or replacement.

Indemnity—Indemnity is the legal principle that ensures that a policyholder is restored to the same financial position after the loss as he was in immediately prior to the loss.

Independent Agent: an independent business person who usually represents two or more insurance companies in a sales and service capacity and who is paid on a commission basis.

Independent Agency System: Type of property and liability insurance marketing system, sometimes called the American agency system, in which the agent is an independent businessperson representing several companies. The agency owns the expirations or renewal rights to the business, and the agent is compensated by commissions that vary by line of insurance.

Indeterminate Premium Whole Life Insurance: Nonparticipating whole life policy that permits the insurer to adjust premiums based on anticipated future experience. Initial premiums are guaranteed for a certain period. After the initial guaranteed period expires, the insurer can increase premiums up to some maximum limit.

Indexing: Adjusting of values over time to reflect the impact of inflation.

Individual Contract: A contract of health insurance made with an individual called the policy holder or the insured, which normally covers such individual and, in certain instances, members of his family.

Individual Insurance: Policies which provide protection to the policyholder and/or his/her family. Sometimes called Personal Insurance as distinct from group and blanket insurance.

Industrial Life Insurance: Life insurance issued in small amounts, usually less than $1,000, with premiums payable on a weekly or monthly basis. The premiums are generally collected at the home by an agent of the company. Sometimes referred to as debit insurance.

Inheritance tax: A tax on the right of an heir to receive property at the death of another.

Initial Reserve: In life insurance, the reserve at the beginning of any policy year.

Insolvent: Having insufficient financial resources (assets) to meet financial obligations (liabilities).

Inspection Report: A report (usually written) of an investigation of an applicant, conducted by an independent agency that specializes in insurance investigations. The report covers such matters as occupation, financial status, health history, and moral problems.

Insurability: Acceptability to the company of an applicant for insurance.

Insurable interest—The insured's financial interest in the subject matter of the insurance. A policy where the insured is without such interest is unenforceable.

Insurable Risk: The conditions that make a risk insurable are (a) the peril insured against must produce a definite loss not under the control of the insured, (b) there must be a large number of homogeneous exposures subject to the same perils, (c) the loss must be calculable and the cost of insuring it must be economically feasible, (d) the peril must be unlikely to affect all insureds simultaneously, and (e) the loss produced by a risk must be definite and have a potential to be financially serious.

Insurance—(1) A means whereby the losses of the few are distributed over the many. (2) A system under which individuals, businesses, and other organizations or entities, in exchange for payment of a sum of money (a premium), are guaranteed compensation for losses resulting from certain perils under specified conditions.

Insurance Age: Age based on the individuals nearest birthday. If the individual is more than 6 months or 182 days into their birthday year, the birthday would be treated as if it had already occurred that year (also referred to as Age Nearest).

Insurance Company: Any corporation primarily engaged in the business of furnishing insurance protection to the public.

Insurance Commissioner: The top insurance regulatory official in a state.

Insurance Examiner: The representative of a state insurance department assigned to participate in the official audit and examination of the affairs of an insurance company.

Insurance Guaranty Funds: State Funds that provide for the payment of unpaid claims of insolvent insurers.

Insured: A person or organization covered by an insurance policy, including the "named insured" and any other parties for whom protection is provided under the policy terms.

Insurer: The party to the insurance contract who promises to pay losses or benefits. Also, any corporation engaged primarily in the business of furnishing insurance to the public.

Insuring Agreement: That part of an insurance contract that states the promises of the insurer.

Insuring Clause: The clause which sets forth the type of loss being covered by the policy and the parties to the insurance contract.

Inter Vivos Trust: A trust created while the creator of the trust is living. Also known as a living trust.

Interest: Money paid for the use of money.

Interest-Adjusted Method: Method of determining cost to an insured of a life insurance policy that considers the time cost of money by applying an interest factor to each element of cost. See Also Net payment cost index; surrender cost index.

Interest Crediting—New Money Method: A method under which for purposes of crediting interest under the company's dividend scale or other non-guaranteed pricing structure, the company's policies are subdivided into generations based on year(s) of issue. The crediting rate is determined separately for each generation. Each crediting rate is based on the investment earnings of the funds underlying the particular group of policies and the reinvestment frequency.

Interest Crediting—Portfolio Method: The method under which, for purposes of crediting interest under the company's dividend scale or other non-guaranteed pricing structure, the same rate applies to all policies. The crediting rate is based on the investment earnings of all of the investments underlying the entire block of policies. The portfolio method may apply to all policy types issued by a company, or there may separate portfolios for different policy types or years of issue.

Interest Maintenance Reserve (IMR)—A statutory accounting method adopted by the National Association of Insurance Commissioners, that is designed to capture all realized fixed income investment capital gains and losses resulting from the changes in the overall level of interest rates and amortize them over the remaining original investment period.

Interest Option: Life insurance settlement option in which the principal is retained by the insurer and interest is paid periodically.

Intestate: Without a will.

Investment Income: The income generated by a company's portfolio of investments (such as in bonds, stocks, or other financial ventures).

Irrevocable Beneficiary: Beneficiary designation allowing no change to be made in the beneficiary of an insurance policy without the beneficiary's consent.

Irrevocable Trust: A trust in which the creator does not reserve the right to reacquire the trust property.

Issue Age: The age of the insured at the time the policy is being issued.

Joint Tenants: A form of joint property ownership with right of survivorship, i.e., in which the survivors automatically own the share of a deceased co-owner.

Jumbo Risk: A risk involving exceptionally high benefits.

Jumping Juvenile Insurance Policy: Life insurance purchased by parents for children under a specified age. Provides permanent life insurance that increases in face value five times at age twenty-one with no increase in premium.

Key-Person Insurance: Insurance designed to protect a business firm against the loss of income resulting from the death or disability of a key employee.

Lapse: The termination or discontinuance of an insurance policy due to non-payment of a premium.

Lapsed Policy: A policy terminated for non-payment of premiums. The term is sometimes limited to a termination occurring before the policy has a cash or other surrender value.

Lapse Supported Pricing: A pricing structure that uses gains from terminated policies to support subsequent values of policies remaining in-force. If policy lapses are lower than assumed, the pricing will prove to be inadequate for the persisting policies in that block.

Law of Large Numbers: Concept that the greater the number of exposures, the more closely will actual results approach the probable results expected from an infinite number of exposures.

Legal Reserve: The minimum reserve which a company must keep to meet future claims and obligations as they are calculated under the state insurance code.

Legal Reserve Life Insurance Company: A life insurance company operating under state insurance laws specifying the minimum basis for the reserves the company must maintain on its policies.

Level Commission Scale: A commission scale providing for payment of commissions at the same rate every year the policy is in-force.

Level Premium: A premium which remains unchanged throughout the life of a policy.

Level Premium Life Insurance: Life insurance for which the premium remains the same from year to year. The premium is more than the actual cost of protection during the earlier years of the policy and less than the actual cost in the later years. The building of a reserve is a natural result of level premiums. The overpayments in the early years, together with the interest that is earned, serve to balance out the underpayments of the later years.

Liability: Any legally enforceable obligation. Also, funds required for payment of future claims and expenses, including Asset Valuation Reserve

Life Expectancy: The average number of years of life remaining for a group of persons of a given age according to a particular mortality table.

Life Income Option: Life insurance settlement option in which the policy proceeds are paid during the lifetime of the beneficiary. A certain number of guaranteed payments may also be payable.

Life Insurance: Insurance providing for payment of a specified amount on the insured's death, either to his or her estate or to a designated beneficiary; or in the case of an endowment policy, to the policy holder at a specified date.

Life Insurance in-force: The sum of the face amounts, plus dividend additions, of life insurance polices outstanding at a given time. Additional amounts payable under accidental death or other special provisions are not included.

Life Insurance Programming: Systematic method of determining the insured's financial goals, which are translated into specific amounts of life insurance, then periodically reviewed for possible changes.

Limited Payment Life Insurance: Whole life insurance on which premiums are payable for a specified number of years or until death if death occurs before the end of the specified period.

Liquidation: Dissolving a company by selling its assets for cash.

Living Benefits Rider: A rider that allows insureds who are terminally ill or who suffer from certain catastrophic diseases to collect part of their life insurance benefits before they die, primarily to pay for the care they require.

Living Trust: A trust created while the creator of the trust is living. Also known as an inter vivos trust.

Lloyd's of London: insurance marketplace where brokers, representing clients with insurable risks, deal with Lloyd's underwriters, who in turn represent investors. The investors are grouped together into syndicates that provide capital to insure the risks.

Loading: The amount that must be added to the pure premium for expenses, profit, and a margin for contingencies. See Expense Loading

Loan value—The amount which can be borrowed at a specified rate of interest from the issuing company by the policyholder, using the value of the policy as collateral. In the event the policyholder dies with the debt partially or fully unpaid, then the amount borrowed plus any interest is deducted from the amount payable.

Loss—A claim under a policy. The financial loss caused to the insured by the happening of the event insured against.

Loss Prevention: Any measure which reduces the probability or frequency of a particular loss but does not eliminate completely all possibility of that loss

Loss Ratio: A ratio calculated by dividing claims into premiums. It may be calculated in several different ways, using paid premiums or earned premiums, and using paid claims with or without changes in claim reserves and with or without changes in active reserves.

Loss Reserve: The amount set up as the estimated cost of a claim. (See IBNR Reserve)

Loss Reserve Development: how the latest estimate of an insurance company's claim obligations compares to an earlier projection.

Lump-Sum Distribution: Payment within one taxable year of the entire balance payable to an employee from a trust which forms part of a qualified pension or employee annuity plan on account of that person's death, separation from service or attainment of age 59.

Mail Order Insurer: Type of insurance company that sells policies through the mail or other mass media, eliminating need for agents.

Master Policy (or Master Contract): The policy issued to a group policyholder setting forth the provisions of the group insurance plan. The individuals insure under the policy are then issued certificates of insurance.

Material facts: Any fact or circumstance which would affect the judgment of a prudent underwriter in considering whether he would accept the risk or not, and at which rate of premium.

Material representation: A statement made to the underwriter before acceptance of risk, which is material to his decision in accepting and rating the risk.

Maximum Premium: The maximum periodic payment a company will require regardless of age and face amount to keep a policy in-force.

McCarran-Ferguson Act: Federal law passed in 1945 stating that continued regulation of the insurance industry by the states is in the public interest and that federal antitrust laws apply to insurance only to the extent that the industry is not regulated by state law.

Medical Examination: The examination given by a qualified physician to determine to the insurability of an applicant. A medical examination may also be used to determine whether an insured claiming disability is actually disabled.

Minimum Group: The least number of employees permitted under a state law to affect a group for insurance purposes; the purpose is to maintain some sort of proper division between individual policy insurance and the group forms.

Minimum Premium: The minimum periodic payment a company will allow regardless of face amount to keep a policy in-force.

Misquote: An incorrect estimate of the insurance premium.

Misrepresentation: A misstatement of fact made by the insured or his broker to the underwriter before acceptance of the risk that misleads the underwriter in assessing the risk and induces the contract. If the representation is material and amounts to misrepresentation, it is a breach of utmost good faith.

Mode of Premium Payment: The frequency with which premiums are paid monthly, quarterly, semiannually, or annually.

Moral Hazard: Hazard arising from any nonphysical, personal characteristic of a risk that increases the possibility of loss or may intensify the severity of loss for instance, bad habits, low integrity, poor financial standing.

Mortality Table: A statistical table showing the death rate at each age usually expressed as so many per thousand.

Mutual Life Insurance Company—is organized and incorporated under a state's laws and has no stockholders. The policy owner is the customer and, in effect, an owner. A portion of surplus earnings may return to policyholders in the form of dividends. This is in contrast to a stock company, where the policy owner is a customer only.

MVR: motor vehicle report

National Association of Insurance Commissioners (NAIC): The association of insurance commissioners of various states formed to promote national uniformity in the regulation of insurance.

NAIC Certified: Products that have been certified by the NAIC.

NAIC Compliant State: A state that has passed the NAIC model illustration regulations.

Negligence: Failure to use the care that a reasonable and prudent person would have used under the same or similar circumstances.

Net Premium: The portion of the premium rate which is designed to cover benefits of the policy, but not expenses, contingencies, or profit. The term is also used to describe the portion of the premium remitted to the home office by an agent after deduction of the agent's commission.

Net Present Value (NPV): Means of evaluating which products offer the lowest cost, taking into account the time value of money for the life of the policy.

Net written premiums: premium income retained by insurance companies, directly or through reinsurance, after payments made for reinsurance.

Non-admitted Assets—Assets which are not recognized by regulatory authorities in assessing solvency and include items such as furniture, certain equipment and agent's balances. These assets are listed in exhibit 13 of the annual statement that insurers provide to insurance regulators.

Non-admitted Insurance Company: An insurance company not licensed to do business in a particular state; such a company, however, may sell excess and surplus insurance in that state if admitted insurers lack the capacity or expertise.

Non-cancelable Guaranteed Renewable Policy: An individual policy which the insured person has the right to continue to force until a specified age, such as to age 65, by the timely payment of premiums. During this period, the insurer has no right to unilaterally make any changes in any provision of the policy while it is in-force.

Non-disclosure—Failure by the insured or his broker to disclose a material fact or circumstance to the underwriter before acceptance of the risk.

Non-forfeiture Option: One of the choices available if the policyholder discontinues premium payments on a policy with a cash value. This, if any, may be taken in cash, as extended term insurance or as reduced paid-up insurance.

Non-medical Limit: The maximum face value of a policy that a given company will issue without the applicant taking a medical examination.

Non-occupational Policy: Contract which insures a person against off-the-job accident or sickness. It does not cover disability resulting from injury or sickness covered by Workers' Compensation. Group accident and sickness policies are frequently non-occupational.

Non-occupational Policy: One that provides off-the-job coverage only; it does not cover loss resulting from accidents or sickness arising out of or in the course of employment or covered under any workers' compensation law.

Non-participating Policy: A life insurance policy in which the company does not distribute to policyholders any part of its surplus. Note should be taken that premiums for nonparticipating polices are usually lower than for comparable participating polices. Note should also be taken that some nonparticipating polices have both a maximum premium and a current lower premium. The current premium reflects anticipated experience that is more favorable than the company is willing to guarantee, and it may be changed from time to time for the entire block of business to which the policy belongs. (See also: Participating policy)

Non-Tobacco Status: No cigarette or tobacco usage based upon company guidelines.

Occupational Hazards: Occupations which expose the insured to greater than normal physical danger by the very nature of the work in which the insured is engaged, and the varying periods of absence from the occupation, due to the disability, that can be expected.

Operating Ratio: The sum of expenses and losses expressed as a percent of earned premium.

Ordinary Life: Synonymous with Whole Life and Straight Life: The three terms are applied to the type of policy which continues during the whole of the insured's life and provides for the payment of amount insured at this death.

Other Insured Rider: Rider which provides coverage to an eligible business or family member other than the insured.

Override commission: Commission payable in addition to the original commission.

Paid-up Insurance: Insurance on which all required premiums have been paid. The term is frequently used to mean the reduced paid-up insurance available as a nonforfeiture option.

Paramedical Examination: Physical examination of an applicant by a trained person other than a physician.

Participating Policy: A life insurance policy under which the company agrees to distribute to policyholders the part of its surplus which its Board of Directors determines is not needed at the end of the business year. Such a distribution serves to reduce the premium the policy-holder had paid. (See also: Policy dividend; Nonparticipating policy)

Pegging: Pegging is a practical smoothing device used to arbitrarily increase the actual dividend(s) paid on a new lower dividend scale to eliminate a temporary reduction in the actual dividends paid from year to year on a policy. Usually only base policy dividends are pegged; dividends on riders and Paid Up Additions (PUA) are not. (See Substitution). Pegging compares (normally before any adjust-ments for loans) the following:(a)The smaller of the dividend amount actually paid in the prior policy year and the prior year's dividend schedule payable in the current policy year, and (b) The current policy year's formula payment under the current year's schedule. This distri-bution does not follow the contribution method. It's done infrequently to enhance persistency.

Per Capita: this means that if a beneficiary dies before the insured, the remaining beneficiaries will equally divide that share of the proceeds in addition to receiving their own shares when the insured dies. (1) By head or by individual; (2) to share equally

Peril: The cause of a loss insured against in a policy.

Permanent Life Insurance—Type of life insurance (other than term insurance) which accrues cash value and is designed for long-term, or permanent, needs of a policyholder. Includes universal and variable life, among others.

Persistency: The degree to which policies stay in-force through the continued payment of renewal premiums.

Persistency Bonus (Policy owner's): An enhancement to the policy's benefits, usually in the form of additional interest credits and/or reduced charges, for policies that remain in-force for a certain period. The bonus may or may not be guaranteed in the contract.

Personal representative: A person appointed through the will of a deceased or by a court to settle the estate of one who dies.

Per Stirpes: this means that if a beneficiary dies before the insured, that beneficiary's share of the proceed will pass upon that beneficiary's heirs rather going to the remaining beneficiaries when the insured dies. It means by family branches. A method of dividing benefits among living members of a class of beneficiaries and the descendants of deceased members.

Physical hazard: The risk associated with the subject matter of insurance.

Policy: The legal document issued by the company to the policyholder, which outlines the conditions and terms of the insurance; also called the policy contract or the contract.

Policy Dividend: A refund of part of the premium on a participating life insurance policy reflecting the difference between the premium charged and actual experience.

Policy Fee: Fee added to the periodic premium payments to cover undefined policy costs.

Policy Loan: A loan made by a life insurance company from its general funds to a policyholder on the security of the cash value of a policy.

Policy Owner: The person or business that owns the policy and is responsible for premium payments.

Policy Reserves: The measure of the funds that a life insurance company holds specifically for fulfillment of its policy obligations. Reserves are required by law to be so calculated that, together with future premium payments and anticipated interest earnings, they will enable the company to pay all future claims.

Policy Term: That period for which an insurance policy provides coverage.

Policyholder: The person who owns a life insurance policy. This is usually the insured person, but it may also be a relative of the insured, a partnership or a corporation.

Policyholders' Surplus: Sum left after liabilities are deducted from assets. Sums such as paid-in capital and special voluntary reserves are also included in this term. This surplus is an additional financial protection to policyholders in the event a company suffers unexpected or catastrophic losses. In effect, it is the financial base that permits a company to sell insurance.

Pool: An organization of insurers or re-insurers through which particular types of risk are underwritten and premiums, losses and expenses are shared in agreed-upon amounts.

Pooling arrangement: An agreement to divide any losses that might occur equally among two or more people, typically with each paying the average loss.

Premium: The amount paid to an insurer or re-insurer in consideration of his acceptance of a risk.

Premium Discount: Periodic Payment discount given by a company.

Premium financing: A policyholder contracts with a lender to pay the insurance premium on his/her behalf. The policyholder agrees to repay the lender for the cost of the premium, plus interest and fees.

Premium Loan: A policy loan made for the purpose of paying premiums.

Premium Tax: A tax, imposed by each state, on the premium income of insurers doing business in the state.

Pricing Elements: The elements used in pricing a policy, principally investment earnings, mortality and expenses. If actual experience is better than the assumptions made in determining the policy guarantees, the difference after reflecting surplus needs is available for distribution to policyholders through the company's dividend scale or other non-guaranteed pricing structure.

Primary Beneficiary: See Beneficiary.

Principal: One for whom an agent acts, especially as to contractual dealings with third persons.

Principal Sum: The amount payable in one sum in the event of accidental death and in, some cases, accidental dismemberment. When a contract provides benefits for both accidental death and accidental dismemberment, each dismemberment benefit is an amount equal to the principal sum or some fraction thereof.

Privacy: (1) The right to be let alone; (2) in insurance contexts, the right to fair personal information practices.

Probate: The court-supervised process of validating or establishing a distribution for assets of a deceased including the payment of outstanding obligations.

Probate estate: That portion of the assets and liabilities whose distribution is supervised by the courts in the probate process.

Projected Rates: Policy payment that is currently being charged by the company after the guarantee period.

Proof of Loss: Documentation presented to the insurance company by the insured in support of a claim so that the insurer can determine its liability under the policy.

Pro rata cancellation: When the policy is terminated midterm by the insurance company, the earned premium is calculated only for the period coverage was provided. For example: an annual policy with premium of $1,000 is cancelled after 40 days of coverage at the company's election. The earned premium would be calculated as follows: 40/365 days X $1,000=$110 X $1,000=$110.

Profit Commission: A commission payable on the profit generated under an insurance or reinsurance contract as an encouragement to maintain the flow of profitable business.

Proportional reinsurance: A type of reinsurance where the ceding insurer cedes to its reinsurer a predetermined proportion of the liability and premium of those policies subject to the reinsurance agreement.

Prospectus: A guide to the various sub-accounts and other required information by the National Association of Security Dealers (NASD) and Security & Exchange Commission (SEC). This is required with any variable insurance product.

Prototype Plan: A standardized plan, approved and qualified as to its concept by the Internal Revenue Service, which is made available by life insurance companies, banks and mutual funds for employers' use.

Risk Classification: The process by which a company decides how its premium rates for life insurance should differ according to the risk characteristics of individuals insured (e.g., age, occupation, sex, state of health) and then applies the resulting rules to individual applications. (See: Underwriting)

Risk control: any conscious action (or decision not to act) intended to reduce the frequency, severity, or unpredictability of accidental losses.

Risk pooling arrangement: see Pooling arrangement.

Risk Retention Group: An alternative form of insurance in which members of a similar profession or business band together to self insure their risks.

Select Mortality: Descriptive of the mortality experience of newly underwritten insured's. This period of discernibly different (favorable) mortality usually lasts 5 to 15 years.

Separate Account: An asset account established by a life insurance company separate from other funds, used primarily for pension plans and variable life products. This arrangement permits wider latitude in the choice of investments, particularly in equities.

Settlement Options—The ways in which policyholders or beneficiaries may choose to have benefits paid other than a lump sum.

Skip person: a beneficiary who is at least two generations younger than the person making the transfer.

Smoker Status: Cigarette or tobacco use based upon company guidelines.

Special Risk Insurance: Coverage for risks or hazards of a special or unusual nature.

Spousal Rider: Rider which provides coverage to the insured's spouse.

Standard Insurance: Insurance written on the basis of regular morbidity underwriting assumption used by an insurance company and issued at normal rates.

Standard Markets: insurance companies for which the vast majority of people qualify

Standard Provision: Those contract provisions generally required by state statutes until superseded by the uniform policy provision.

Standard Risk: A person, who, according to a company's underwriting standards, is entitled to purchase insurance protection without extra rating or special restrictions.

State Insurance Department: A department of a state government whose duty is to regulate the business of insurance and give the public information on insurance.

Statutory Accounting Principles (SAP): Principles required by statute which must be followed by an insurance company when submitting its financial statements to the various state insurance departments. They are designed to provide greater protection for the public against potential insolvency of these essential institutions. Such principles differ from the Generally Accepted Accounting Principles (GAAP).

Statutory Reserve: Reserves calculated on the basis of state requirements.

Statutory Surplus: the amount left after a company's liabilities are subtracted from assets when both those values are computed using Statutory Accounting Principles (SAP)

Statutory Underwriting Profit or Loss: Premiums earned less losses and expenses.

Step-Rate Premium: A rating structure in which the premiums increase periodically at pre-determined times such as policy years or attained ages.

Stock Life Insurance Company: A life insurance company owned by stockholders who elect a board to direct the company's management. Stock companies, in general, issue nonparticipating insurance, but may also issue participating insurance.

Stock Redemption Plan: an entity purchase form of buy-sell agreement within a corporation that involves the corporation buying back shares from a departing owner.

Straight Life Insurance: Whole life insurance on which premiums are payable for life.

Subagent: The agent of an agent.

Substandard Risk: An individual, who, because of health history or physical limitations, does not measure up to the qualification of a standard risk.

Substantial Compliance Rule: The rule that, where a policyholder has done everything possible to comply with the beneficiary change procedure set forth in the policy, but has failed because of circumstances beyond his or her control, the change will be effective.

Substitution: Substitution replaces the dividend formula that would have been used in the current policy year (normally before any adjustments for loans), with a prior formula if greater. Usually substitution is only used for very small base policy dividends in the first few years of a policy. (See Pegging).

Supplementary Contract: An agreement between a life insurance company and a policyholder or beneficiary by which the company retains the cash sum payable under an insurance policy and makes payments in accordance with the settlement option chosen.

Surplus: The amount by which the value of an insurer's assets exceeds its liabilities, i.e., the net worth of an insurance company.

Surrender—To terminate or cancel a life insurance policy before the maturity date. In the case of a cash value policy, the policyholder may exercise one of the non-forfeiture options at the time of surrender.

Surrender charge: an amount retained by the issuer of a life insurance policy when a policy is canceled, typically assessed only during the first five to ten years of a policy.

Tax Basis: The cost from which your profits or losses are calculated for income tax purposes.

Taxable estate: The value upon which estate taxes are calculated by the federal government.

Tenants in common: A form of joint property ownership in which the owners may have unequal shares and which does not involve a right of survivorship.

Term Insurance: Life insurance protection during a limited number of years but expiring without value if the insured survives the stated period.

Termination Dividend: An additional dividend payable when a policy terminates (either by maturity, death or surrender), reflecting a return to terminating policyholders of part of the company surplus held for this policy.

Tobacco Status: Status given to an individual who, in the past or present, has used any type of tobacco or nicotine product other than cigarettes.

Tort: A civil wrong, other than a breach of contract, for which a court of law will afford legal relief

Treaty: An agreement between a reinsurer and a ceding insurer setting forth details of the reinsurance arrangement.

Trust: A legal instrument allowing one party to control property for the benefit of another.

Twisting: The practice of inducing by misrepresentation, or inaccurate or incomplete comparison, a policyholder in one company to lapse, forfeit or surrender his insurance for the purpose of taking out a policy in another company.

Ultimate Mortality—Descriptive of the insured's mortality experience after the select period (5-15 years from issue), when mortality increases due to health deterioration.

Underwriter—Underwriters are the professionals upon whose experience and judgment the market depends for its expertise and reputation. It is the underwriter's responsibility to assess the merits of each risk and decide a suitable price, or premium, for accepting all or part of the risk.

Underwriting—The process of selecting applicants for insurance and classifying them according to their degrees of insurability so that the appropriate premium rates may be charged. The process includes rejection of unacceptable risks.

Underwriting Classes: Classification given to an individual based on personal and family health history.

Underwriting Profit or Loss: The amount of money which an insurance company gains or loses as a result of its insurance operations. It excludes investment transactions and federal income taxes.

Unearned Premium: The portion of a premium that a company has collected but has yet to earn because the policy still has unexpired time to run.

Unified Credit: a one-time credit of $192,800, usually applied against Federal Estate Taxes that is available to every individual's estate. The credit also can be used for payment of Federal Gift Taxes during that individual's lifetime.

Uniform Premium: A rating structure in which one premium applies to all insureds, regardless of age, sex, or occupation.

Unilateral Contract: A contract having promises by one party only.

Uninsurable Risk: One not acceptable for insurance due to excessive risk.

Unisex Rates: Rates that are used for both male and females

Universal Life Insurance: A flexible premium life insurance policy under which the policyholder may change the death benefit from time to time (with satisfactory evidence of insurability for increases) and vary the amount or timing of premium payments. Premiums (less expense charges) are credited to a policy account from which mortality charges are deducted and to which interest is credited at rate which may change from time to time.

Variable Life Insurance: A permanent whole life insurance policy under which the death benefits and/or cash values vary (the death benefit is guaranteed to be at least as large as the initial face amount) reflecting the investment experience of a separate pool(s) of assets supporting the reserves for such policies.

Variable Universal Life Insurance: Similar to universal life in that the policy owner chooses the premium to be paid each period, and has the option to increase or decrease the policy death benefit. However, the assets supporting the policy are maintained in one or more separate accounts and the policy owner's values fluctuate (no guarantees).

Vested Commissions: Renewal commissions payable to the writing agent or his estate, whether or not he remains with the company.

Viatical Settlement: Payment of a portion of the proceeds from life insurance to an insured who is terminally ill.

Void policy—One which legally does not exist.

Voidable policy—Where the underwriter or insured has the right to avoid a policy (for example in the event of a breach of utmost good faith) the policy is termed 'voidable'.

Voluntary Market: The market where one seeking insurance obtains insurance in the open market with no help from the state, through an insurer of his or her own selection.

Waiting period—A period of time set forth in a policy that must pass before some or all coverages begin (see "also Elimination Period").

Waiver of Premium: A provision in some policies to relieve the insured of premium payments falling due during a period of continuous total disability that has lasted for a specified length of time, such as three or six months.

Warranty: A statement guaranteed to be true in all respects. If the statement is untrue in any respect, even if it is not material, the contract of which it is a part can be rescinded.

Whole Life Insurance: Life insurance payable to a beneficiary at the death of the insured whenever that occurs. Premiums may be payable for a specified number of years (limited payment life) or for life (straight life).

Will: The legal statement of a person's wishes concerning the disposal of his or her property after death.

Written Premiums: The entire amount of premiums due in a year for all polices issued by an insurance company.

INDEX

SERVICES OFFERED

As you've seen through this book, I offer a unique approach to life insurance planning, consulting and analysis to allow individuals, trust officers, advisors, trustees and other fiduciaries a wide range of consulting and advisory services on a fee basis. Also offered are traditional commission based products. This allows you to make the choice.

As we've discussed, keep in mind that life insurance advisors who have the proper licensing to work on a fee only basis have no financial interest in a client's life insurance decisions on a more objective basis.

Please note that under any fee arrangement; no commission will be accepted. And on any commission based product, no fee would be accepted. On some occasions, a project may start out as a fee based arrangement and may call for the use of a commission based product; in that event the fee will be returned. The fee services offered include:

- Life Insurance Policy Evaluations:
    o Basic Life Insurance Policy Evaluation Service
      (See Sample in page #'s)
    o Comprehensive Life Insurance Evaluation Service
      (See Sample in page #'s)

Just imagine not tuning up your car and having the performance steadily decline. Even though your life insurance policy is safely tucked away in that filing cabinet, it, too, is facing many bumps along the road of a changing investment and interest rate environment. Your cash value life insurance policy—whether it's whole life, universal life, variable life, survivorship life, etc. is similar. It's made up of a variety of components that can each affect the overall performance of your life insurance policy.

In fact, as many as 90% of the life insurance policies purchased in the 1980's will not perform as originally expected due to changes in interest rates, costs of insurance and expenses.

- Trust Officer Fiduciary Due Care—Assist Trust Officers, Advisors, Trustees and Fiduciaries in fulfilling and meeting their fiduciary duty by reviewing and monitoring life insurance policies for which they are responsible under the Prudent Trustee Rule for new and existing policies using the Comprehensive Life Insurance Valuation Service (See Sample in page #'s).

- Life Insurance Consulting and Analysis Services (Hourly and Flat Project Fee)

   o General Life Insurance Issues: Needs planning, Illustrations, New Policies, In Force policies, Marketing
   o Estate Planning Life Insurance—Assisting in the use of life insurance as a funding vehicle for estate liquidity, equalization and wealth transfer.
   o Business Life Insurance—Assisting in analyzing and implementing in the use of life insurance (and where applicable disability income insurance) to fund buy-sell agreements, split-dollar, pension maximization, deferred compensation and other business uses of life insurance.

- No-load/low load permanent/cash value life insurance purchases (Hourly and Flat Project Fee)

- Continuous Policy Management—Life insurance, like other complex financial assets, must be managed on a regular basis. Annual reviews of the life insurance policy(ies)—The services offered would be a periodic Basic Evaluation Report or Comprehensive Evaluation Report—please contact me to discuss further.

- Litigation Consulting—Expert Witness and Consulting—life insurance marketing, contracts and illustrations.

- Disability Insurance—Analyzing existing disability insurance policies and assisting in the purchase of new disability insurance.

- Qualified Appraisals for Charitable and Non-Charitable Life Insurance Gifts

- Policy Valuations

- Content Writing—available for articles, education material and other content.

FOR MORE INFORMATION ON ANY SERVICE, PLEASE CONTACT ME, OR VISIT MY WEBSITE FOR INFORMATION ON REQUESTING THESE SERVICES

June 6, 2006

BASIC LIFE INSURANCE EVALUATION SERVICE

Is Your Current Insurance Policy Meeting Your Expectations? Will It Deliver What You've Paid For?

This service can help you answer these questions by providing customized reports that will evaluate your current policy

Your customized report will provide you with the following:

- **Review the Policy's Projected Long Term Performance**—to determine if based on current assumptions that your policy will continue to its contractual termination date as well as to your life expectancy. If it won't, the report will include suggestions on possible adjustments to have the policy continue to meet planning objectives based on a current Inforce Illustration(s) which is required for this service (see instructions to download a sample request letter).
- **Rate of Return for your policy**—Determine the rate of return on your policy on year by year basis. This will help you estimate the "actual" return on your cash value life insurance policy. You'll receive a summary showing the internal rate of return for certain time periods (5, 10, 20 and 30 years).
- **Life Insurance Company Quality and Financial Strength Overview**—current ratings from the major rating services— (A.M. Best, Moody's, Standard & Poor's, Fitch, and Weiss Ratings), as available.

How you use the information is up to you. Please note that this service provides information that allows you to make your own decision and is not to be construed as advice.

The report will provide you with the information to see if your policy is on track to reach the needs established for it. If it is on track, then nothing needs to be done. If it is not meeting your expectations, then your options will be on the report.

Basic Evaluation Report Information—Continued Please see Evaluation Request Form on Pages 466-467 for Instructions.

Further services are available for comparing a current policy with a new policy.

Please note that on reviews for Variable Life Policies the focus is strictly on the insurance component and the gross hypothetical rate of return on the submitted inforce (or proposed) policy illustration. There is no review or evaluation of the investment components.

Each report is designed for your particular policy. With over 1,500 active companies offering a multitude of constantly changing life insurance products, there are options, riders etc. that may not be shown on the information submitted and that may have a material impact on a policy.

Anthony Steuer Insurance Services   Prepared for:
Client Name
Client Address
City, State, Zip Code

Sample Basic Evaluation Report: COMPANY Universal Life Insurance Policy #XXXXX

Rate of Return:

This table represents your policy's projected one-year internal rate of return on the accumulated cash value based on the information submitted over certain periods. This statement is a snapshot of your policy today based on current interest rates and/or dividends, cost of insurance, premium loads and expenses. Your insurance company can change these factors at any time. Only periodic evaluations, such as this one, will capture those changes.

Age	Year	Premium	Accumulated Cash Value	Death Benefit	Accumulated Cash Value Internal Rate of Return
50	5	$9,232	$32,832	$1,000,000	
55	10	$9,232	$74,666	$1,000,000	-5.25%
65	20	$9,232	$195,040	$1,000,000	-3.87%
75	30	$9,232	$360,327	$1,000,000	-9.17%

The figures represented in this table are based on a universal life insurance illustration with a level annual premium for a newly issued individual universal life insurance policy insuring a male, preferred health classification, non-tobacco user age 45 with a $1,000,000 level death benefit. This policy assumes a credited interest rate of 4.85% with current mortality and expense charges. The rate of return formula utilizes IRS Table 2001 term rates and the cash value from five years prior. The resulting rate of return is based on a before tax internal buildup. The evaluation report for an inforce policy would commence from the date of the inforce illustration.

8863 Greenback Lane, PMB 207, Orangevale, CA 95662
916/989-3938 (Phone), 800/450-8909 (Toll-Free Phone), 916/989-3699 (Fax)
e-mail: tony@tonysteuer.com, web: www.tonysteuer.com
Life & Disability Insurance License #LX0721016

Anthony Steuer Insurance Services   Prepared for:
Client Name
Client Address
City, State, Zip Code

Evaluation:

For a new policy: The evaluation would be the facts above as a disclosure of what to expect in terms of a cash build-up along with the financial strength ratings on the other side of this report.

For an existing policy: The evaluation would read as follows: Your policy was originally projected to stay inforce until your policy [age]. Your policy is projected to go your policy [age] based on the submitted projections [dated] as provided by your [life insurance company]. As your life expectancy is [years], this policy will continue past your life expectancy or terminate prior to your life expectancy. (Life Expectancy is based on: Commissioners 2001 Standard Ordinary Mortality Table (Society of Actuaries)).

Recommended Action:

This section would address whether any changes might be necessary at this time. If the policy is underperforming, then a recommendation of action(s) such as increasing planned premiums; reduce the death benefit or other applicable options would be listed here.

*__This evaluation was performed on October 24, 2006
and is only valid for that date.
This evaluation was based on the information provided and makes
no guarantees or obligations__*

Continued Monitoring Of Your Policy:

Remember, factors such as current interest rates and/or dividends, cost of insurance, premium loads and expenses will change over time

8863 Greenback Lane, PMB 207, Orangevale, CA 95662
916/989-3938 (Phone), 800/450-8909 (Toll-Free Phone), 916/989-3699 (Fax)
e-mail: tony@tonysteuer.com, web: www.tonysteuer.com
Life & Disability Insurance License #LX0721016

Anthony Steuer Insurance Services   Prepared for:
Client Name
Client Address
City, State, Zip Code

and those changes will affect the return rates quoted in this check-up and the overall ability of the policy to meet your objectives. The only thing that is guaranteed about a life insurance illustration provided at the date of sale is that it will not come true. It would be nearly impossible for a life insurance company to pay out the same interest rate (or dividend rate each year. This applies to the other components as well.

Annual statements are a snapshot of a certain point in time, inforce ledgers are a look into a potential future. Sometimes there is no way to know that a component, (or components) have been changed except by the ongoing evaluation of inforce illustrations. Therefore, it is highly recommended to actively monitor your policy's performance by requesting these (and a check-up) every two to three years.

Reading your life insurance contract will help you understand what rights you have and what rights the insurance company has. However this is easier said than done as a life insurance contract is very complex so take your time and re-read as much as you need or want to.

Loans will negatively affect the return and performance of the policy. If loan interest is not paid, then, as shown on the inforce illustration, the policy's cash will quickly decline, lapsing (terminating) the policy quickly.

Financial Strength Ratings:

The financial strength of a life insurance is highly important as a life insurance policy is a long term investment. Life insurance companies are evaluated by ratings services and represent their independent opinions after evaluating a company's financial condition and operating

Anthony Steuer Insurance Services   Prepared for:
Client Name
Client Address
City, State, Zip Code

performance, using their specific criteria. The ratings agencies assign ratings of a company's financial strength and ability to meet obligations to policyholders. The following are the financial strength ratings for your submitted life insurance policy's current company (due to mergers and spin-offs), your current company may not be the same as the original company which is a good reason to continue to monitor the financial strength. The relative rank is included to give you a sense of how the ratings compare. Some insurance companies are not rated by all of the rating services. For further information on ratings (and contact information for the rating services), please visit the ratings area on my main website at www.tonysteuer.com in the resources section:

Sample: [NAME OF INSURANCE COMPANY]- Life Insurer Financial Strength Ratings as of [DATE]:

Agency	Rating	Description	Relative Ranking
A.M. Best Company Rating	A	Excellent	3 out of 15
Standard & Poor's Financial Strength Rating	AA	Very Strong	3 out of 20
Moody's Financial Strength Rating	Aa3	Excellent	4 out of 21
Fitch/Duff & Phelps Claim s Paying Ability	AA-	Very High	4 out of 18
Weiss Safety Rating	B	Good	5 out of 16

October 24, 2006

COMPREHENSIVE LIFE INSURANCE EVALUATION SERVICE

Is Your Current Insurance Policy (Or Your Client's Policy) Meeting Expectations?

This service is designed to assist you in answering these questions by providing customized reports that will evaluate your current policy (or your client's current policy).

Your customized report will provide you with the following:

- **Review the Policy's Potential Lifetime Performance**—to determine if based on current assumptions that your policy will continue to it's contractual termination date as well as to your life expectancy. If it won't, the report will include suggestions on possible adjustments to have the policy continue to meet planning objectives based on a current Inforce Illustration(s) which is required for this service (see instructions to download a sample request letter).
- **Rate of Return for your policy**—Determine the rate of return on your policy on year by year basis. This will help you estimate the "actual" return on your cash value life insurance policy. You'll receive a summary showing annual Rate of Return's 5, 10, 20 and 30 years from the date of inforce illustration.
- **Rate of Return on Death Benefit**—illustrates the year by year internal rate of return on the death benefit. You'll receive a summary for 5, 10, 20 and 30 years from the date of inforce illustration.
- **Net Amount At Risk**—Measure of Life Insurance, Total Death Benefit less Total Cash Surrender Value—You'll receive a summary for 5, 10, 20 and 30 years from the date of inforce illustration.
- **Present Value Of The Death Benefit As Measured Against The Present Value Of Premiums**—You'll receive a summary for 5, 10, 20 and 30 years from the date of inforce illustration.
- **Present Value Of Cash Surrender Values As Measured Against The Present Value Of Premiums**—You'll receive a summary for 5, 10, 20 and 30 years from the date of inforce illustration.

- **Future Value Of Premium Payments (Opportunity Cost)**— Calculated at a 5% Return on Investment (ROI). You'll receive a summary for 5, 10, 20 and 30 years from the date of inforce illustration.
- **Future Value Of Cash Surrender Value**—calculated at a 5% Return on Investment. You'll receive a summary for 5, 10, 20 and 30 years from the date of inforce illustration.
- **Income Tax Data for Policy**—provides taxable gain and assume income tax incurred if surrendered for each year. Total premiums paid to date of inforce illustration (these may be on inforce illustration) and your income tax rate (federal and state) or a requested rate.
- **Life Insurance Company Quality and Financial Strength Overview**—current ratings from the five major rating services-(A.M. Best, Moody's, Standard & Poor's, Fitch, and Weiss Ratings), as available with an in-depth life.
- **Detailed Company Financial Information and Ratios (3 Year History)**—
  - o Total Admitted Assets, Separate Accounts, Total Liabilities, New Policies Written, Life Insurance in Force
  - o Profitability Tests: Net Premiums Written, Benefits Paid to Net Premiums Written Ratio, Net Operating Gain to Total Assets, Return on Equity, Net Yield and Total Return
  - o Leverage Tests: Changes in Net Premiums Written, Net Premiums Written to Capital & Surplus Funds Ratio, Surplus Relief and Leverage (Capital & Surplus to Liabilities Ratio)
  - o Liquidity Tests: Current Liquidity, Quick Liquidity, Non-Investment Grade Bonds to Capital & Surplus (NAIC Classes 3-6), Delinquent & Foreclosed Mortgage to Capital & Surplus,
  - o Investment Quality: Breakdown of Invested Assets and Invested Asset Analysis, Asset Quality Analysis, Total Investment Return and Bond Portfolio Return

How you use the information is up to you. Please note that this service provides information that allows you to make your own decision and is not to be construed as advice.

The report will provide you with the information to see if the policy is on track to meet the needs established for it. If it is on track, then nothing needs to be done. If expectations are not being met, then possible options will be on the report.

Please see Evaluation Request Form on Pages Pages 466-467 for Instructions.

Further services are available for comparing a current policy with a new policy.

Please note that on reviews for Variable Life Policies the focus is strictly on the insurance component and the gross hypothetical rate of return on the submitted inforce (or proposed) policy illustration. There is no review or evaluation of the investment components.

Each report is designed for your particular policy. With over 1,500 active companies offering a multitude of constantly changing life insurance products, there are options, riders etc. that may not be shown on the information submitted and that may have a material impact on a policy.

Anthony Steuer Insurance Services   Prepared for:
Client Name
Client Address
City, State, Zip Code

Sample Comprehensive Evaluation Report: COMPANY Universal Life Insurance Policy #XXXXX

Rate of Return:

This table represents your policy's projected internal rate of return on the accumulated cash value based on the information submitted over certain periods. he information submitted. This table represents the cash value's internal rate of return on your policy over five year periods. The death benefit internal rate of return is the actual return on premiums as compared to the death benefit. This statement is a snapshot of your policy today based on current interest rates and/or dividends, cost of insurance, premium loads and expenses. Your insurance company can change these factors at any time. Only periodic evaluations, such as this one, will capture those changes.

Age	Year	Premium	Accumulated Cash Value	Death Benefit	Accumulated Cash Value Internal Rate of Return	Death Benefit Internal Rate of Return
50	5	$9,232	$32,832	$1,000,000		2,166%
55	10	$9,232	$74,666	$1,000,000	-14.98%	1,083%
65	20	$9,232	$195,040	$1,000,000	-3.87%	542%
75	30	$9,232	$360,327	$1,000,000	-1.52%	361%

The figures represented in this table are based on a universal life insurance illustration with a level annual premium for a newly issued individual universal life insurance policy insuring a male, preferred health classification, non-tobacco user age 45 with a $1,000,000 level death benefit. This policy assumes a credited interest rate of 4.85% with cur-

8863 Greenback Lane, PMB 207, Orangevale, CA 95662
916/989-3938 (Phone), 800/450-8909 (Toll-Free Phone), 916/989-3699 (Fax)
e-mail: tony@tonysteuer.com, web: www.tonysteuer.com
Life & Disability Insurance License #LX0721016

Anthony Steuer Insurance Services

Prepared for:
Client Name
Client Address
City, State, Zip Code

rent mortality and expense charges. The rate of return formula utilizes IRS Table 2001 term rates and the cash value from five years prior. The resulting rate of return is based on a before tax internal buildup. <u>The evaluation report for an inforce policy would commence from the date of the inforce illustration.</u>

Income Tax Data for Policy:

The following table illustrates the potential income tax on the surrender value at certain time periods assuming a 35% gross overall income tax rate. This is for a traditional, non-modified endowment contract (policies held within a qualified retirement plan are subject to different tax rules).

<u>Age</u>	<u>Year</u>	Sum of Premiums Paid	Surrender Cash Value	Taxable Gain	Estimated Income Tax Incurred on Gain at 35% Gross Tax Rate	Net Surrender Value After Taxes
50	5	$46,161	$14,872	-31,289	None	$14,872
55	10	$92,321	$74,666	-17,655	None	$74,666
65	20	$184,643	$195,040	10,397	$3,639	$191,401
75	30	$276,964	$360,327	83,363	$29,177	$331,150

Present Value Calculations:

The following table illustrates the sum of premiums paid and the death benefit as measured in today's dollars utilizing present value and net present value calculations.

8863 Greenback Lane, PMB 207, Orangevale, CA 95662
916/989-3938 (Phone), 800/450-8909 (Toll-Free Phone), 916/989-3699 (Fax)
e-mail: tony@tonysteuer.com, web: www.tonysteuer.com
Life & Disability Insurance License #LX0721016

Anthony Steuer Insurance Services   Prepared for:
Client Name
Client Address
City, State, Zip Code

Present Value (PV) is the amount of cash in today's dollars of a future sum (or stream of payments). Net Present Value (NPV) is the present value of a future sum (or stream of payments) less the cost.

These calculations utilize a 5% discount rate at 5, 10, 20 and 30 year time periods. This rate was chosen as it is a conservative long term rate of return based on the long term historical rate of return on U.S. Treasuries.

The Net Present Value calculation is the net present value at the 5% discount rate of the future death benefit less the premiums paid.

The percentage return ratio illustrates the present value of the future death benefit as compared to the present value of the premiums paid. The higher the ratio the greater the amount, as measured in death benefits that is being returned to the policyholder.

Age	Year	Sum of Premiums:	Death Benefit:	Present Value at 5% discount rate— Total Premiums	Present Value at 5% discount rate— Death Benefit	Net Present Value at 5% discount rate on Death Benefit & Premiums	Percentage Return at 5% discount Rate— Present Value of Death Benefits to Present Value of Premiums
50	5	$46,161	$1,000,000	$39,970	$783,526	$706,245	1,960.27%
55	10	$92,231	$1,000,000	$771,288	$613,913	$513,391	861.17%
65	20	$184,643	$1,000,000	$115,053	$376,889	$243,889	327.58%
75	30	$276,964	$1,000,000	$141,921	$231,377	$78,439	163.08%

8863 Greenback Lane, PMB 207, Orangevale, CA 95662
916/989-3938 (Phone), 800/450-8909 (Toll-Free Phone), 916/989-3699 (Fax)
e-mail: tony@tonysteuer.com, web: www.tonysteuer.com
Life & Disability Insurance License #LX0721016

Anthony Steuer Insurance Services

Prepared for:
Client Name
Client Address
City, State, Zip Code

Evaluation:

For a new policy: The evaluation would be the facts above as a disclosure of what to expect in terms of a cash build-up along with the financial strength ratings on the other side of this report.

For an existing policy: The evaluation would read as follows: Your policy was originally projected to stay inforce until your policy [age]. Your policy is projected to go your policy [age] based on the submitted projections [dated] as provided by your [life insurance company]. As your life expectancy is [years], this policy will continue past your life expectancy (or terminate prior to your life expectancy).

Life Expectancy is based on: Commissioners 2001 Standard Ordinary Mortality Table (Society of Actuaries)

Recommended Action:

This section would address whether any changes might be necessary at this time. If the policy is underperforming, then a recommendation of action(s) such as increasing planned premiums; reduce the death benefit or other applicable options would be listed here.

*This evaluation was performed on October 24, 2006
and is only valid for that date.
The evaluation was based on the information provided
and makes no guarantees or obligations*

CONTINUED MONITORING OF YOUR POLICY:

8863 Greenback Lane, PMB 207, Orangevale, CA 95662
916/989-3938 (Phone), 800/450-8909 (Toll-Free Phone), 916/989-3699 (Fax)
e-mail: tony@tonysteuer.com, web: www.tonysteuer.com
Life & Disability Insurance License #LX0721016

Anthony Steuer Insurance Services   Prepared for:
Client Name
Client Address
City, State, Zip Code

Remember, factors such as current interest rates and/or dividends, cost of insurance, premium loads and expenses will change over time and those changes will affect the return rates quoted in this check-up and the overall ability of the policy to meet your objectives. The only thing that is guaranteed about a life insurance illustration provided at the date of sale is that it will not come true. It would be nearly impossible for a life insurance company to pay out the same interest rate (or dividend rate each year. This applies to the other components as well.

Annual statements are a snapshot of a certain point in time, inforce ledgers are a look into a potential future. Sometimes there is no way to know that a component (or components) have been changed except by the ongoing evaluation of inforce illustrations. Therefore, it is highly recommended to actively monitor your policy's performance by requesting these (and a check-up) every two to three years.

Reading your life insurance contract will help you understand what rights you have and what rights the insurance company has. However this is easier said than done as a life insurance contract is very complex so take your time and re-read as much as you need or want to.

Loans will negatively affect the return and performance of the policy. If loan interest is not paid, then as shown on the inforce illustration, the policy's cash will quickly decline, lapsing (terminating) the policy quickly.

FINANCIAL STRENGTH RATINGS:

The financial strength of a life insurance is highly important as a life insurance policy is a long term investment. Life insurance companies are evaluated by ratings services and represent their independent opinions after evaluating a company's financial condition and operat-

8863 Greenback Lane, PMB 207, Orangevale, CA 95662
916/989-3938 (Phone), 800/450-8909 (Toll-Free Phone), 916/989-3699 (Fax)
e-mail: tony@tonysteuer.com, web: www.tonysteuer.com
Life & Disability Insurance License #LX0721016

Anthony Steuer Insurance Services   Prepared for:
                                      Client Name
                                      Client Address
                                      City, State, Zip Code

---

ing performance, using their specific criteria. The ratings agencies assign ratings of a company's financial strength and ability to meet obligations to policyholders. The following are the financial strength ratings for your submitted life insurance policy's current company (due to mergers and spin-offs), your current company may not be the same as the original company which is a good reason to continue to monitor the financial strength. The relative rank is included to give you a sense of how the ratings compare. Some insurance companies are not rated by all of the rating services. For further information on ratings (and contact information for the rating services), please visit the ratings area on my main website at www.tonysteuer.com in the resources section:

[NAME OF INSURANCE COMPANY]

Group Affiliation:	[name]
Address:	[Address]
Phone Number:	[Phone Number]
Web Site:	[Website]
Date of Incorporation:	[19xx]
Company Type:	[Stock, Mutual, other]
NAIC Number:	[xxx]

Life Insurer Financial Strength Ratings as of [DATE]:

Anthony Steuer Insurance Services   Prepared for:
Client Name
Client Address
City, State, Zip Code

Agency	Rating	Description	Relative Ranking
A.M. Best Company Rating	A	Excellent	3 out of 15
Standard & Poor's Financial Strength Rating	AA	Very Strong	3 out of 20
Moody's Financial Strength Rating	Aa3	Excellent	4 out of 21
Fitch/Duff & Phelps Claim s Paying Ability	AA-	Very High	4 out of 18
Weiss Safety Rating	B	Good	5 out of 16

Insurance Marketplace Standards Association Membership (IMSA): YES OR NO

[COMPANY] is a member of IMSA as of [DATE]. IMSA stands for the Insurance Marketplace Standards Association. IMSA promotes high ethical standards in the sale and service of individually-sold life insurance, annuity and long-term care products.

IMSA member companies are insurers who have agreed to adopt and abide by IMSA's Principles and Code of Ethical Market Conduct to earn your trust and gain your confidence. For additional information please visit www.imsaethics.org.

	Year End- 2003	Year End - 2004	Year end- 2005
Total Admitted Assets: Assets permitted to be included in an insurance company's annual statement. Also includes separate accounts.			
Total Liabilities: Funds required for payment of future payments of fu ture claims and expenses, including asset valuation & reserve			
Total Capital, Surplus & Asset Valuation Reserve(AVR):			
Life Insurance Inforce:			

8863 Greenback Lane, PMB 207, Orangevale, CA 95662
916/989-3938 (Phone), 800/450-8909 (Toll-Free Phone), 916/989-3699 (Fax)
e-mail: tony@tonysteuer.com, web: www.tonysteuer.com
Life & Disability Insurance License #LX0721016

Anthony Steuer Insurance Services

Prepared for:
Client Name
Client Address
City, State, Zip Code

Invested Assets - $xxxxxxxx

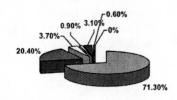

0.60%
0.90% 3.10%
0%
3.70%
20.40%
71.30%

- ▨ Bonds
- ☐ Policy Loans
- ▧ Stocks
- ▨ Cash & Short-Term
- ▧ Mortgages
- ☐ Other
- ▧ Real Estate

Investment Yields:

Year	Company	Industry Average
2001	7.02%	7.01%
2002	6.40%	6.42%
2003	6.00%	5.82%
2004	5.87%	5.50%
2005	5.84%	5.52%
5 Year Average:	6.23%	6.05%

Net investment income expressed as a percent of mean cash and invested assets plus accrued investment income minus borrowed money. Industry average source—Vital Signs

Bond Quality:

Class 1 (Highest):   67.3%
Class 2 (Higher):   26.6%
Class 3 (Medium):   3.6%
Class 4 (Low):   1.9%
Class 5 (Lower):   0.4%
Class 6 (In or Near Default): 0.2%

Non-Performing Assets:

Bonds In or Near Default:	1.3%
Problem Mortgages:	0.1%
Real Estate Acquired by Foreclosure:	0.2%
Total Non-Performing Assets/Surplus & AVR:	1.6%
As a Percent of Invested Assets:	0.2%

Source: Year-End 2005 Data from the life insurance companies' statutory annual statements

8863 Greenback Lane, PMB 207, Orangevale, CA 95662
916/989-3938 (Phone), 800/450-8909 (Toll-Free Phone), 916/989-3699 (Fax)
e-mail: tony@tonysteuer.com, web: www.tonysteuer.com
Life & Disability Insurance License #LX0721016

Anthony Steuer Insurance Services   Prepared for:
Client Name
Client Address
City, State, Zip Code

[COMPANY] Key Financial Information and Ratios (in thousands)— Continued:

	Year End - 2003	Year End - 2004	Year end - 2005

PROFITABILITY TESTS: (See also Investment Yield – page 6):

Net Premiums Written (NPW): Total Premiums Written (Direct & Reinsured) less amounts which were forwarded to other reinsurance companies

Benefits paid to NPW: Total benefits paid as a percentage of net premiums written (ratio)

Leverage: Ratio of Capital & Surplus to Liabilities reflects the extent to which the company has leveraged it's capital and surplus base, and is a good test of a company's ability to pay claims in a crisis

LEVERAGE TESTS:

Change in Net Premiums Written: The annual percentage change in net premiums written is a measure of growth in underwriting commitments

Net Premiums Written to Capital & Surplus Funds Rati o: Measures a company's exposure to pricing errors in it's current book of business

Surplus Relief: The relationship of commissions and expense allowances on reinsurance ceded to capital and surplus funds. The use of surplus relief can be the result of "surplus strain", a term used to describe an insurance transaction wherein the funds collected are not sufficient under statutory accounting guidelines to cover the liabilities established

Leverage: Ratio of Capital & Surplus to Liabilities reflects the extent to which the company has leveraged it's capital and surplus base, and is a good test of a company's ability to pay claims in a crisis

LIQUIDITY TESTS:

Current Liquidity: Proportion of net liabilities covered by cash & unrelated investments. Current liquidity of less than 100% may mean that the company is relying on unpaid premiums and outstanding loads to pay current obligations. Liquidity of greater than 100% can mean that the company is not investing a sufficient amount of assets and therefore receiving a lower overall return on assets

Quick Liquidity: The ratio of unaffiliated quick assets to liabilities. This test measures the proportion of liabilities (excluding Asset Valuation Reserve (AVR), conditional reserves and separate accounts) covered by cash and quickly convertible investments. It indicated a company's ability to meet it's maturing obligations without requiring the sale of long term investments or the borrowing of money

Source: Year-End Data from the life insurance companies' statutory annual statements (Best's Key Rating Guide)

8863 Greenback Lane, PMB 207, Orangevale, CA 95662
916/989-3938 (Phone), 800/450-8909 (Toll-Free Phone), 916/989-3699 (Fax)
e-mail: tony@tonysteuer.com, web: www.tonysteuer.com
Life & Disability Insurance License #LX0721016

Anthony Steuer Insurance Services   Prepared for:
                                          Client Name
                                          Client Address
                                          City, State, Zip Code

To Request A Life Insurance Policy Evaluation Report:

1) Print and complete the attached Evaluation Request Form (please complete one per policy).

2) Send copies of the following items:

- Policy Data Pages
- Current Inforce Illustrations (existing policy(ies))—Download Applicable Sample Request Letter from www.tonysteuer.com (Whole Life, Universal Life, Variable (Universal) Life)
- Original Illustration (If Available)
- Most Recent Annual Statement

3) Include check payable to "Anthony Steuer Life Insurance Services"

- $149 for Basic Evaluation Service or
- $449 for Comprehensive Evaluation Service

Optional:

- $10—Additional Fee if you would prefer to receive your evaluation report by mail
- Copy of "Questions and Answers on Life Insurance" by Anthony Steuer Writers Notes Magazine (Notable Mention Award-Business Category—2006)—"Understanding life insurance can be daunting, but Steuer brings it down to earth. The book includes the steps needed to evaluate a company or agent, the business of underwriting, how to monitor policies, tracking

8863 Greenback Lane, PMB 207, Orangevale, CA 95662
916/989-3938 (Phone), 800/450-8909 (Toll-Free Phone), 916/989-3699 (Fax)
e-mail: tony@tonysteuer.com, web: www.tonysteuer.com
Life & Disability Insurance License #LX0721016

Anthony Steuer Insurance Services   Prepared for:
Client Name
Client Address
City, State, Zip Code

down lost policies, and over-looked issues such as replacements, loans, and taxes. Glossaries give contact information and a list of terms."—WNM

- 10% Discount off of the $27.95 Cover Price with the Basic Evaluation Report—$25.16
- 25% Discount off of the $27.95 Cover Price with the Comprehensive Evaluation Report—$20.96
  (No Shipping and Handling Fee or Taxes)

4) Mail to address below.

Please Note:

Submitted materials will not be returned, please retain originals for your records.

You will be notified by email upon receipt

Once your materials are received they will be reviewed and a report will be generated and delivered to you by email in PDF format in approximately 10 business days ($10 fee to receive report by mail).

8863 Greenback Lane, PMB 207, Orangevale, CA 95662
916/989-3938 (Phone), 800/450-8909 (Toll-Free Phone), 916/989-3699 (Fax)
e-mail: tony@tonysteuer.com, web: www.tonysteuer.com
Life & Disability Insurance License #LX0721016

Anthony Steuer Insurance Services   Prepared for:
Client Name
Client Address
City, State, Zip Code

Life Insurance Policy Evaluation Request Form

Requestor Information

First Name: _____Last Name: _____
Mailing Address: _____
City: _____State: _____Zip Code: _____
Email Address: _____Daytime Phone Number: _____

Policy Information (Use separate sheets for each policy):

Insurance company name: _____
Policy Number: _____Type of Policy: _____

Insured's First Name: _____Last Name: _____
Sex: _____   Date of Birth: _____
Policy owner's full name (or name of trust): _____

For Comprehensive Service: Total Estimated Income Tax Bracket: _____%

Please send a copy of this page along with the Services Selection on the next page.

8863 Greenback Lane, PMB 207, Orangevale, CA 95662
916/989-3938 (Phone), 800/450-8909 (Toll-Free Phone), 916/989-3699 (Fax)
e-mail: tony@tonysteuer.com, web: www.tonysteuer.com
Life & Disability Insurance License #LX0721016

Anthony Steuer Insurance Services   Prepared for:
Client Name
Client Address
City, State, Zip Code

	Price	Quantity	Total
Basic Evaluation Service	$149		$
Comprehensive Evaluation Service	$449		$
Fee to receive copy by U.S. Mail	$10		$
Questions and Answers on Life Insurance—Book—	$25.16 (with Basic Report) $20.96 (with Comprehensive Report)		$
Grand Total:	-----------------------------	------------	$

Please make check payable to Anthony Steuer Insurance Services

Additional information and Comments (please attach extra page(s) if needed):

_____

_____

_____

Please send a copy of this page along with the Life Insurance Policy Evaluation Request Form on the prior page.

8863 Greenback Lane, PMB 207, Orangevale, CA 95662
916/989-3938 (Phone), 800/450-8909 (Toll-Free Phone), 916/989-3699 (Fax)
e-mail: tony@tonysteuer.com, web: www.tonysteuer.com
Life & Disability Insurance License #LX0721016

Anthony Steuer Insurance Services

Life and Disability Insurance Analyst   'Your Life Insurance Center'

PROFESSIONAL BIOGRAPHY: ANTHONY STEUER, CLU, LA

Anthony Steuer is a specially licensed Individual Life and Disability Insurance Analyst. There are only about 30 such analysts licensed by the State of California. As an analyst, Tony has the knowledge, and the authority, to provide non-biased advice regarding life insurance. Tony is a member of the Society of Financial Service Professionals and is also a registered limited principal with the National Association of Securities Dealers

Tony specializes in the analysis of life insurance products and provides fee based analytical services directly to clients and to attorneys, CPA's and investment advisors. He also performs fee based due diligence and due care analysis for professional advisors and trust officers. Tony is a specialist at analyzing a life insurance policy from the carrier to examine and evaluate potential scenarios.

Writing, Teaching and Speaking:
- Author of "Questions and Answers on Life Insurance"—
    - o Writer's Notes—Notable Achievement Award—Business Category (2006)
    - o Editor's Choice Award—iUniverse Publishing (2006)
    - o Book of the Day—Insurance Newscast (6/14/05)
- www.lovetoknow.com   Interview—Life   Insurance   Expert (9/2006)
- A.M. Best Company—Best's Directory of Recommended Expert Service Providers
- Contributed articles for A.M. Best's Best Review Magazine
- Frequent speaker at various professional meetings
- Technical editor for the "The Retirement Bible" and the "Investing Bible"

- Author of Online Continuing Education Courses
- Moderator of Courses for Life Underwriter Training Council
- Instructor for Courses for Continuing Education for Society of Financial Service Professionals.
- Appearance on the Wall Journal Morning Radio Show, regarding life insurance needs

He has also served the following organizations:

- Board of Directors, Marin Community Institute for Psychotherapy
- Past Director—San Francisco & Marin Life Underwriters Associations
- President (1993)—Leading Life Insurance Producers of No.Cal.
- President (1996-1997)—S.F. Chapter Society of Financial Service Professionals
- Regional Liaison- Society of Financial Service Professionals

Prior to commencing his own practice in 1995, Tony was an Assistant Vice President with Acordia-Lloyd a multi-line insurance brokerage. His responsibilities were as a lead on an endorsed life insurance program with the State Bar of California as well as working with Health Insurance Producers and Property & Casualty Producers to assist in developing life insurance programs for their clients.

Tony earned his Bachelor of Science in Finance degree from California State University at Chico.

Tony can be reached by E-mail at: tony@tonysteuer.com

Or visit www.tonysteuer.com on the Web

California Life and Disability Insurance Analyst License #LX0721016

978-0-595-32147-6
0-595-32147-X

Printed in the United States
65081LVS00003B/32

9 780595 321476